Kamisama Kiss

Story & Art by

Julietta Suzuki

Kamisama Kiss

Volume 19
CONTENTS

CHARACTERS

Tomoe
The shinshi who serves Nanami now that she's a tochigami. Originally a wild fox ayakashi. He controls powerful kitsunebi.

Nanami Momozono
A high school student who was turned into a kamisama by the tochigami Mikage. She likes Tomoe.

Onikiri
Onibi-warashi, spirits of the shrine.

Kotetsu
Onibi-warashi, spirits of the shrine.

Mamoru
Nanami's shikigami. He can create a spiritual barrier to keep out evil.

Kurama
A super-popular idol. He's actually a tengu.

Mizuki
Nanami's second shinshi. The incarnation of a white snake. Used to be the shinshi of Yonomori shrine.

Unari
The chief of the mermaids who rule over the Okinawan sea. Kirihito stole her robe of feathers.

Kirihito
A human whose body was taken over by the great yokai Akura-oh. He is attended by shikigami minions.

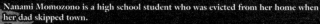

Nanami Momozono is a high school student who was evicted from her home when her dad skipped town.
She meets the tochigami Mikage at a park, and he leaves his shrine and his kami powers to her.
Now Nanami spends her days with Tomoe and Mizuki, her shinshi, and with Onikiri and Kotetsu, the onibi-warashi spirits of the shrine.
Nanami has been slowly gaining powers as kamisama by holding a festival at her shrine, attending a big kami conference, and all sorts of other adventures.
Nanami's and Tomoe's feelings for each other are finally out in the open and they have started to date!
Nanami and her classmates go on a school trip to Okinawa. The mermaid Unari suspects Ami of stealing her robe of feathers and kidnaps her. Kikuichi, Kirihito's minion, bargains with Nanami to help Kirihito in exchange for the robe, and then...

Story
so
far

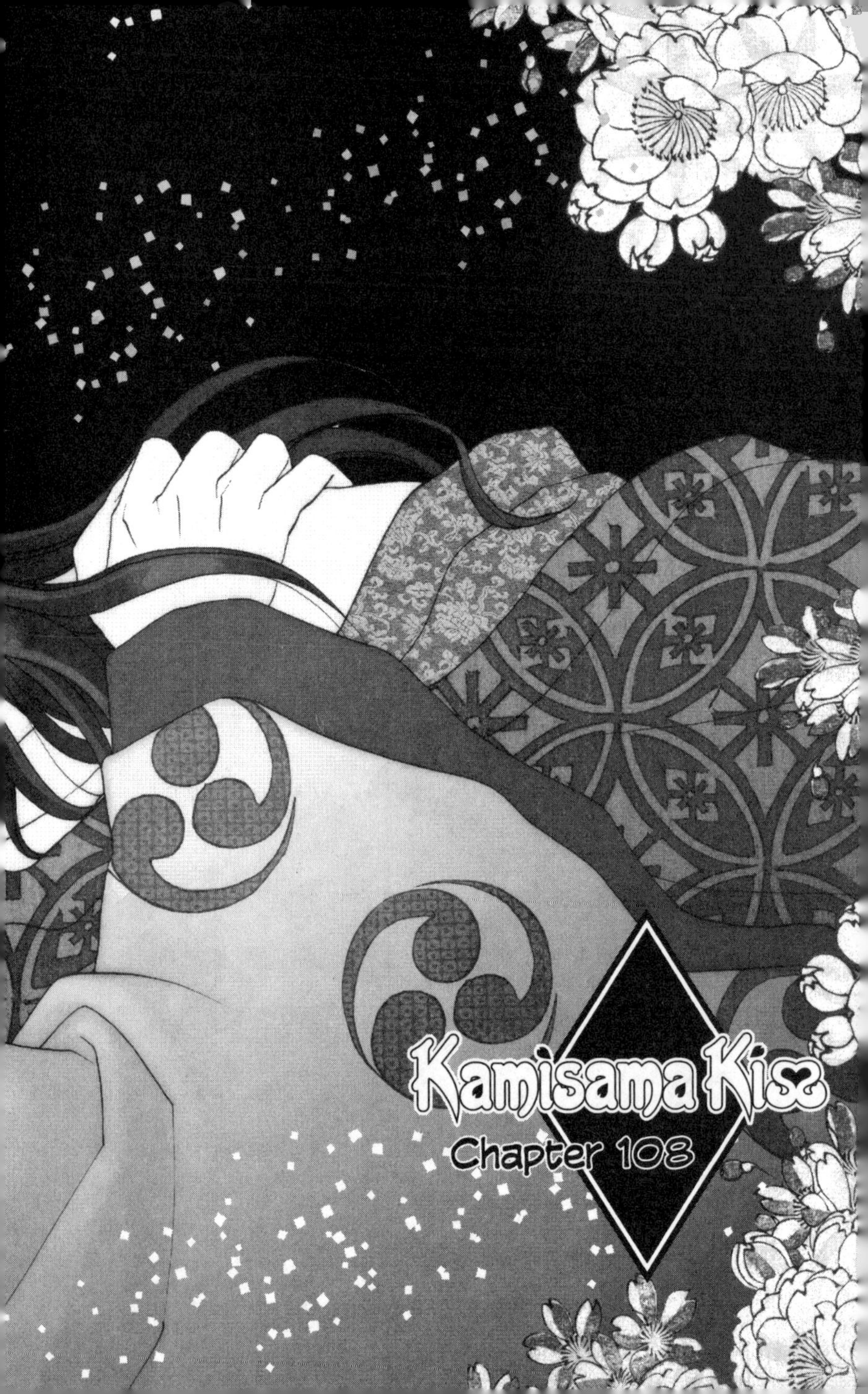
Kamisama Kiss
Chapter 108

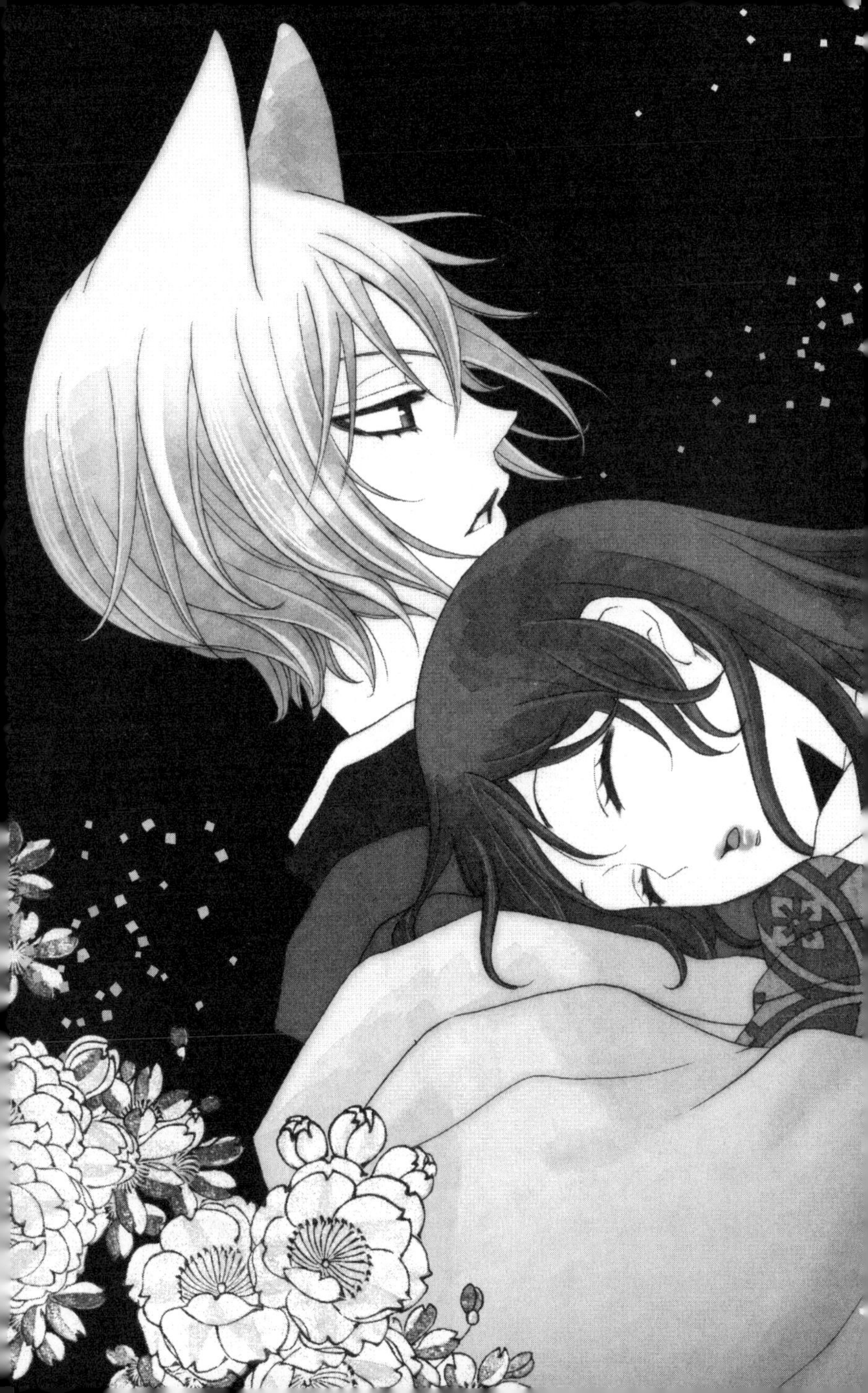

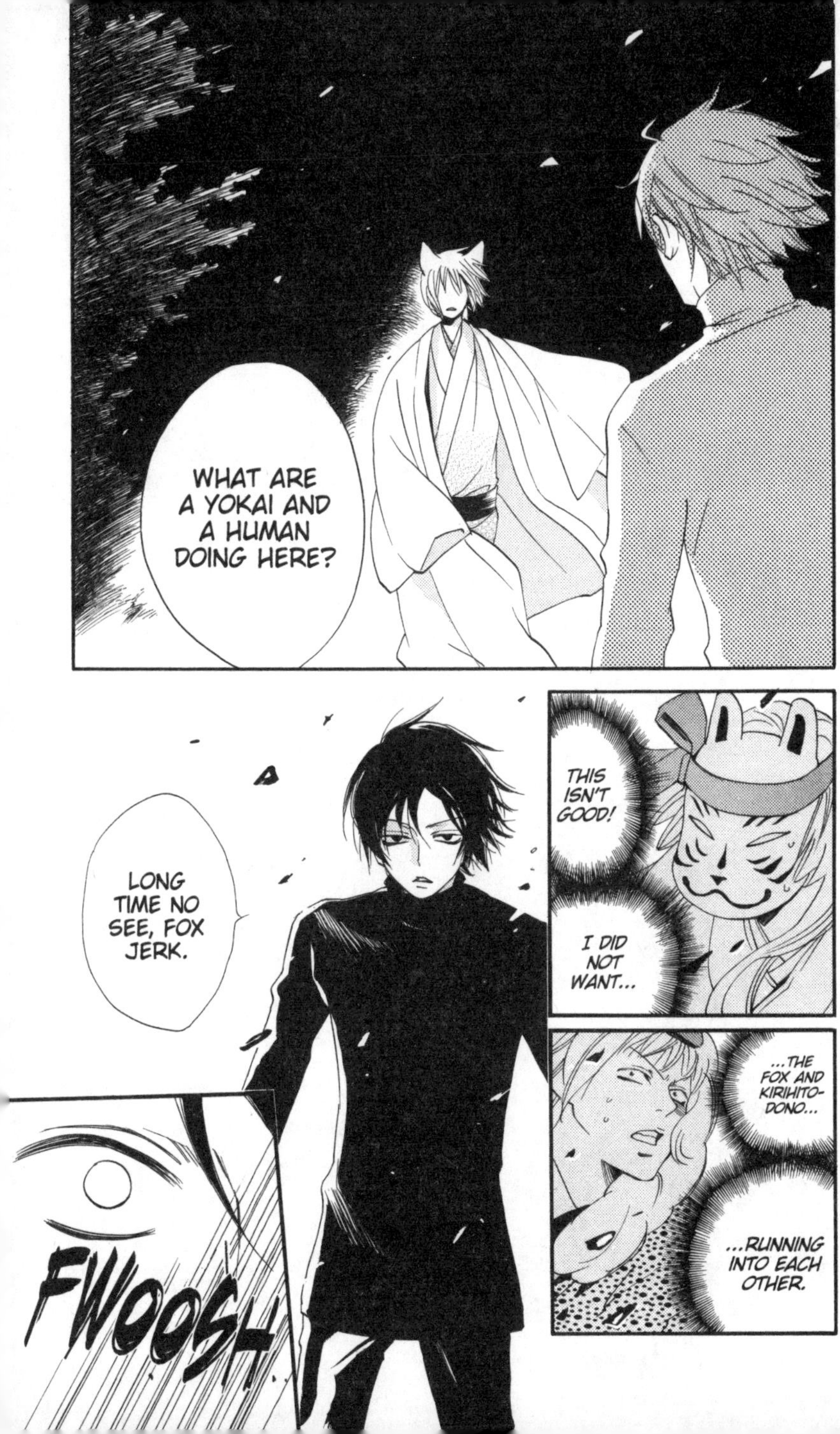
WHAT ARE A YOKAI AND A HUMAN DOING HERE?
THIS ISN'T GOOD!
I DID NOT WANT...
...THE FOX AND KIRIHITO-DONO...
...RUNNING INTO EACH OTHER.
LONG TIME NO SEE, FOX JERK.
FWOOSH

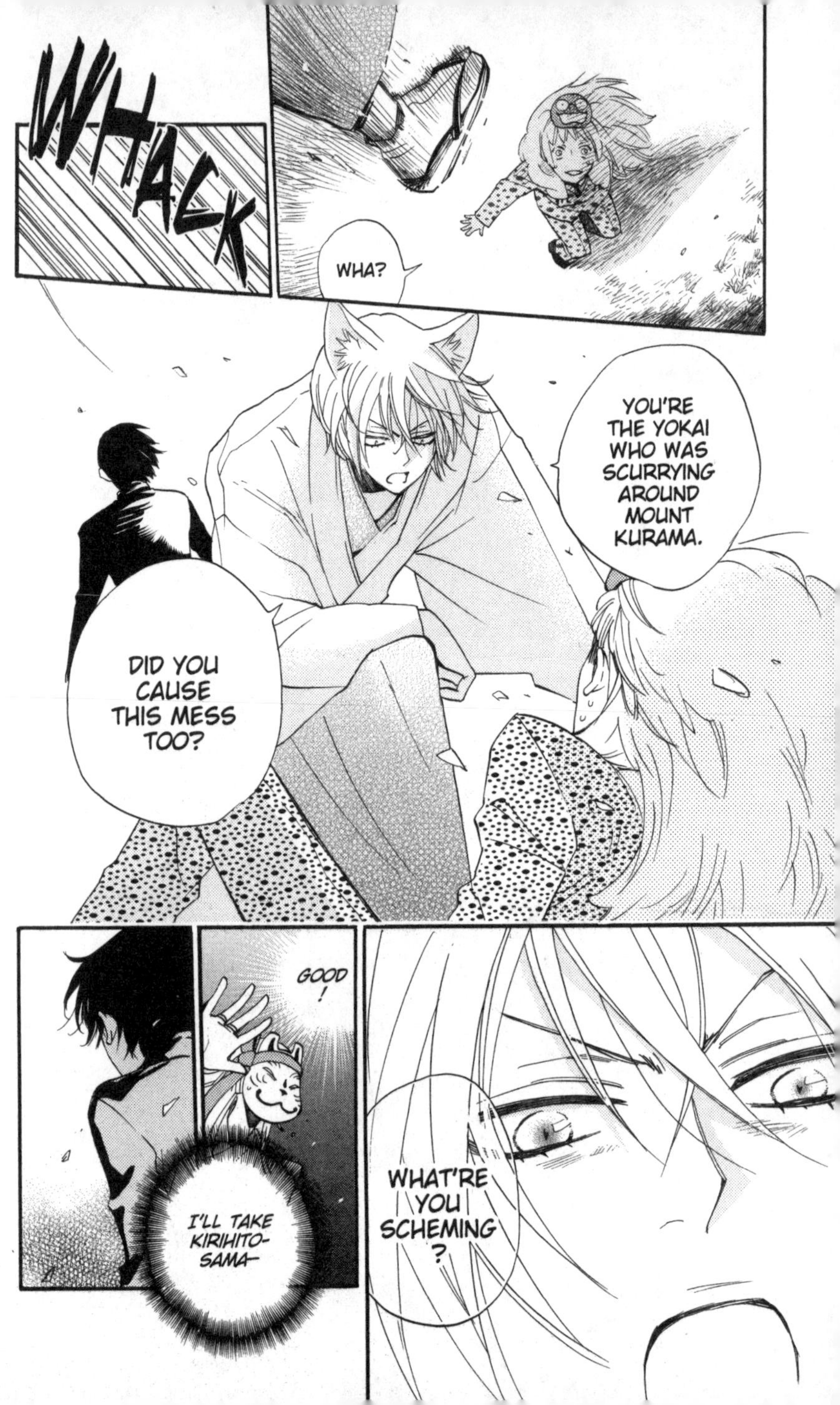
WHA?
WHACK
YOU'RE THE YOKAI WHO WAS SCURRYING AROUND MOUNT KURAMA.
DID YOU CAUSE THIS MESS TOO?
WHAT'RE YOU SCHEMING?
GOOD!
I'LL TAKE KIRIHITO-SAMA—

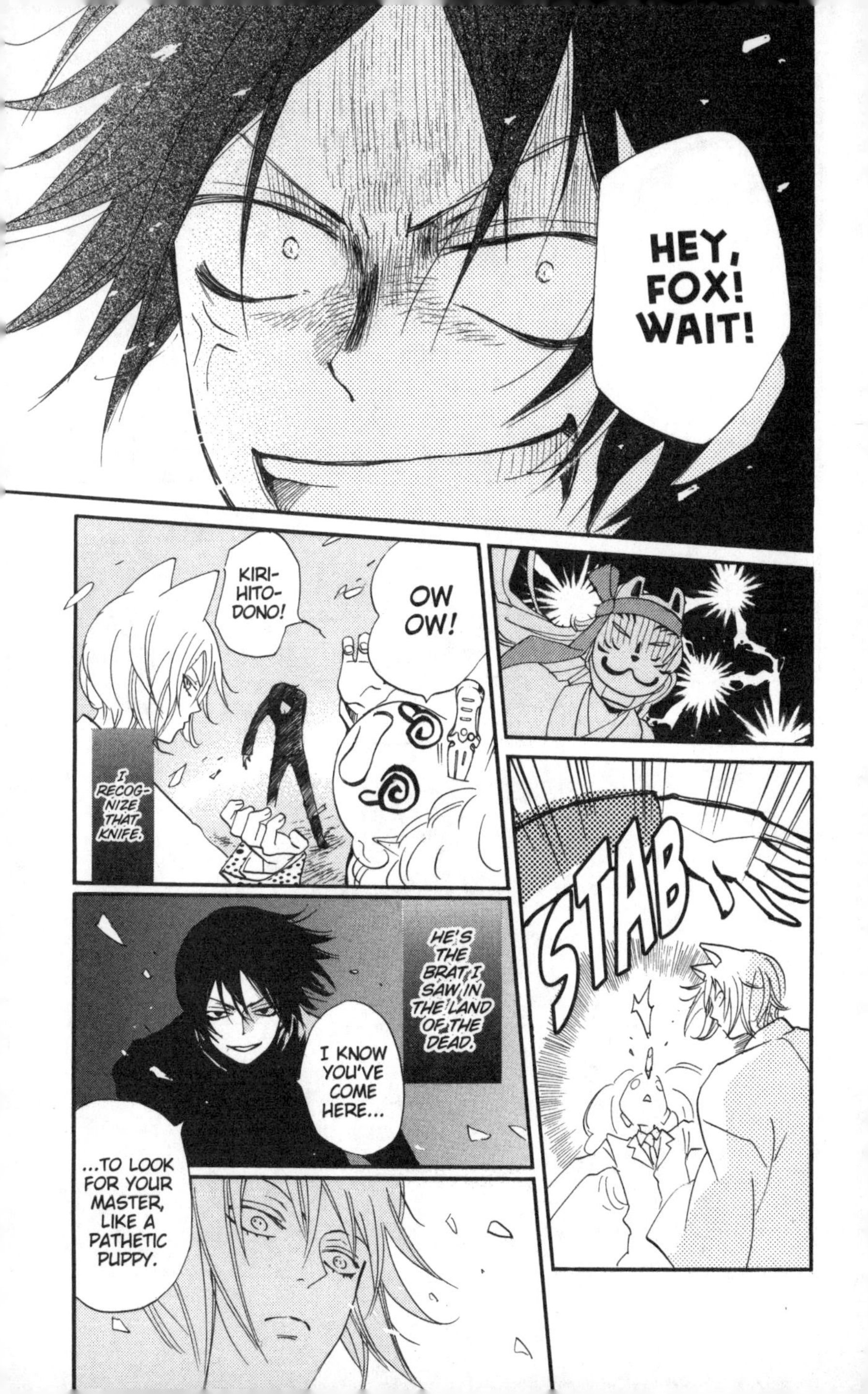
HEY, FOX! WAIT!
OW OW!
KIRI-HITO-DONO!
I RECOG-NIZE THAT KNIFE.
STAB
HE'S THE BRAT I SAW IN THE LAND OF THE DEAD.
I KNOW YOU'VE COME HERE...
...TO LOOK FOR YOUR MASTER, LIKE A PATHETIC PUPPY.

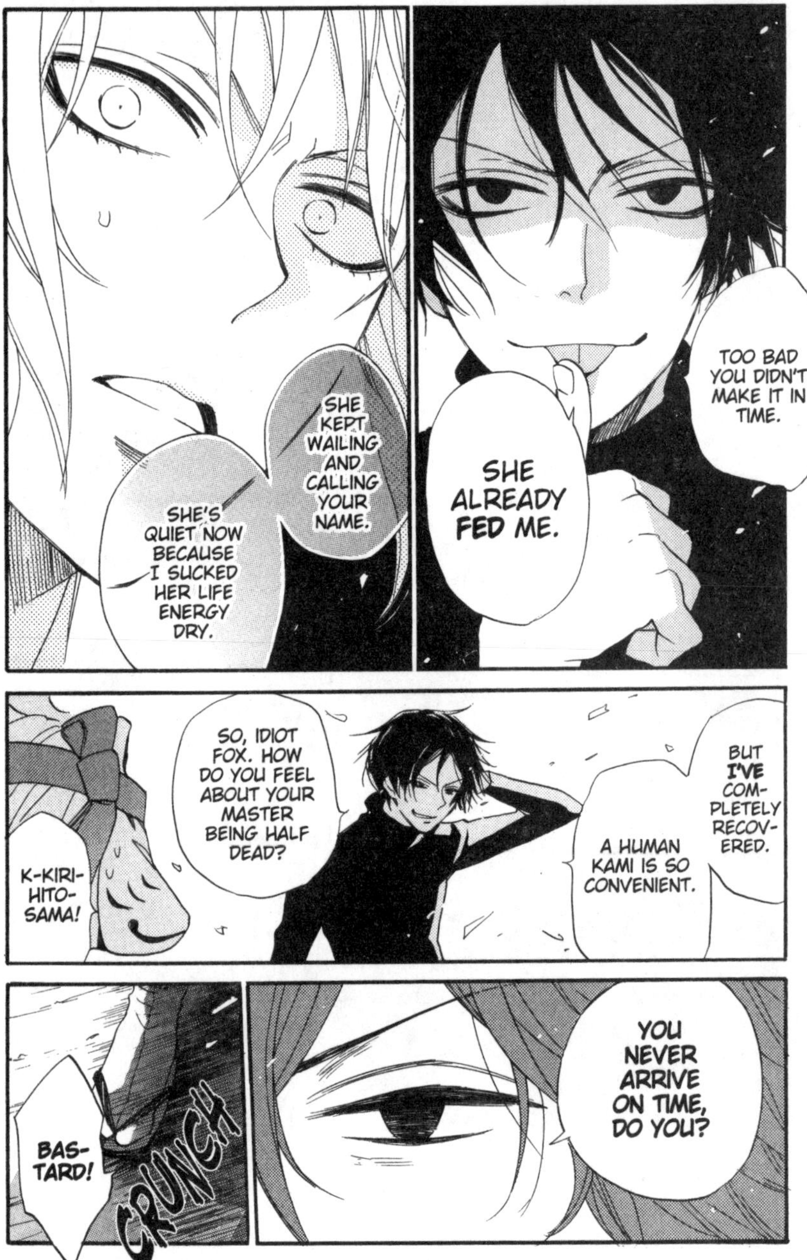
TOO BAD YOU DIDN'T MAKE IT IN TIME.
SHE ALREADY FED ME.
SHE KEPT WAILING AND CALLING YOUR NAME.
SHE'S QUIET NOW BECAUSE I SUCKED HER LIFE ENERGY DRY.
BUT I'VE COMPLETELY RECOVERED.
A HUMAN KAMI IS SO CONVENIENT.
SO, IDIOT FOX. HOW DO YOU FEEL ABOUT YOUR MASTER BEING HALF DEAD?
K-KIRIHITO-SAMA!
YOU NEVER ARRIVE ON TIME, DO YOU?
BASTARD!
CRUNCH

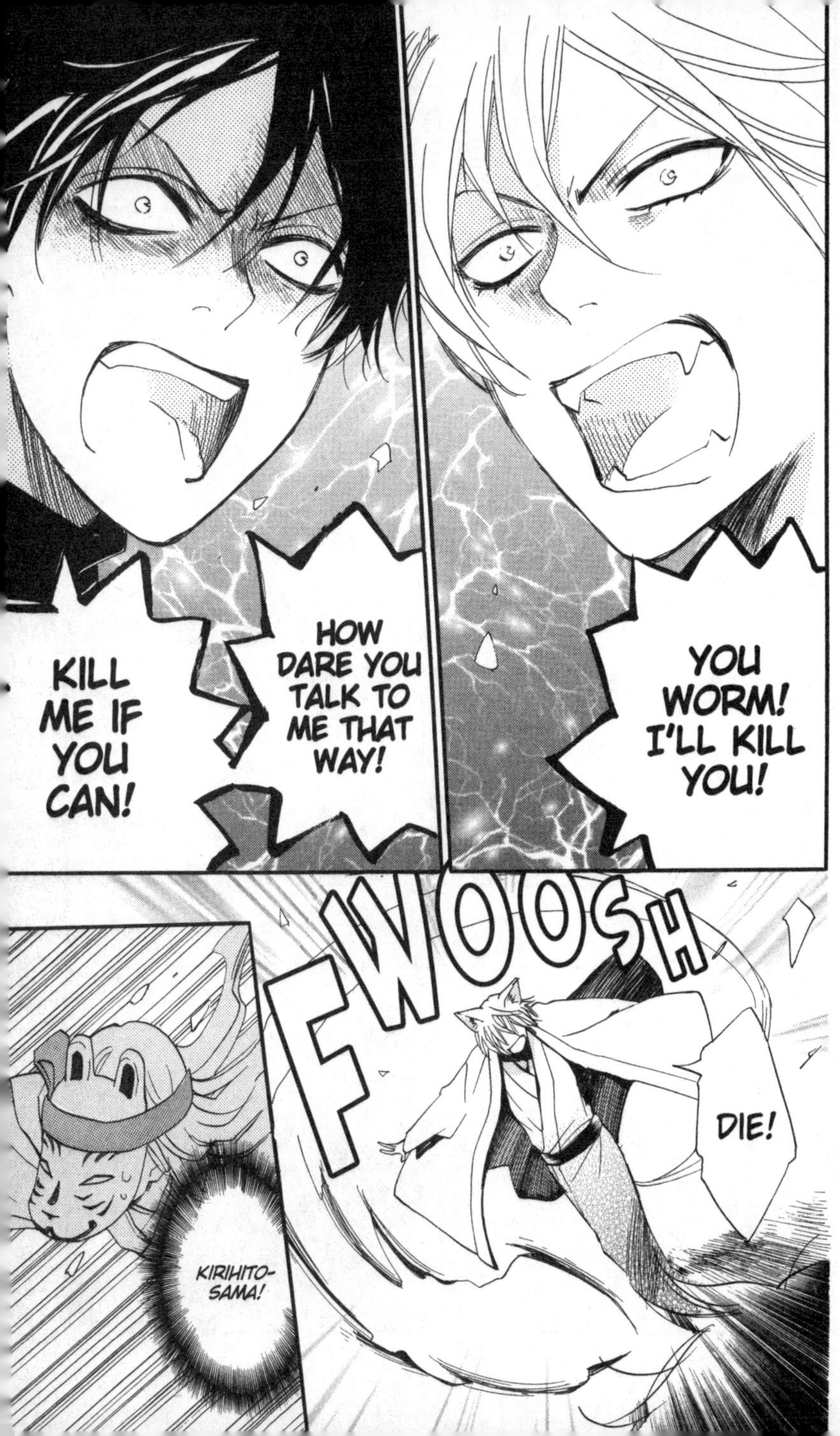
YOU WORM! I'LL KILL YOU!
HOW DARE YOU TALK TO ME THAT WAY!
KILL ME IF YOU CAN!
FWOOSH
DIE!
KIRIHITO-SAMA!

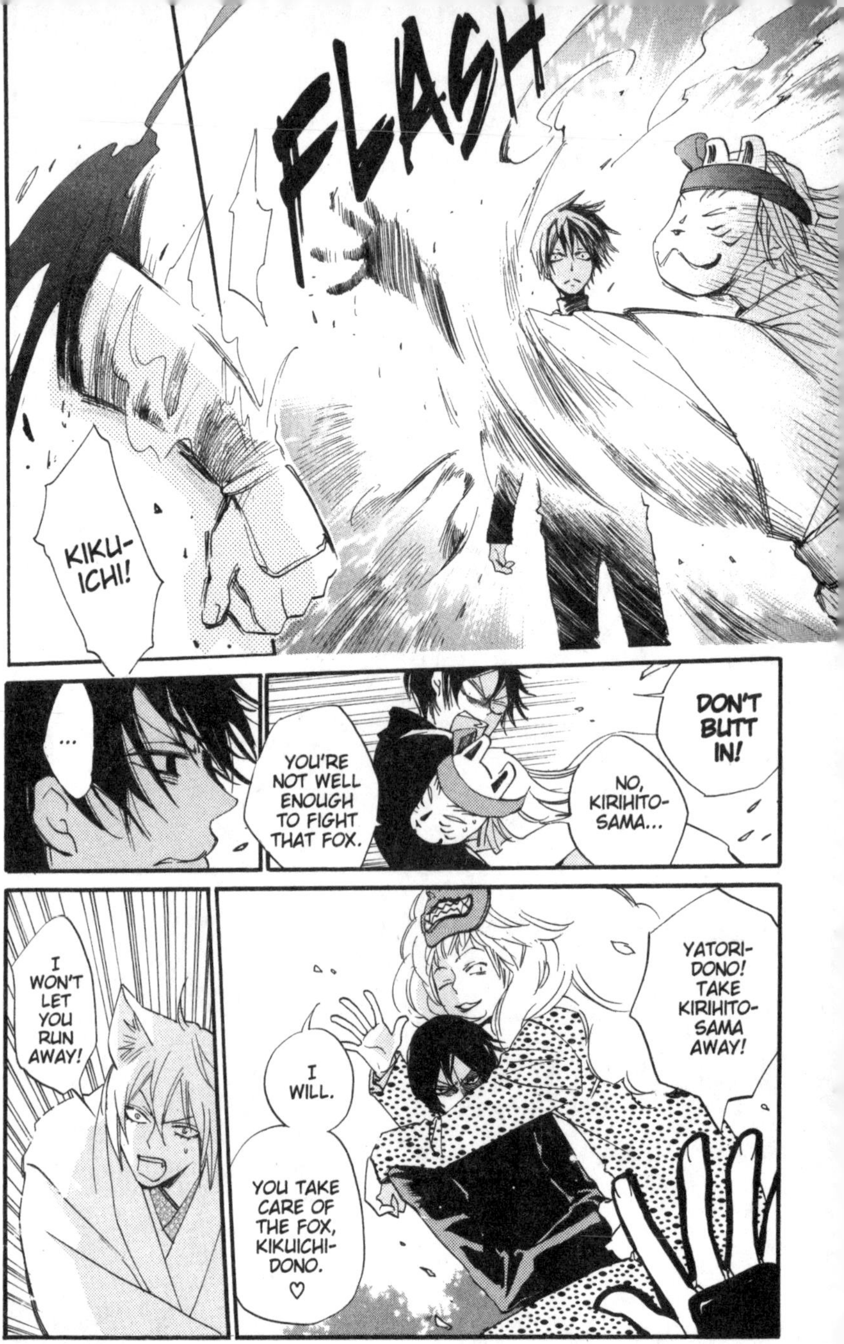
FLASH
KIKU-ICHI!
DON'T BUTT IN!
NO, KIRIHITO-SAMA...
YOU'RE NOT WELL ENOUGH TO FIGHT THAT FOX.
...
YATORI-DONO! TAKE KIRIHITO-SAMA AWAY!
I WILL.
YOU TAKE CARE OF THE FOX, KIKUICHI-DONO. ♡
I WON'T LET YOU RUN AWAY!

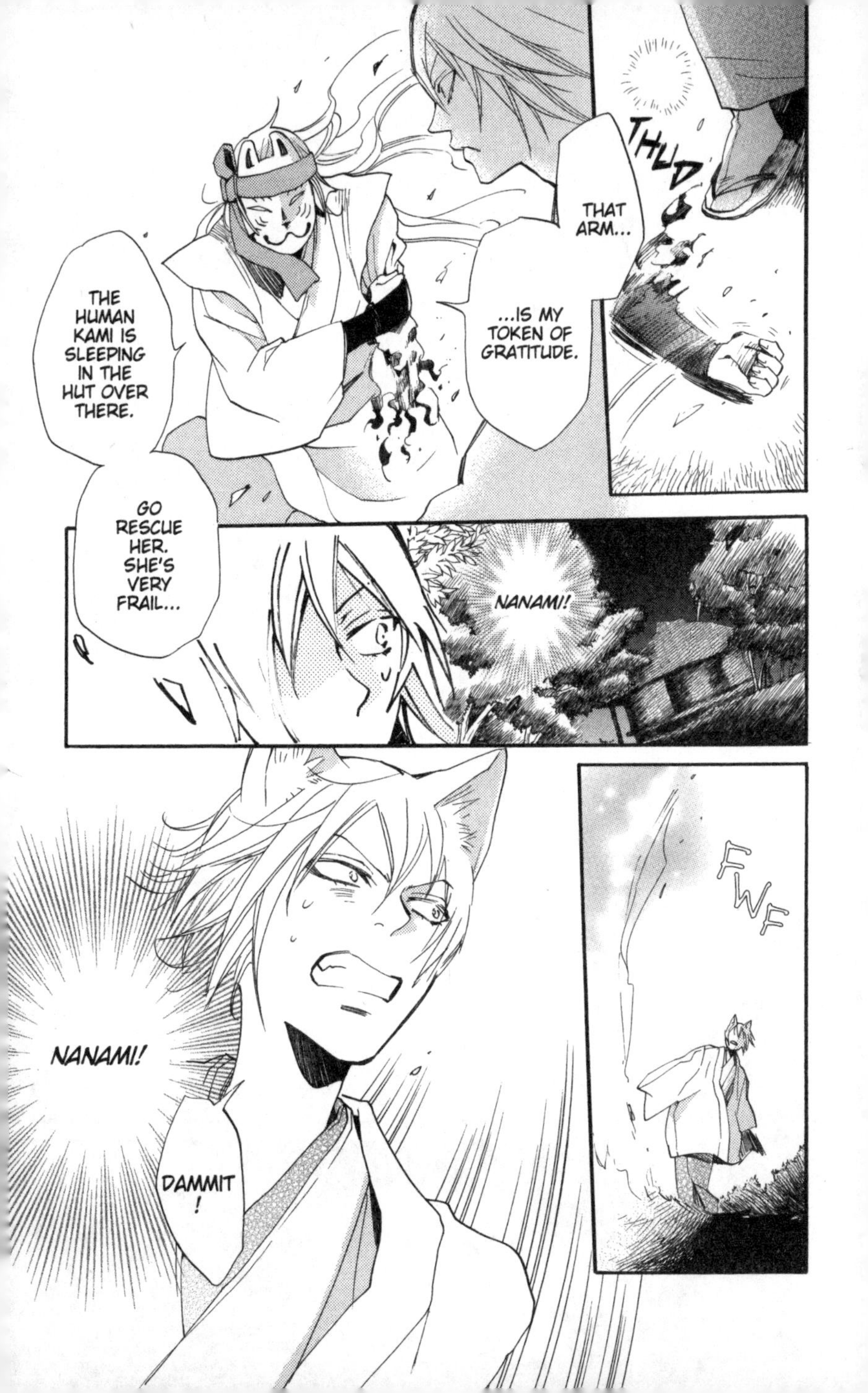
THUD
THAT ARM...
...IS MY TOKEN OF GRATITUDE.
THE HUMAN KAMI IS SLEEPING IN THE HUT OVER THERE.
GO RESCUE HER. SHE'S VERY FRAIL...
NANAMI!
FWF
NANAMI!
DAMMIT!

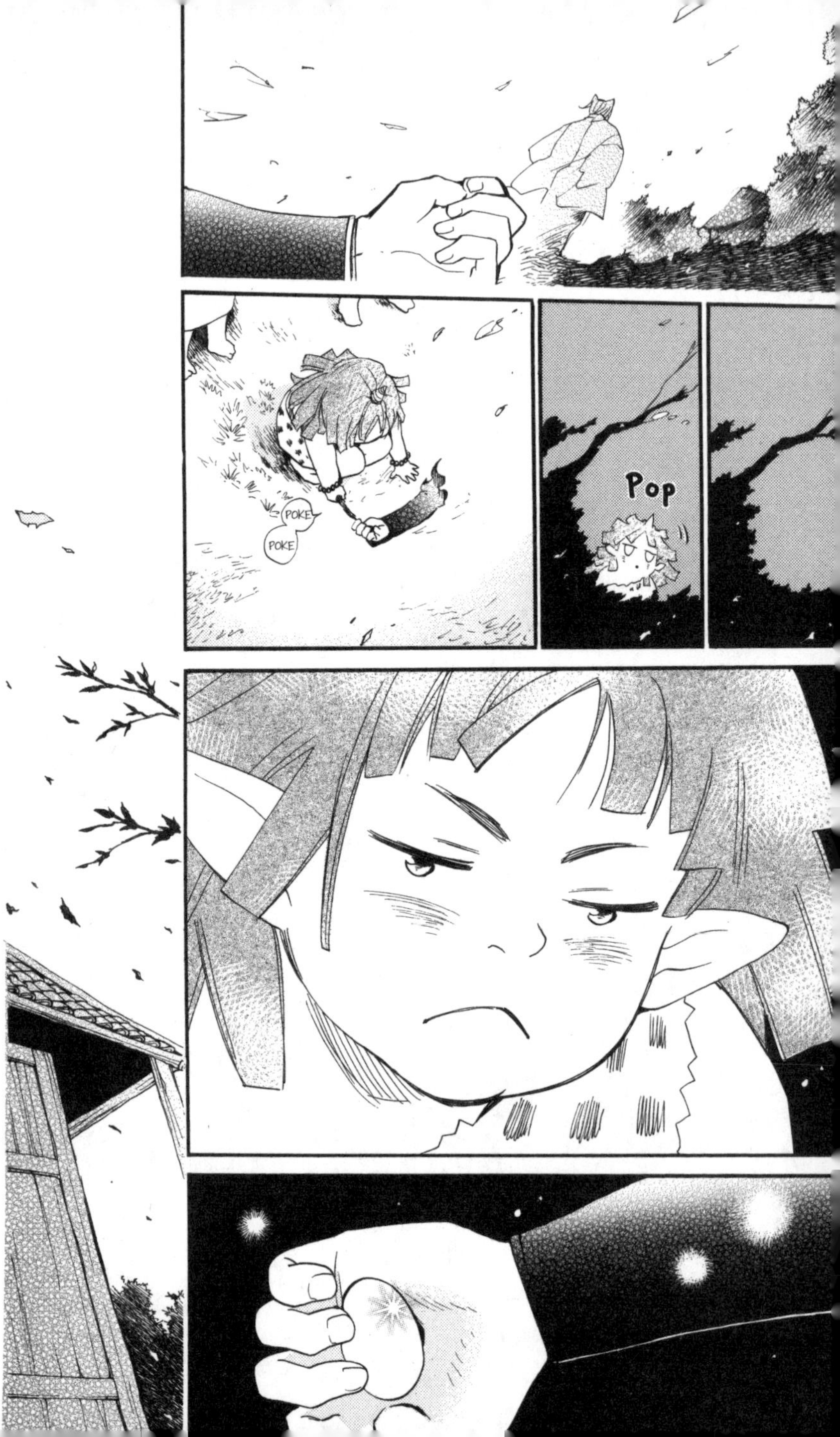
Pop
POKE
POKE

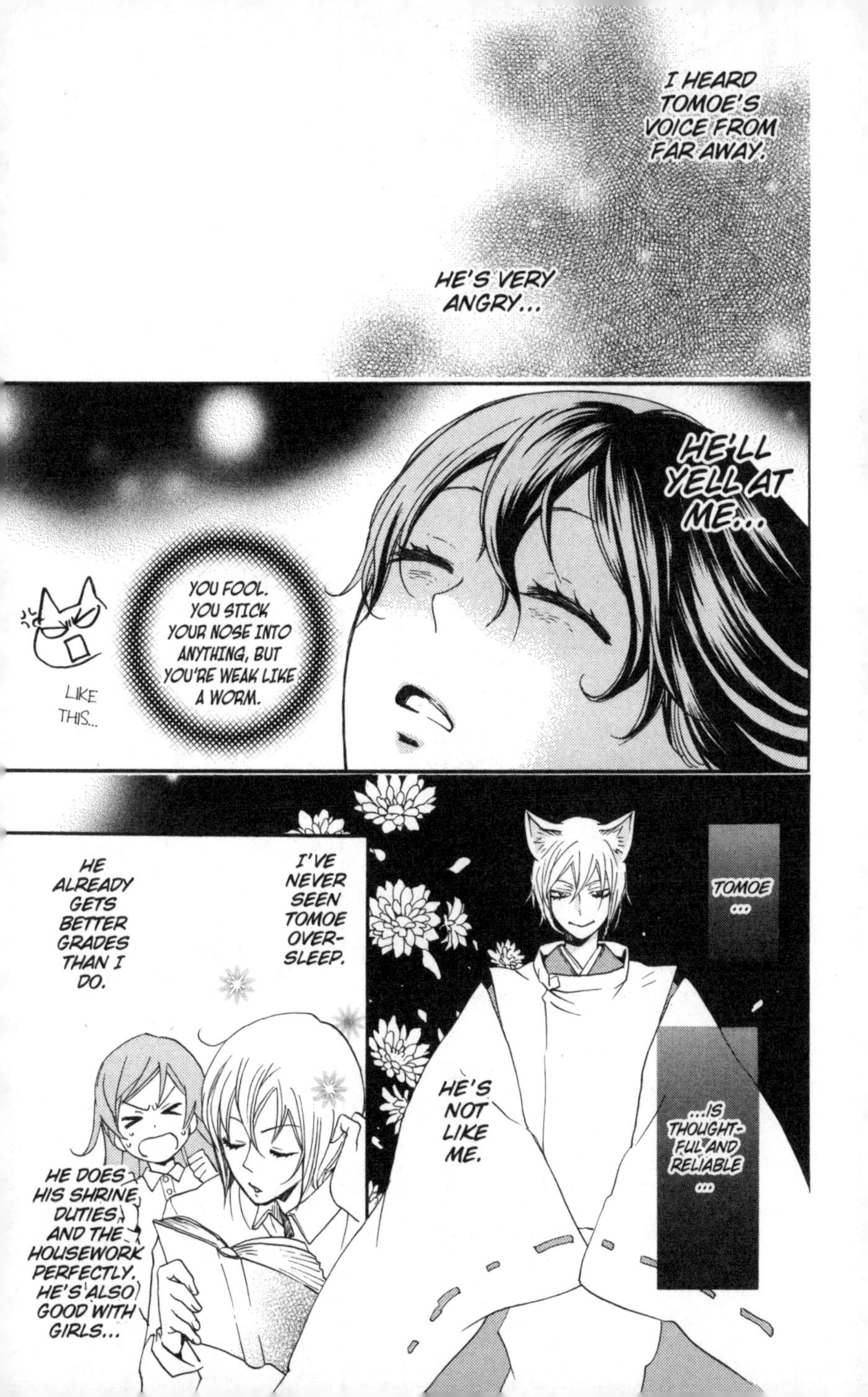
I HEARD TOMOE'S VOICE FROM FAR AWAY.
HE'S VERY ANGRY...
HE'LL YELL AT ME...
YOU FOOL. YOU STICK YOUR NOSE INTO ANYTHING, BUT YOU'RE WEAK LIKE A WORM.
LIKE THIS...
TOMOE...
...IS THOUGHTFUL AND RELIABLE...
HE'S NOT LIKE ME.
I'VE NEVER SEEN TOMOE OVERSLEEP.
HE ALREADY GETS BETTER GRADES THAN I DO.
HE DOES HIS SHRINE DUTIES AND THE HOUSEWORK PERFECTLY. HE'S ALSO GOOD WITH GIRLS...

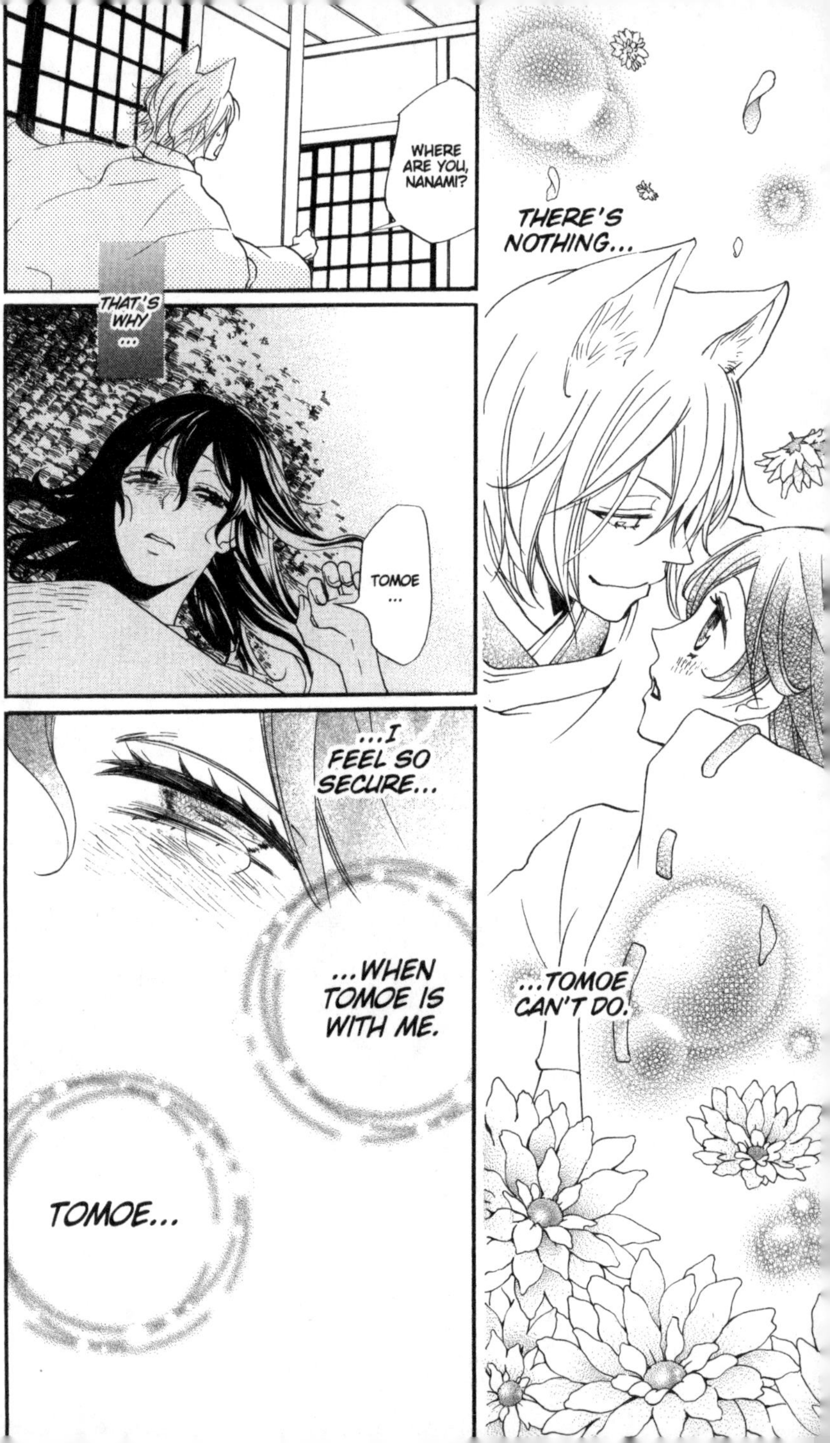
THERE'S NOTHING...
...TOMOE CAN'T DO.
WHERE ARE YOU, NANAMI?
THAT'S WHY ...
TOMOE ...
...I FEEL SO SECURE...
...WHEN TOMOE IS WITH ME.
TOMOE...

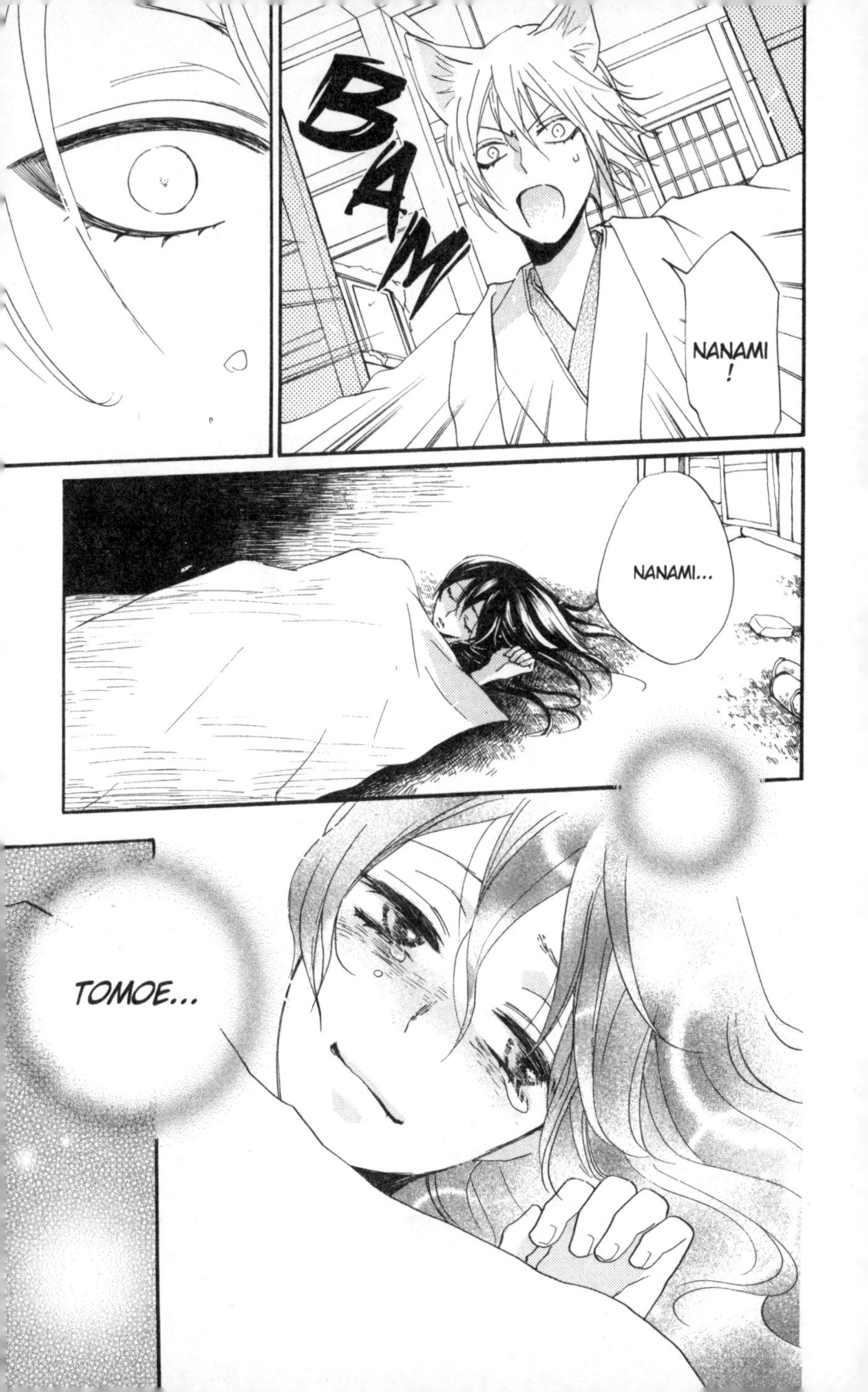
BAM
NANAMI!
NANAMI...
TOMOE...

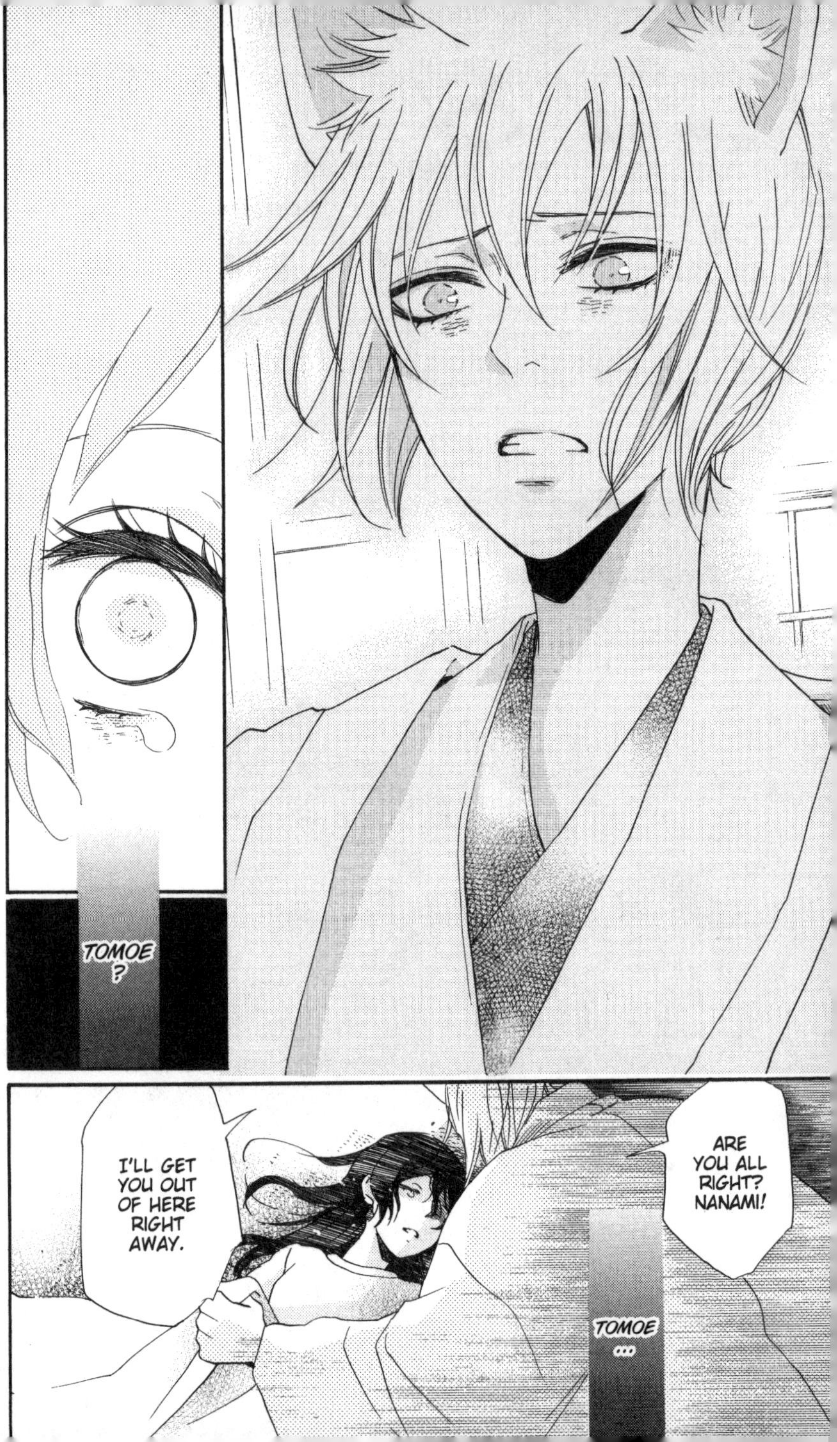
TOMOE ?
ARE YOU ALL RIGHT? NANAMI!
I'LL GET YOU OUT OF HERE RIGHT AWAY.
TOMOE ...

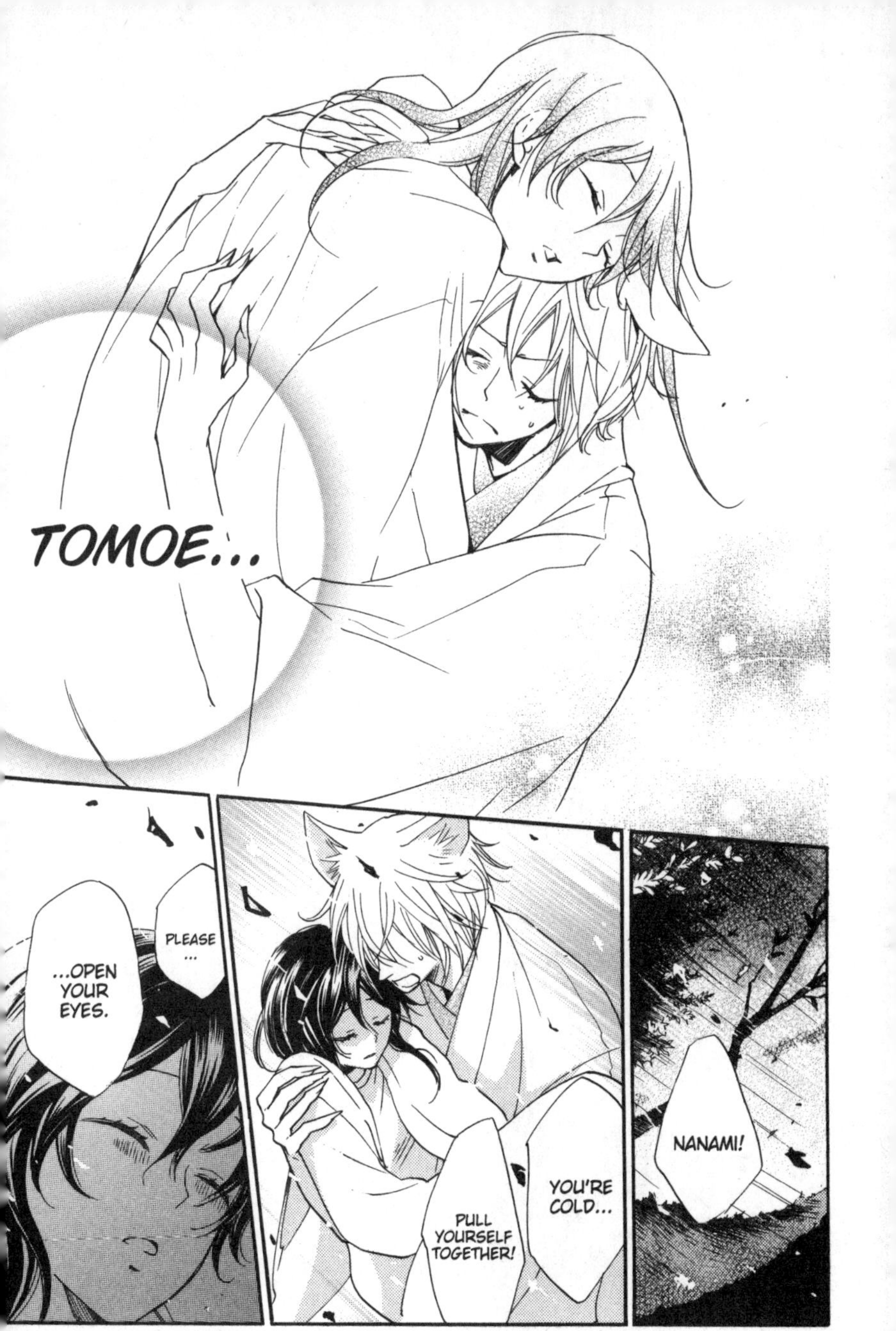
TOMOE...
NANAMI!
YOU'RE COLD...
PULL YOURSELF TOGETHER!
PLEASE...
...OPEN YOUR EYES.

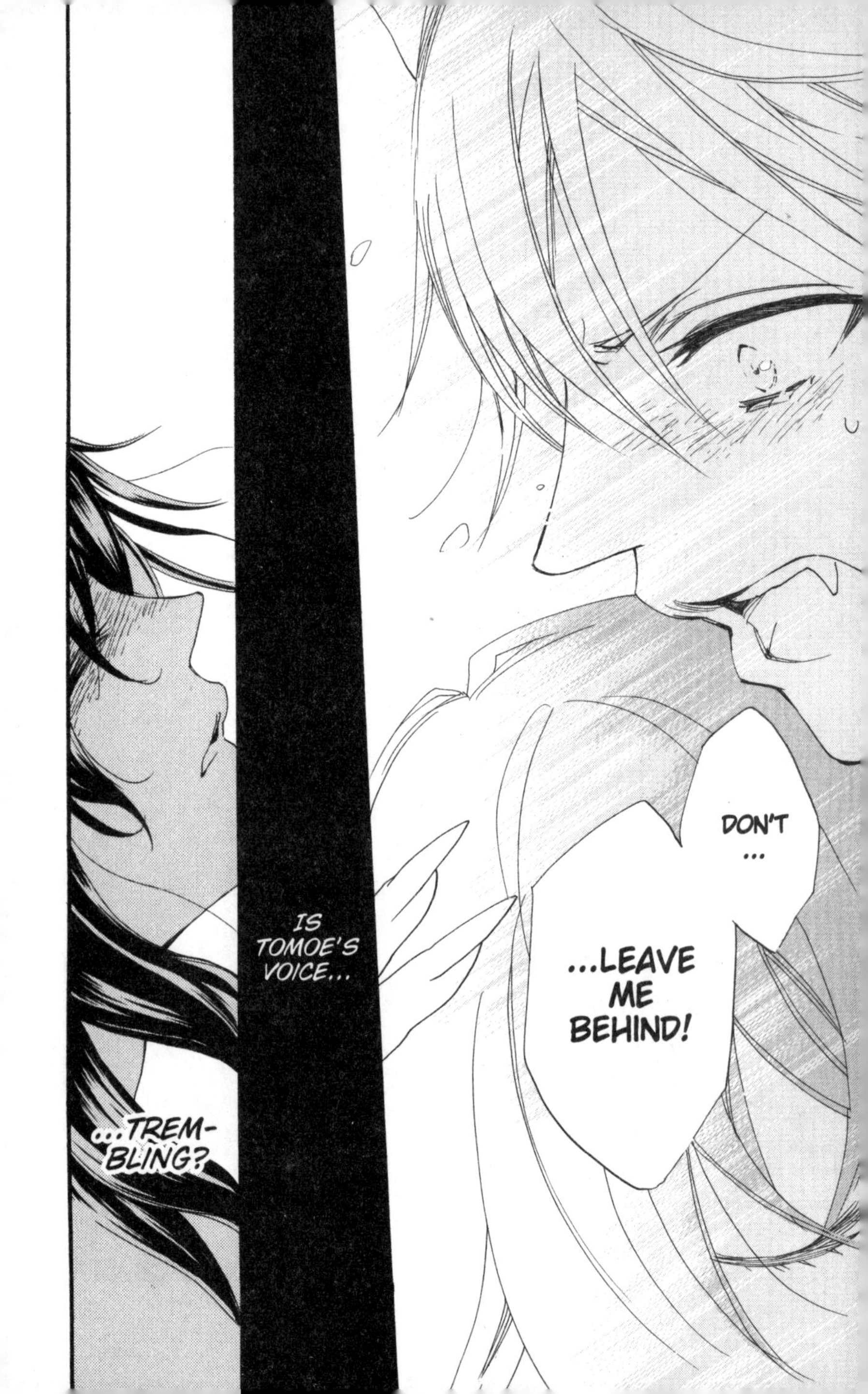
DON'T ...
...LEAVE ME BEHIND!
IS TOMOE'S VOICE...
...TREM-BLING?

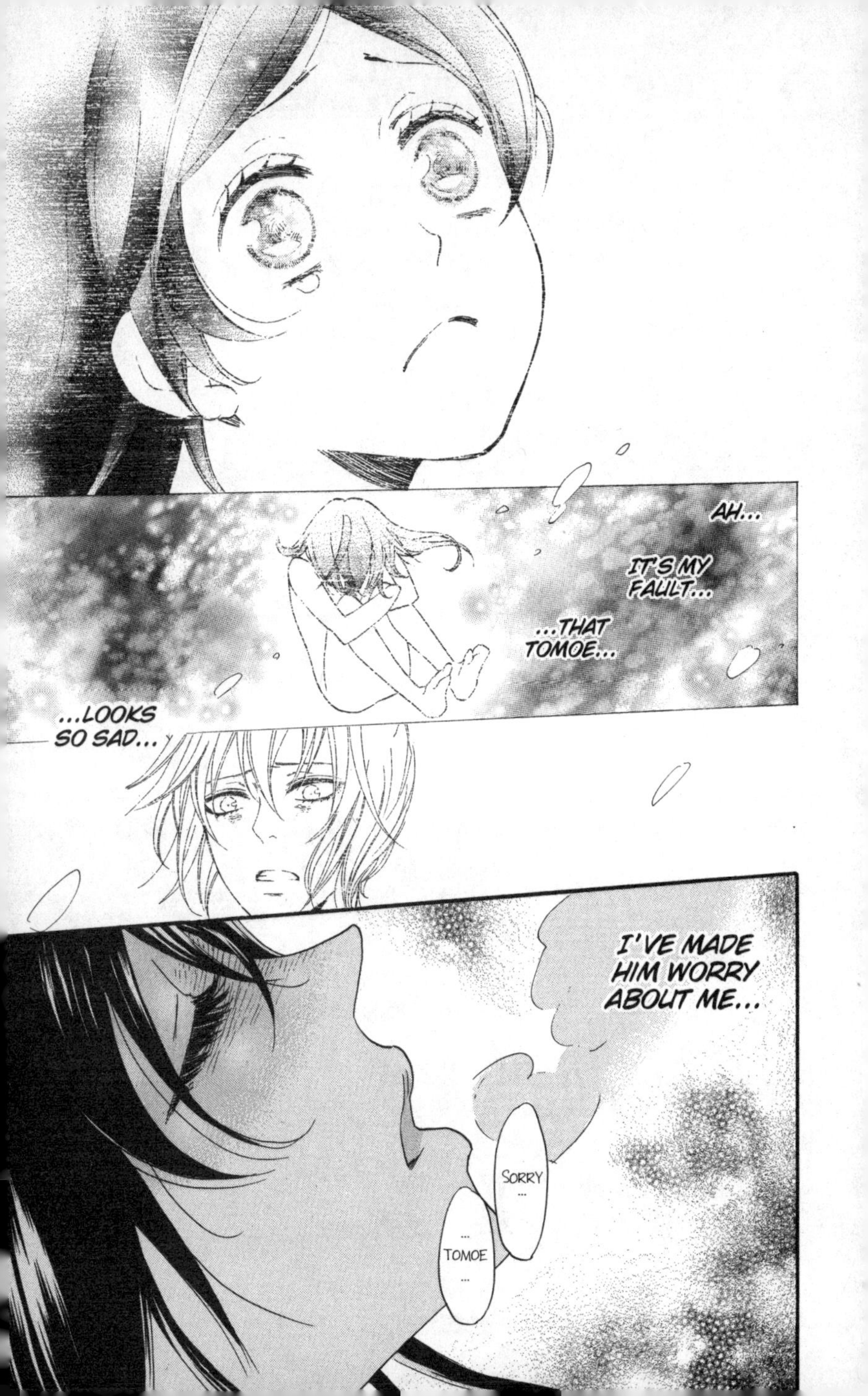
AH...
IT'S MY FAULT...
...THAT TOMOE...
...LOOKS SO SAD...
I'VE MADE HIM WORRY ABOUT ME...
SORRY...
...TOMOE...

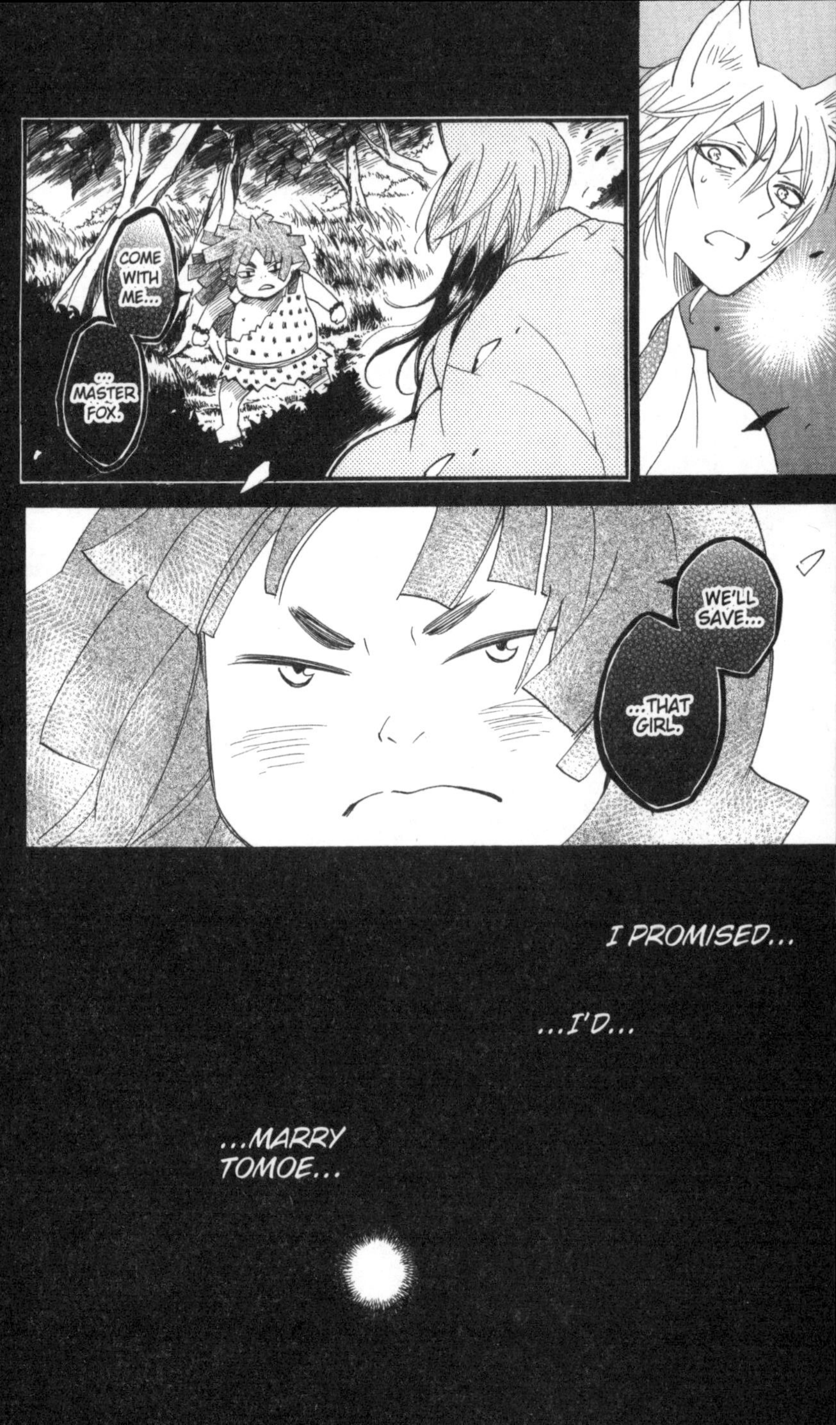
COME WITH ME...
...MASTER FOX.
WE'LL SAVE...
...THAT GIRL.
I PROMISED...
...I'D...
...MARRY TOMOE...

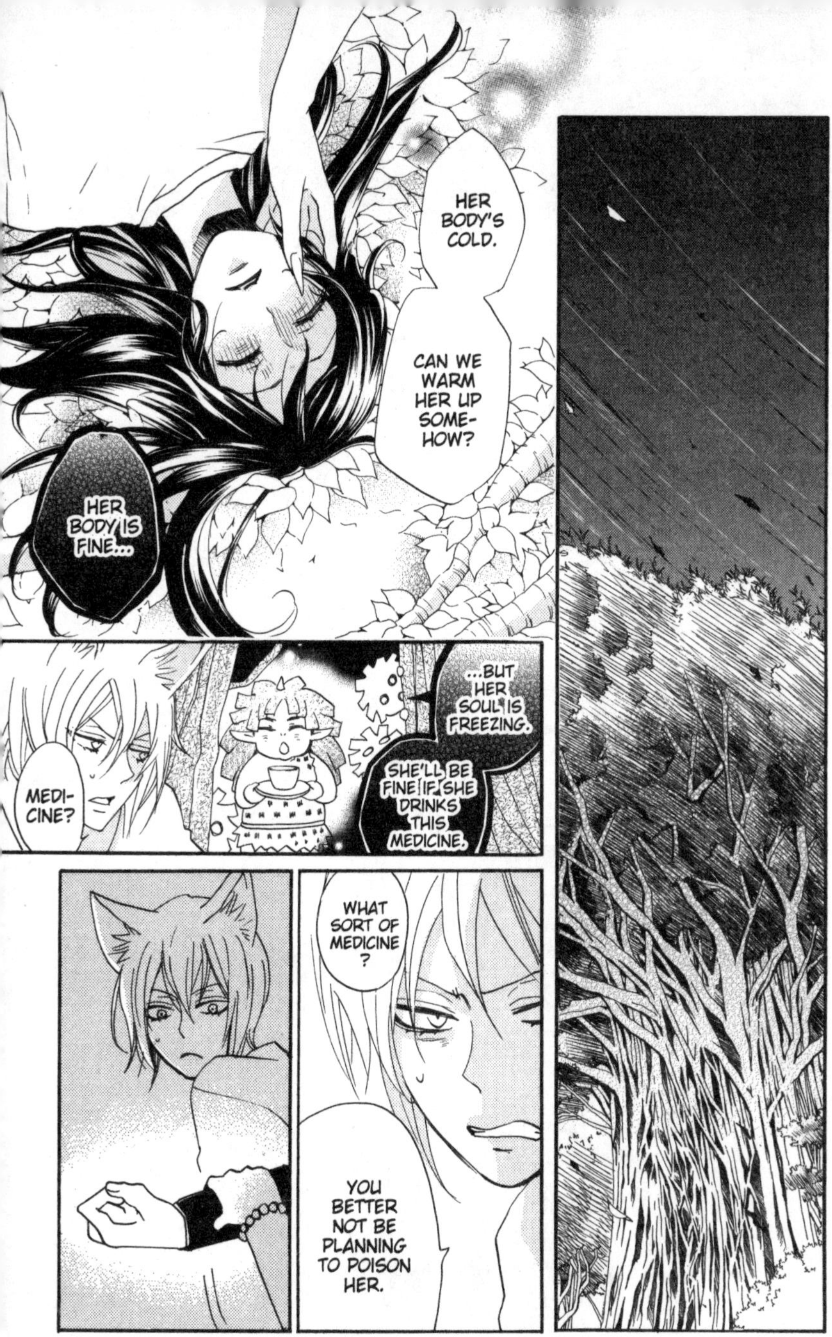
HER BODY'S COLD.
CAN WE WARM HER UP SOME-HOW?
HER BODY IS FINE...
...BUT HER SOUL IS FREEZING.
SHE'LL BE FINE IF SHE DRINKS THIS MEDICINE.
MEDI-CINE?
WHAT SORT OF MEDICINE ?
YOU BETTER NOT BE PLANNING TO POISON HER.

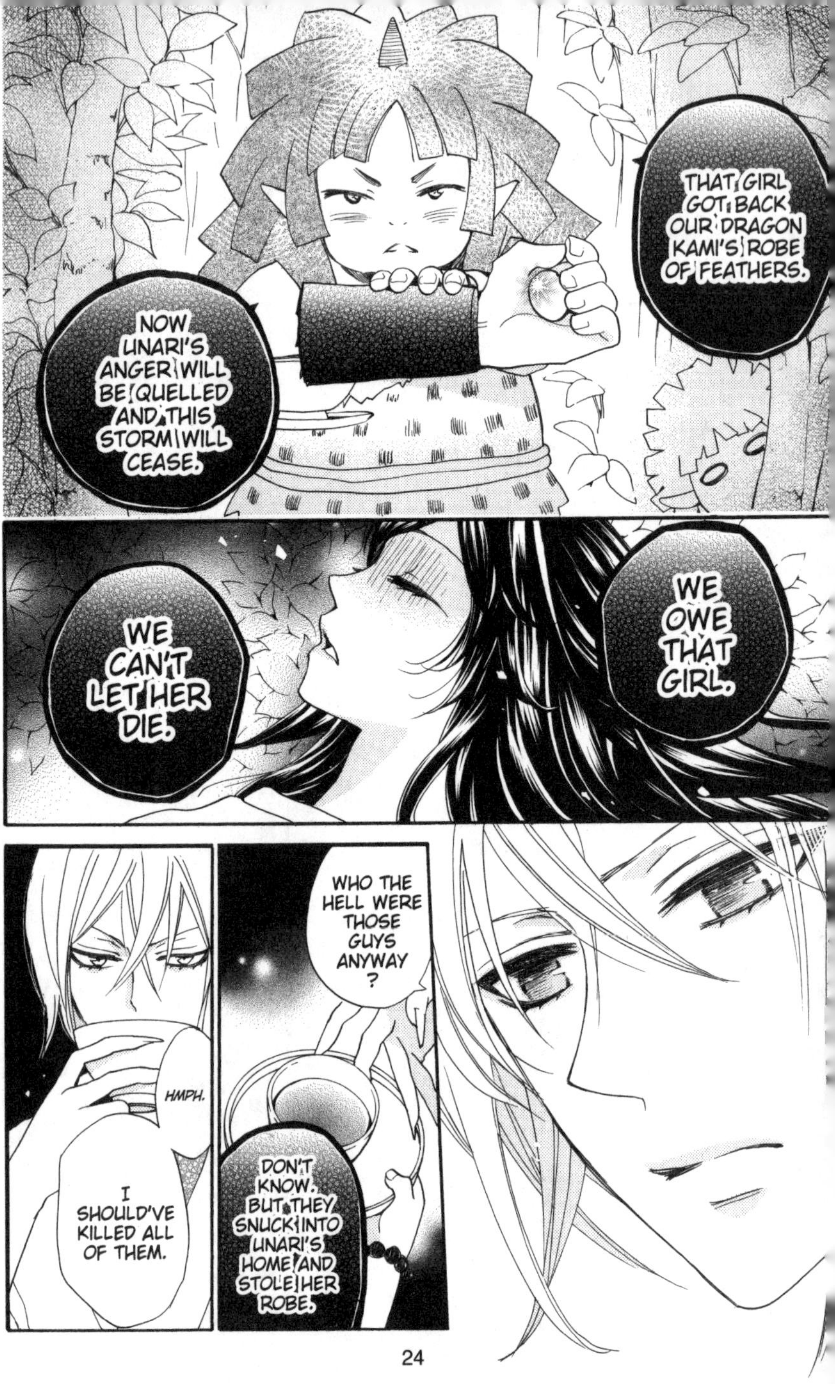
THAT GIRL GOT BACK OUR DRAGON KAMI'S ROBE OF FEATHERS.
NOW UNARI'S ANGER WILL BE QUELLED AND THIS STORM WILL CEASE.
WE OWE THAT GIRL.
WE CAN'T LET HER DIE.
WHO THE HELL WERE THOSE GUYS ANYWAY?
DON'T KNOW. BUT THEY SNUCK INTO UNARI'S HOME AND STOLE HER ROBE.
HMPH.
I SHOULD'VE KILLED ALL OF THEM.

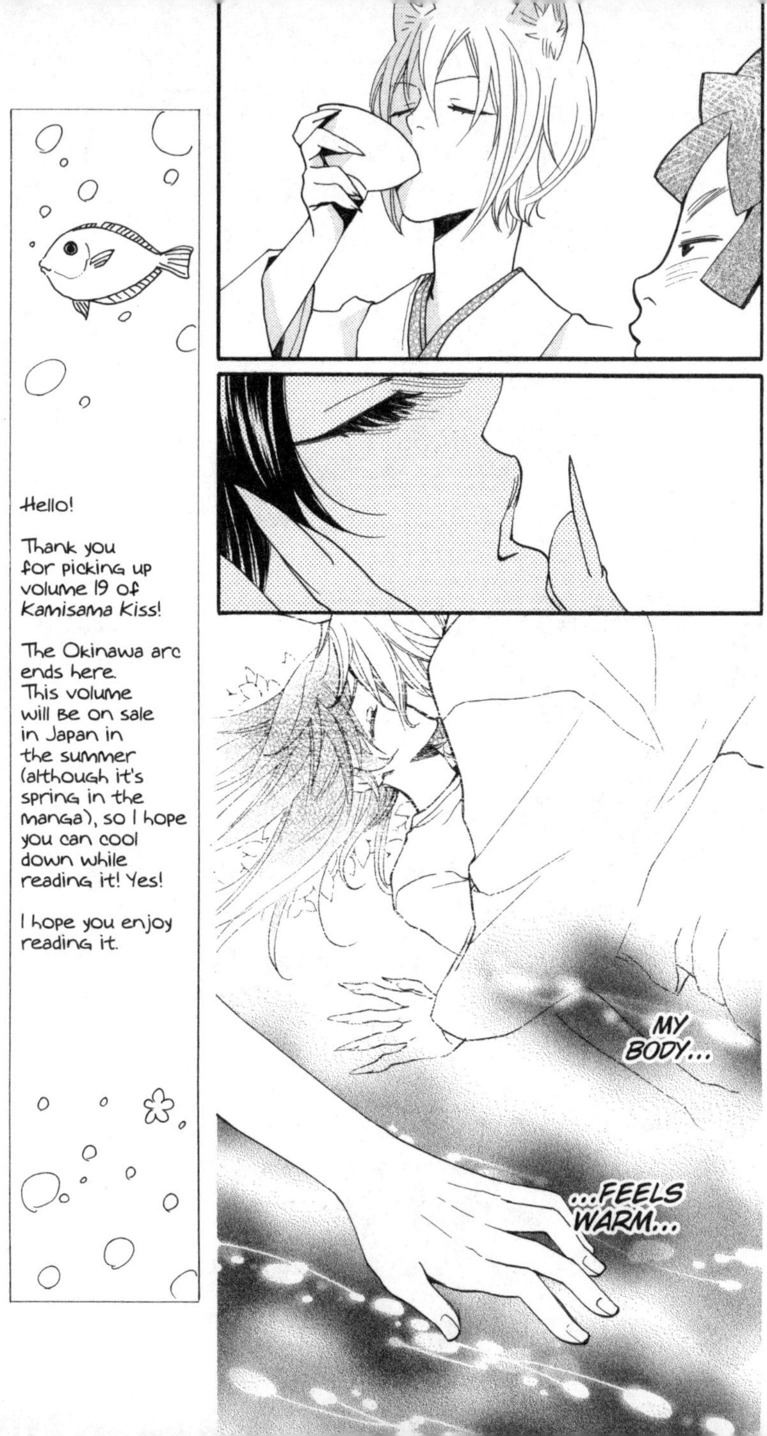
MY BODY...
...FEELS WARM...

Hello!

Thank you for picking up volume 19 of Kamisama Kiss!

The Okinawa arc ends here. This volume will be on sale in Japan in the summer (although it's spring in the manga), so I hope you can cool down while reading it! Yes!

I hope you enjoy reading it.

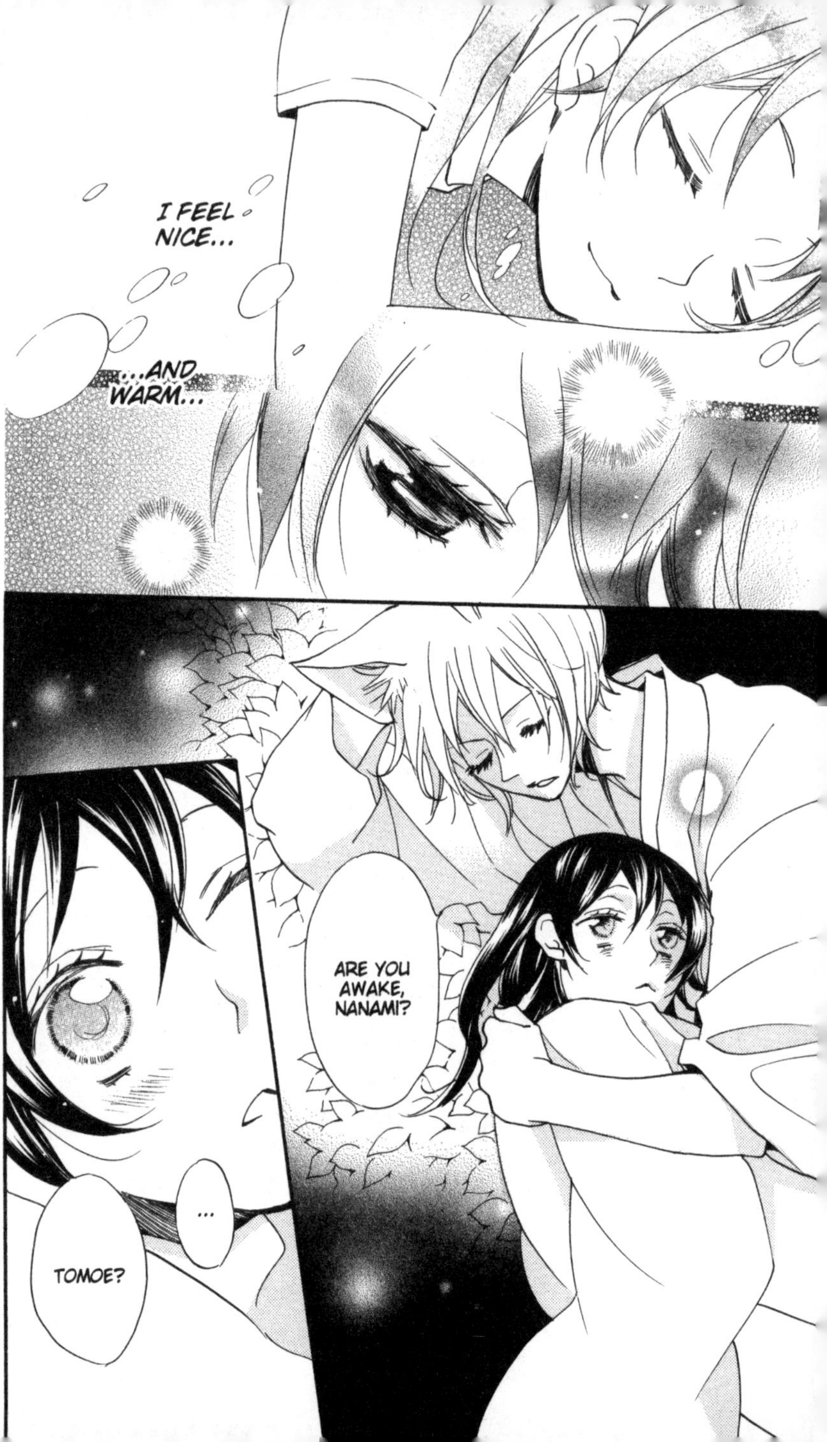
I FEEL NICE...
...AND WARM...
ARE YOU AWAKE, NANAMI?
...
TOMOE?

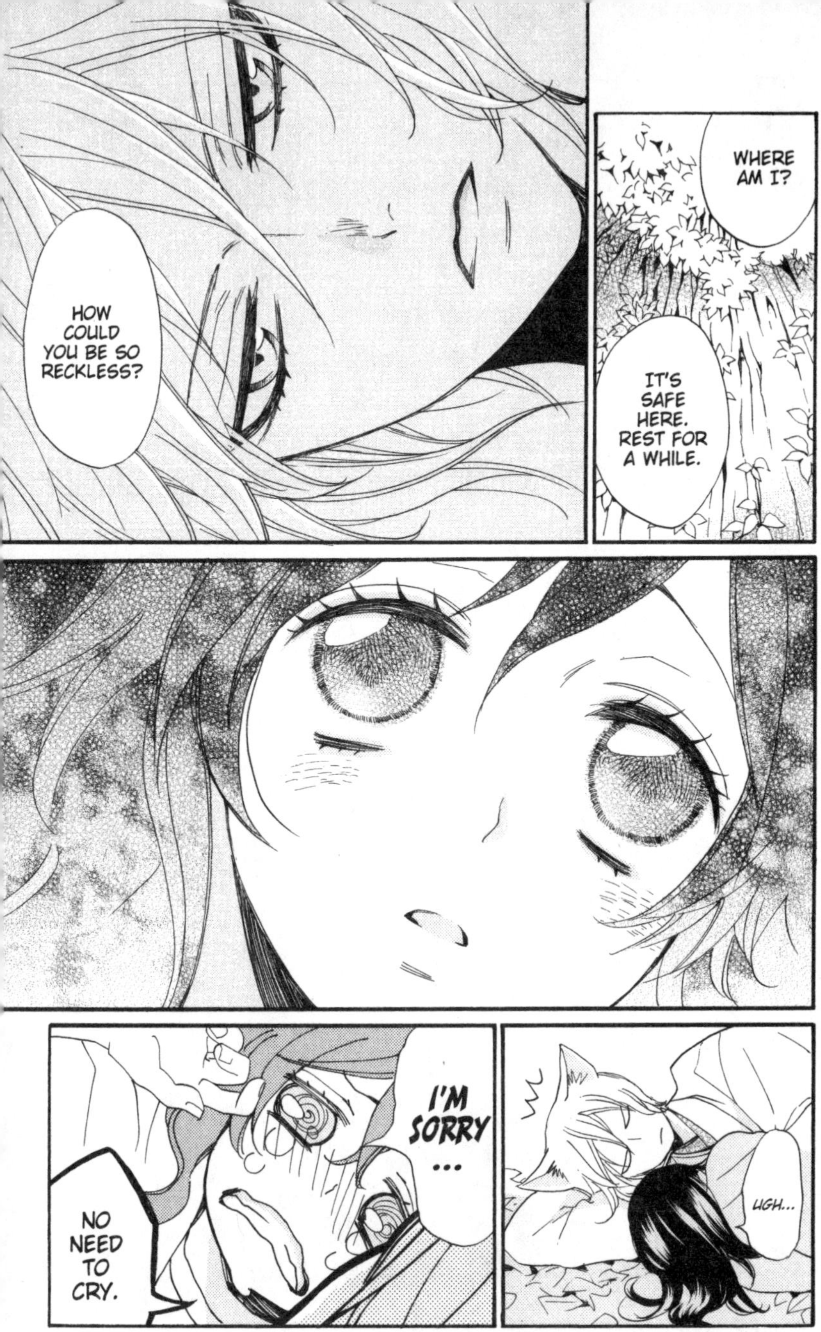
WHERE AM I?
IT'S SAFE HERE. REST FOR A WHILE.
HOW COULD YOU BE SO RECKLESS?
UGH...
I'M SORRY...
NO NEED TO CRY.

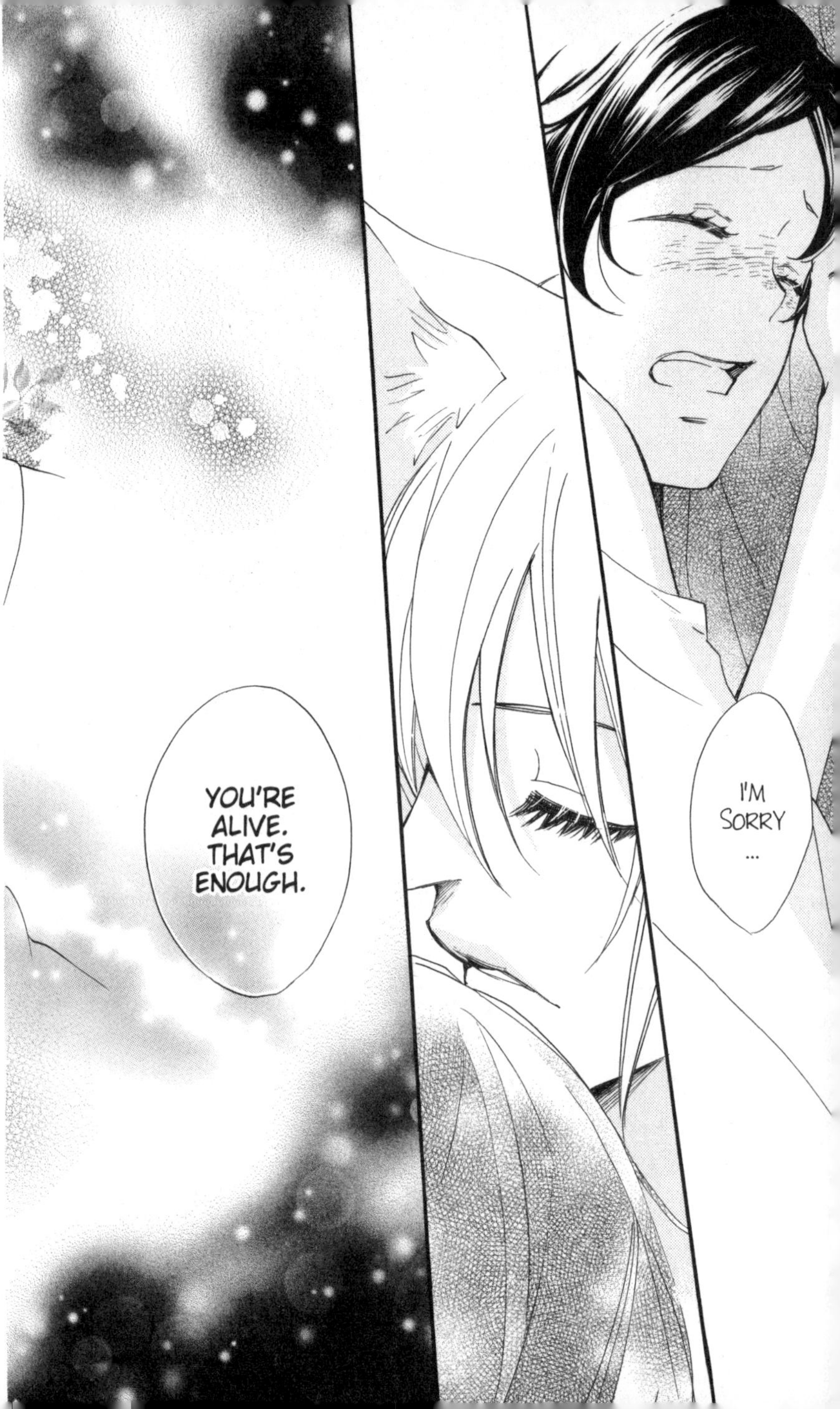
I'M SORRY ...
YOU'RE ALIVE. THAT'S ENOUGH.

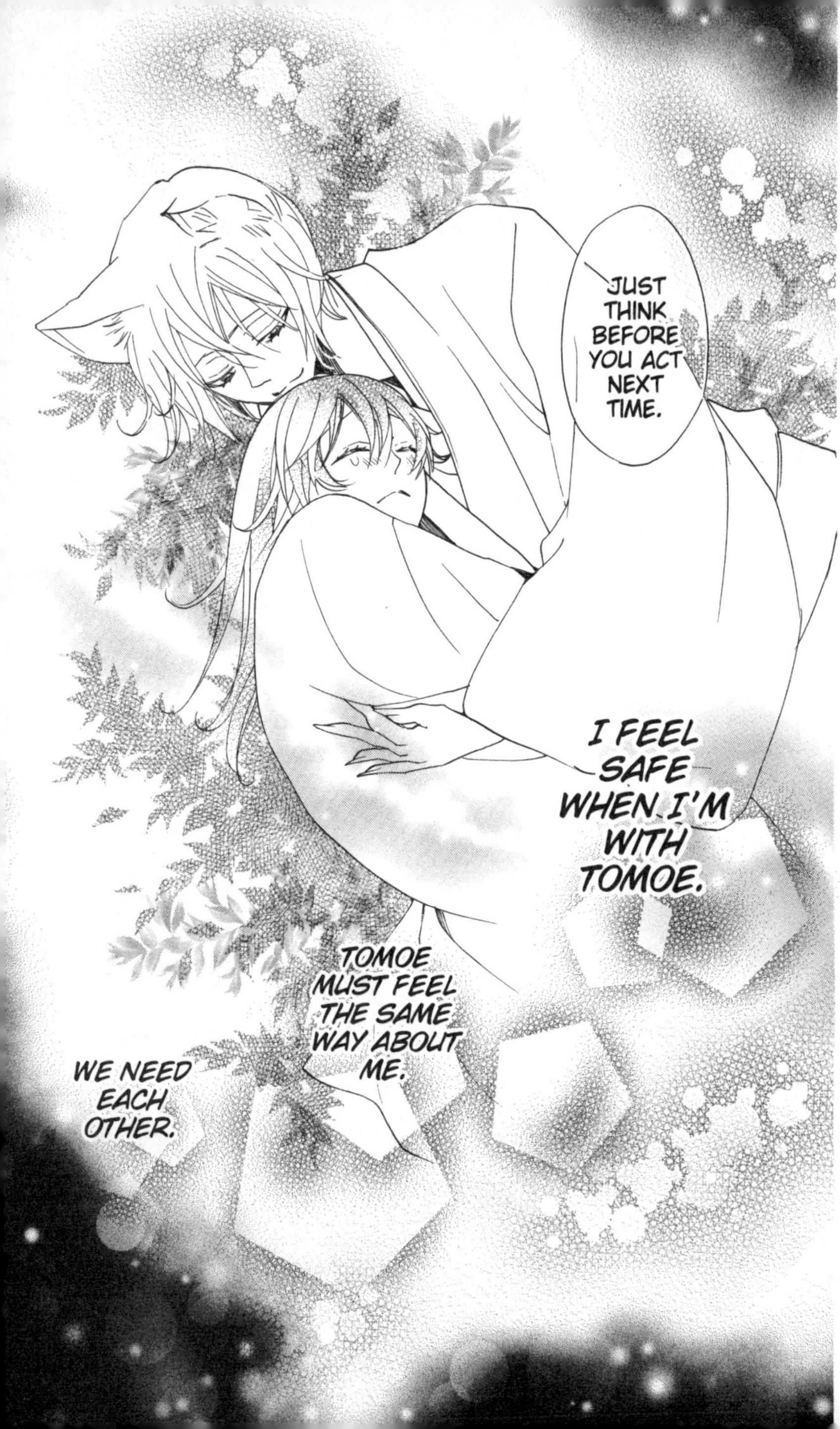
JUST THINK BEFORE YOU ACT NEXT TIME.
I FEEL SAFE WHEN I'M WITH TOMOE.
TOMOE MUST FEEL THE SAME WAY ABOUT ME.
WE NEED EACH OTHER.

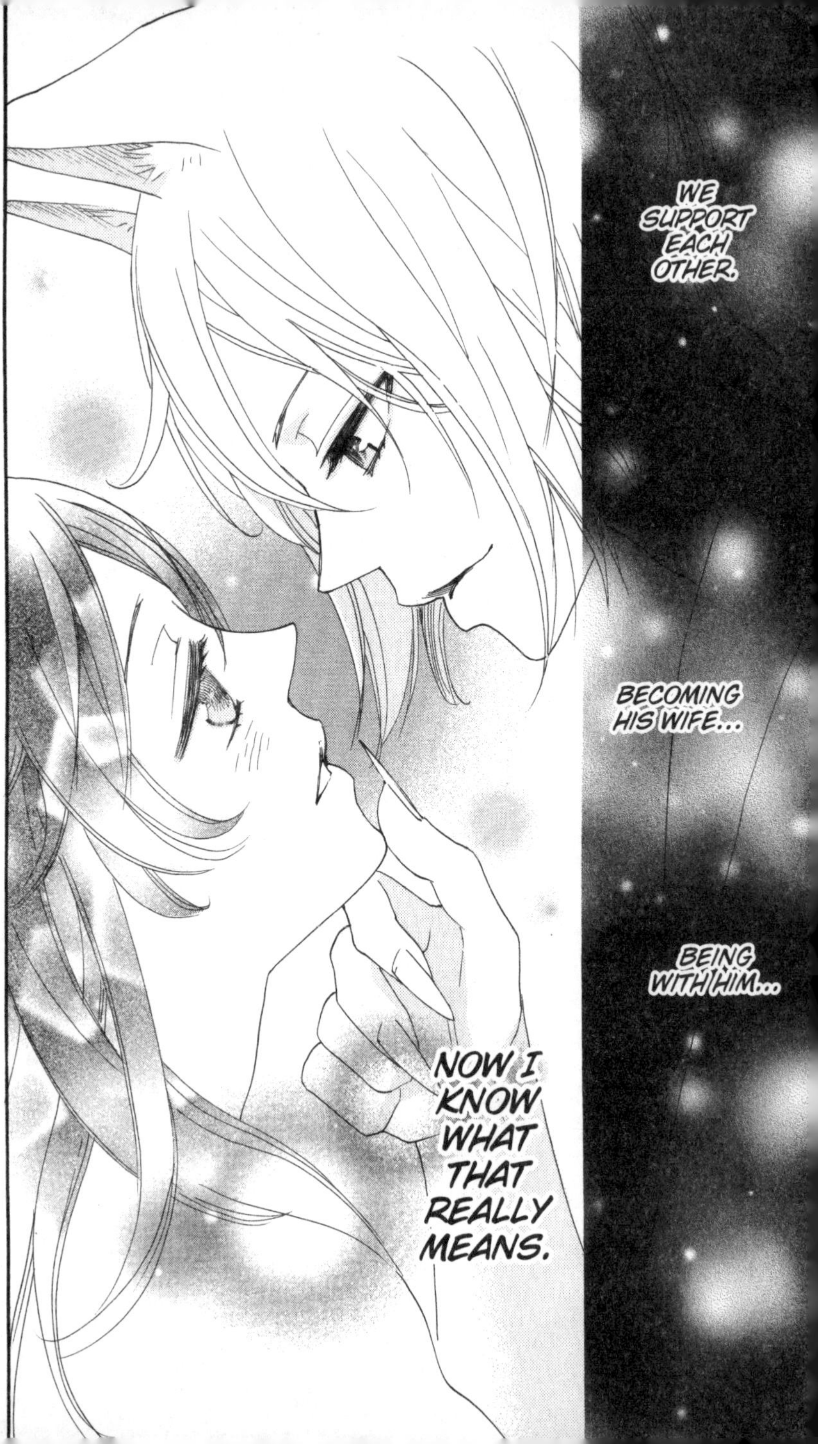
WE SUPPORT EACH OTHER.
BECOMING HIS WIFE...
BEING WITH HIM...
NOW I KNOW WHAT THAT REALLY MEANS.

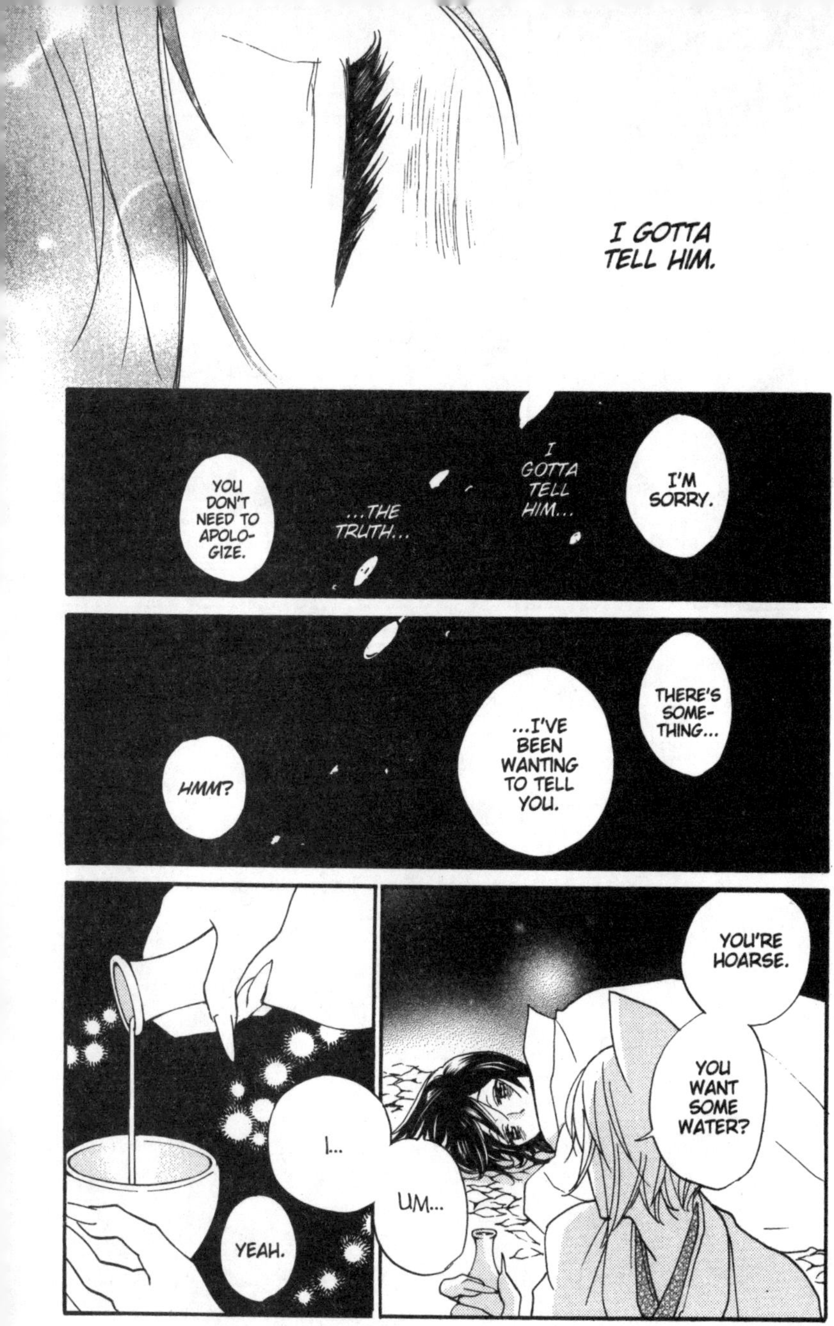
I GOTTA TELL HIM.
I'M SORRY.
I GOTTA TELL HIM...
...THE TRUTH...
YOU DON'T NEED TO APOLOGIZE.
THERE'S SOMETHING...
...I'VE BEEN WANTING TO TELL YOU.
HMM?
YOU'RE HOARSE.
YOU WANT SOME WATER?
I...
UM...
YEAH.

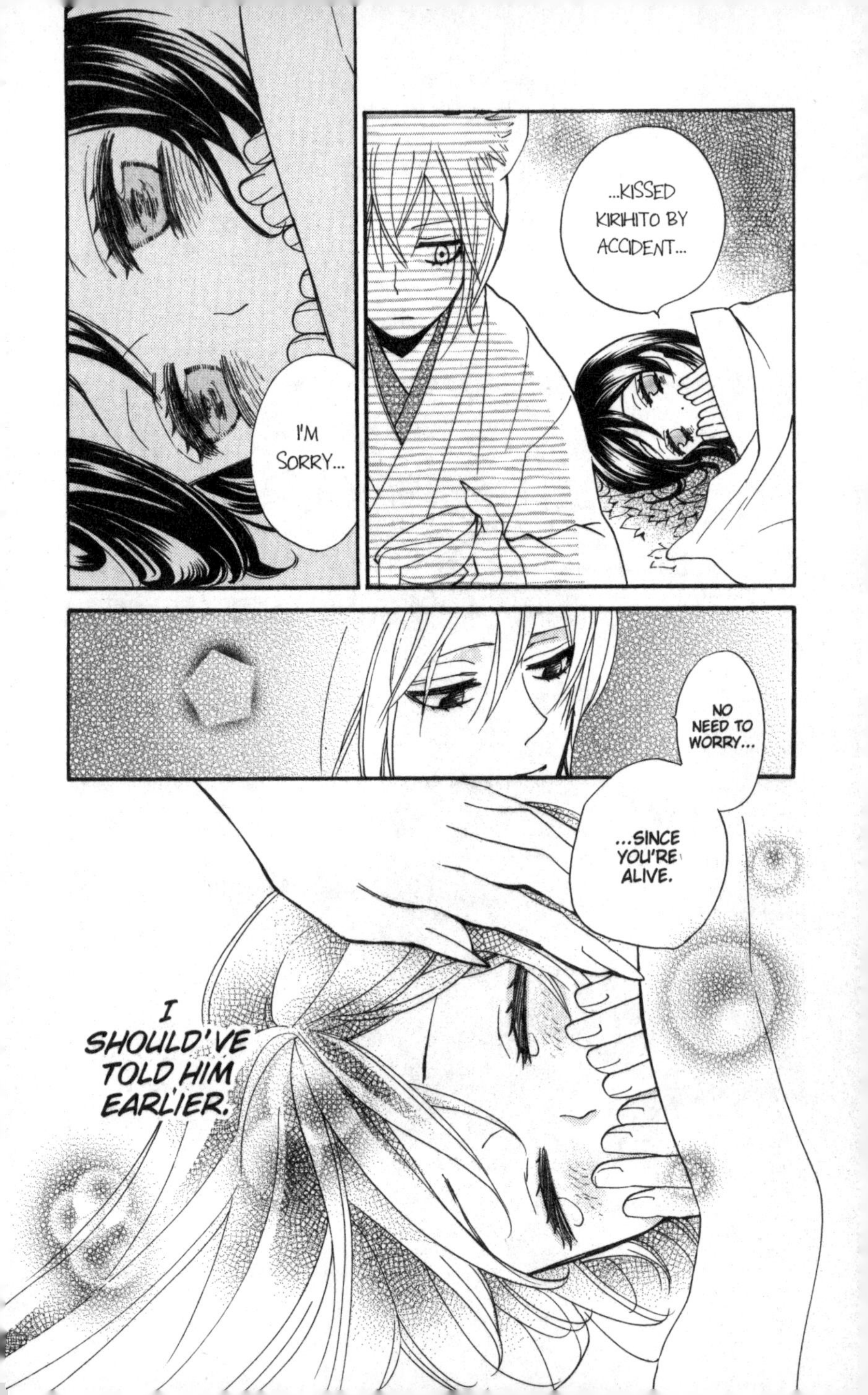
...KISSED KIRIHITO BY ACCIDENT...
I'M SORRY...
NO NEED TO WORRY...
...SINCE YOU'RE ALIVE.
I SHOULD'VE TOLD HIM EARLIER.

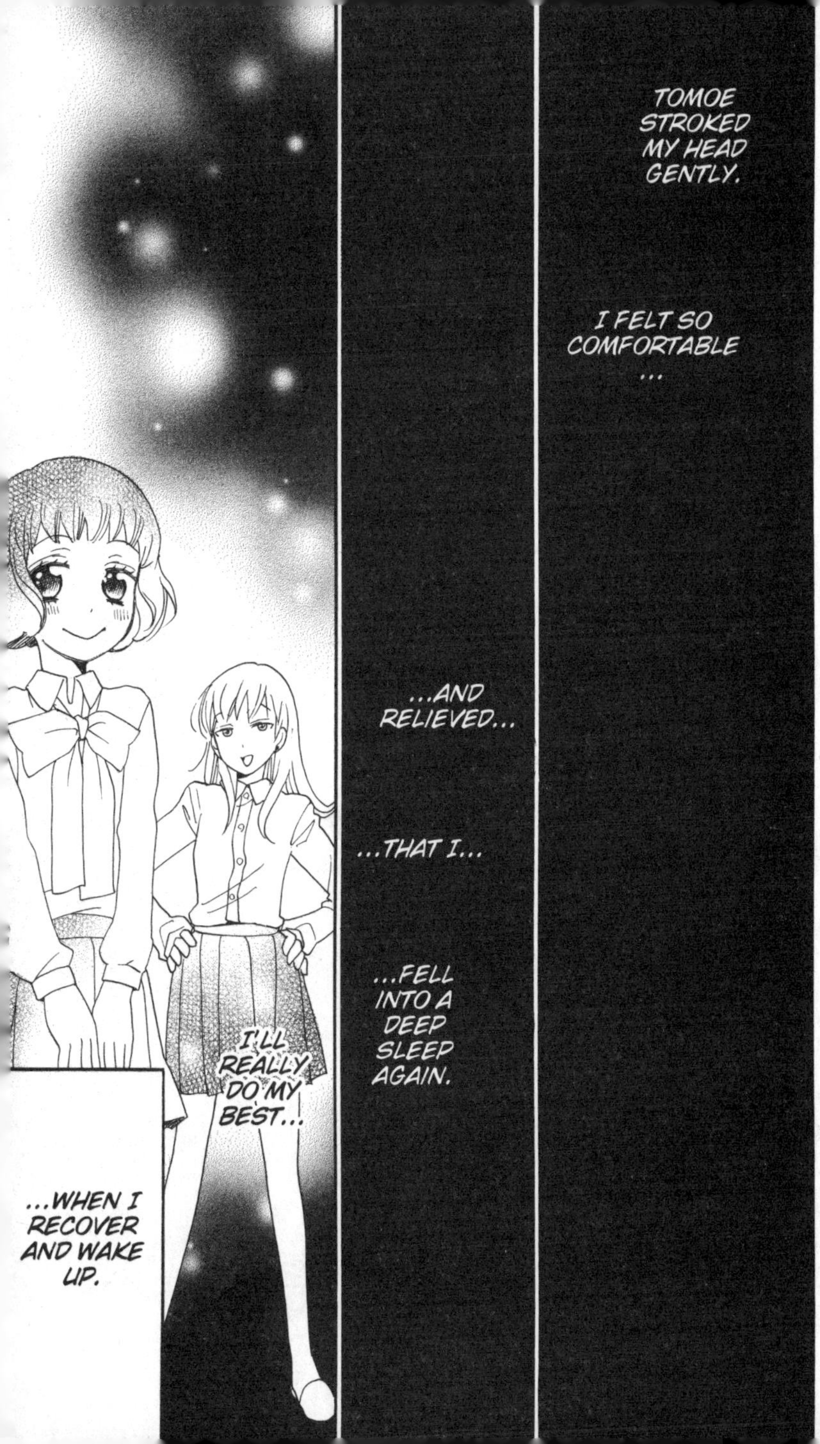
TOMOE STROKED MY HEAD GENTLY.
I FELT SO COMFORTABLE ...
...AND RELIEVED...
...THAT I...
...FELL INTO A DEEP SLEEP AGAIN.
I'LL REALLY DO MY BEST...
...WHEN I RECOVER AND WAKE UP.

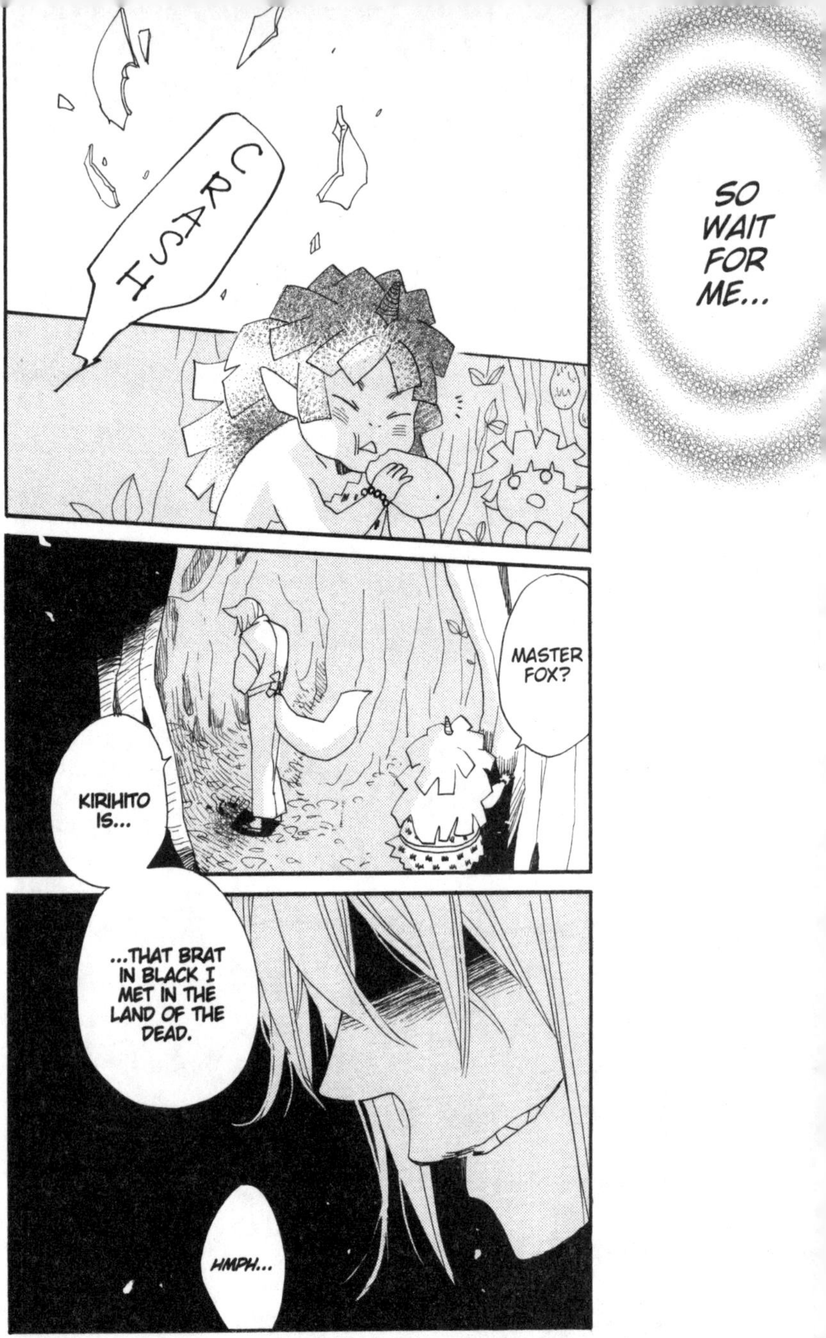
SO WAIT FOR ME...
CRASH
MASTER FOX?
KIRIHITO IS...
...THAT BRAT IN BLACK I MET IN THE LAND OF THE DEAD.
HMPH...

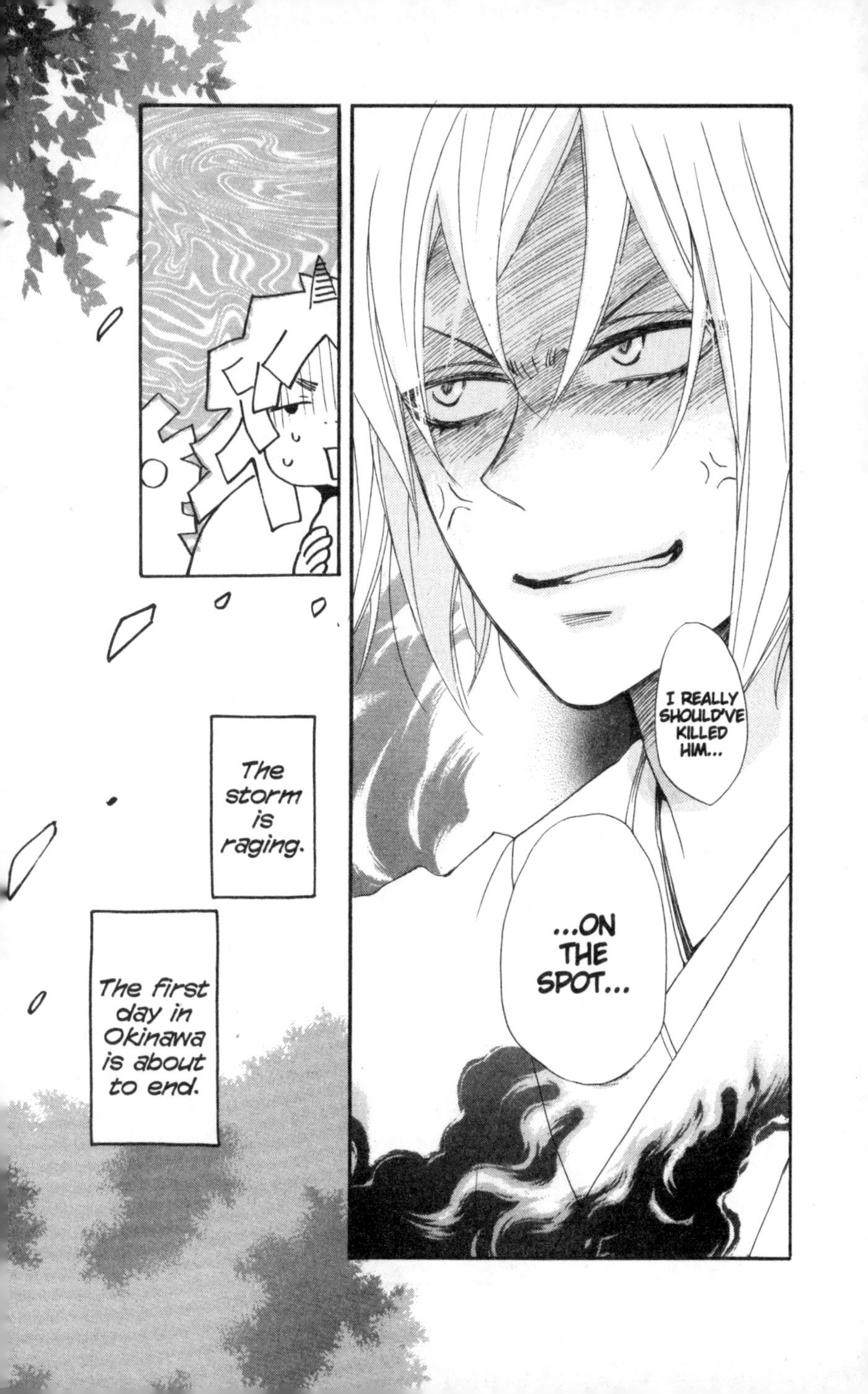
I REALLY SHOULD'VE KILLED HIM...
...ON THE SPOT...
The storm is raging.
The first day in Okinawa is about to end.

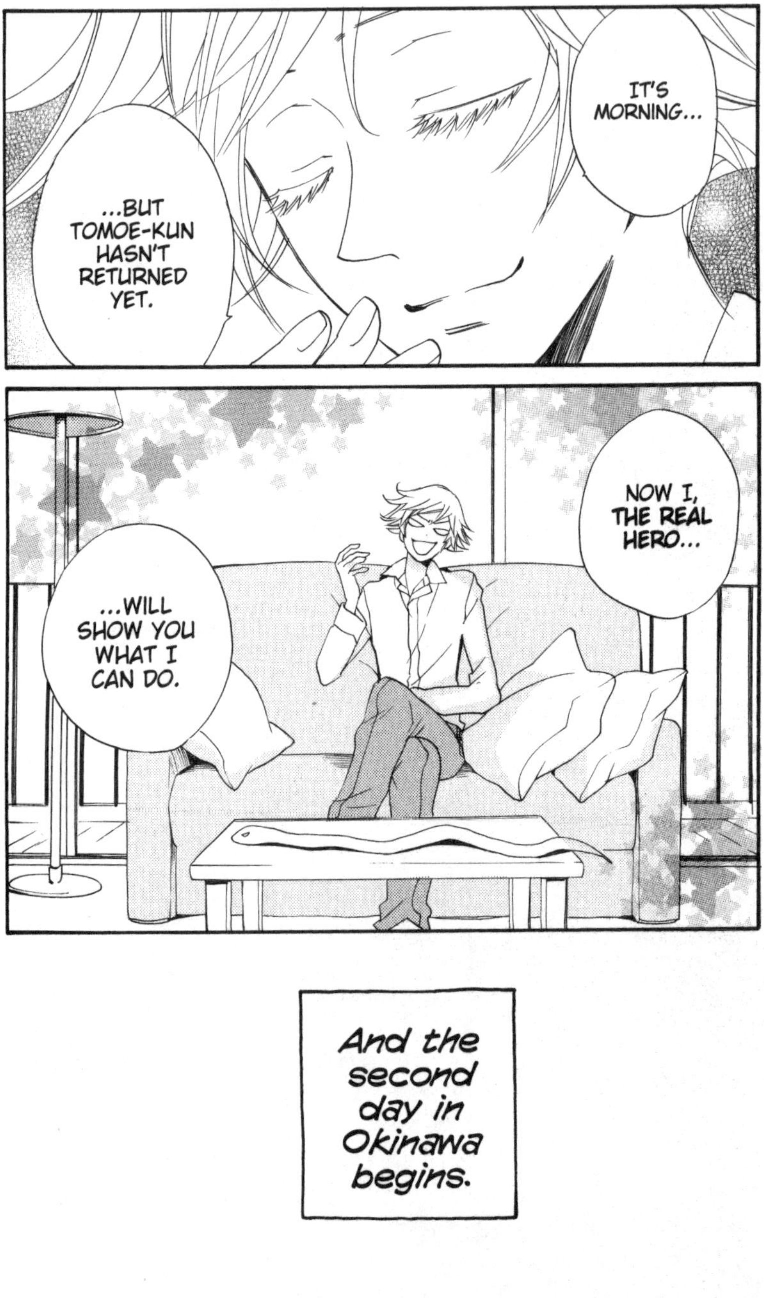
IT'S MORNING...
...BUT TOMOE-KUN HASN'T RETURNED YET.
NOW I, THE REAL HERO...
...WILL SHOW YOU WHAT I CAN DO.
And the second day in Okinawa begins.

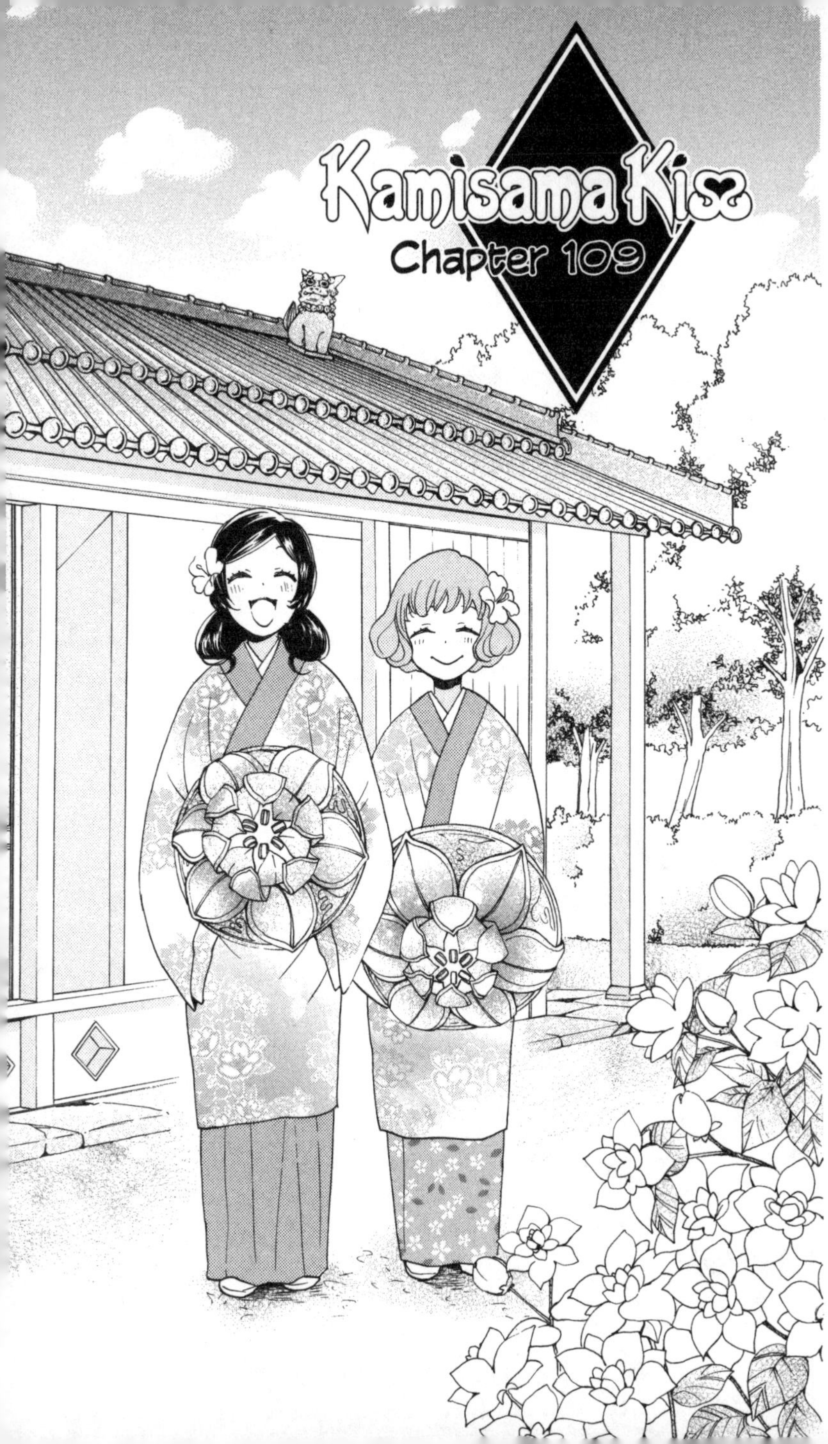
Kamisama Kiss
Chapter 109

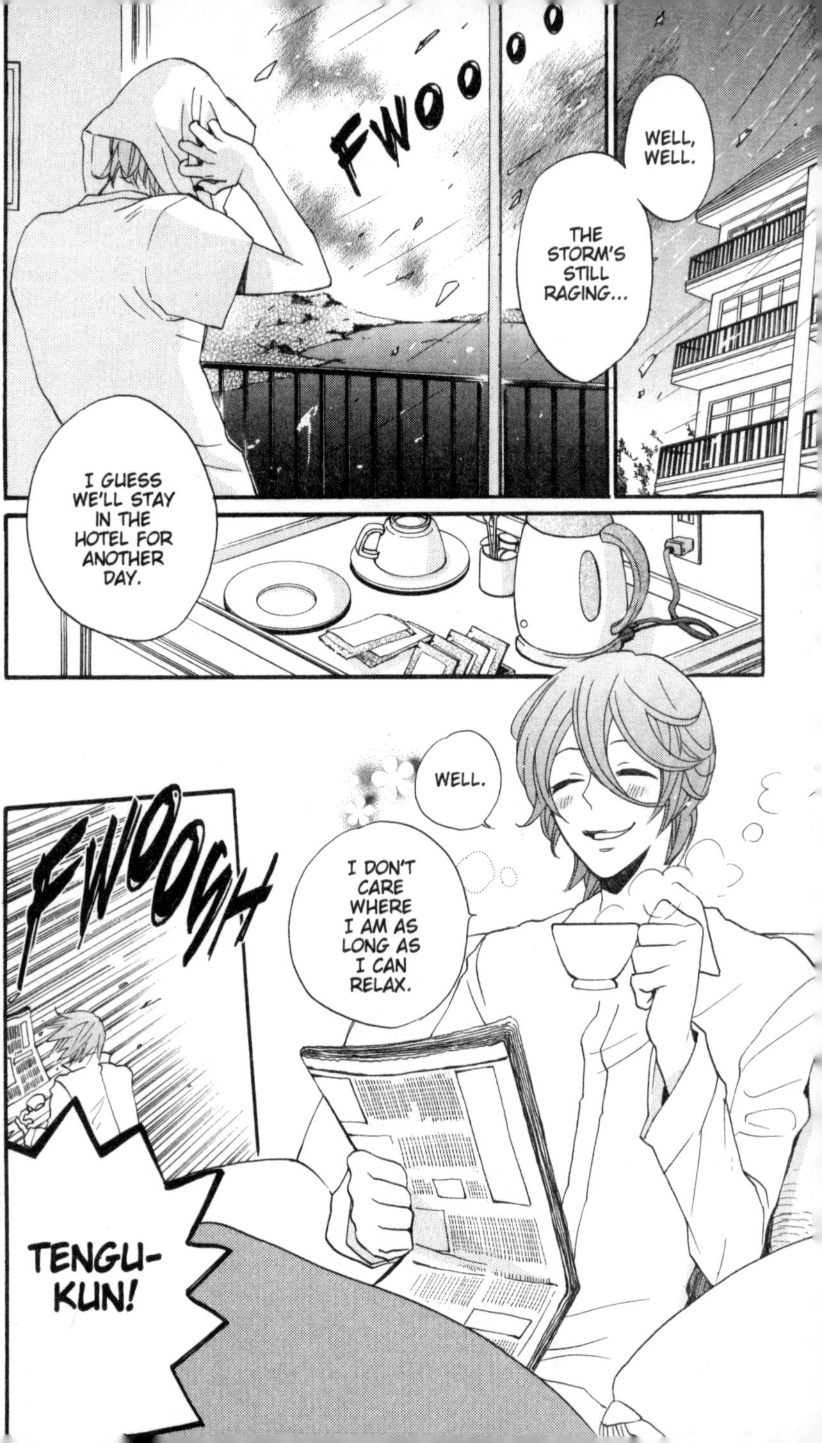
WELL, WELL.
THE STORM'S STILL RAGING...
FWOOOO
I GUESS WE'LL STAY IN THE HOTEL FOR ANOTHER DAY.
WELL.
I DON'T CARE WHERE I AM AS LONG AS I CAN RELAX.
FWOOOSH
TENGU-KUN!

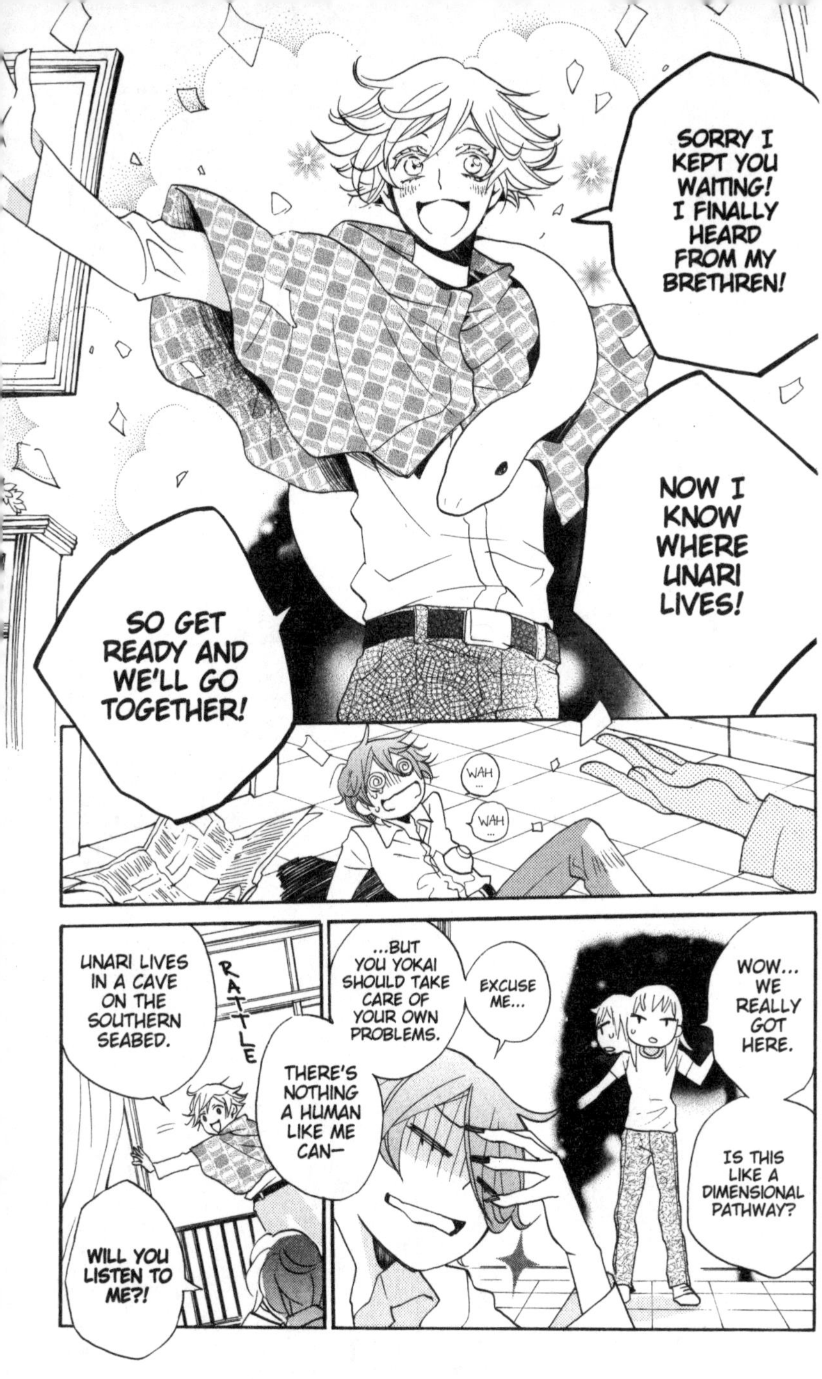
SORRY I KEPT YOU WAITING! I FINALLY HEARD FROM MY BRETHREN!
NOW I KNOW WHERE UNARI LIVES!
SO GET READY AND WE'LL GO TOGETHER!
WAH...
WAH...
WOW... WE REALLY GOT HERE.
IS THIS LIKE A DIMENSIONAL PATHWAY?
EXCUSE ME...
...BUT YOU YOKAI SHOULD TAKE CARE OF YOUR OWN PROBLEMS.
THERE'S NOTHING A HUMAN LIKE ME CAN—
RATTLE
UNARI LIVES IN A CAVE ON THE SOUTHERN SEABED.
WILL YOU LISTEN TO ME?!

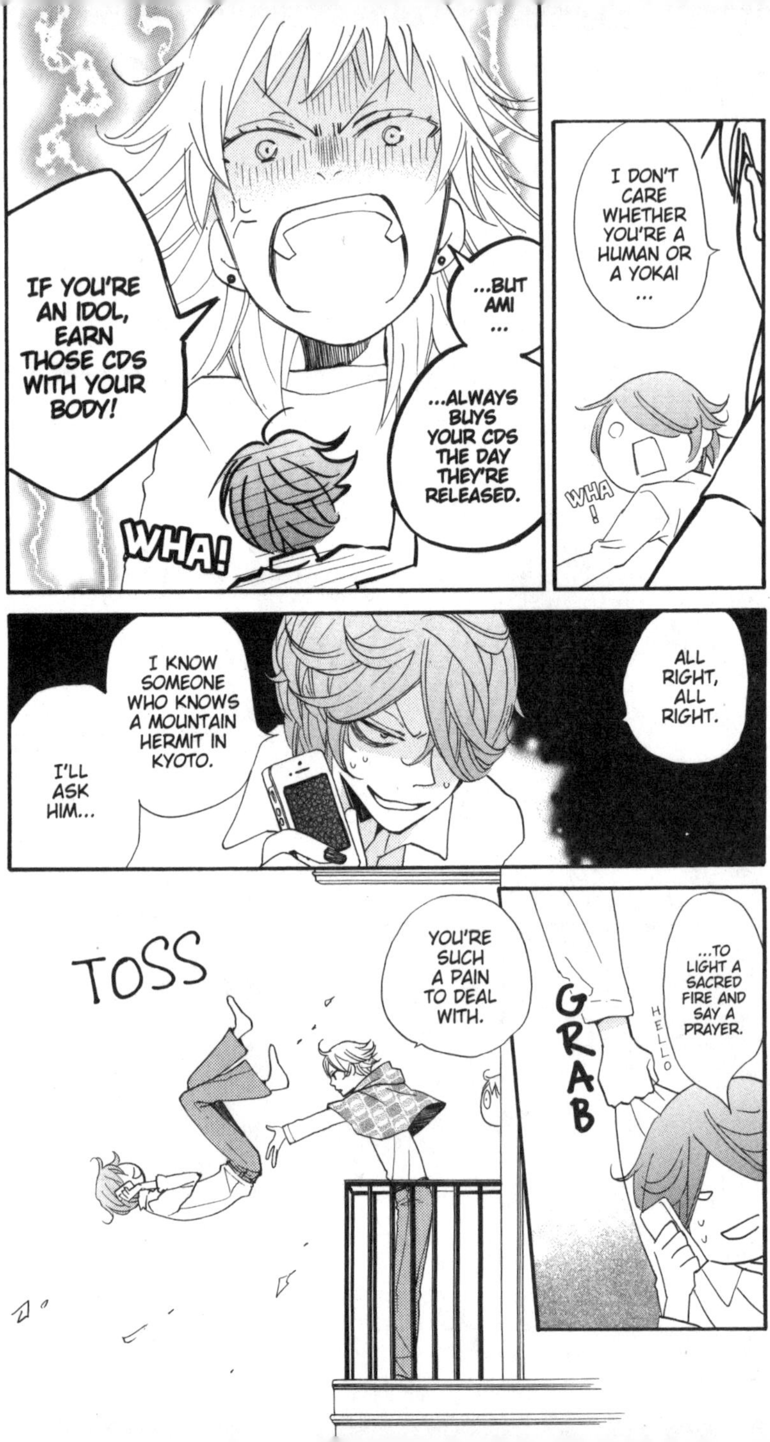
I DON'T CARE WHETHER YOU'RE A HUMAN OR A YOKAI ...
WHA !
...BUT AMI ...
...ALWAYS BUYS YOUR CDS THE DAY THEY'RE RELEASED.
IF YOU'RE AN IDOL, EARN THOSE CDS WITH YOUR BODY!
WHA!
ALL RIGHT, ALL RIGHT.
I KNOW SOMEONE WHO KNOWS A MOUNTAIN HERMIT IN KYOTO.
I'LL ASK HIM...
...TO LIGHT A SACRED FIRE AND SAY A PRAYER.
HELLO
GRAB
YOU'RE SUCH A PAIN TO DEAL WITH.
TOSS

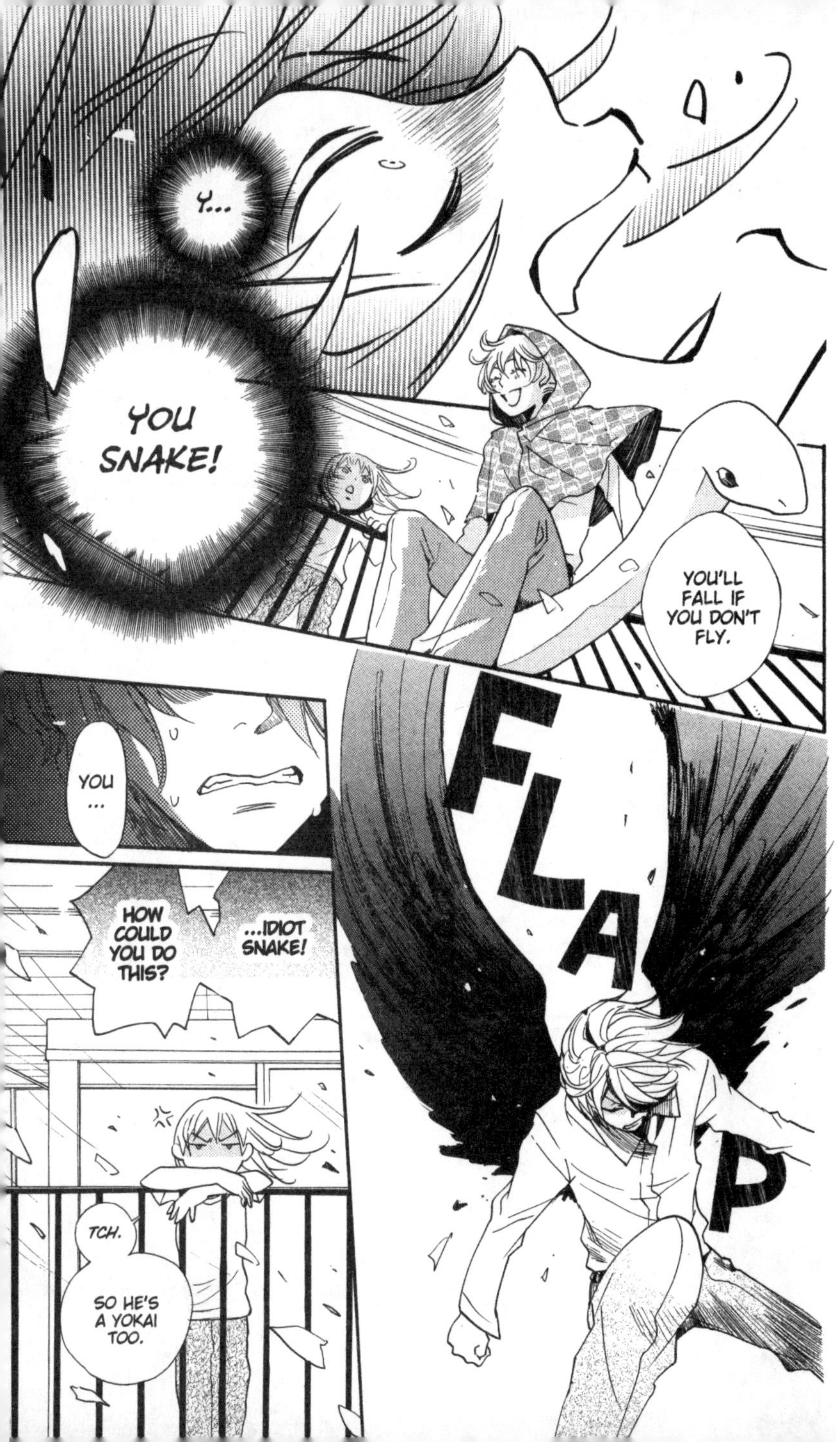
Y...
YOU SNAKE!
YOU'LL FALL IF YOU DON'T FLY.
FLAP
YOU ...
HOW COULD YOU DO THIS?
...IDIOT SNAKE!
TCH.
SO HE'S A YOKAI TOO.

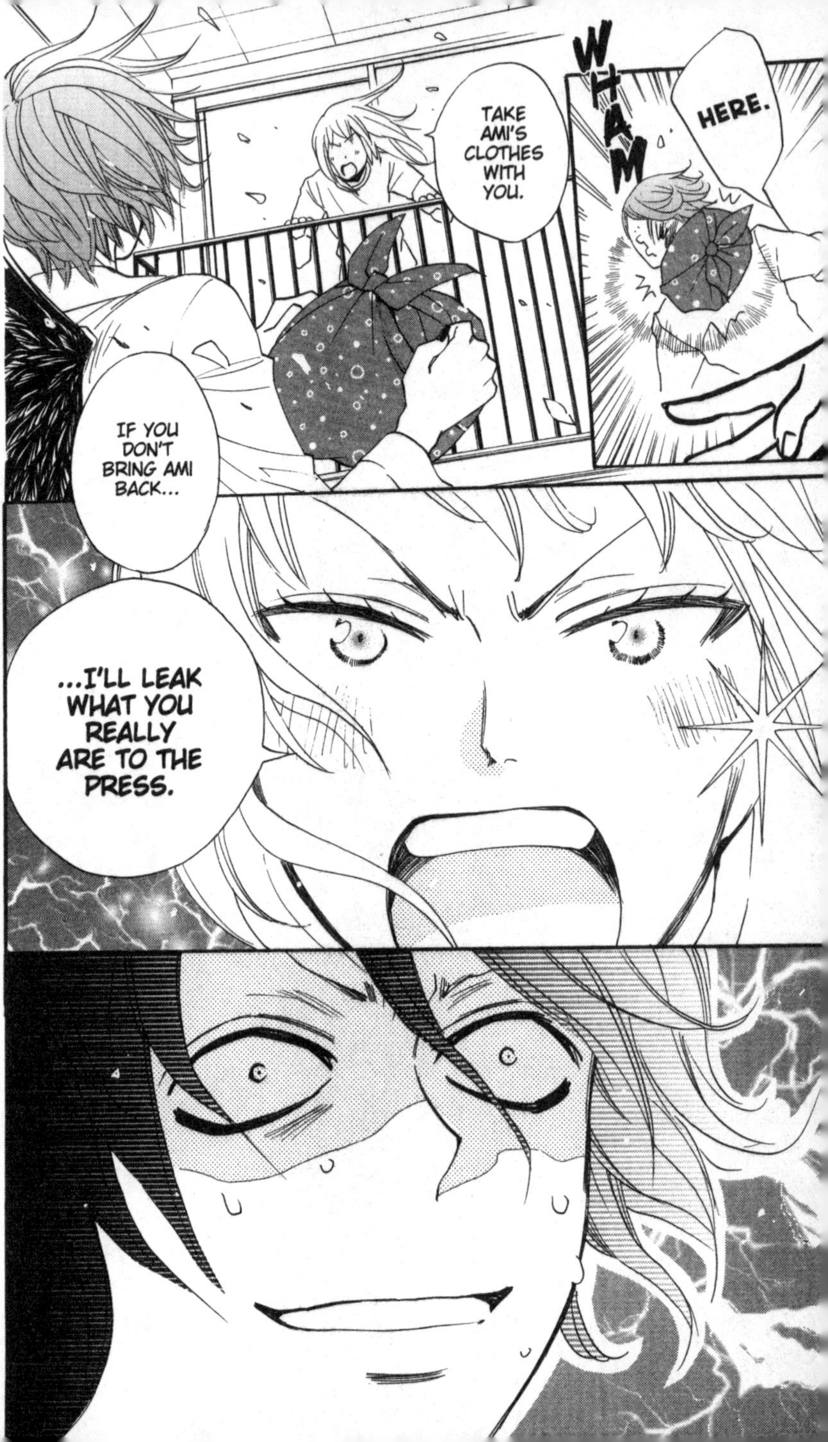
WHAM
HERE.
TAKE AMI'S CLOTHES WITH YOU.
IF YOU DON'T BRING AMI BACK...
...I'LL LEAK WHAT YOU REALLY ARE TO THE PRESS.

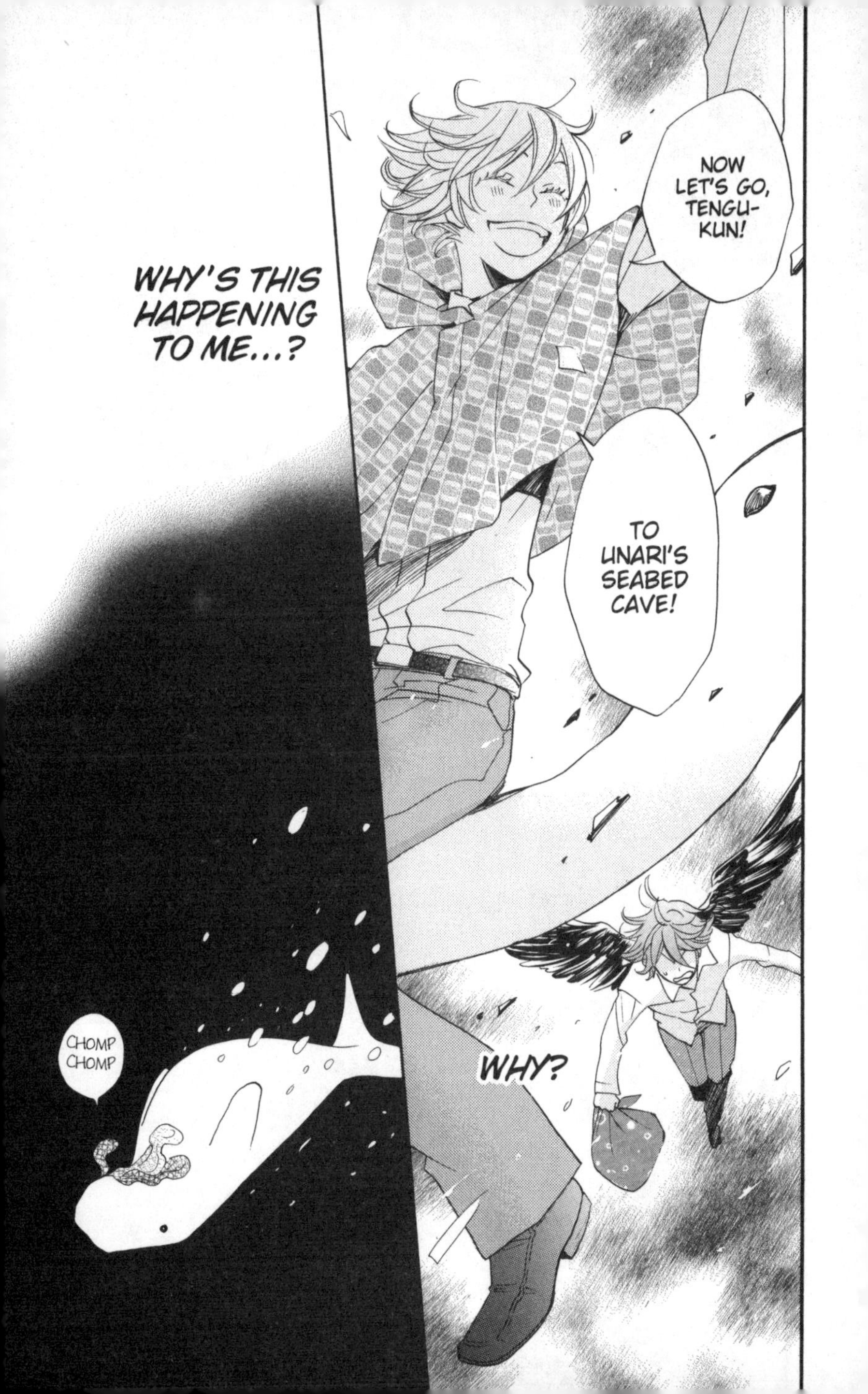
NOW LET'S GO, TENGU-KUN!
TO UNARI'S SEABED CAVE!
WHY'S THIS HAPPENING TO ME...?
WHY?
CHOMP CHOMP

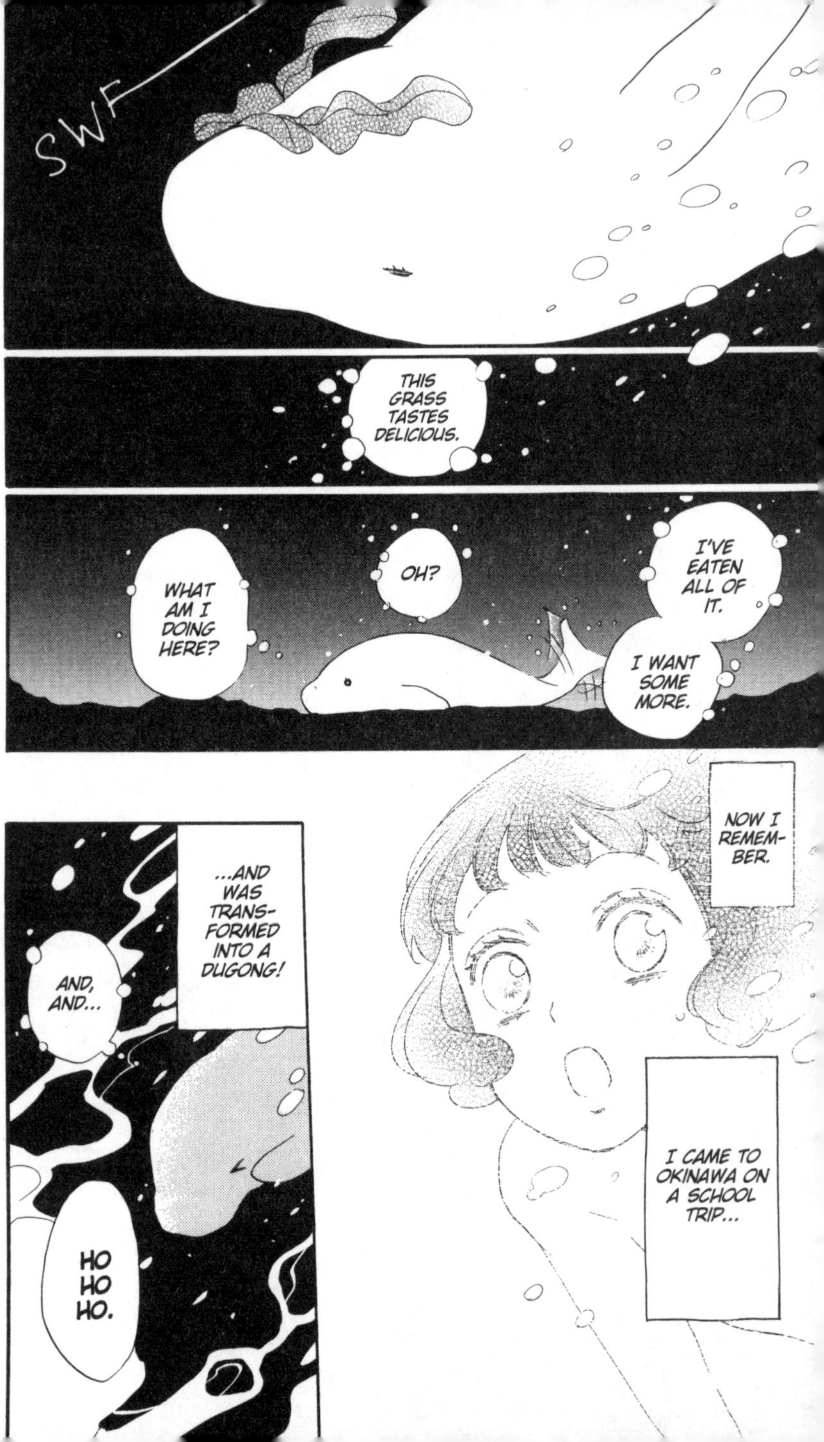
SWF
THIS GRASS TASTES DELICIOUS.
I'VE EATEN ALL OF IT.
I WANT SOME MORE.
OH?
WHAT AM I DOING HERE?
NOW I REMEMBER.
I CAME TO OKINAWA ON A SCHOOL TRIP...
...AND WAS TRANSFORMED INTO A DUGONG!
AND, AND...
HO HO HO.

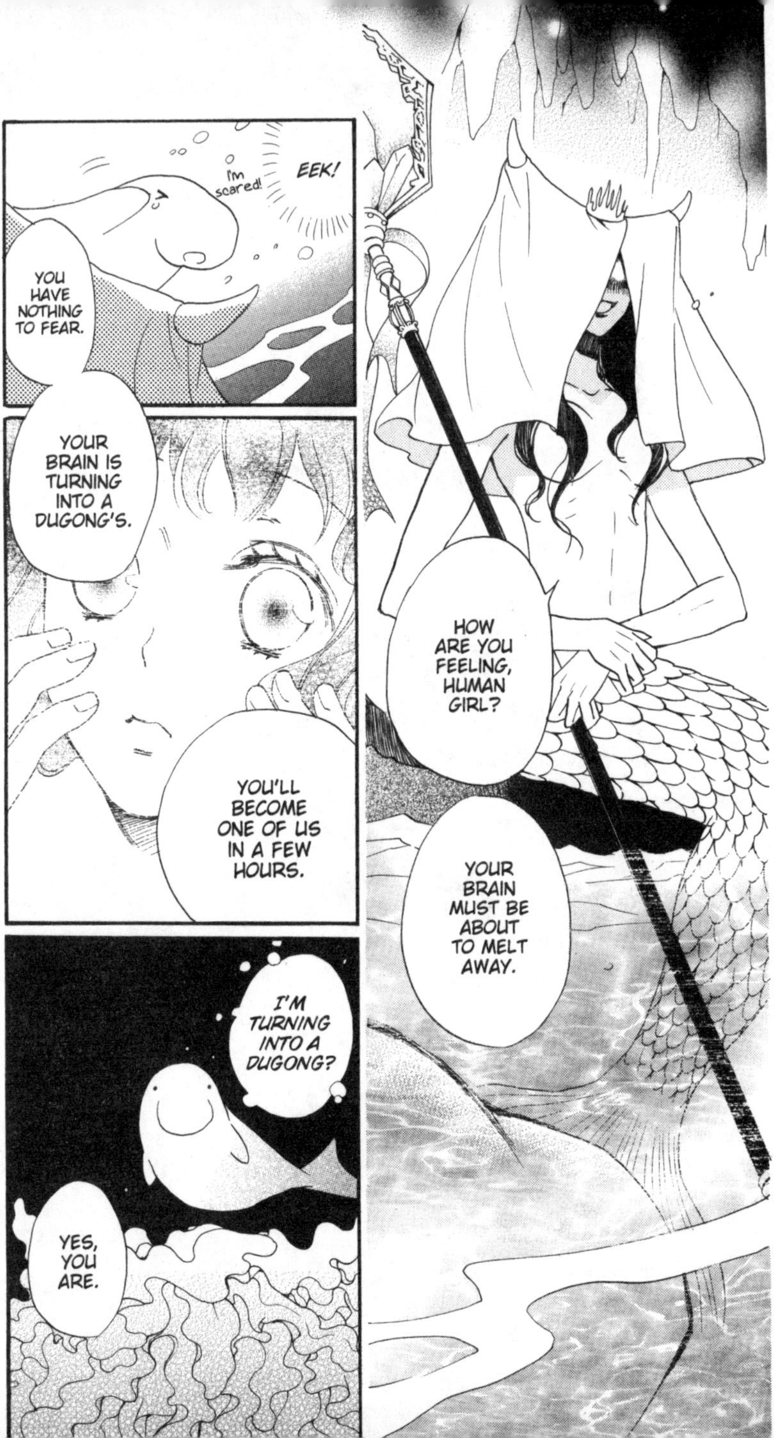
HOW ARE YOU FEELING, HUMAN GIRL?
YOUR BRAIN MUST BE ABOUT TO MELT AWAY.
EEK!
I'm scared!
YOU HAVE NOTHING TO FEAR.
YOUR BRAIN IS TURNING INTO A DUGONG'S.
YOU'LL BECOME ONE OF US IN A FEW HOURS.
I'M TURNING INTO A DUGONG?
YES, YOU ARE.

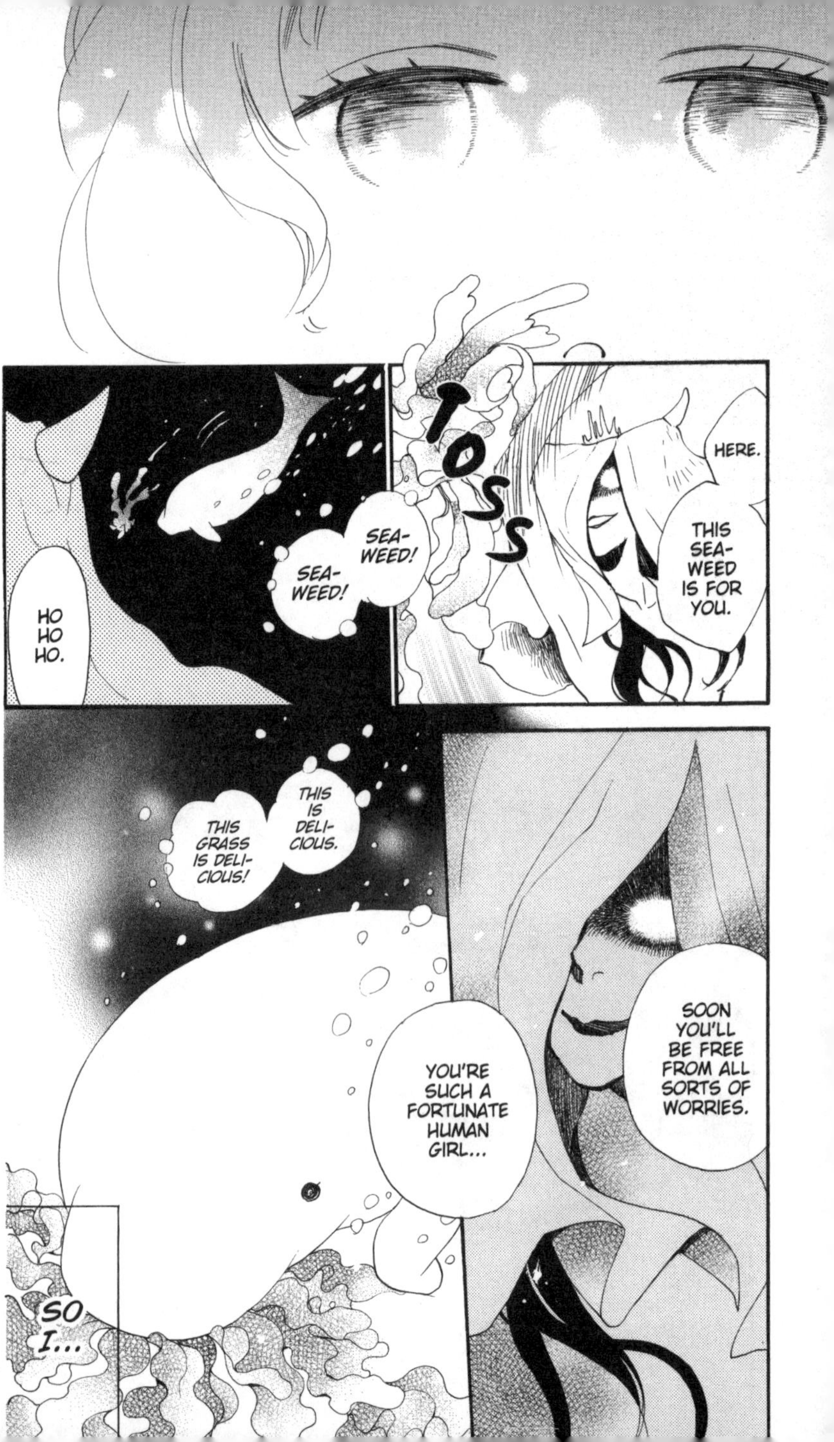
TOSS
HERE.
THIS SEA-WEED IS FOR YOU.
SEA-WEED!
SEA-WEED!
HO HO HO.
SOON YOU'LL BE FREE FROM ALL SORTS OF WORRIES.
YOU'RE SUCH A FORTUNATE HUMAN GIRL...
THIS IS DELI-CIOUS.
THIS GRASS IS DELI-CIOUS!
SO I...

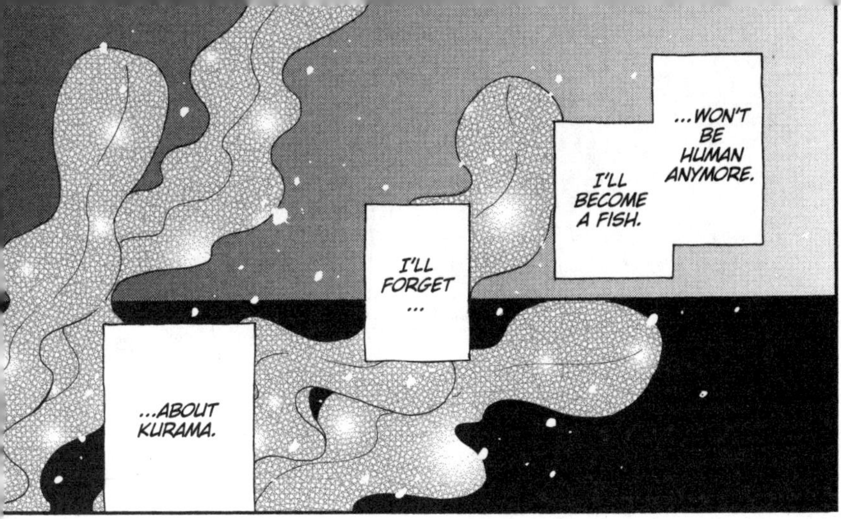
...WON'T BE HUMAN ANYMORE.
I'LL BECOME A FISH.
I'LL FORGET ...
...ABOUT KURAMA.

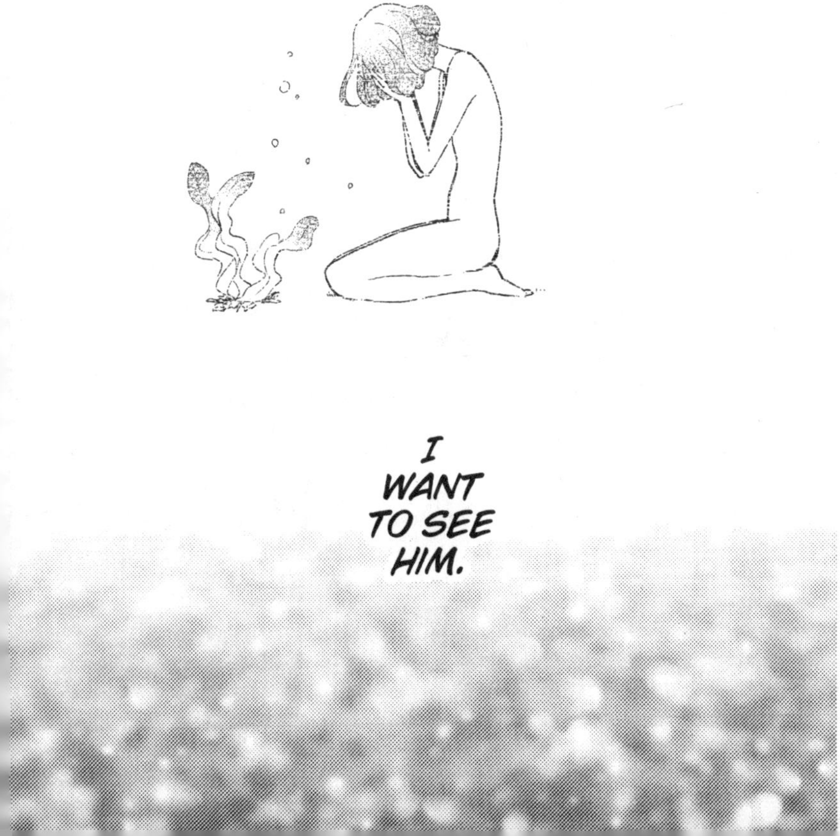
I WANT TO SEE HIM.

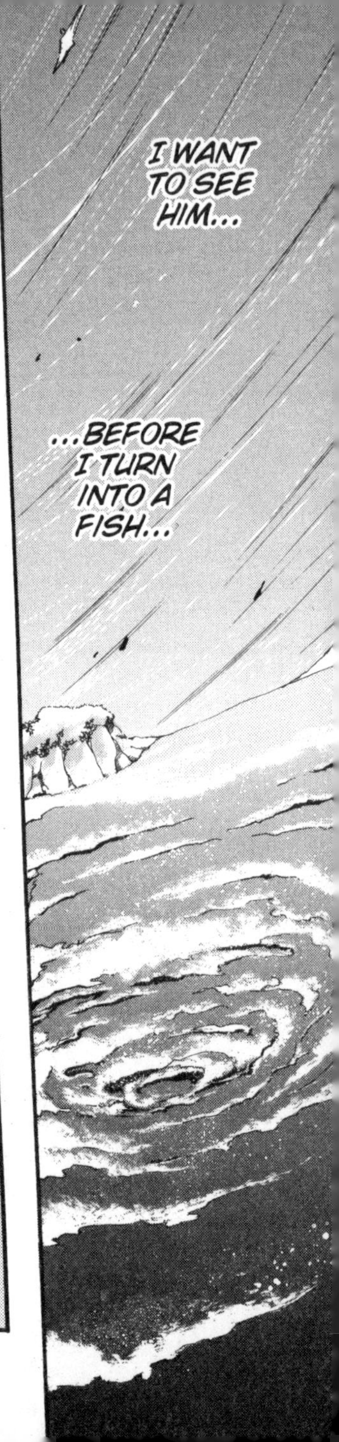
I WANT TO SEE HIM...
...BEFORE I TURN INTO A FISH...

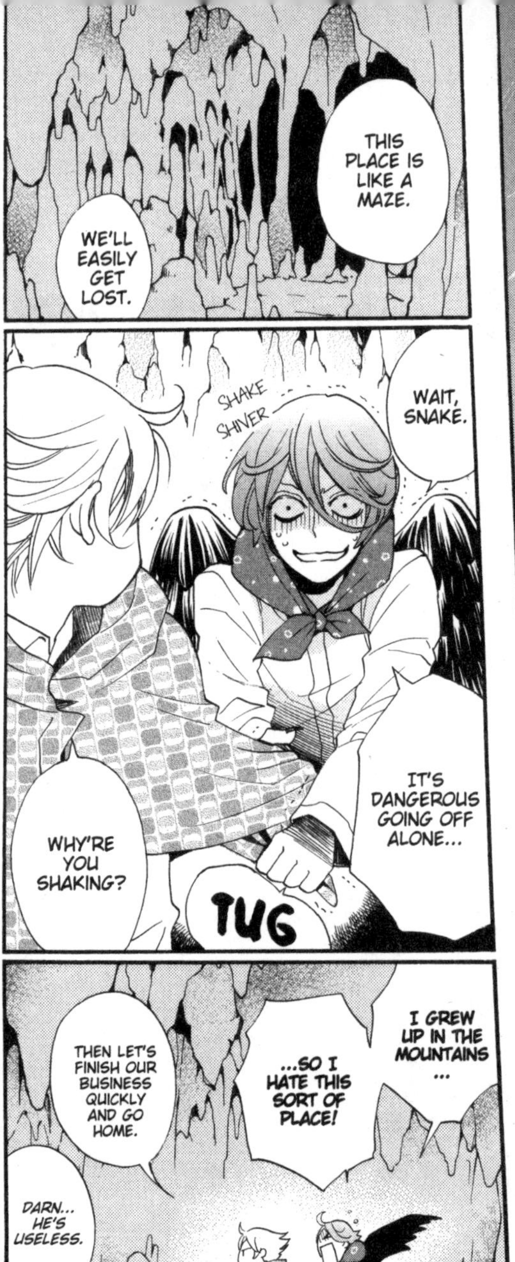
THIS PLACE IS LIKE A MAZE.
WE'LL EASILY GET LOST.
WAIT, SNAKE.
SHAKE SHIVER
IT'S DANGEROUS GOING OFF ALONE...
WHY'RE YOU SHAKING?
TUG
I GREW UP IN THE MOUNTAINS ...
...SO I HATE THIS SORT OF PLACE!
THEN LET'S FINISH OUR BUSINESS QUICKLY AND GO HOME.
DARN... HE'S USELESS.

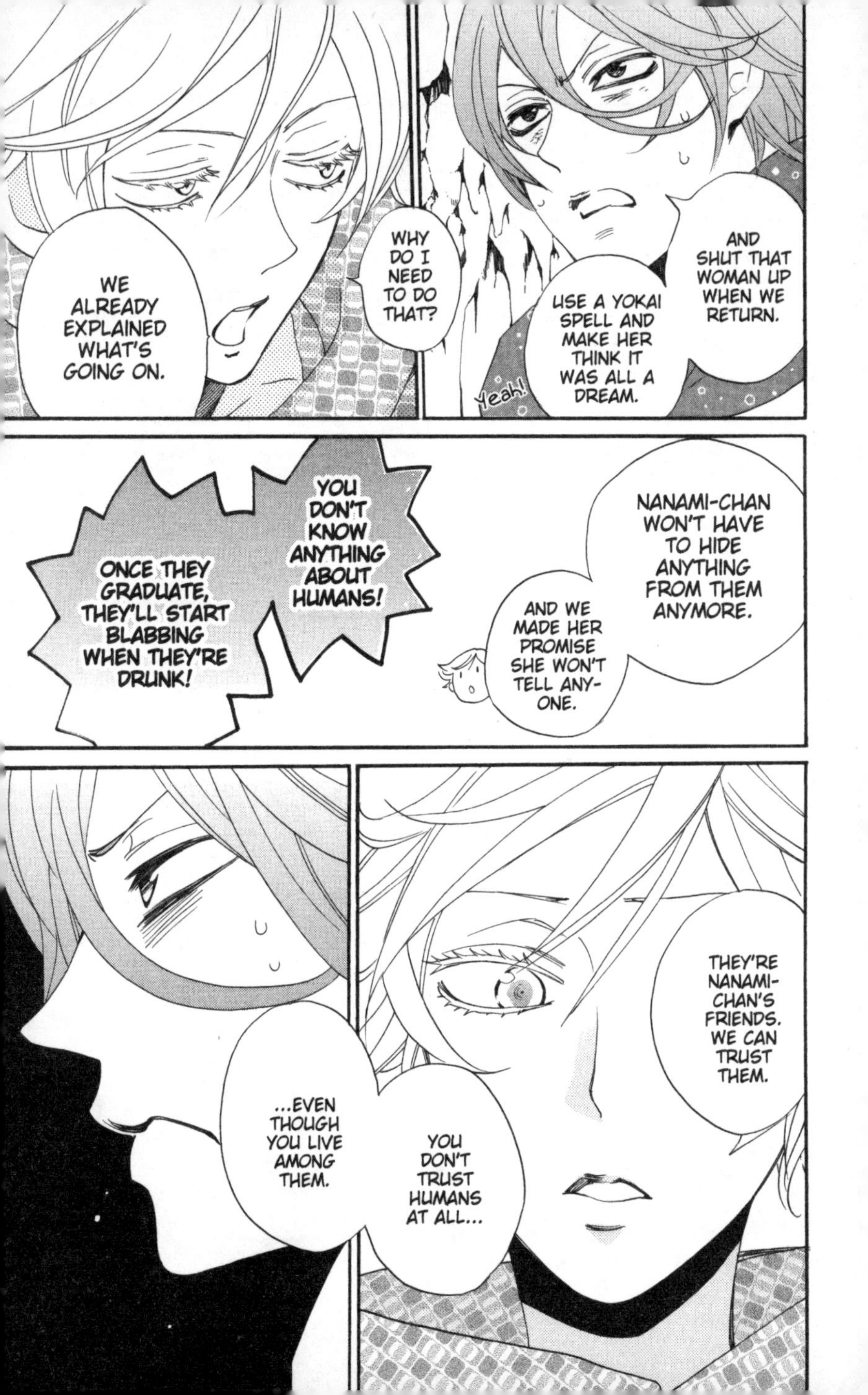
AND SHUT THAT WOMAN UP WHEN WE RETURN.
USE A YOKAI SPELL AND MAKE HER THINK IT WAS ALL A DREAM.
Yeah!
WHY DO I NEED TO DO THAT?
WE ALREADY EXPLAINED WHAT'S GOING ON.
NANAMI-CHAN WON'T HAVE TO HIDE ANYTHING FROM THEM ANYMORE.
AND WE MADE HER PROMISE SHE WON'T TELL ANY-ONE.
YOU DON'T KNOW ANYTHING ABOUT HUMANS!
ONCE THEY GRADUATE, THEY'LL START BLABBING WHEN THEY'RE DRUNK!
THEY'RE NANAMI-CHAN'S FRIENDS. WE CAN TRUST THEM.
YOU DON'T TRUST HUMANS AT ALL...
...EVEN THOUGH YOU LIVE AMONG THEM.

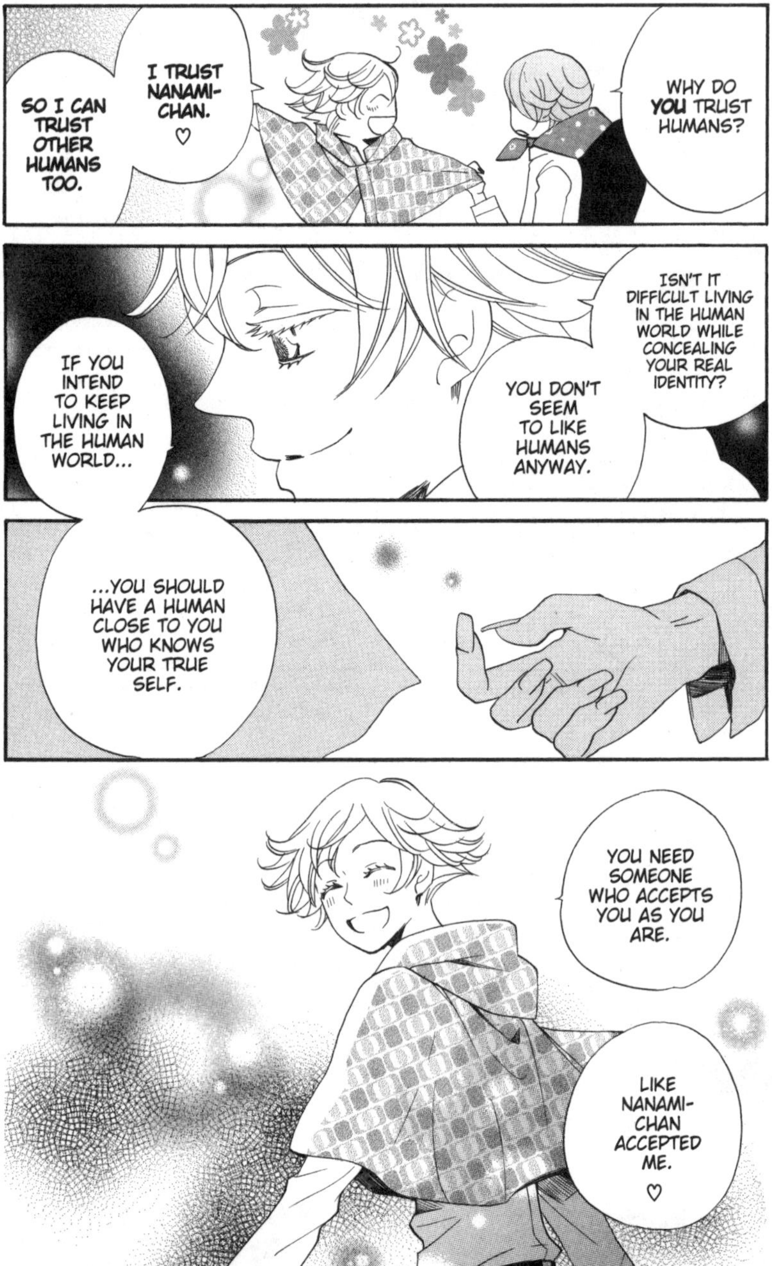
WHY DO **YOU** TRUST HUMANS?
I TRUST NANAMI-CHAN. ♡
SO I CAN TRUST OTHER HUMANS TOO.
ISN'T IT DIFFICULT LIVING IN THE HUMAN WORLD WHILE CONCEALING YOUR REAL IDENTITY?
YOU DON'T SEEM TO LIKE HUMANS ANYWAY.
IF YOU INTEND TO KEEP LIVING IN THE HUMAN WORLD...
...YOU SHOULD HAVE A HUMAN CLOSE TO YOU WHO KNOWS YOUR TRUE SELF.
YOU NEED SOMEONE WHO ACCEPTS YOU AS YOU ARE.
LIKE NANAMI-CHAN ACCEPTED ME. ♡

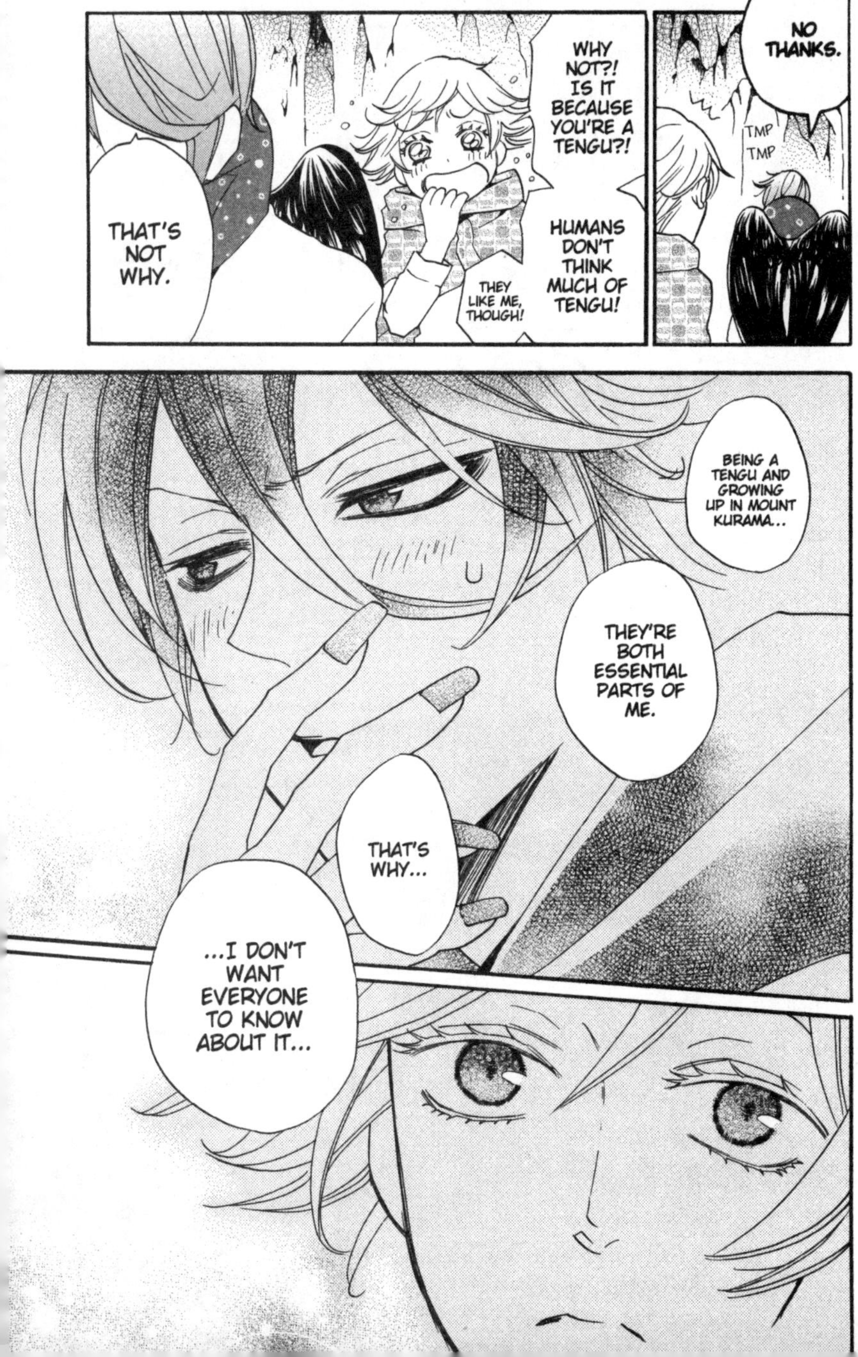
NO THANKS.
TMP
TMP
WHY NOT?! IS IT BECAUSE YOU'RE A TENGU?!
HUMANS DON'T THINK MUCH OF TENGU!
THEY LIKE ME, THOUGH!
THAT'S NOT WHY.
BEING A TENGU AND GROWING UP IN MOUNT KURAMA...
THEY'RE BOTH ESSENTIAL PARTS OF ME.
THAT'S WHY...
...I DON'T WANT EVERYONE TO KNOW ABOUT IT...

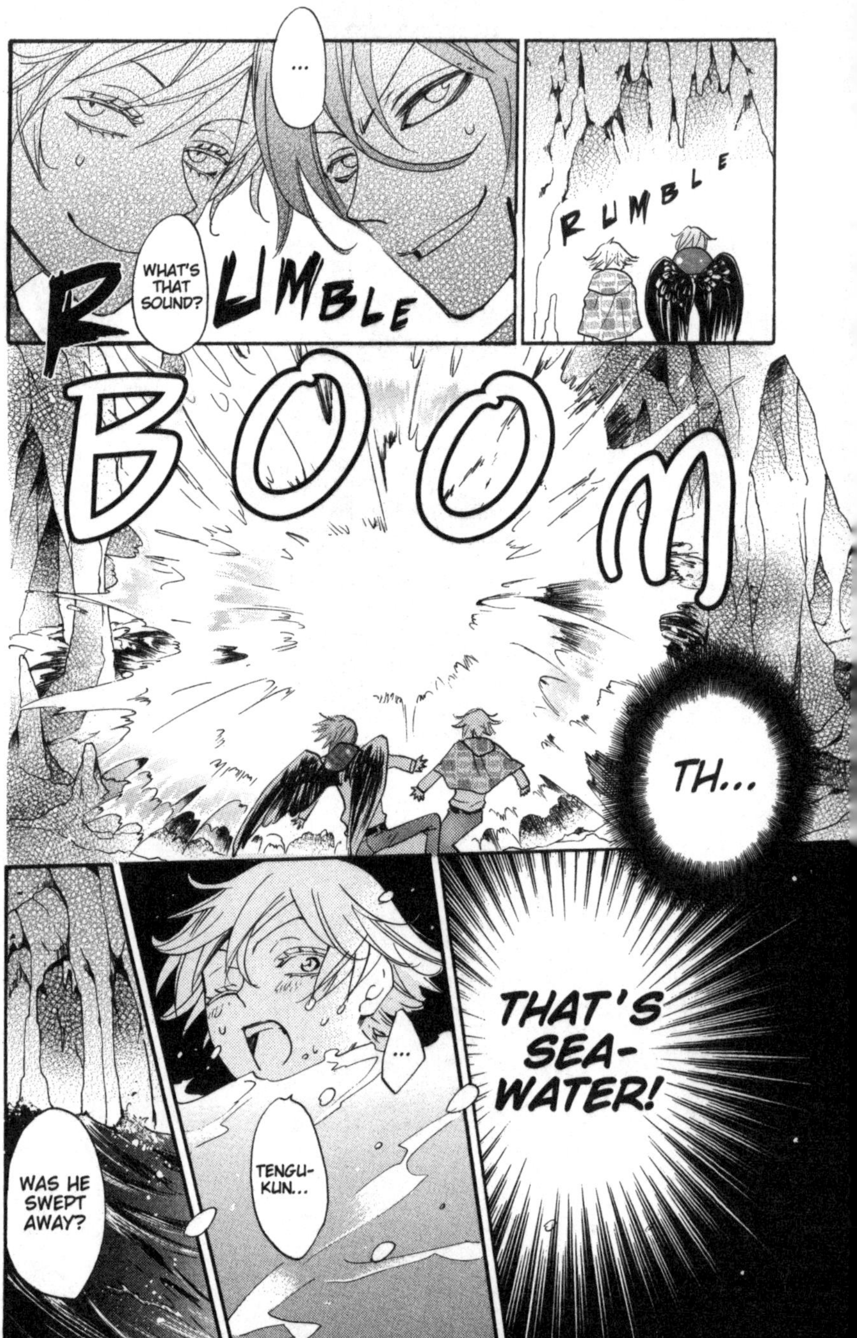
RUMBLE
...
WHAT'S THAT SOUND?
RUMBLE
BOOM
TH...
THAT'S SEA-WATER!
...
TENGU-KUN...
WAS HE SWEPT AWAY?

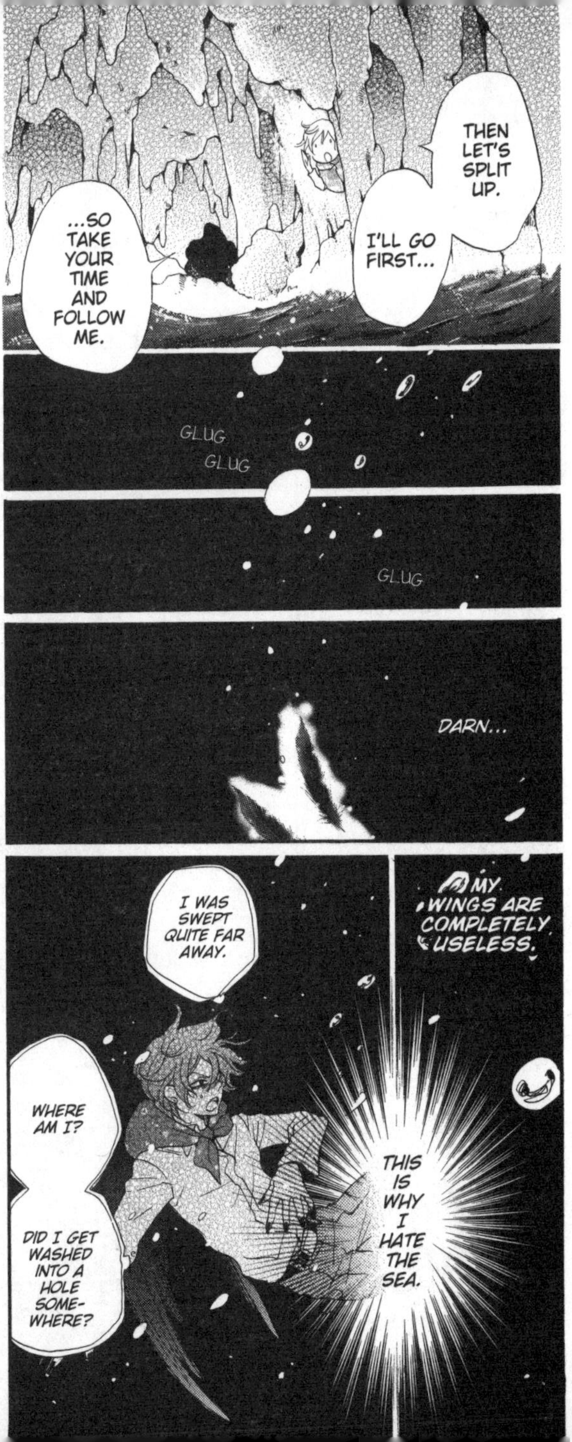
THEN LET'S SPLIT UP.
I'LL GO FIRST...
...SO TAKE YOUR TIME AND FOLLOW ME.
GLUG
GLUG
GLUG
DARN...
MY WINGS ARE COMPLETELY USELESS.
I WAS SWEPT QUITE FAR AWAY.
THIS IS WHY I HATE THE SEA.
WHERE AM I?
DID I GET WASHED INTO A HOLE SOME-WHERE?

It's getting hot.

I started walking outside every season this year because I want to do something good for my health. Nowadays it's difficult to go out while the weather's nice because it starts raining suddenly, or thunder starts to rumble.

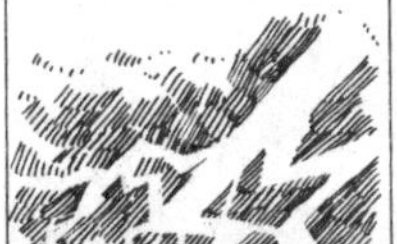

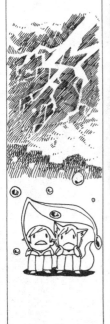

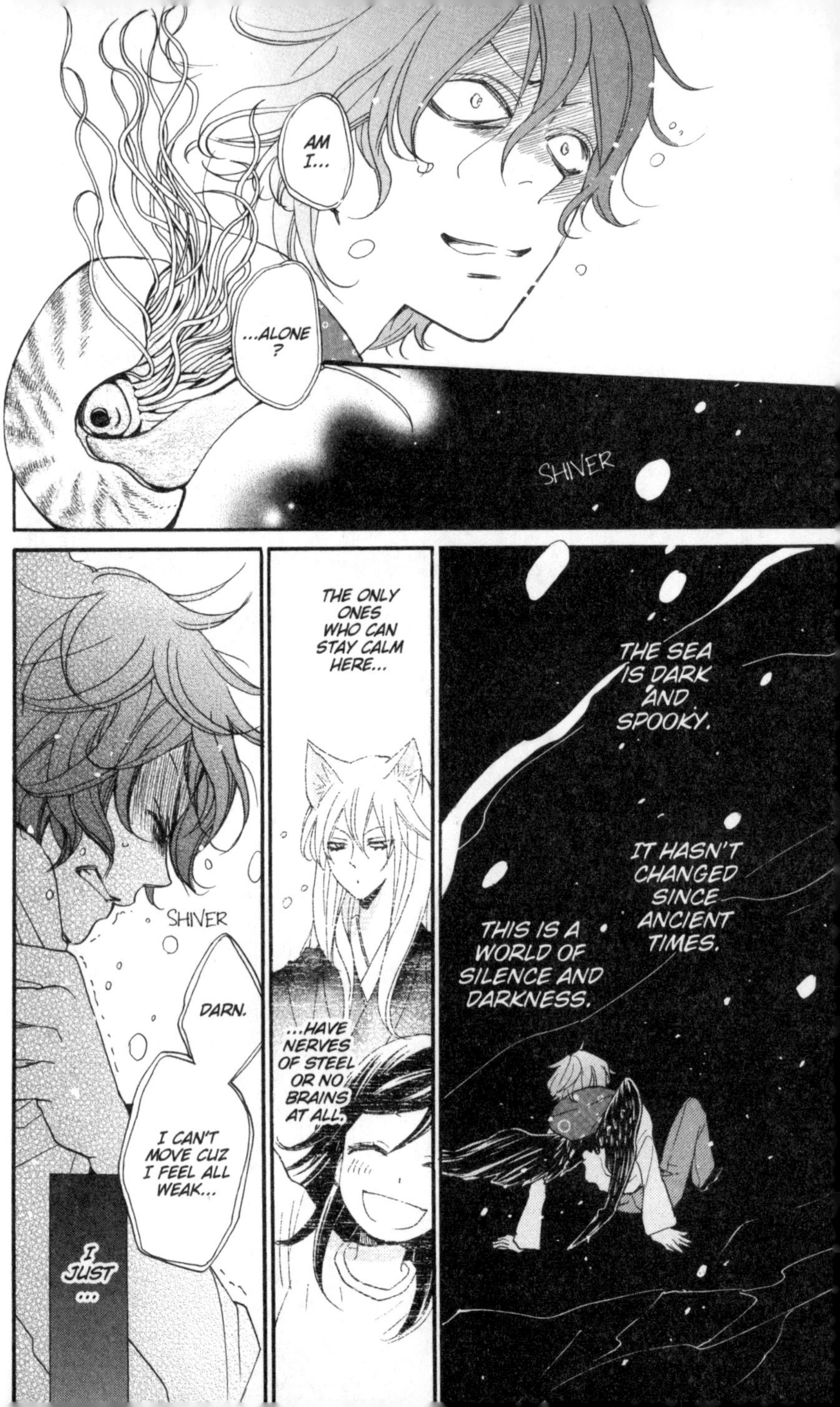
AM I...
...ALONE?
SHIVER
THE SEA IS DARK AND SPOOKY.
IT HASN'T CHANGED SINCE ANCIENT TIMES.
THIS IS A WORLD OF SILENCE AND DARKNESS.
THE ONLY ONES WHO CAN STAY CALM HERE...
...HAVE NERVES OF STEEL OR NO BRAINS AT ALL.
SHIVER
DARN.
I CAN'T MOVE CUZ I FEEL ALL WEAK...
I JUST...

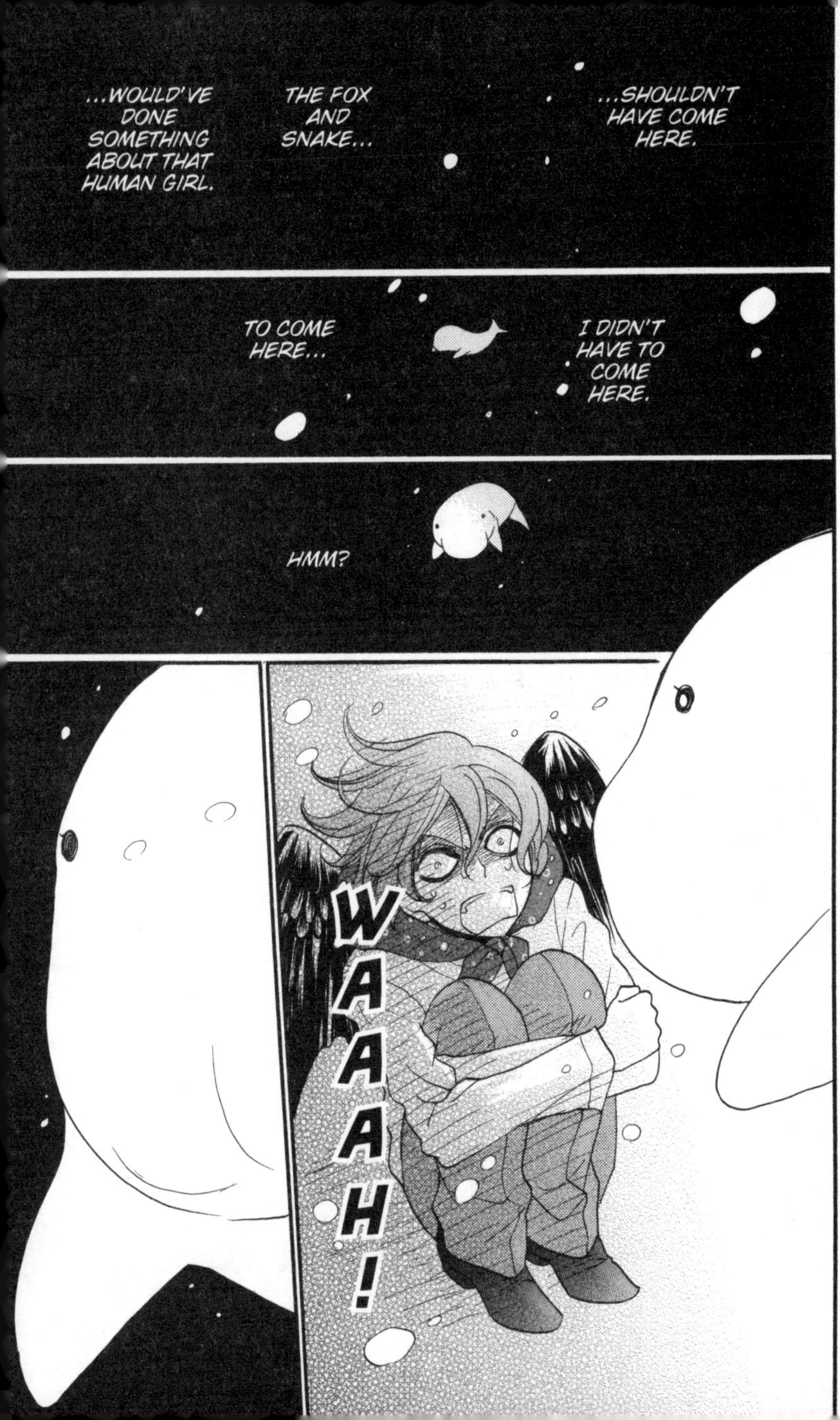
...SHOULDN'T HAVE COME HERE.
THE FOX AND SNAKE...
...WOULD'VE DONE SOMETHING ABOUT THAT HUMAN GIRL.
I DIDN'T HAVE TO COME HERE.
TO COME HERE...
HMM?
WAAAAH!

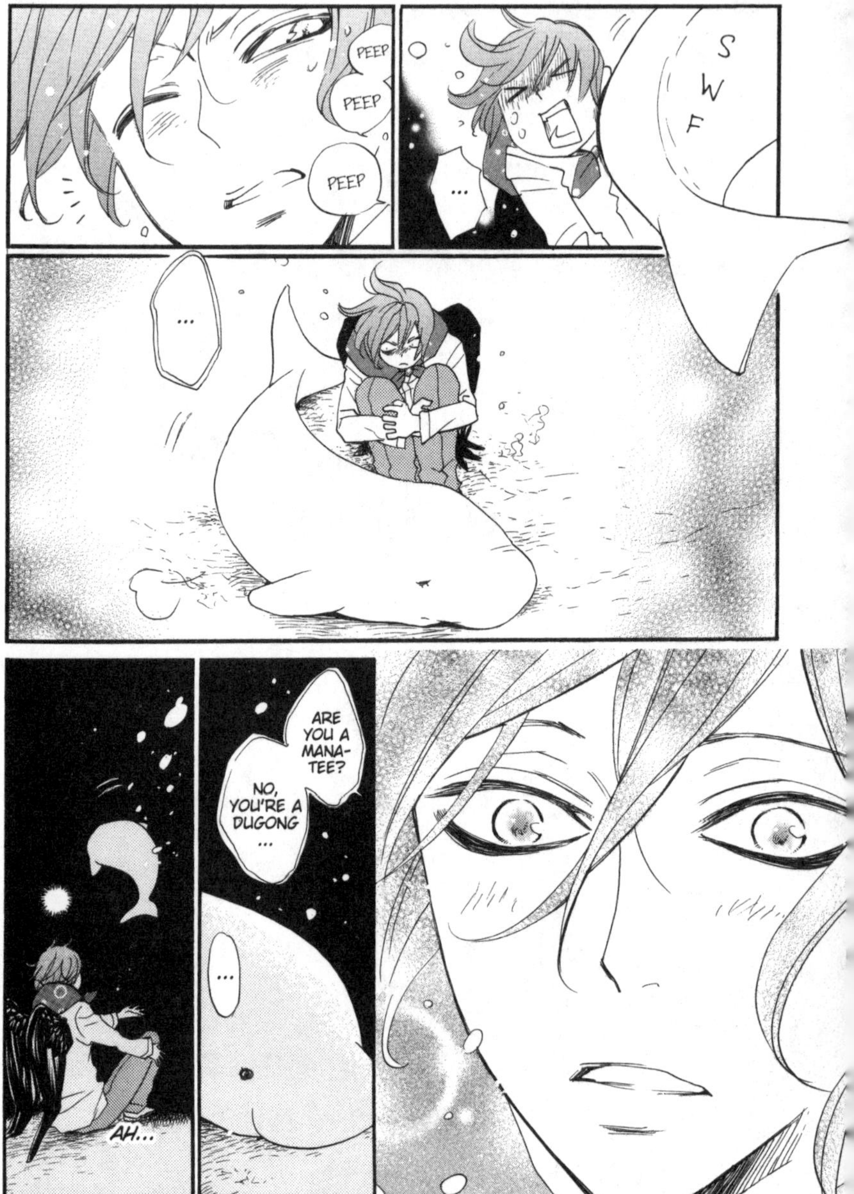
SWF
...
PEEP
PEEP
PEEP
...
ARE YOU A MANATEE?
NO, YOU'RE A DUGONG...
...
AH...

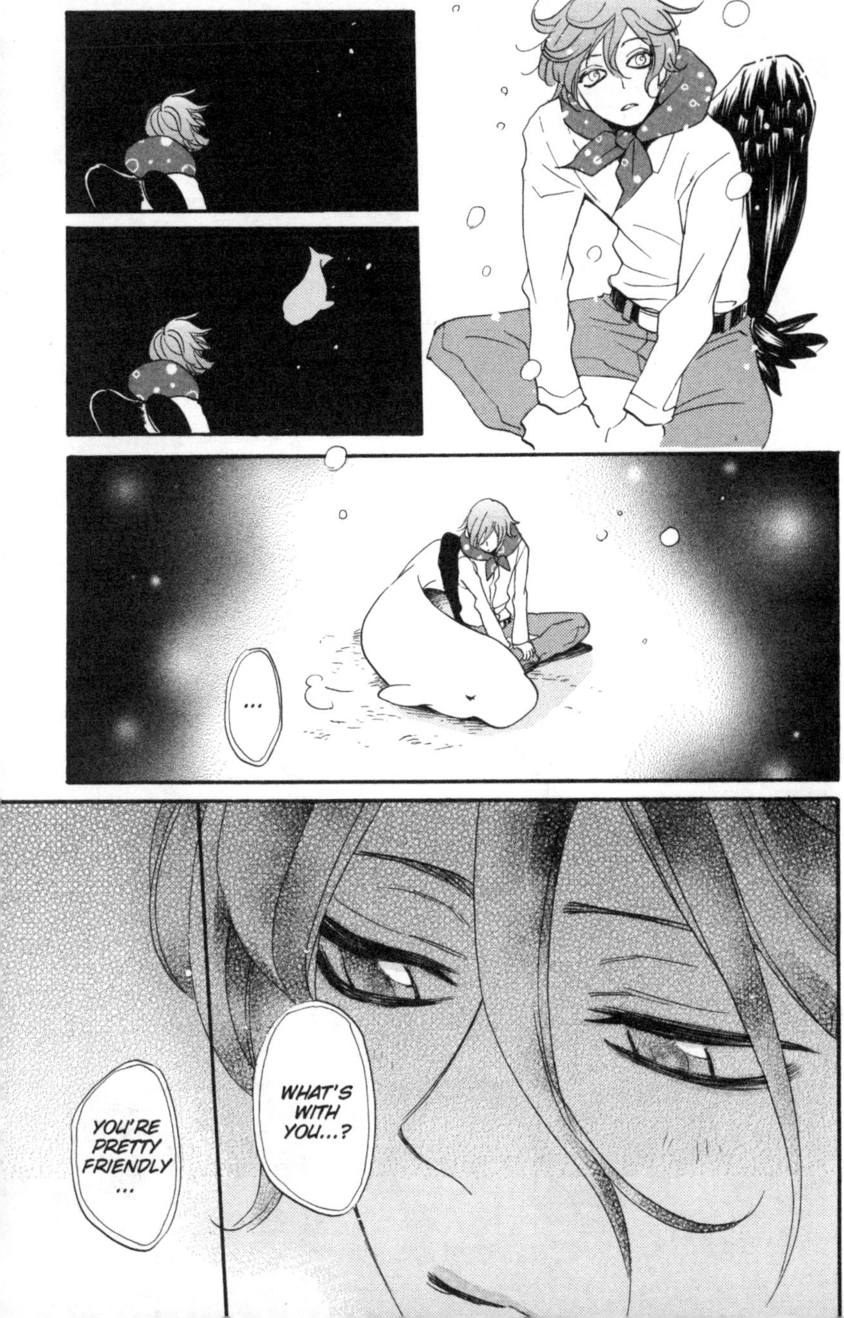
...
WHAT'S WITH YOU...?
YOU'RE PRETTY FRIENDLY ...

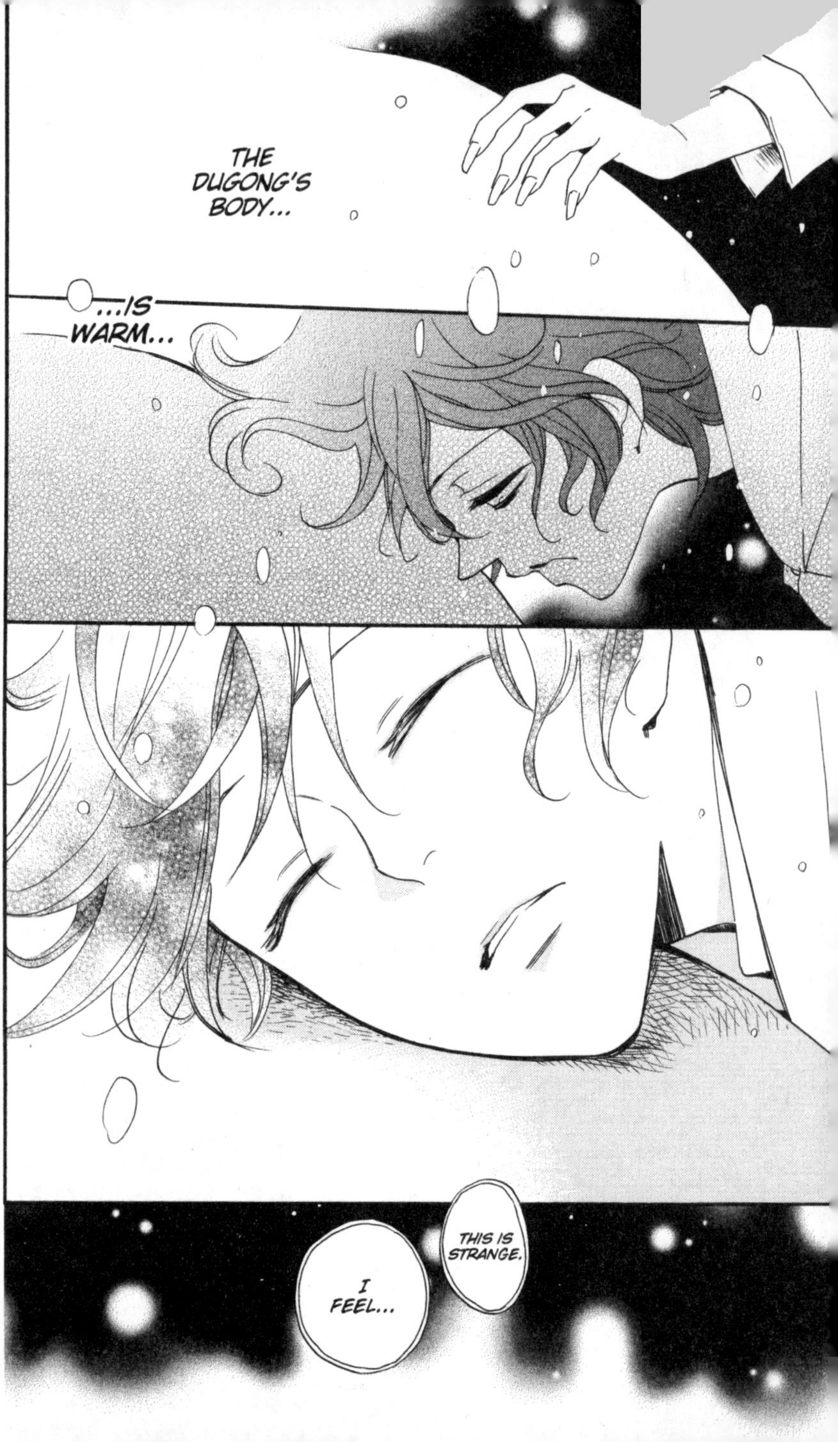
THE DUGONG'S BODY...
...IS WARM...
THIS IS STRANGE.
I FEEL...

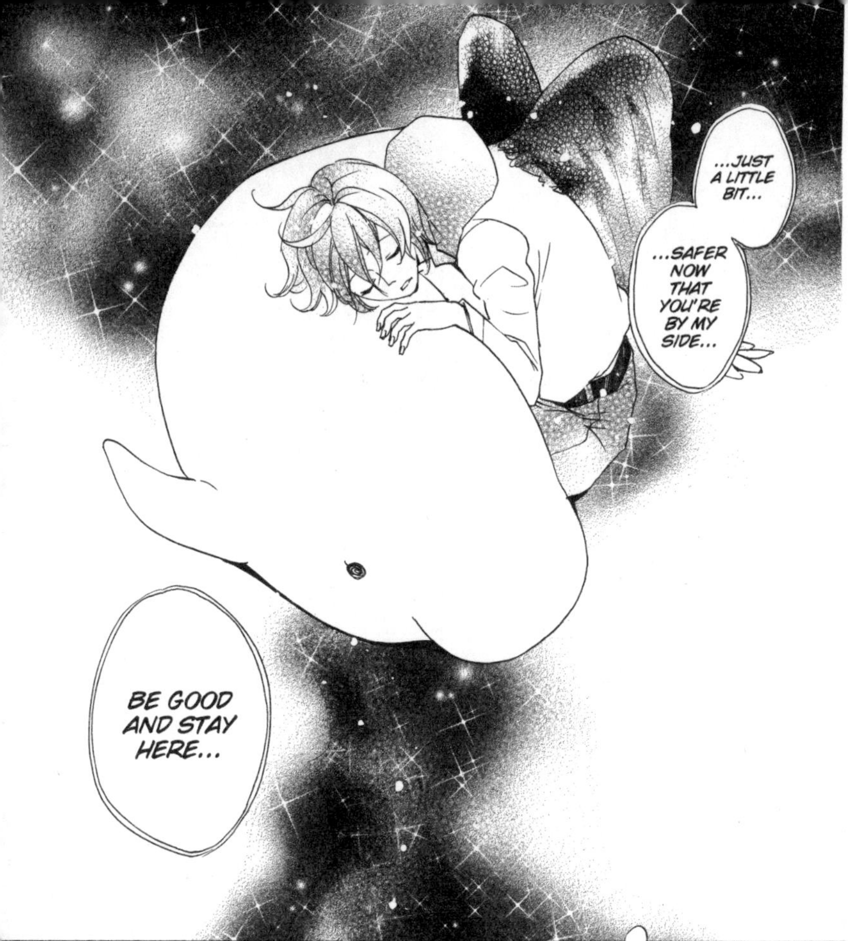
...JUST A LITTLE BIT...
...SAFER NOW THAT YOU'RE BY MY SIDE...
BE GOOD AND STAY HERE...
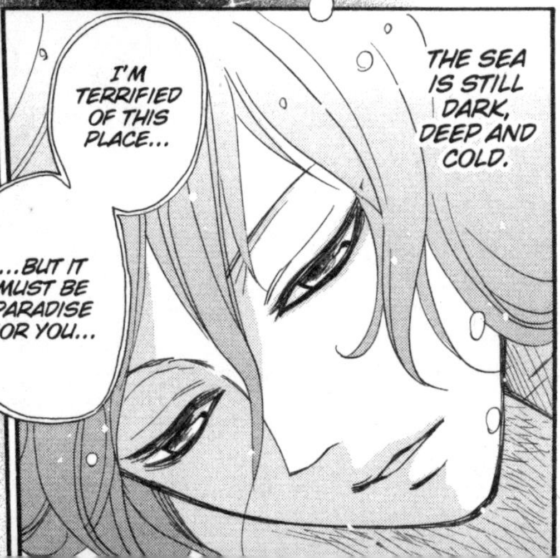
THE SEA IS STILL DARK, DEEP AND COLD.
I'M TERRIFIED OF THIS PLACE...
...BUT IT MUST BE PARADISE FOR YOU...
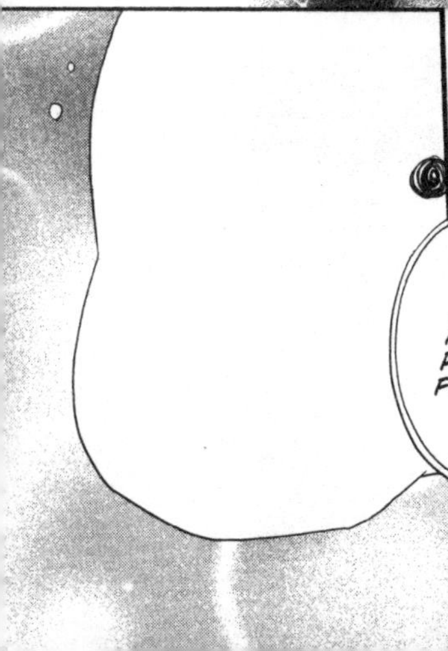

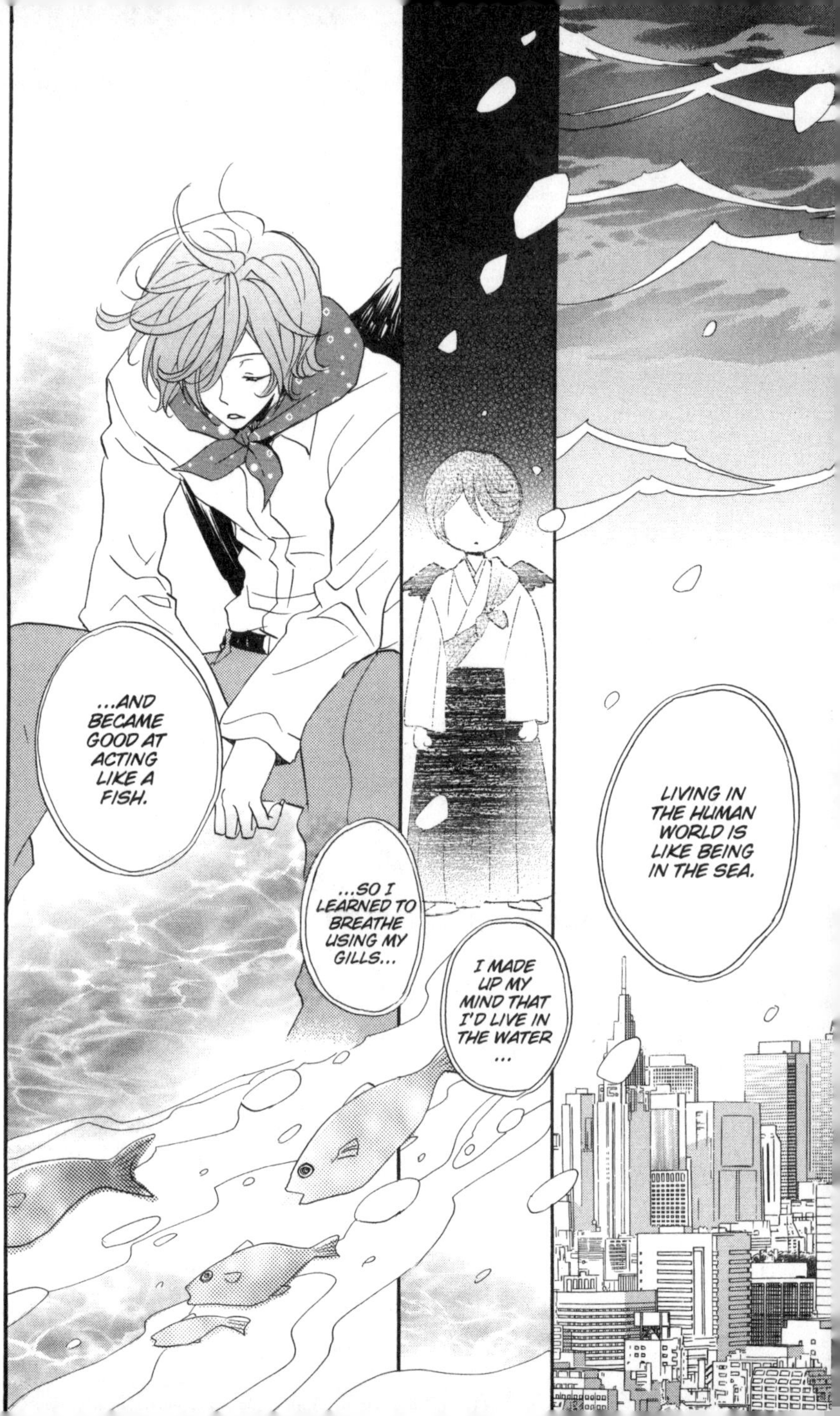
LIVING IN THE HUMAN WORLD IS LIKE BEING IN THE SEA.
I MADE UP MY MIND THAT I'D LIVE IN THE WATER...
...SO I LEARNED TO BREATHE USING MY GILLS...
...AND BECAME GOOD AT ACTING LIKE A FISH.

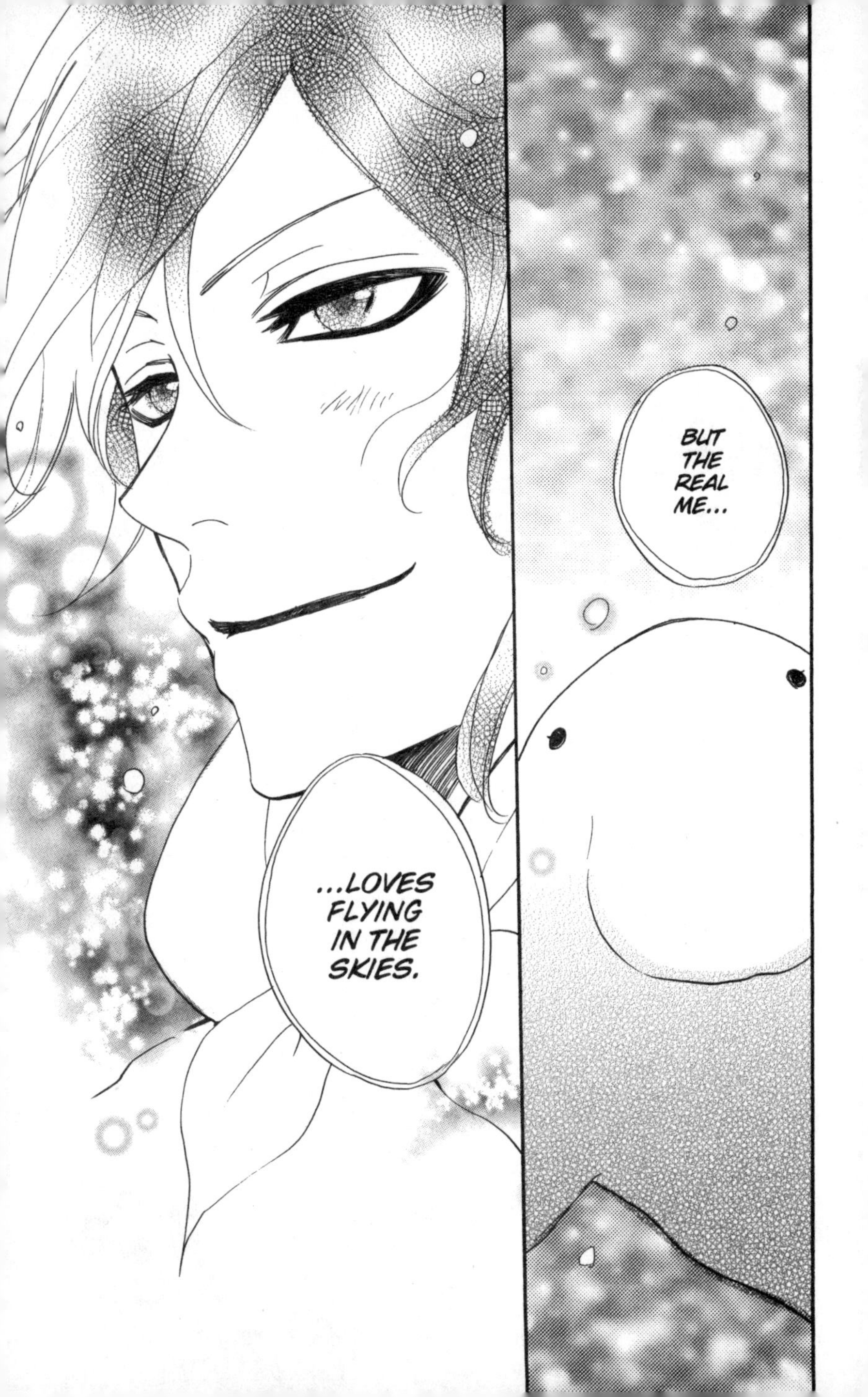
BUT THE REAL ME...
...LOVES FLYING IN THE SKIES.

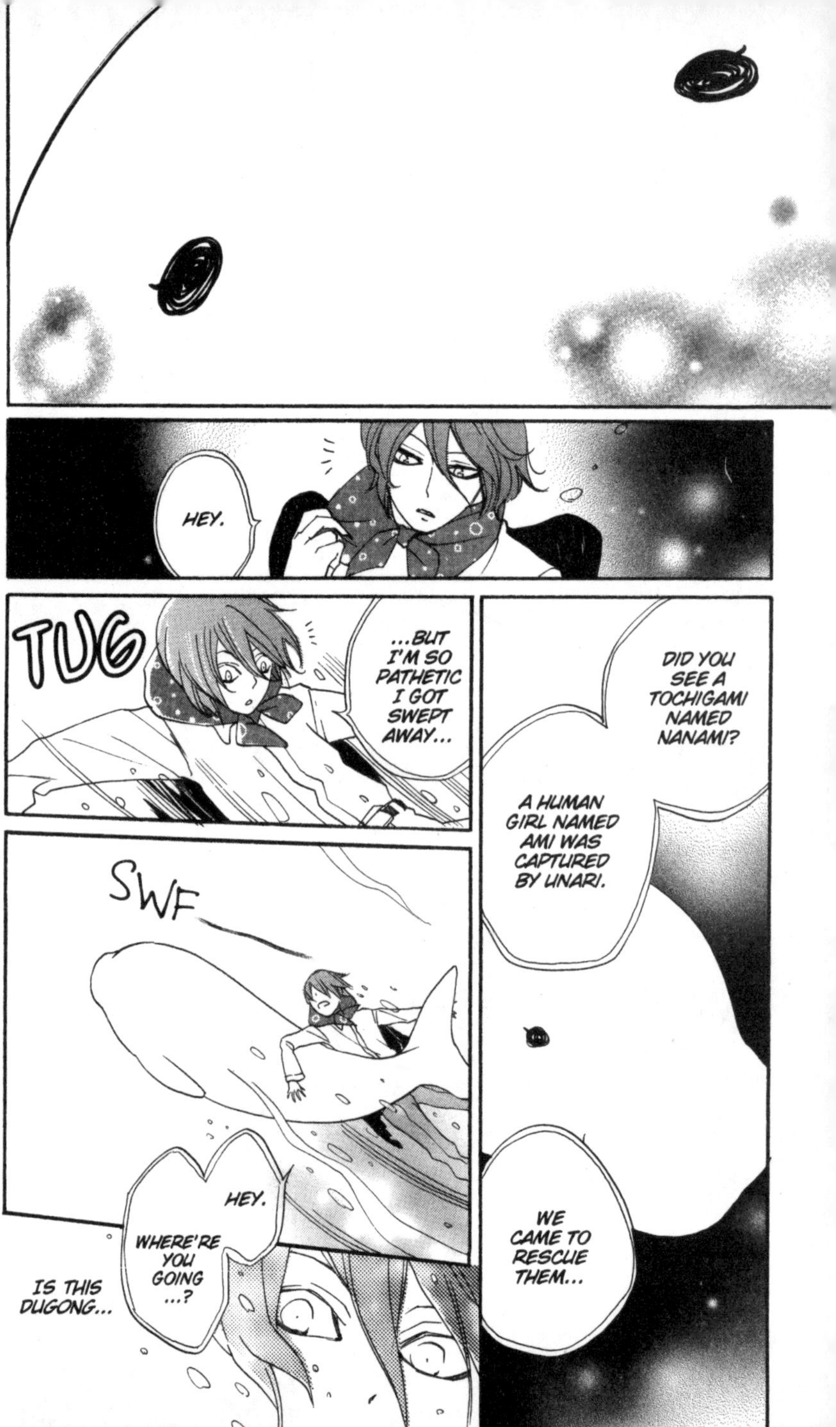
HEY.
DID YOU SEE A TOCHIGAMI NAMED NANAMI?
A HUMAN GIRL NAMED AMI WAS CAPTURED BY UNARI.
WE CAME TO RESCUE THEM...
TUG
...BUT I'M SO PATHETIC I GOT SWEPT AWAY...
SWF
HEY.
WHERE'RE YOU GOING ...?
IS THIS DUGONG...

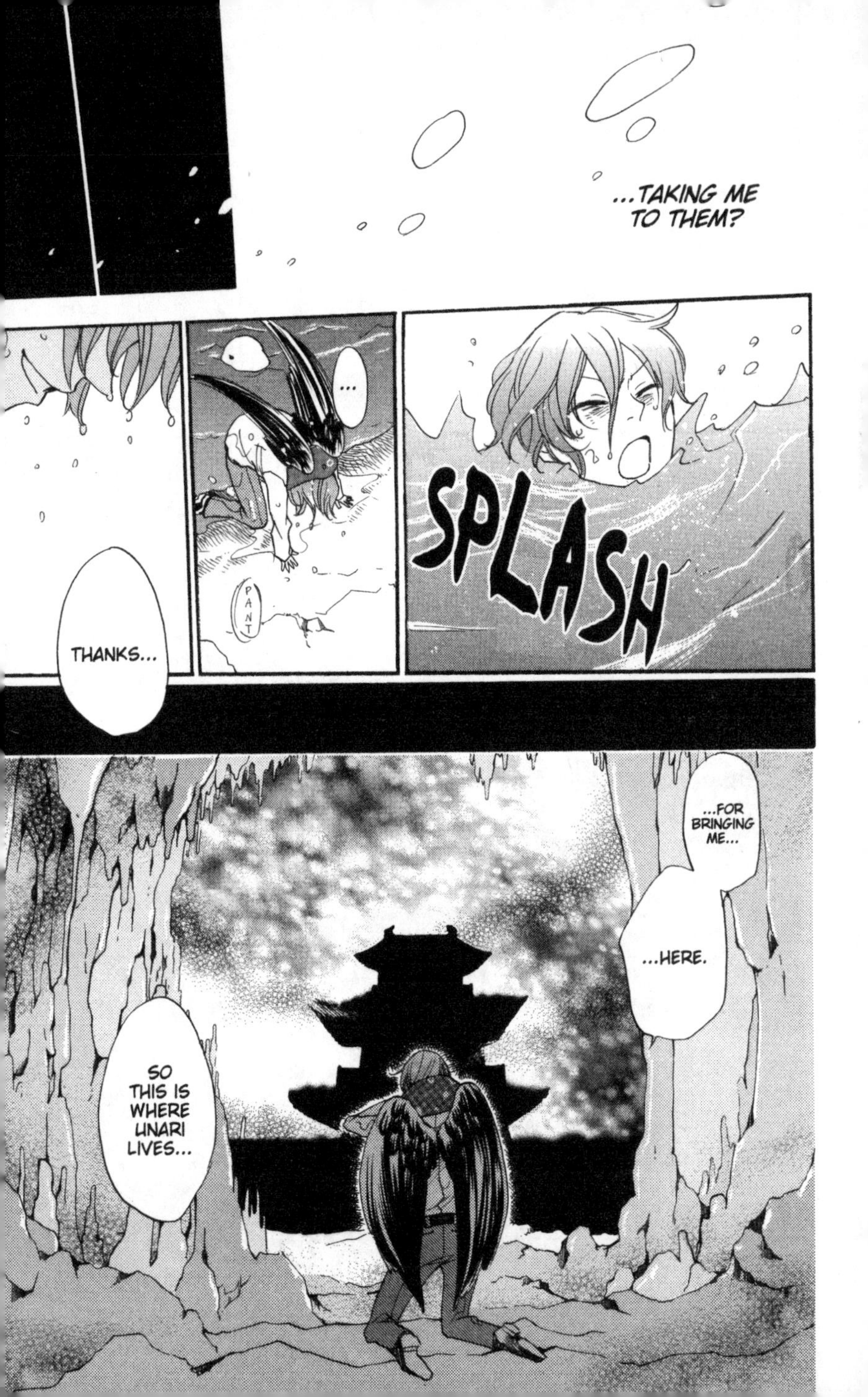
...TAKING ME TO THEM?
SPLASH
...
PANT
THANKS...
...FOR BRINGING ME...
...HERE.
SO THIS IS WHERE UNARI LIVES...

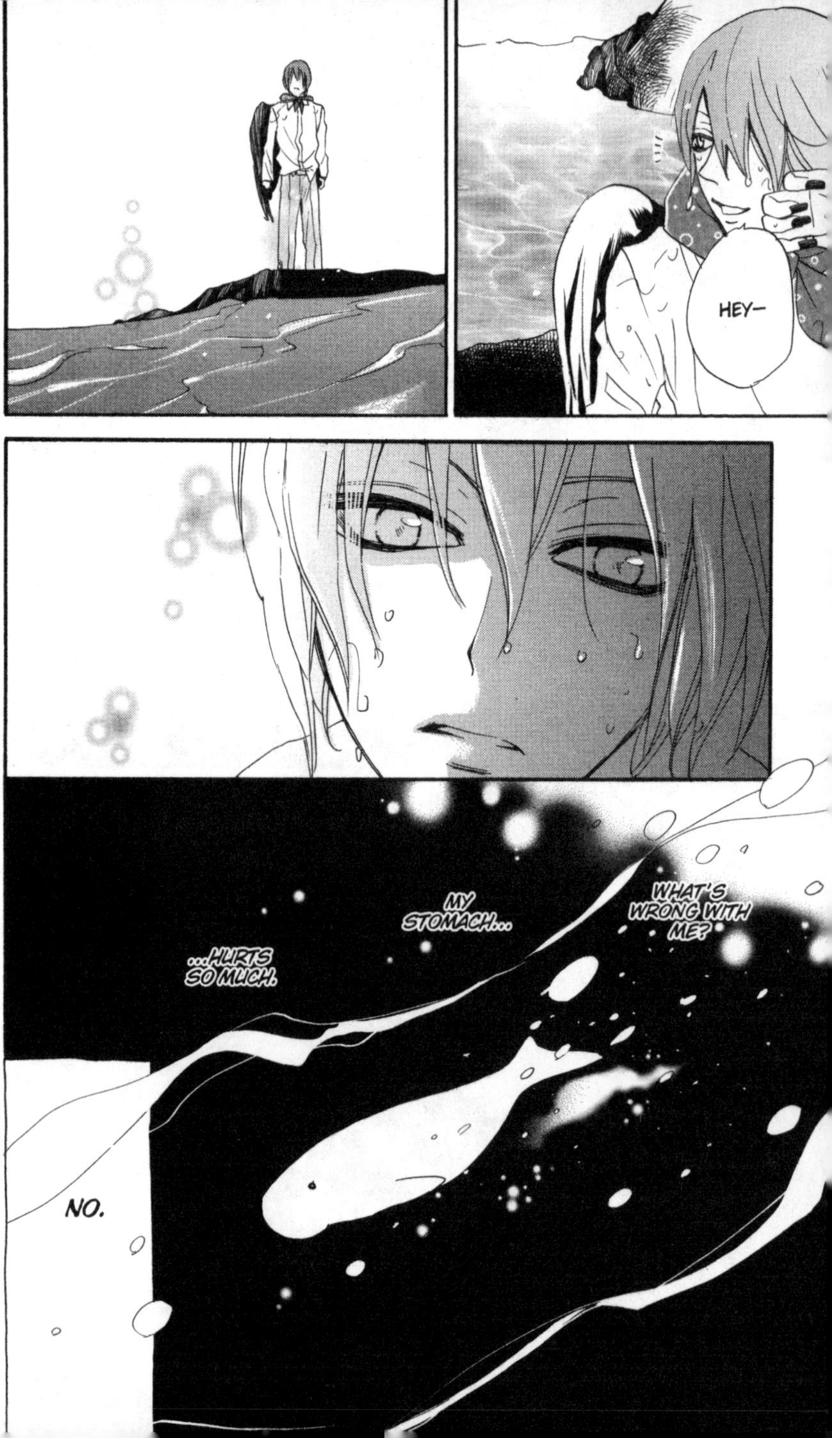
HEY—
WHAT'S WRONG WITH ME?
MY STOMACH...
...HURTS SO MUCH.
NO.

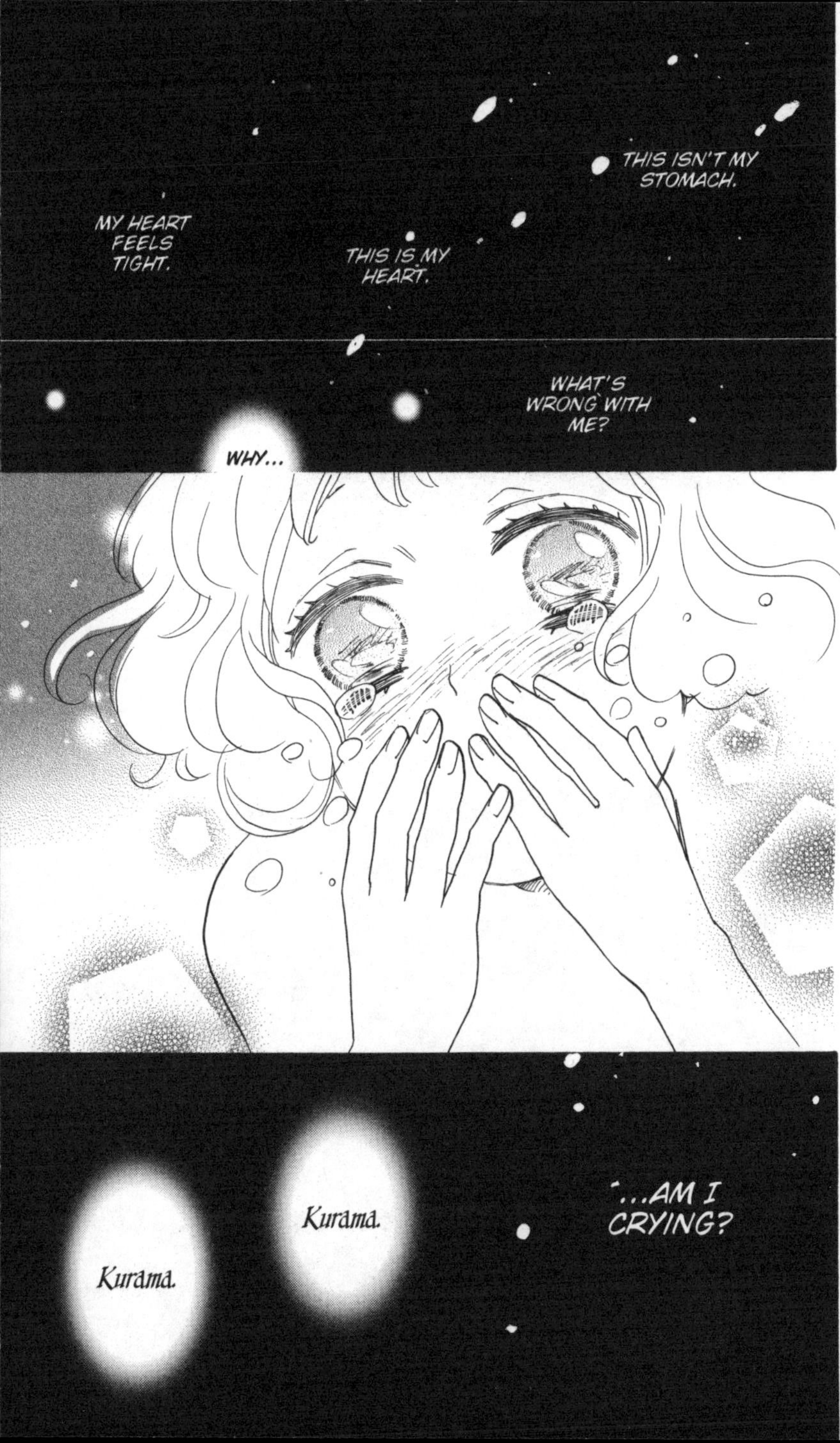
THIS ISN'T MY STOMACH.
THIS IS MY HEART.
MY HEART FEELS TIGHT.
WHAT'S WRONG WITH ME?
WHY...
...AM I CRYING?
Kurama.
Kurama.

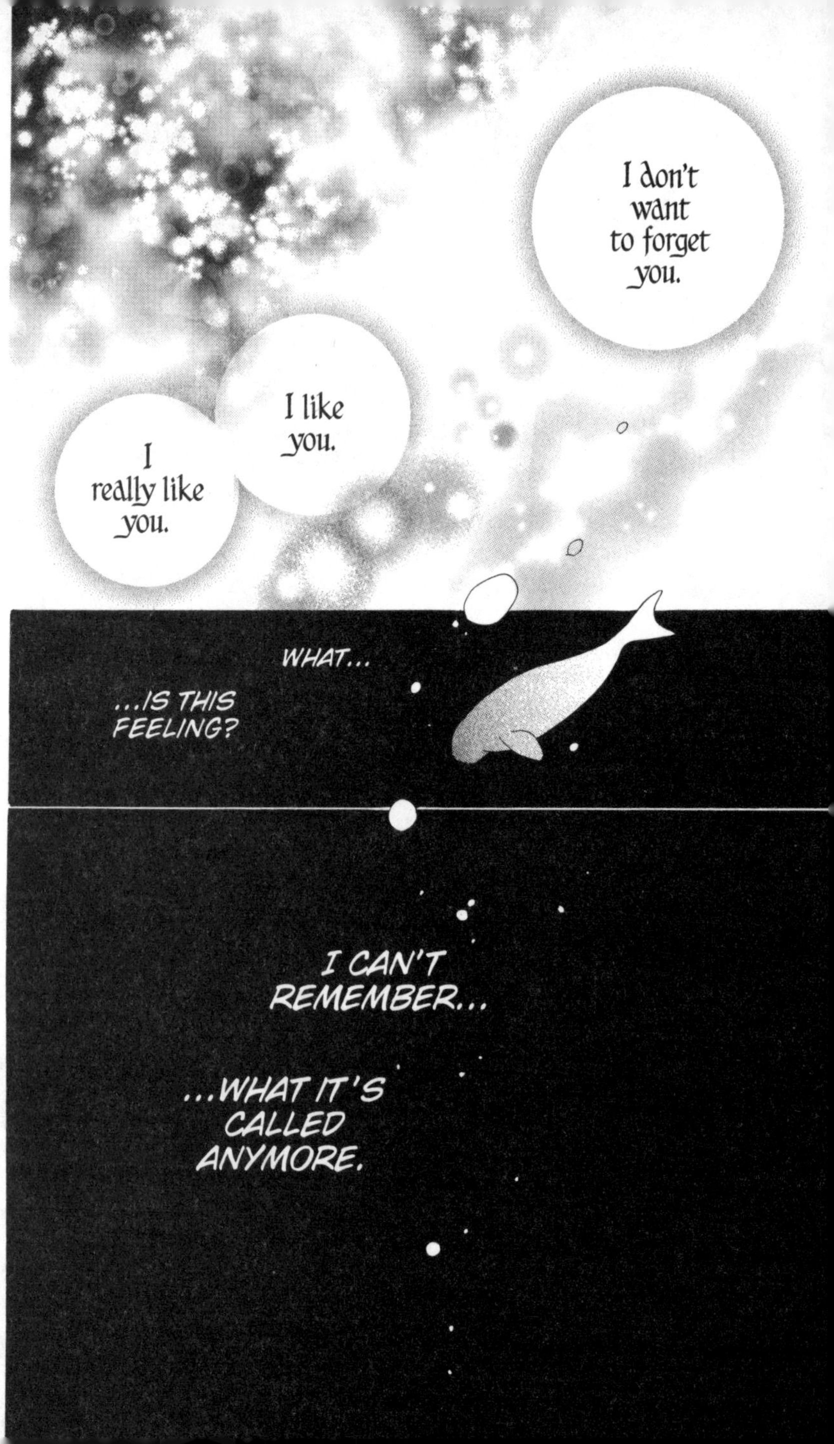
I don't want to forget you.
I like you.
I really like you.
WHAT...
...IS THIS FEELING?
I CAN'T REMEMBER...
...WHAT IT'S CALLED ANYMORE.

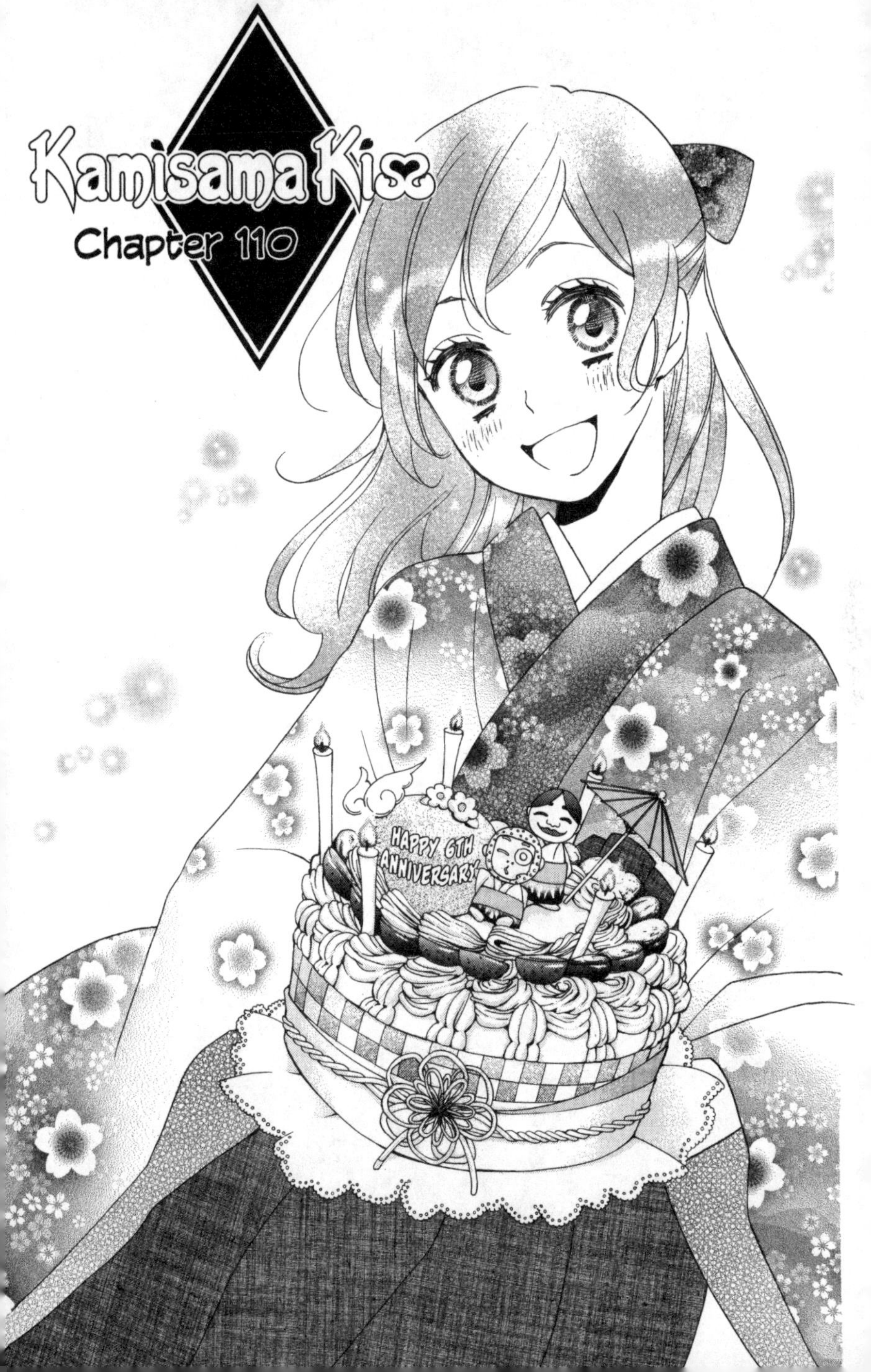
Kamisama Kiss
Chapter 110
HAPPY 6TH ANNIVERSARY

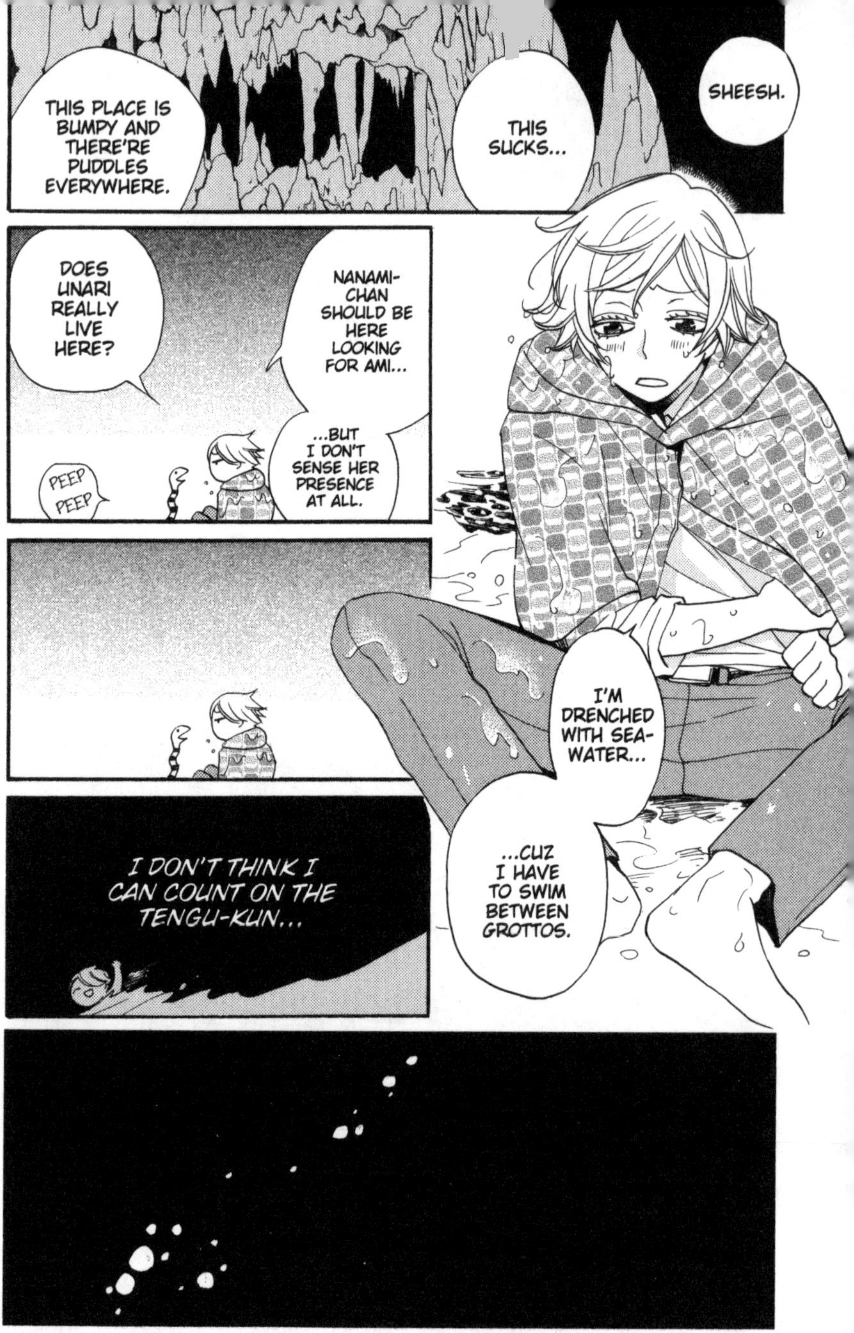

SHEESH.
THIS SUCKS...
THIS PLACE IS BUMPY AND THERE'RE PUDDLES EVERYWHERE.
I'M DRENCHED WITH SEA-WATER...
...CUZ I HAVE TO SWIM BETWEEN GROTTOS.
NANAMI-CHAN SHOULD BE HERE LOOKING FOR AMI...
DOES UNARI REALLY LIVE HERE?
...BUT I DON'T SENSE HER PRESENCE AT ALL.
PEEP PEEP
I DON'T THINK I CAN COUNT ON THE TENGU-KUN...

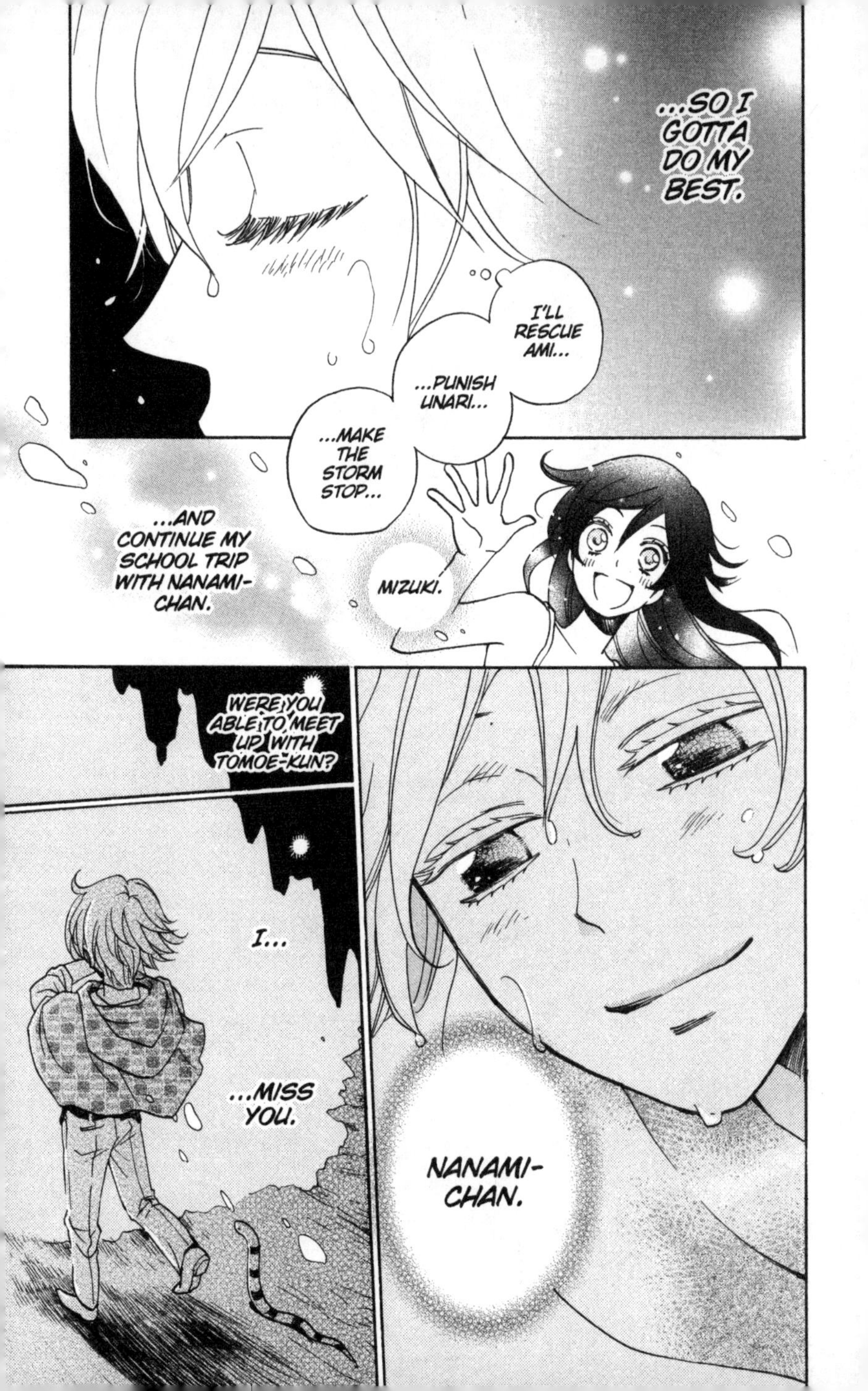
...SO I GOTTA DO MY BEST.
I'LL RESCUE AMI...
...PUNISH UNARI...
...MAKE THE STORM STOP...
...AND CONTINUE MY SCHOOL TRIP WITH NANAMI-CHAN.
MIZUKI.
NANAMI-CHAN.
WERE YOU ABLE TO MEET UP WITH TOMOE-KUN?
I...
...MISS YOU.

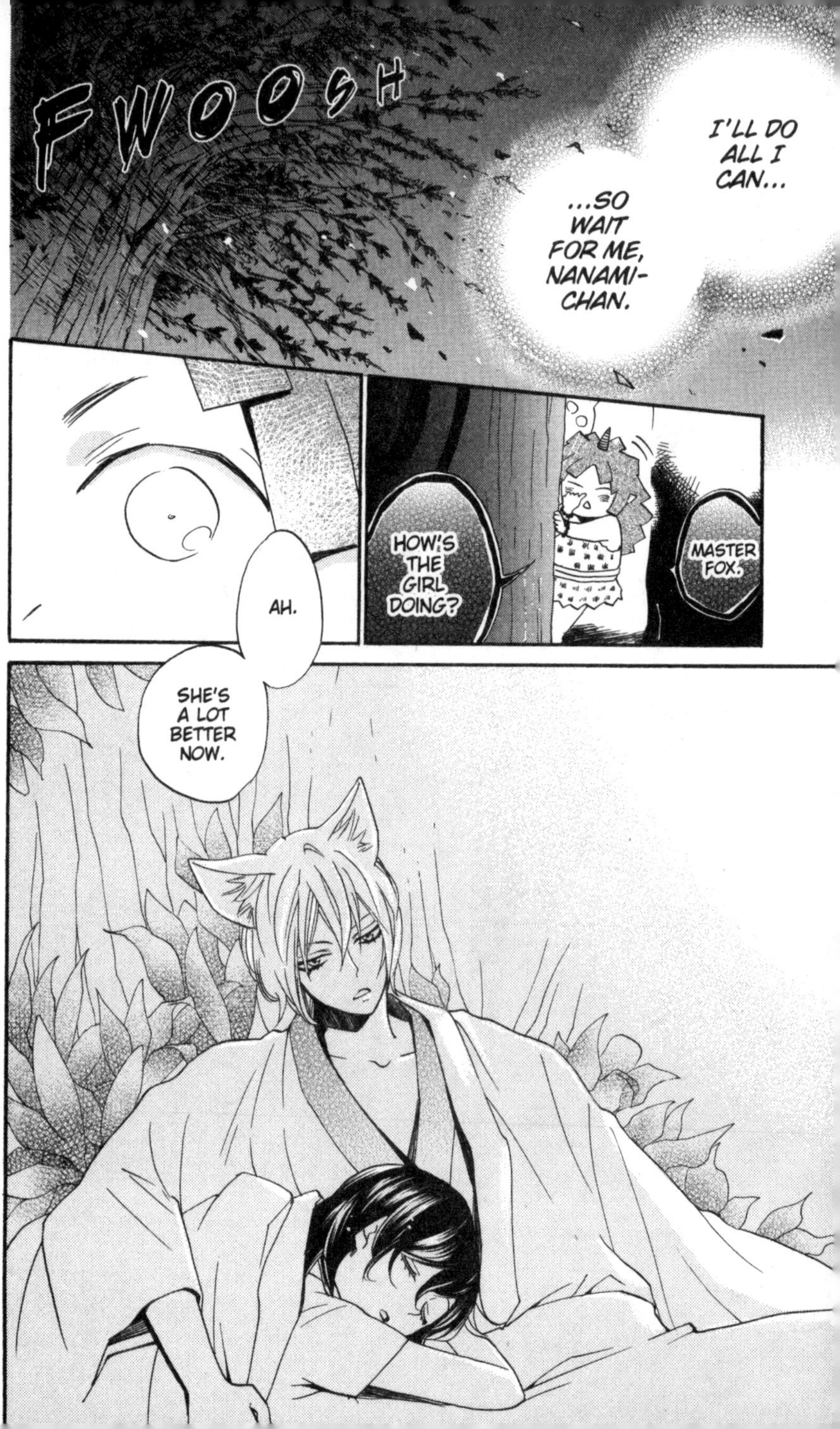
I'LL DO ALL I CAN...
...SO WAIT FOR ME, NANAMI-CHAN.
FWOOSH
MASTER FOX.
HOW'S THE GIRL DOING?
AH.
SHE'S A LOT BETTER NOW.

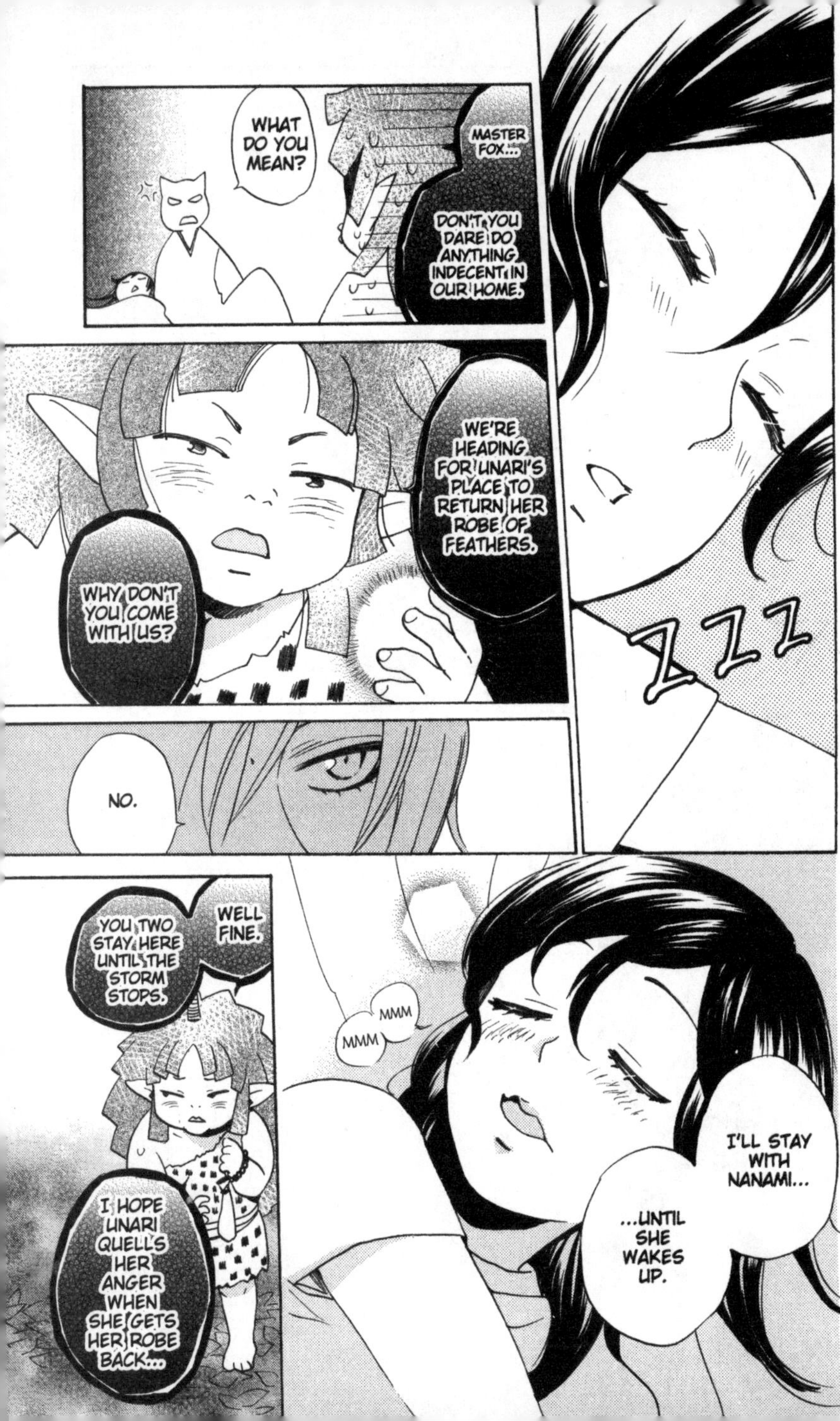
ZZZ
MASTER FOX...
DON'T YOU DARE DO ANYTHING INDECENT IN OUR HOME.
WHAT DO YOU MEAN?
WE'RE HEADING FOR UNARI'S PLACE TO RETURN HER ROBE OF FEATHERS.
WHY DON'T YOU COME WITH US?
NO.
MMM
MMM
I'LL STAY WITH NANAMI...
...UNTIL SHE WAKES UP.
WELL FINE.
YOU TWO STAY HERE UNTIL THE STORM STOPS.
I HOPE UNARI QUELLS HER ANGER WHEN SHE GETS HER ROBE BACK...

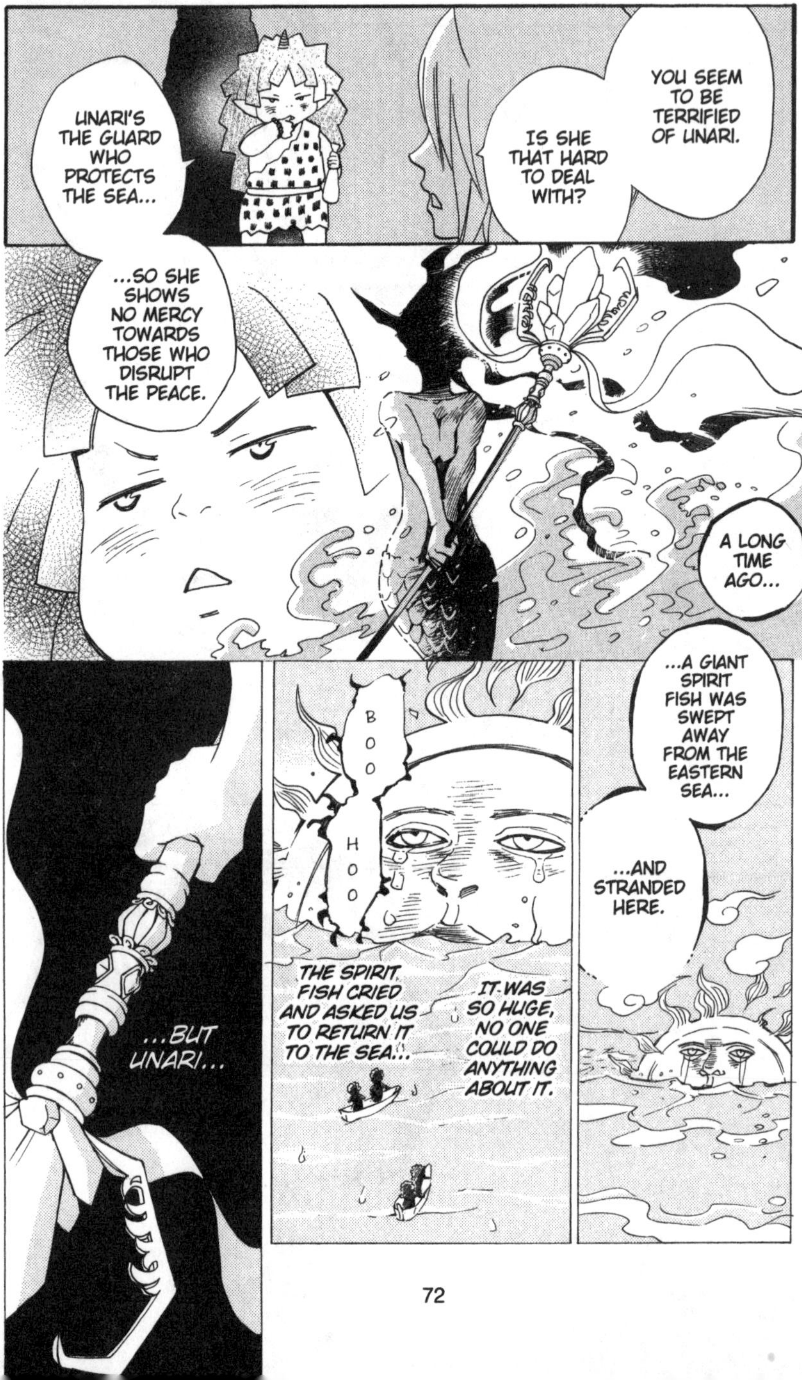
YOU SEEM TO BE TERRIFIED OF UNARI.
IS SHE THAT HARD TO DEAL WITH?
UNARI'S THE GUARD WHO PROTECTS THE SEA...
...SO SHE SHOWS NO MERCY TOWARDS THOSE WHO DISRUPT THE PEACE.
A LONG TIME AGO...
...A GIANT SPIRIT FISH WAS SWEPT AWAY FROM THE EASTERN SEA...
...AND STRANDED HERE.
BOO HOO
IT WAS SO HUGE, NO ONE COULD DO ANYTHING ABOUT IT.
THE SPIRIT FISH CRIED AND ASKED US TO RETURN IT TO THE SEA...
...BUT UNARI...

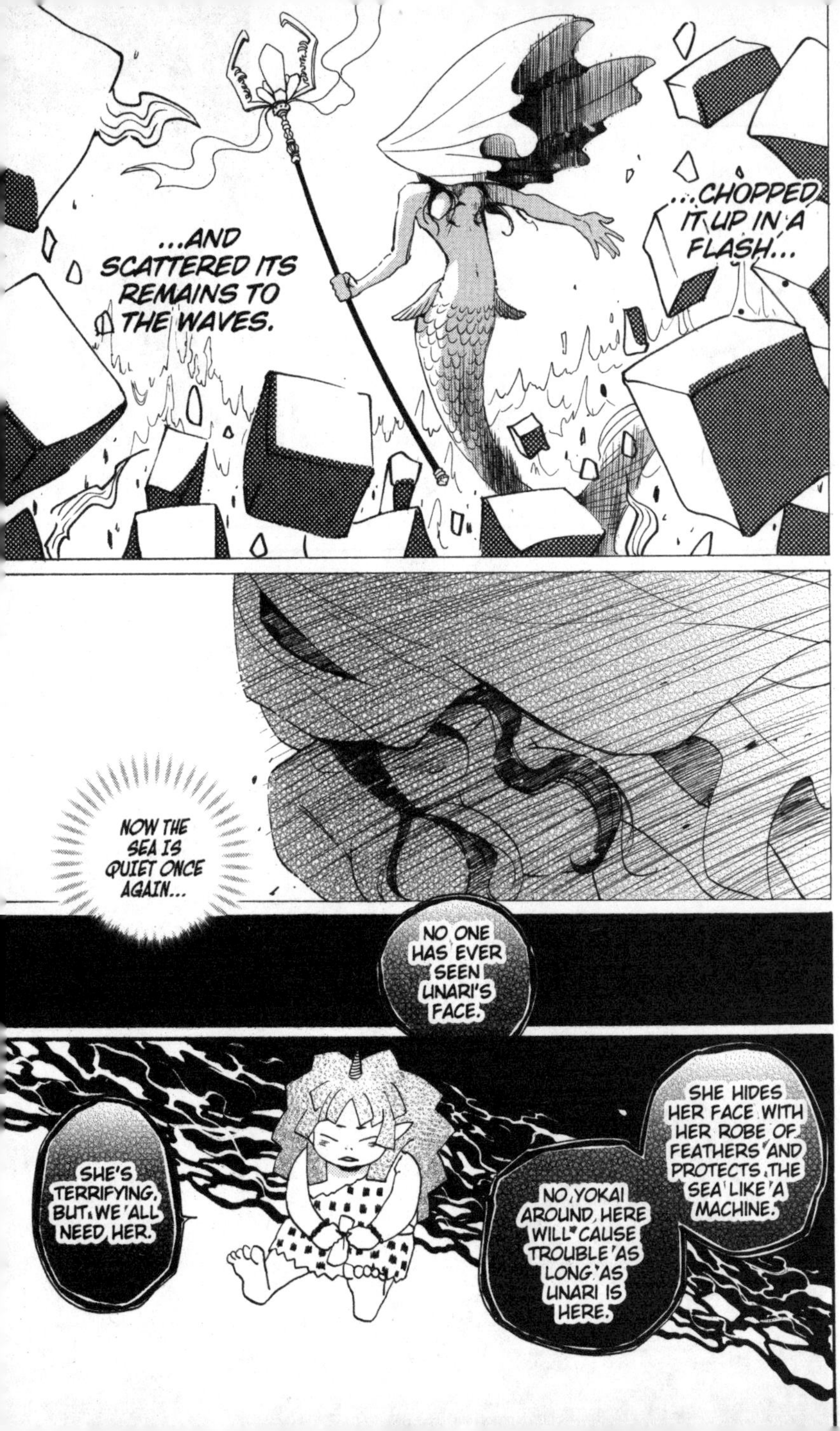
...CHOPPED IT UP IN A FLASH...
...AND SCATTERED ITS REMAINS TO THE WAVES.
NOW THE SEA IS QUIET ONCE AGAIN...
NO ONE HAS EVER SEEN UNARI'S FACE.
SHE HIDES HER FACE WITH HER ROBE OF FEATHERS AND PROTECTS THE SEA LIKE A MACHINE.
NO YOKAI AROUND HERE WILL CAUSE TROUBLE AS LONG AS UNARI IS HERE.
SHE'S TERRIFYING, BUT WE ALL NEED HER.

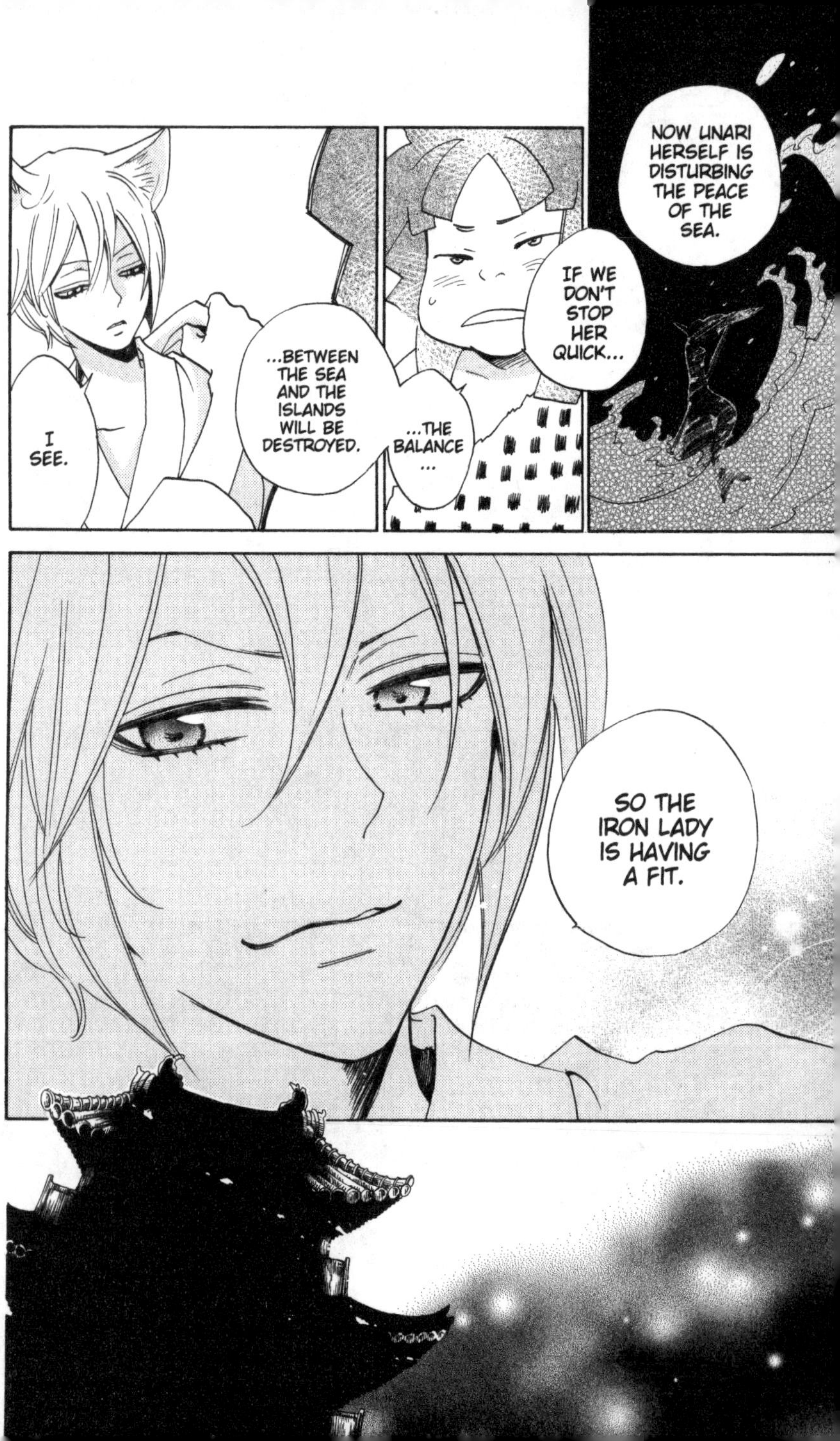
NOW UNARI HERSELF IS DISTURBING THE PEACE OF THE SEA.
IF WE DON'T STOP HER QUICK...
...THE BALANCE ...
...BETWEEN THE SEA AND THE ISLANDS WILL BE DESTROYED.
I SEE.
SO THE IRON LADY IS HAVING A FIT.

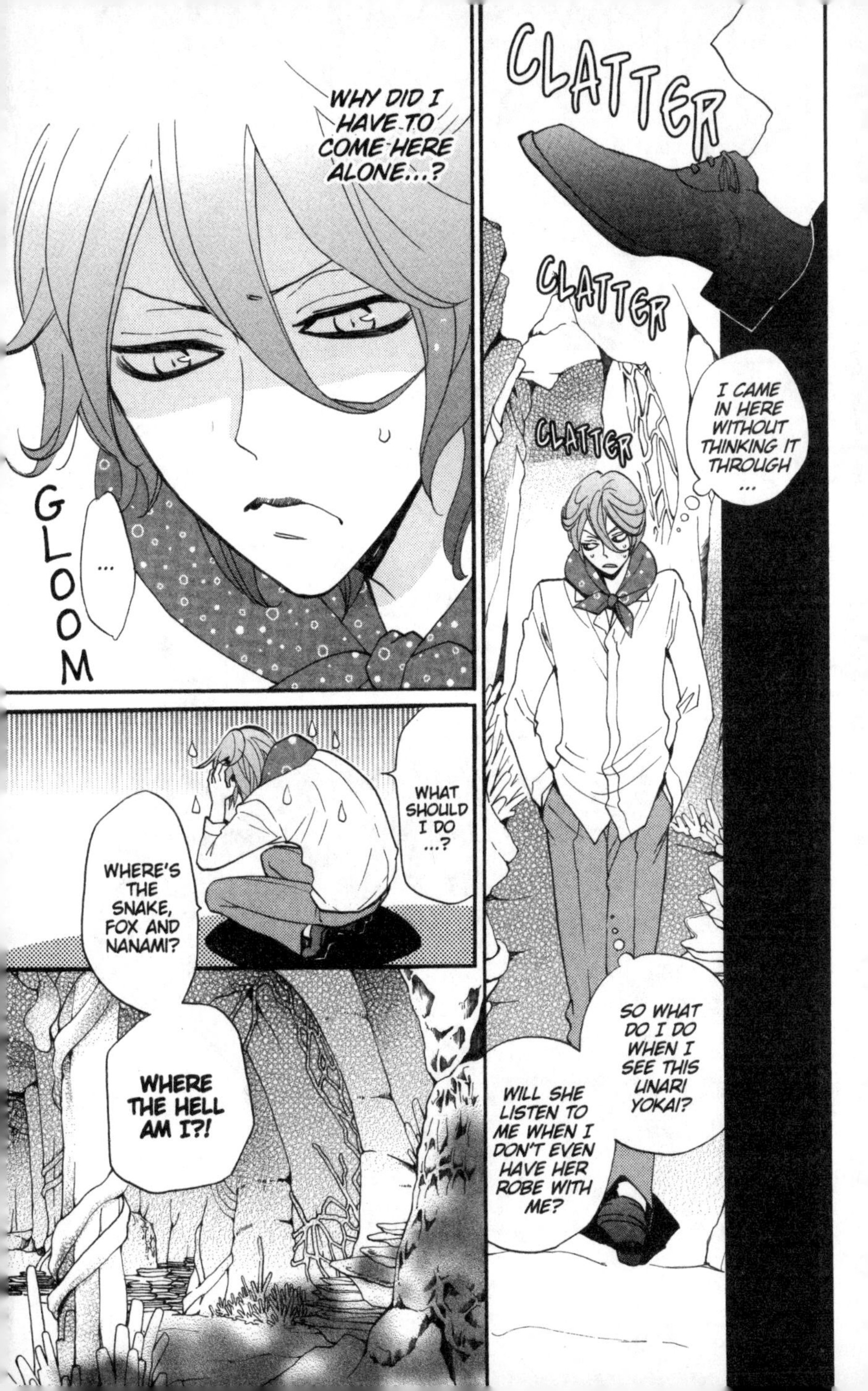
CLATTER
CLATTER
I CAME IN HERE WITHOUT THINKING IT THROUGH...
CLATTER
SO WHAT DO I DO WHEN I SEE THIS UNARI YOKAI?
WILL SHE LISTEN TO ME WHEN I DON'T EVEN HAVE HER ROBE WITH ME?
WHY DID I HAVE TO COME HERE ALONE...?
GLOOM
...
WHAT SHOULD I DO...?
WHERE'S THE SNAKE, FOX AND NANAMI?
WHERE THE HELL AM I?!

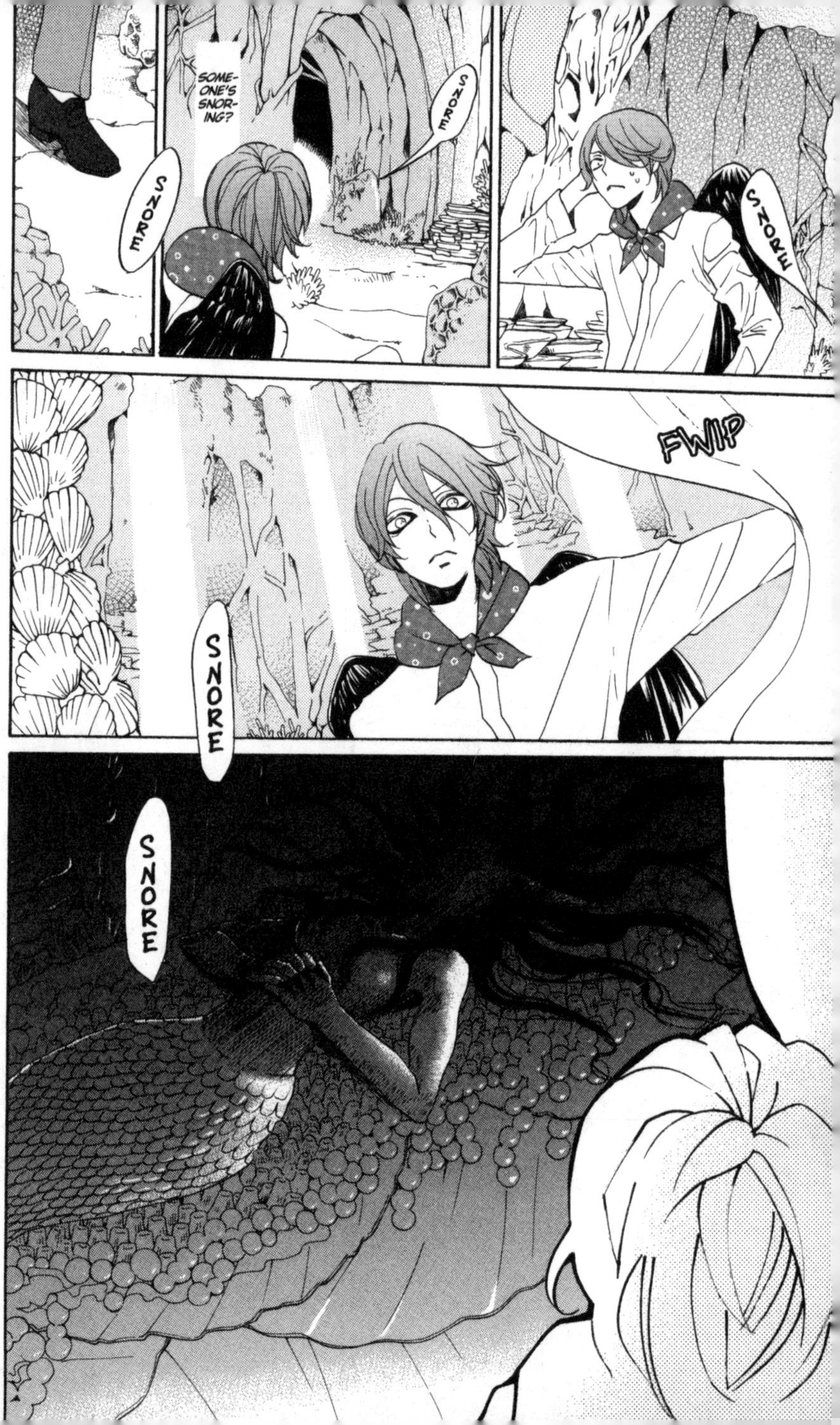
SNORE
SNORE
SOME-ONE'S SNOR-ING?
SNORE
FWIP
SNORE
SNORE

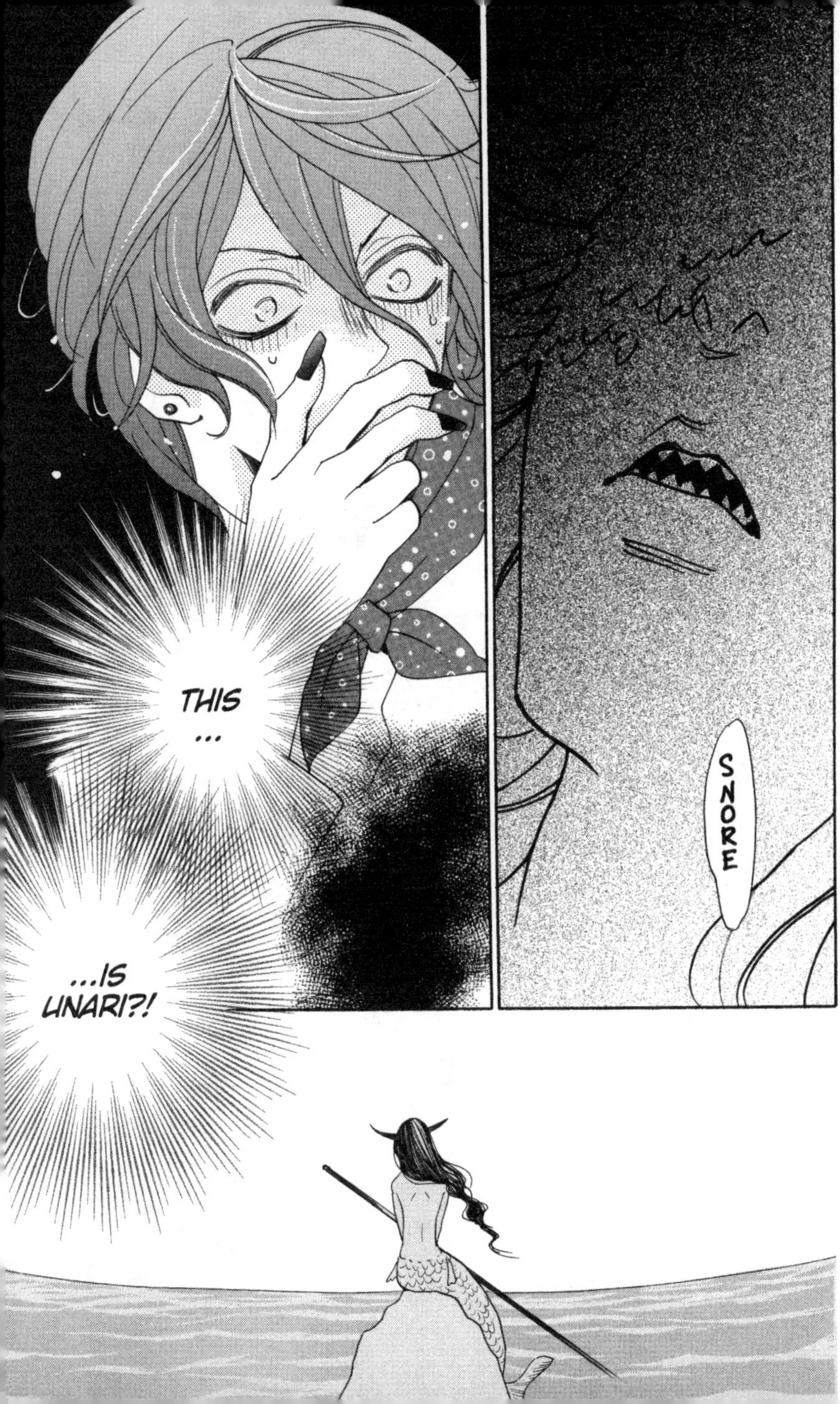
SNORE
THIS ...
...IS UNARI?!

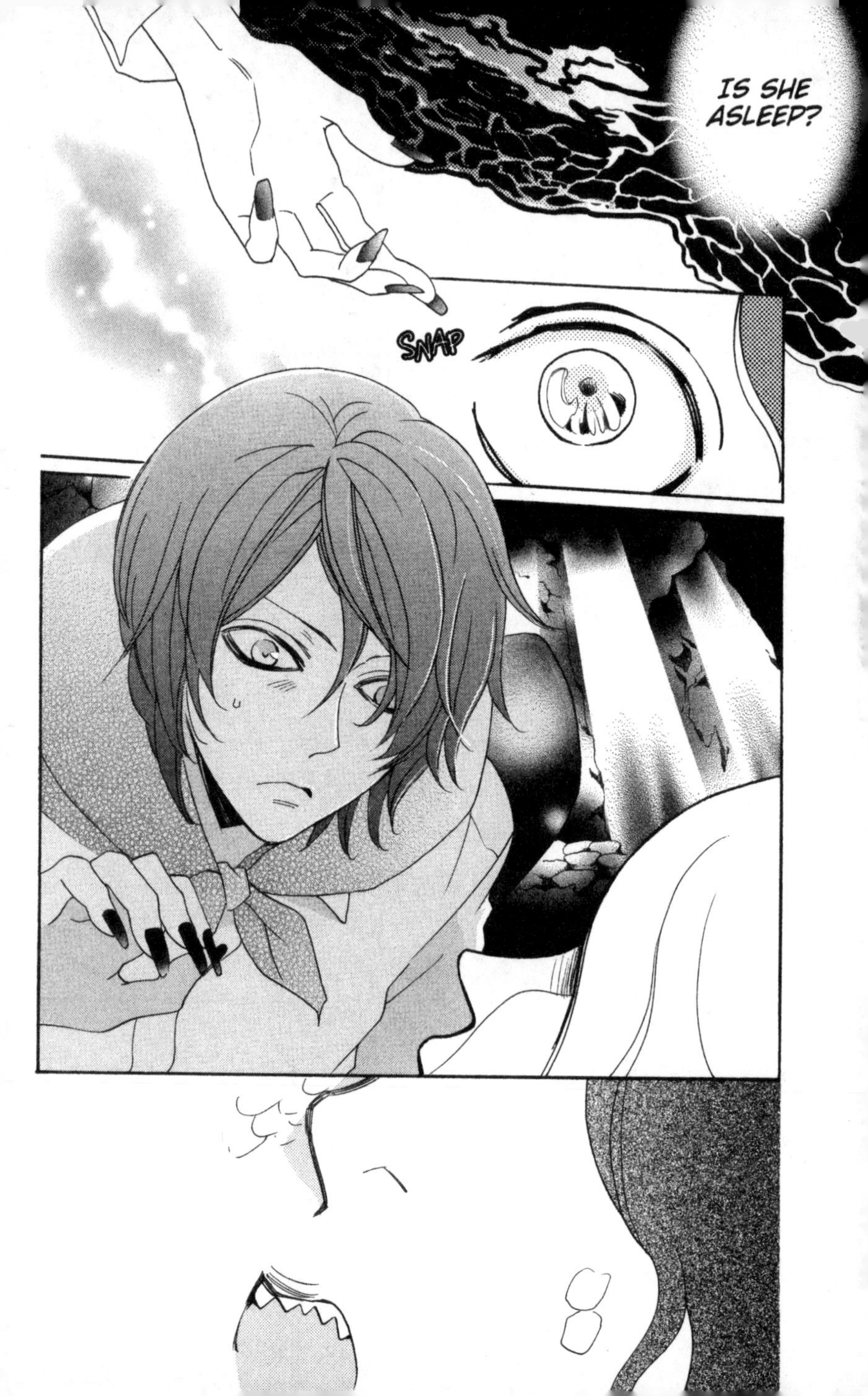
IS SHE ASLEEP?
SNAP

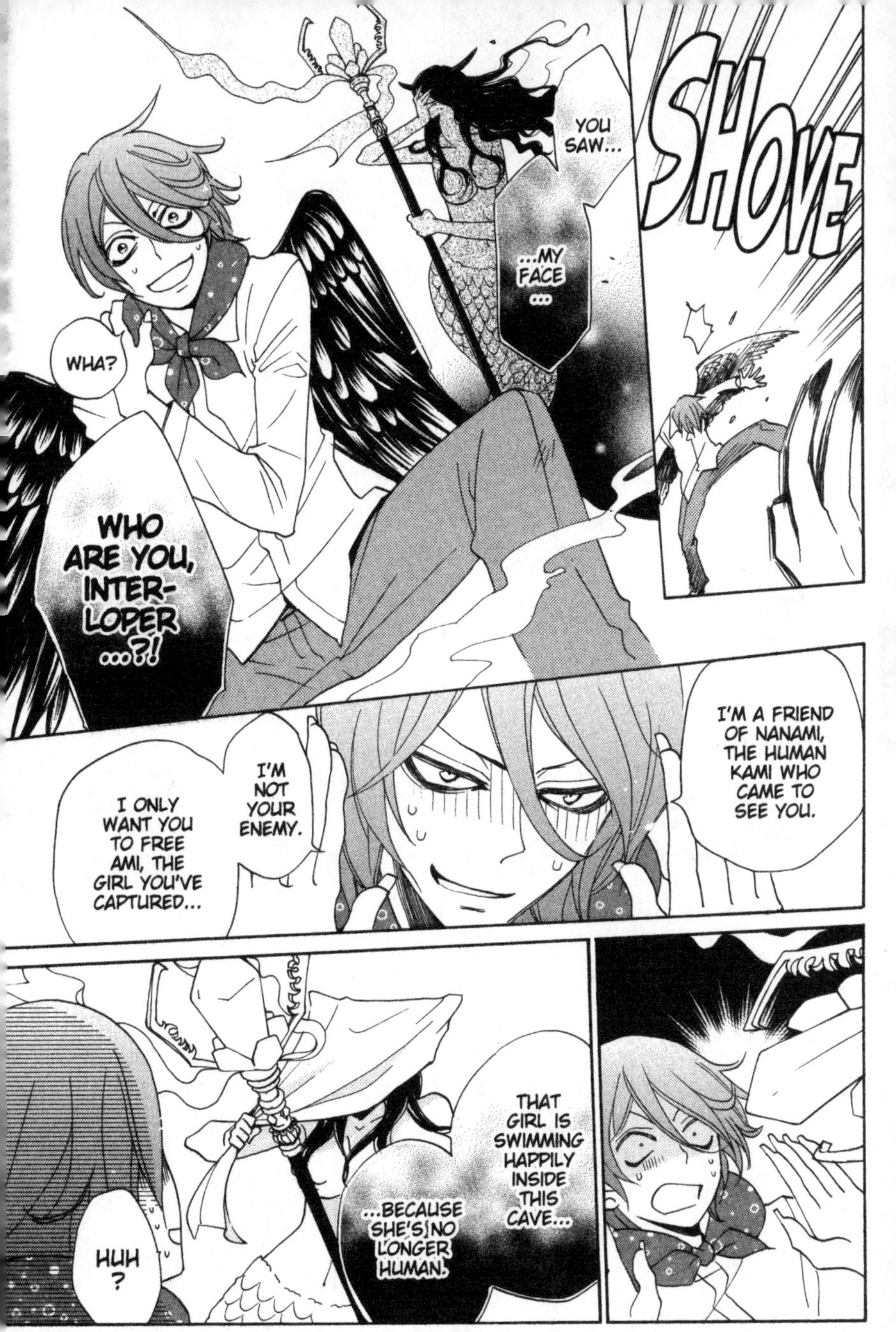
SHOVE
YOU SAW...
...MY FACE...
WHA?
WHO ARE YOU, INTER-LOPER...?!
I'M A FRIEND OF NANAMI, THE HUMAN KAMI WHO CAME TO SEE YOU.
I'M NOT YOUR ENEMY.
I ONLY WANT YOU TO FREE AMI, THE GIRL YOU'VE CAPTURED...
THAT GIRL IS SWIMMING HAPPILY INSIDE THIS CAVE...
...BECAUSE SHE'S NO LONGER HUMAN.
HUH?

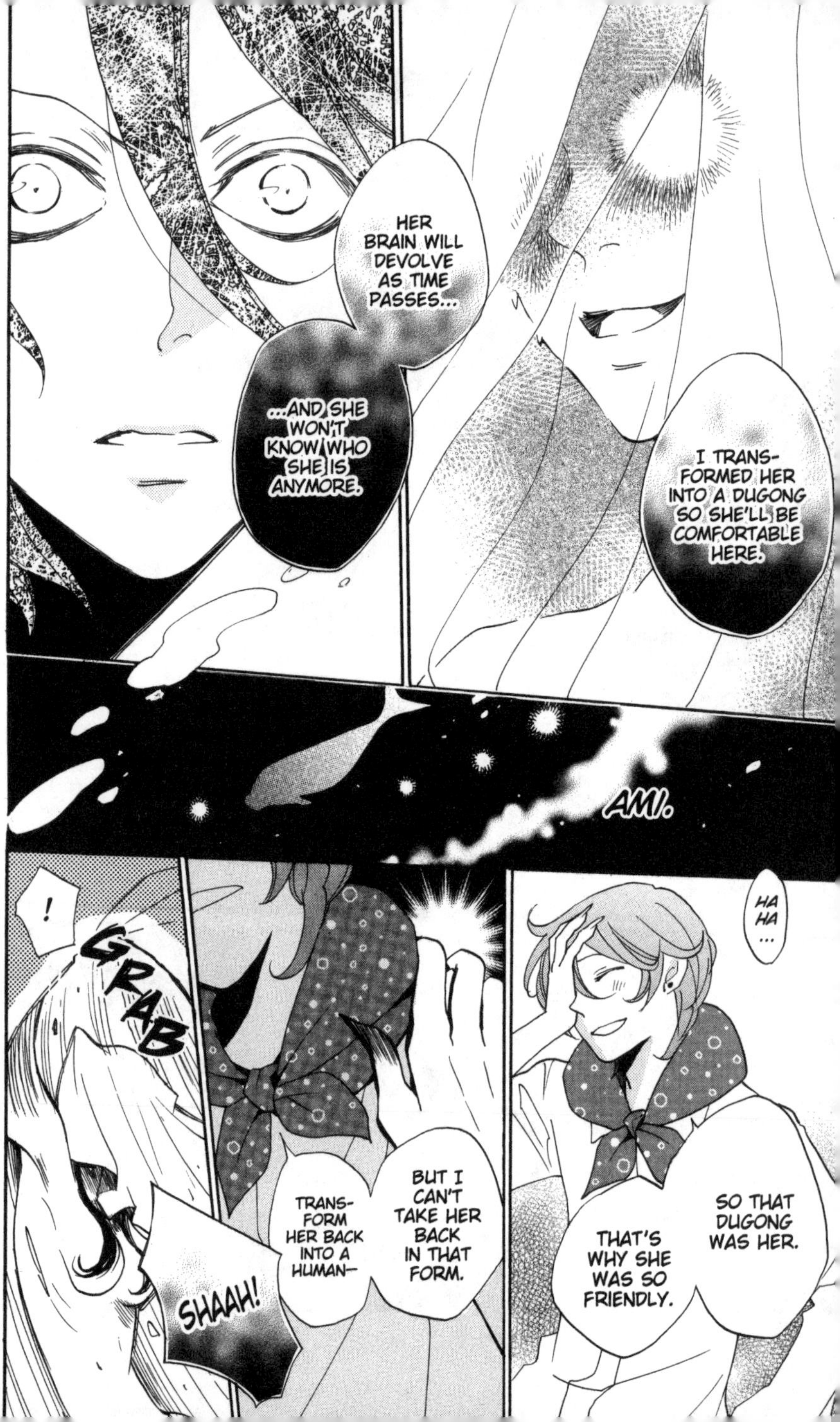
I TRANS-FORMED HER INTO A DUGONG SO SHE'LL BE COMFORTABLE HERE.
HER BRAIN WILL DEVOLVE AS TIME PASSES...
...AND SHE WON'T KNOW WHO SHE IS ANYMORE.
AMI.
HA HA...
SO THAT DUGONG WAS HER.
THAT'S WHY SHE WAS SO FRIENDLY.
BUT I CAN'T TAKE HER BACK IN THAT FORM.
TRANS-FORM HER BACK INTO A HUMAN—
!
GRAB
SHAAH!

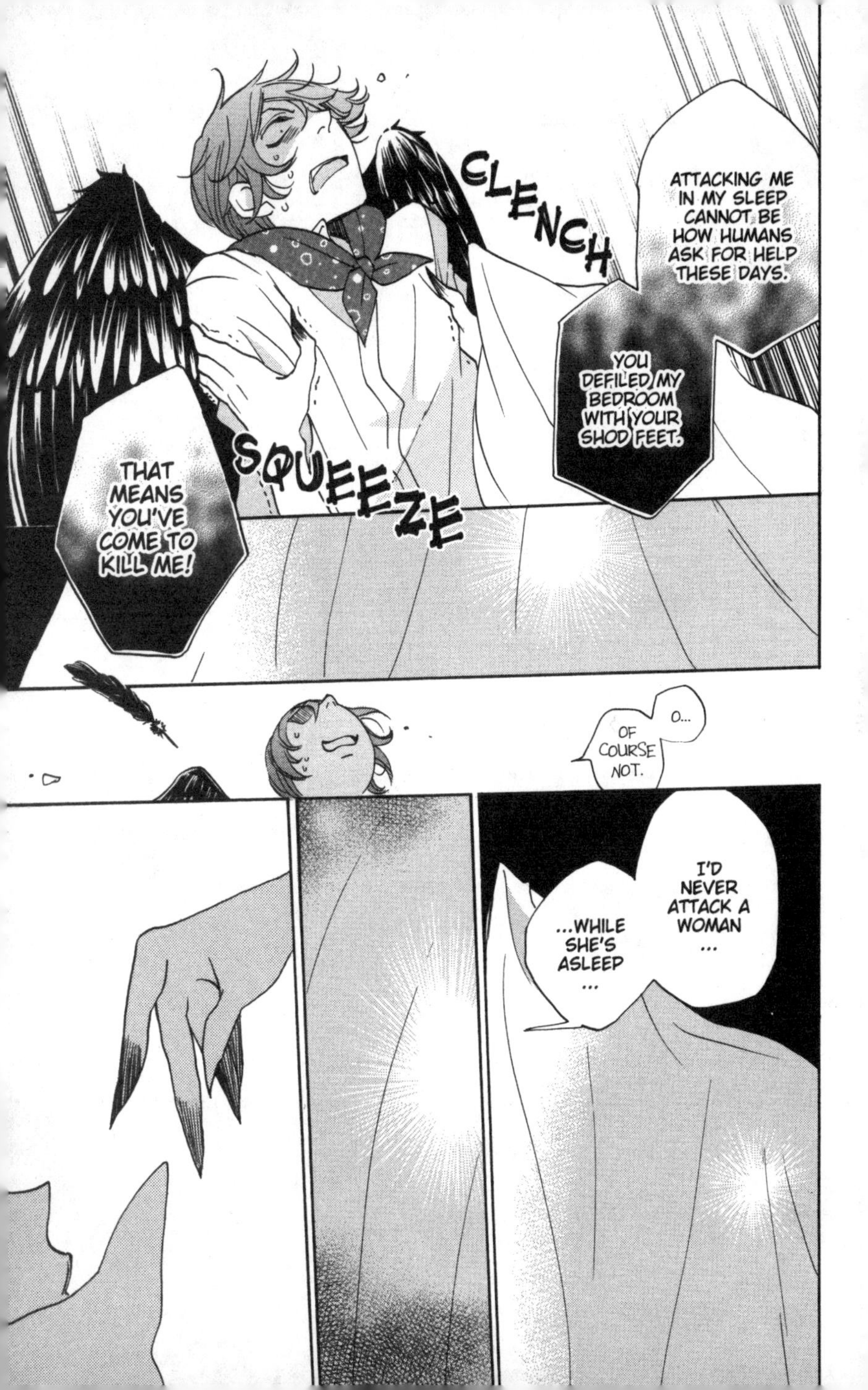
ATTACKING ME IN MY SLEEP CANNOT BE HOW HUMANS ASK FOR HELP THESE DAYS.
CLENCH
YOU DEFILED MY BEDROOM WITH YOUR SHOD FEET.
SQUEEZE
THAT MEANS YOU'VE COME TO KILL ME!
O... OF COURSE NOT.
I'D NEVER ATTACK A WOMAN ...
...WHILE SHE'S ASLEEP ...

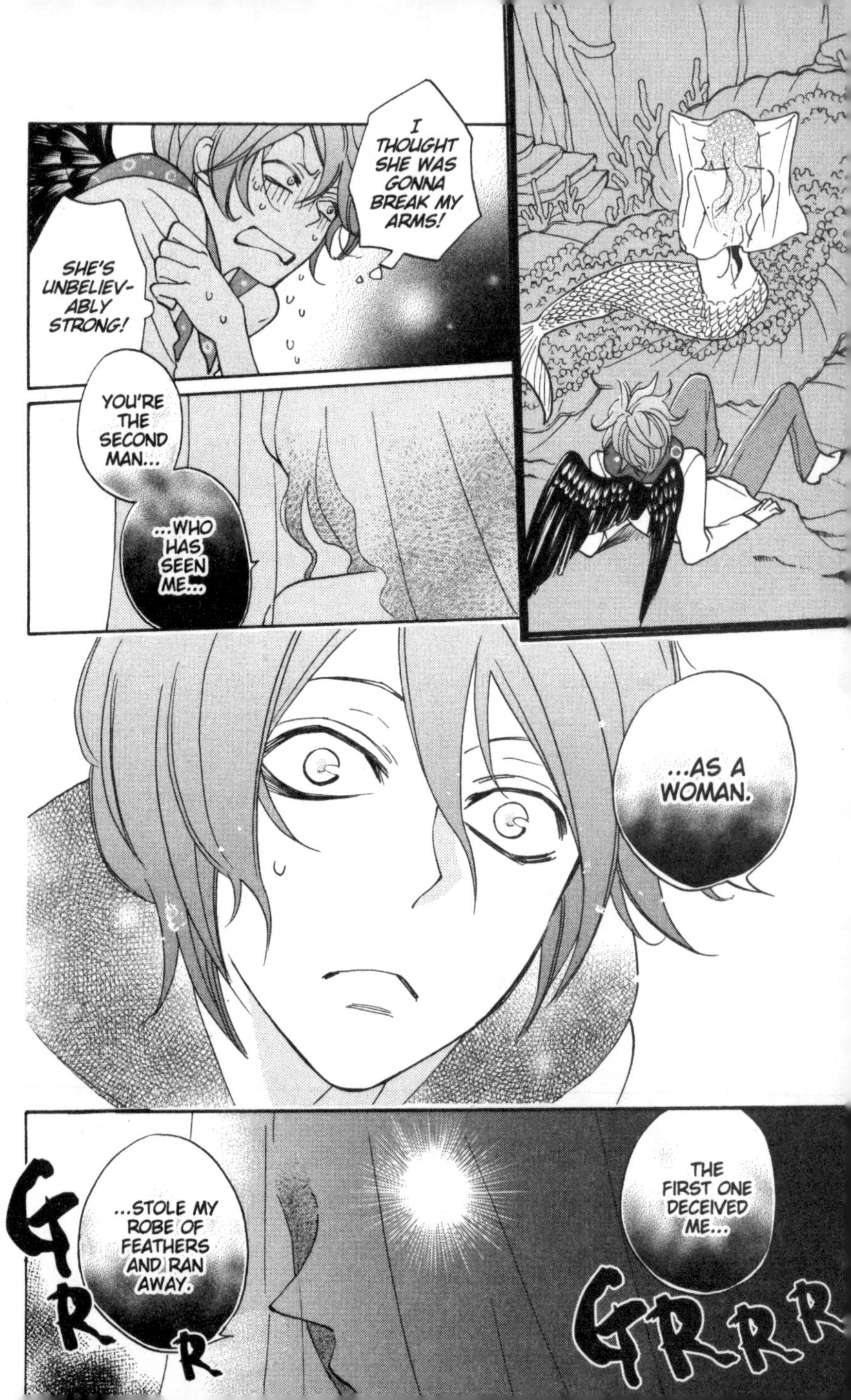
I THOUGHT SHE WAS GONNA BREAK MY ARMS!
SHE'S UNBELIEV-ABLY STRONG!
YOU'RE THE SECOND MAN...
...WHO HAS SEEN ME...
...AS A WOMAN.
THE FIRST ONE DECEIVED ME...
...STOLE MY ROBE OF FEATHERS AND RAN AWAY.
GRRR
GRR

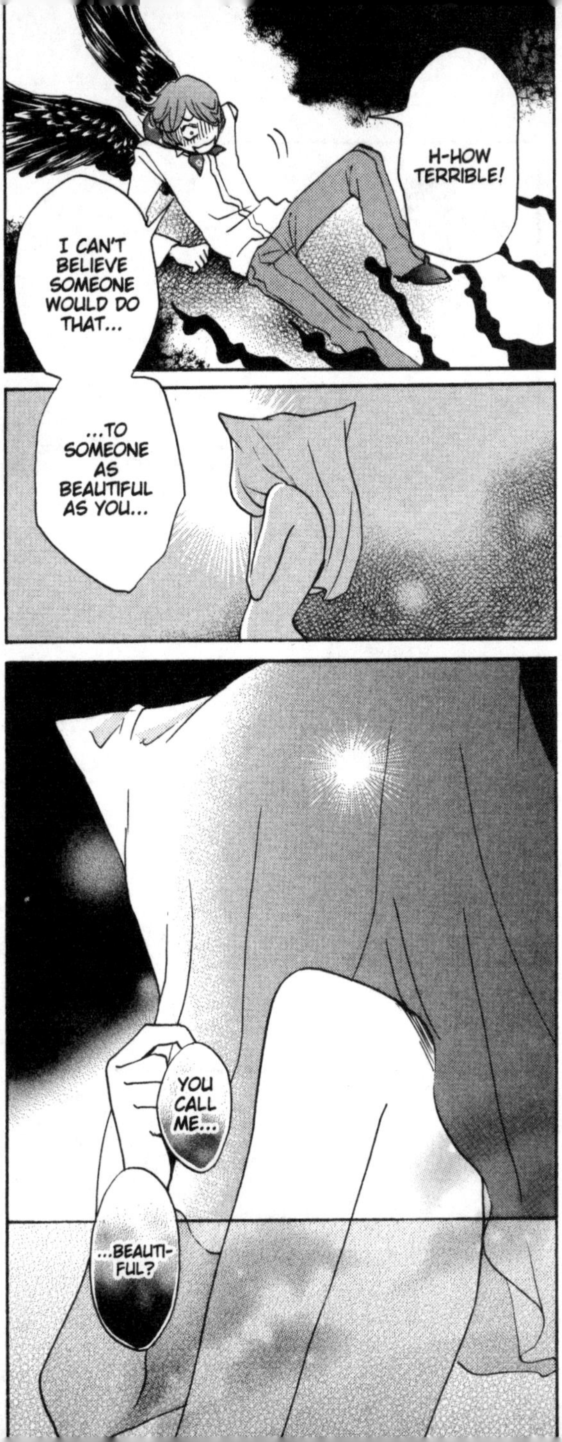
H-HOW TERRIBLE!
I CAN'T BELIEVE SOMEONE WOULD DO THAT...
...TO SOMEONE AS BEAUTIFUL AS YOU...
YOU CALL ME...
...BEAUTIFUL?

I started to turn the air conditioner on since it's getting hot, but then day by day I started to get sick. I couldn't figure out what was happening, but I then found out my body was getting cold internally because of the air conditioner. What a surprise.

"Being cold" and "getting cold internally" are different...!

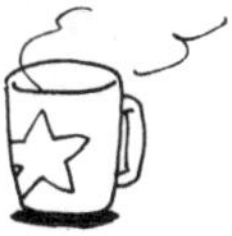

Drinking ginger tea warmed me up.

Everyone watch out for summer fatigue!

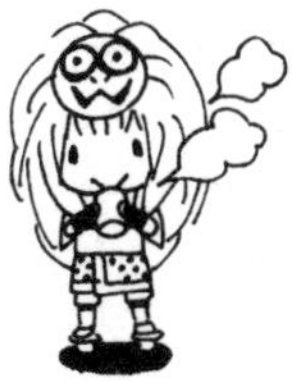

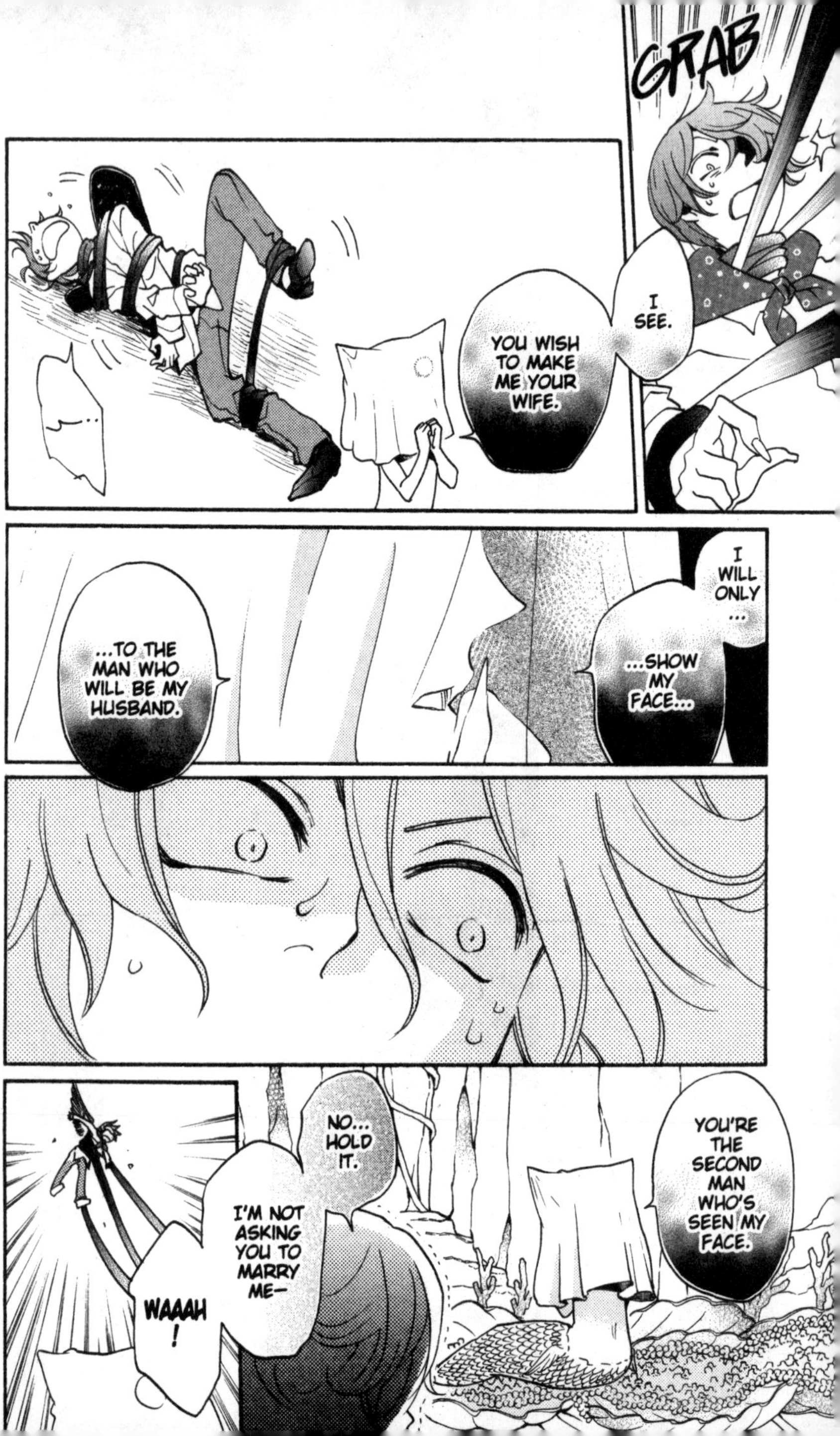
GRAB
I SEE.
YOU WISH TO MAKE ME YOUR WIFE.
...
I WILL ONLY...
...SHOW MY FACE...
...TO THE MAN WHO WILL BE MY HUSBAND.
YOU'RE THE SECOND MAN WHO'S SEEN MY FACE.
NO... HOLD IT.
I'M NOT ASKING YOU TO MARRY ME—
WAAAH!

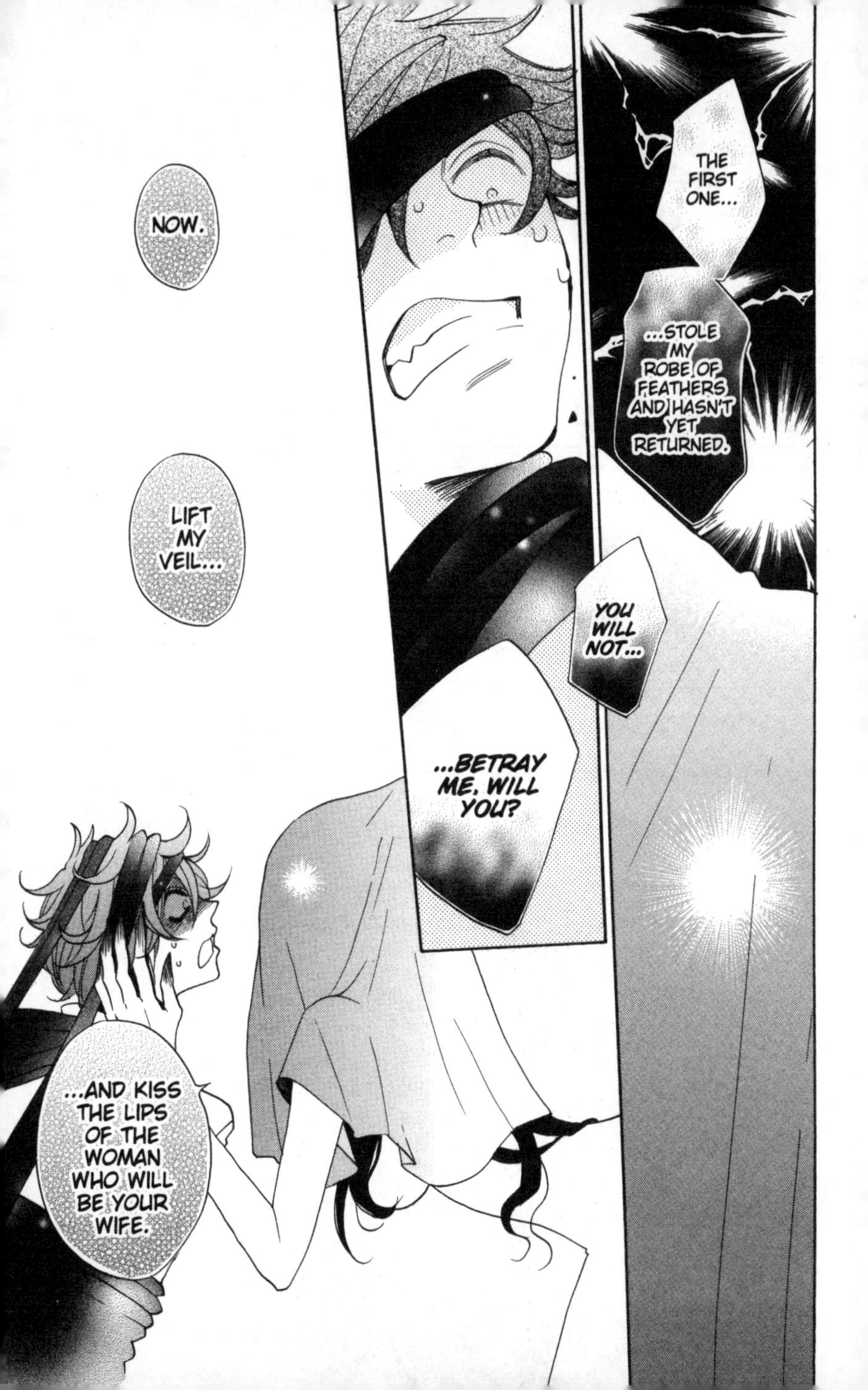
THE FIRST ONE...
...STOLE MY ROBE OF FEATHERS AND HASN'T YET RETURNED.
YOU WILL NOT...
...BETRAY ME, WILL YOU?
NOW.
LIFT MY VEIL...
...AND KISS THE LIPS OF THE WOMAN WHO WILL BE YOUR WIFE.

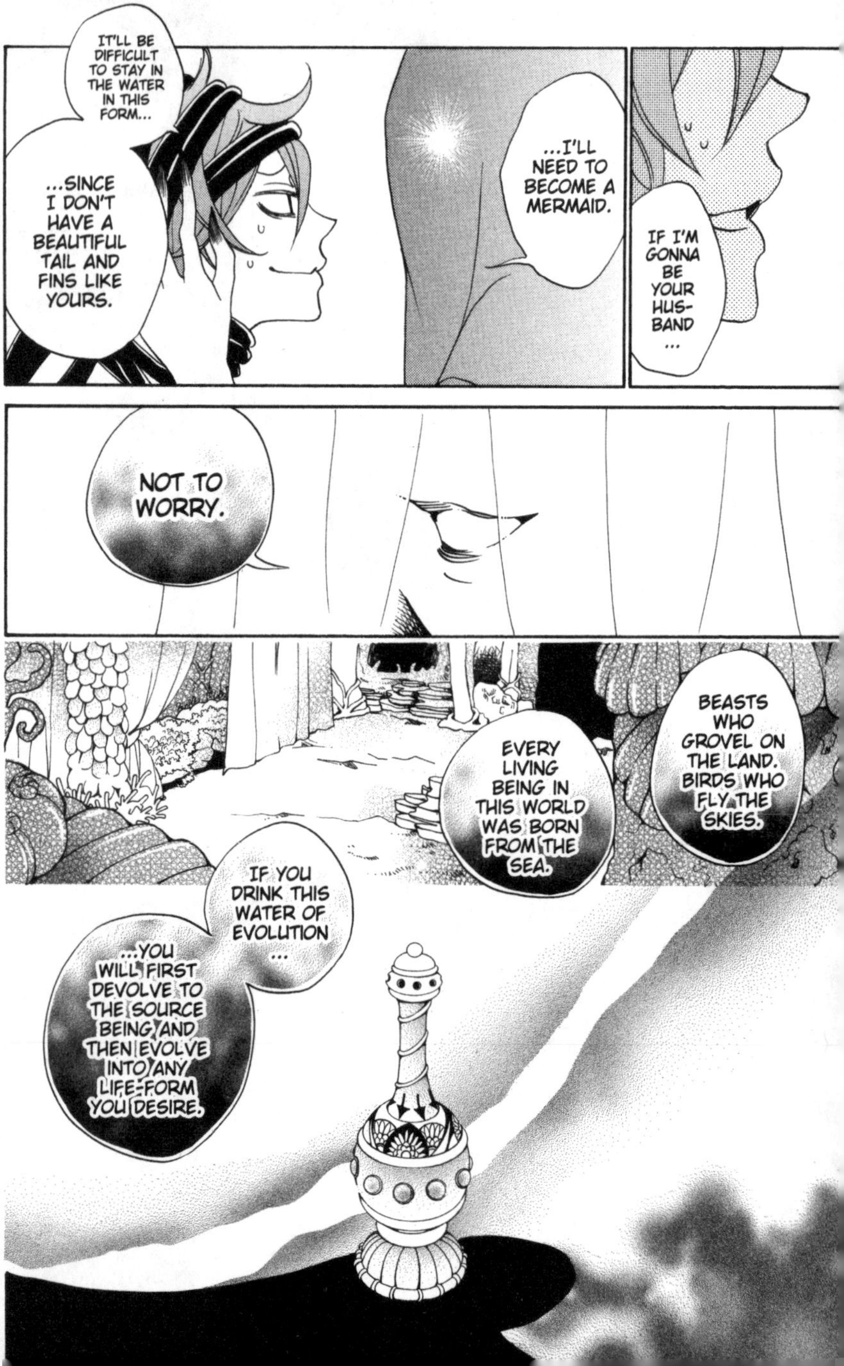
IF I'M GONNA BE YOUR HUS-BAND...
...I'LL NEED TO BECOME A MERMAID.
IT'LL BE DIFFICULT TO STAY IN THE WATER IN THIS FORM...
...SINCE I DON'T HAVE A BEAUTIFUL TAIL AND FINS LIKE YOURS.
NOT TO WORRY.
EVERY LIVING BEING IN THIS WORLD WAS BORN FROM THE SEA.
BEASTS WHO GROVEL ON THE LAND. BIRDS WHO FLY THE SKIES.
IF YOU DRINK THIS WATER OF EVOLUTION...
...YOU WILL FIRST DEVOLVE TO THE SOURCE BEING AND THEN EVOLVE INTO ANY LIFE-FORM YOU DESIRE.

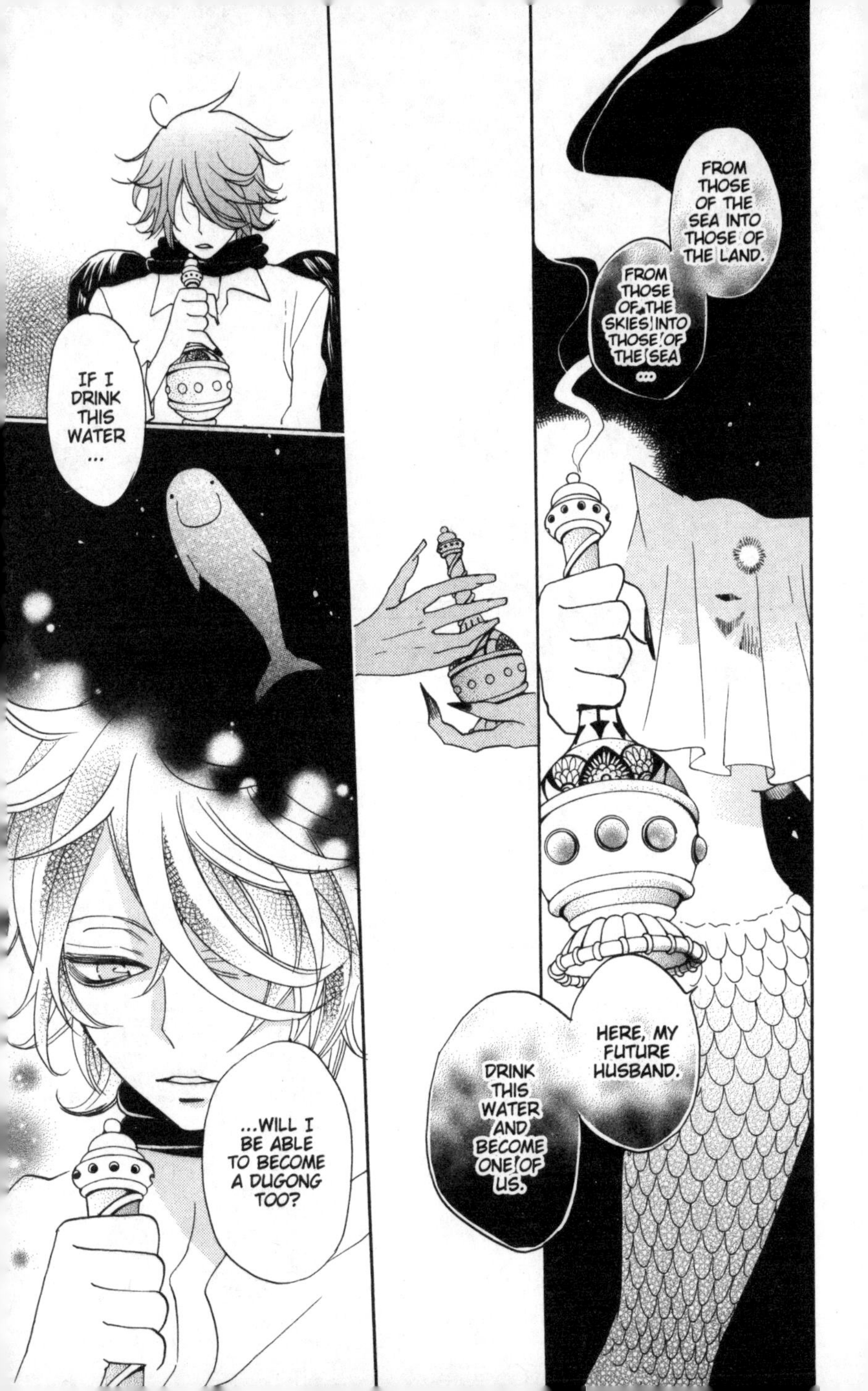
FROM THOSE OF THE SEA INTO THOSE OF THE LAND.
FROM THOSE OF THE SKIES INTO THOSE OF THE SEA...
HERE, MY FUTURE HUSBAND.
DRINK THIS WATER AND BECOME ONE OF US.
IF I DRINK THIS WATER...
...WILL I BE ABLE TO BECOME A DUGONG TOO?

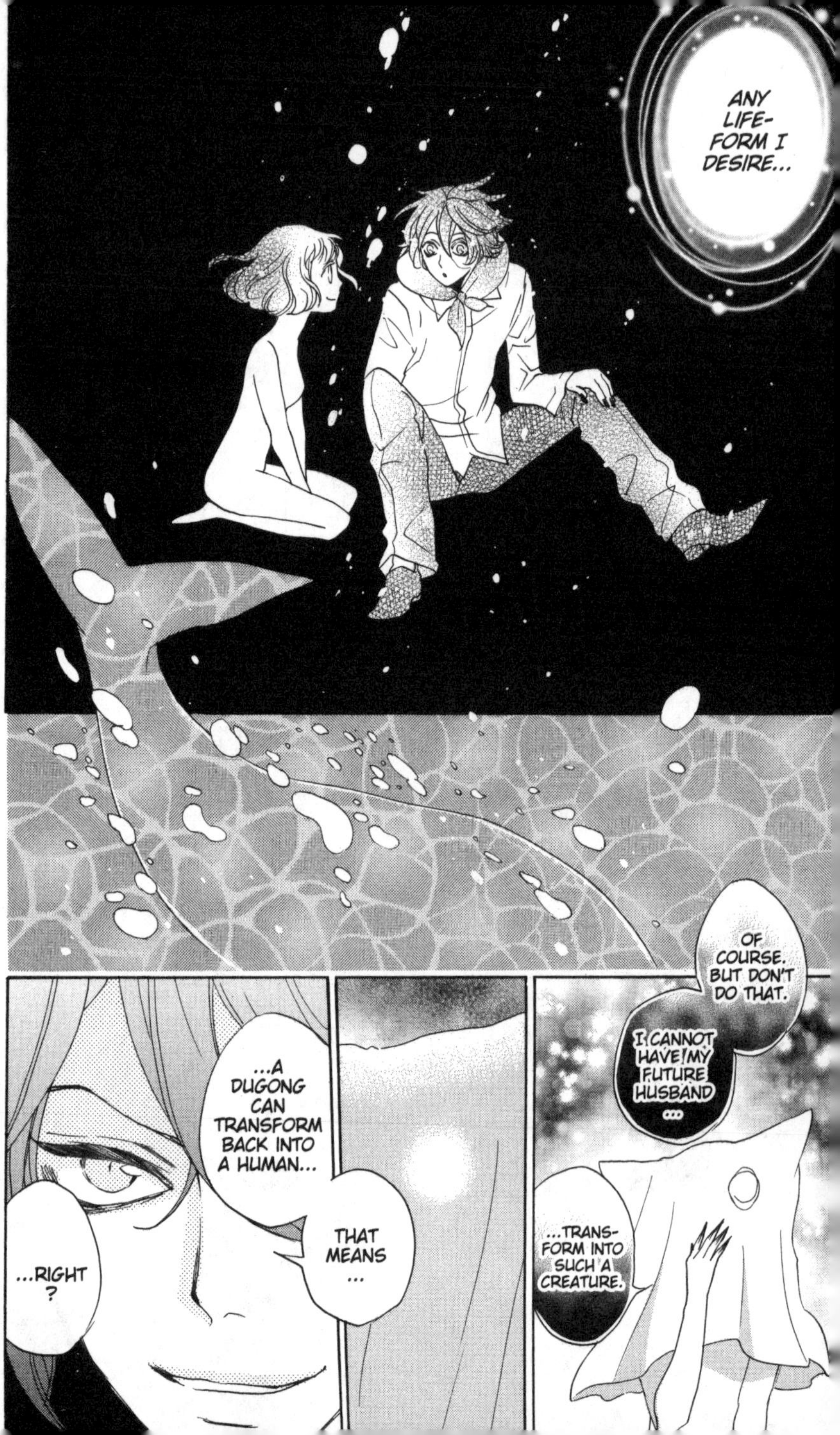
ANY LIFE-FORM I DESIRE...
OF COURSE. BUT DON'T DO THAT.
I CANNOT HAVE MY FUTURE HUSBAND...
...TRANSFORM INTO SUCH A CREATURE.
...A DUGONG CAN TRANSFORM BACK INTO A HUMAN...
THAT MEANS...
...RIGHT?

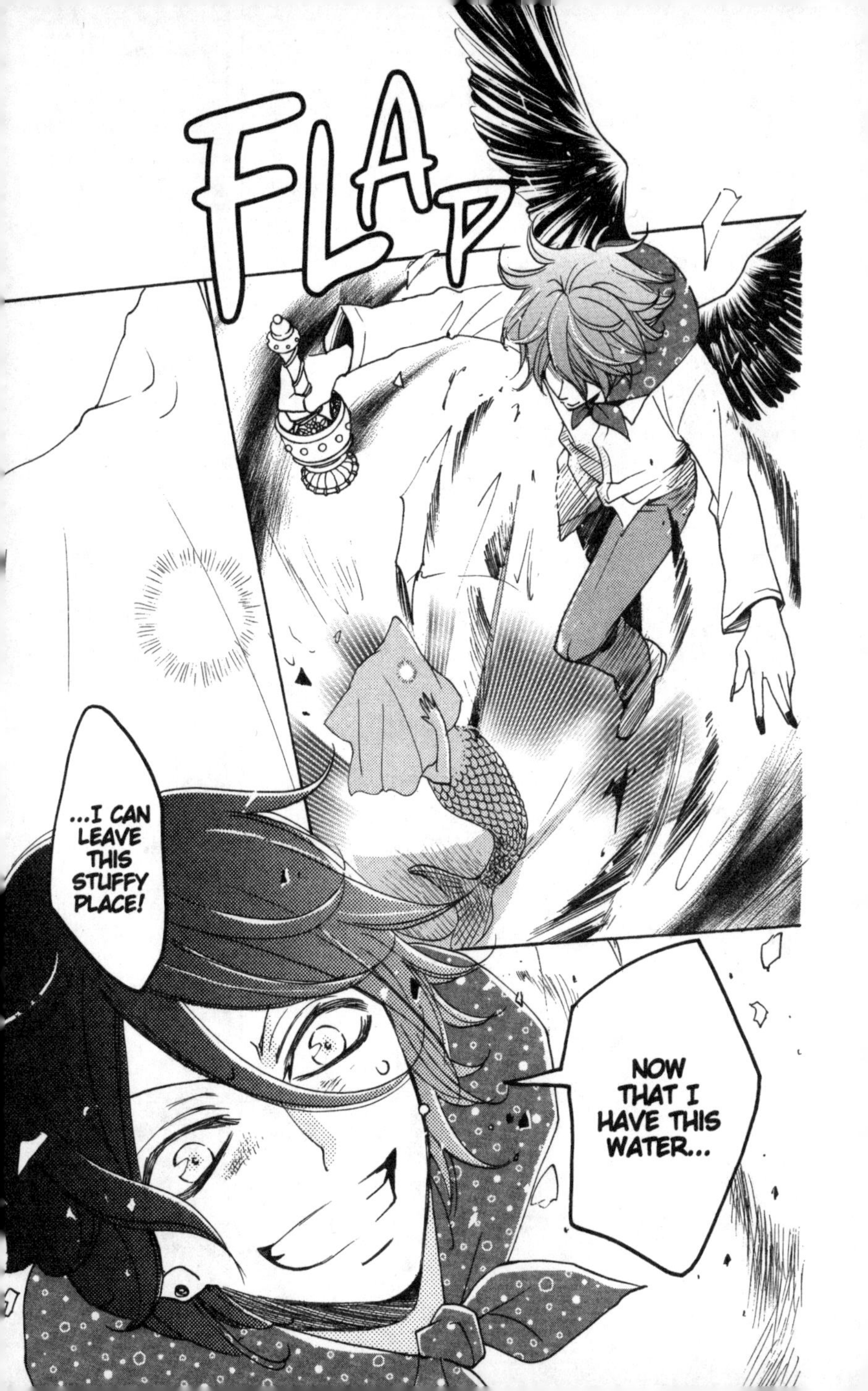
FLAP
NOW THAT I HAVE THIS WATER...
...I CAN LEAVE THIS STUFFY PLACE!

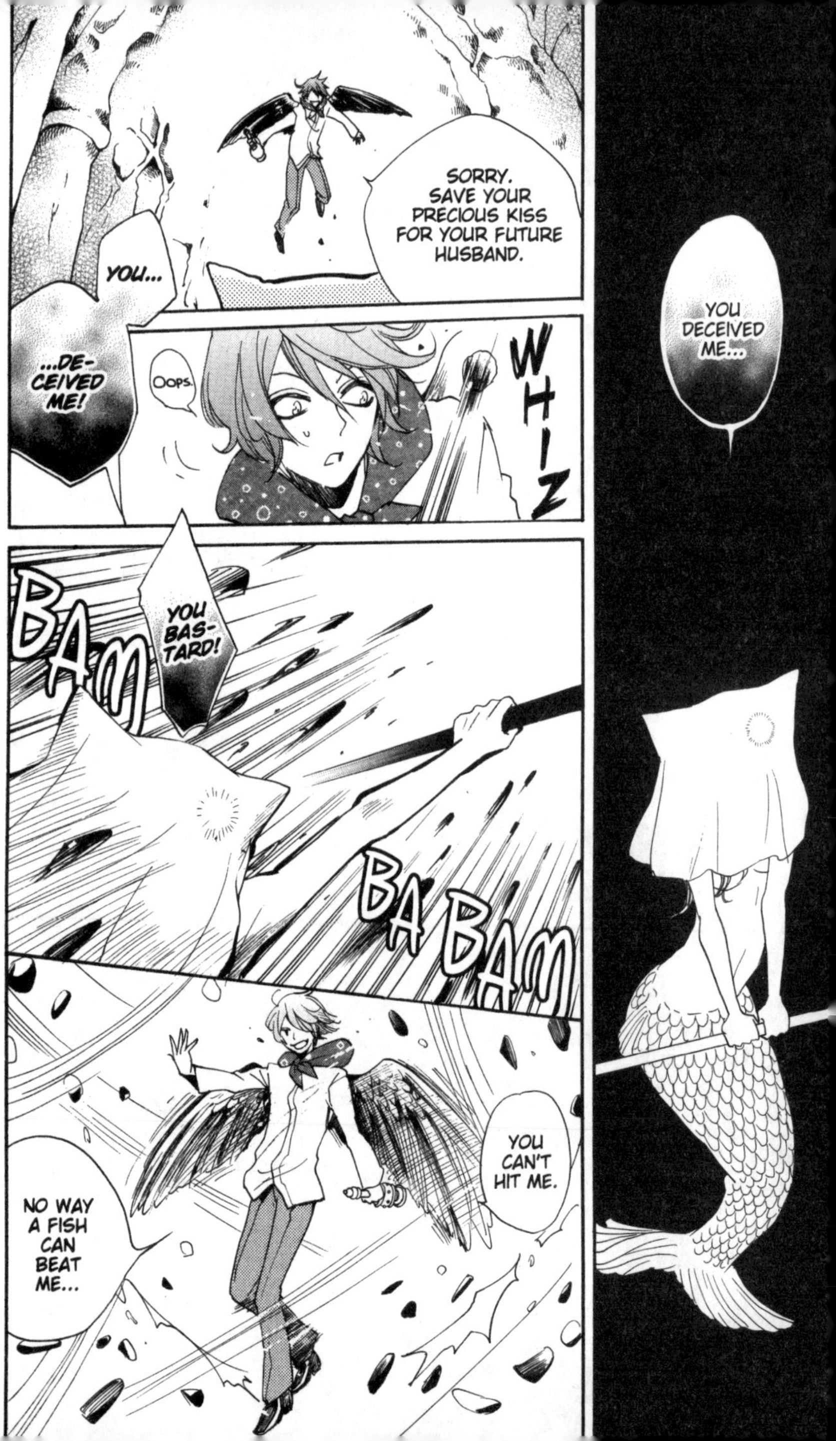
YOU DECEIVED ME...
SORRY. SAVE YOUR PRECIOUS KISS FOR YOUR FUTURE HUSBAND.
YOU...
WHIZ
Oops.
...DE-CEIVED ME!
YOU BAS-TARD!
BAM
BA BAM
YOU CAN'T HIT ME.
NO WAY A FISH CAN BEAT ME...

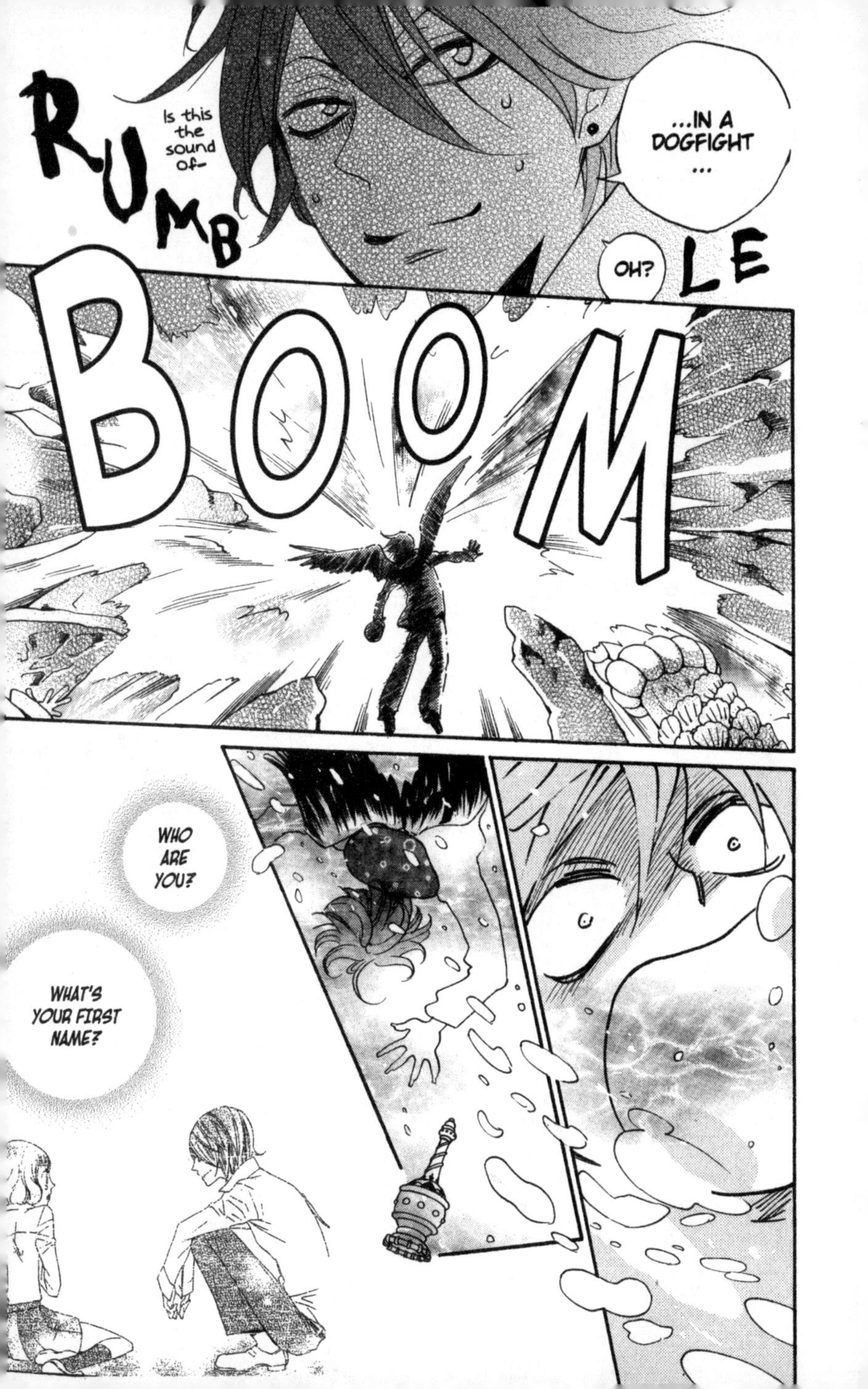
...IN A DOGFIGHT ...
Is this the sound of-
RUMBLE
OH?
BOOM
WHO ARE YOU?
WHAT'S YOUR FIRST NAME?

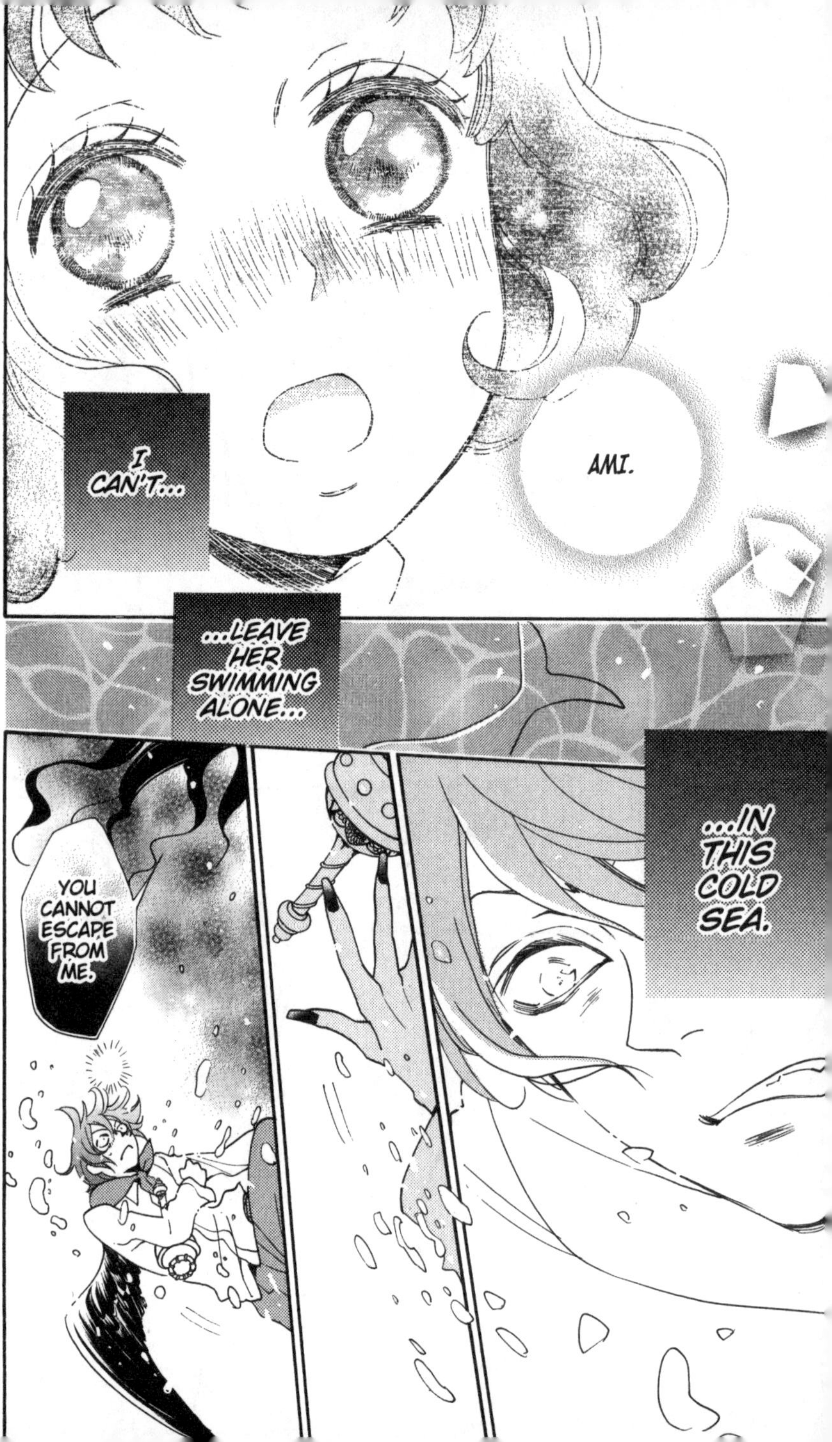
AMI.
I CAN'T...
...LEAVE HER SWIMMING ALONE...
...IN THIS COLD SEA.
YOU CANNOT ESCAPE FROM ME.

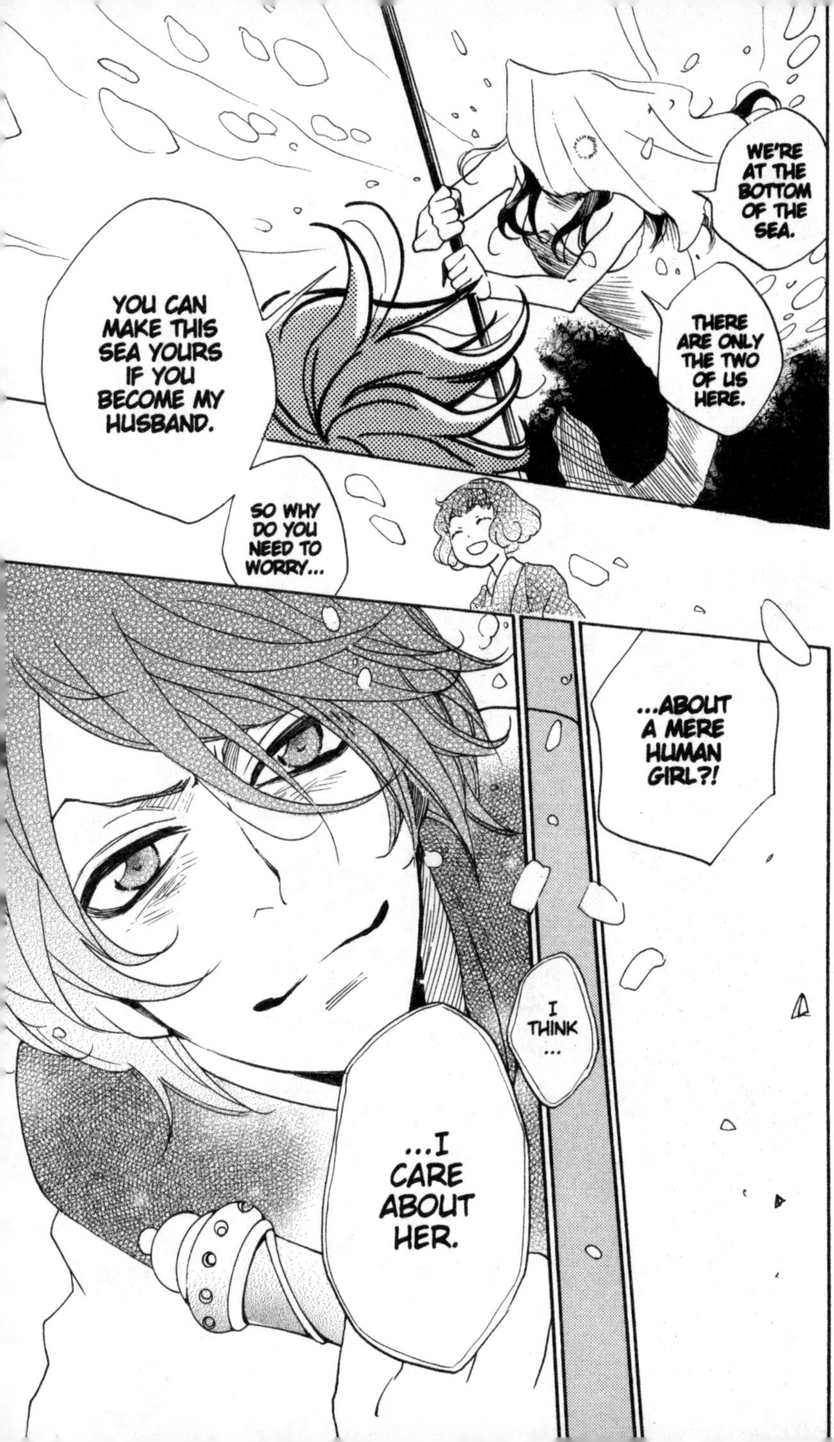
WE'RE AT THE BOTTOM OF THE SEA.
THERE ARE ONLY THE TWO OF US HERE.
YOU CAN MAKE THIS SEA YOURS IF YOU BECOME MY HUSBAND.
SO WHY DO YOU NEED TO WORRY...
...ABOUT A MERE HUMAN GIRL?!
I THINK...
...I CARE ABOUT HER.

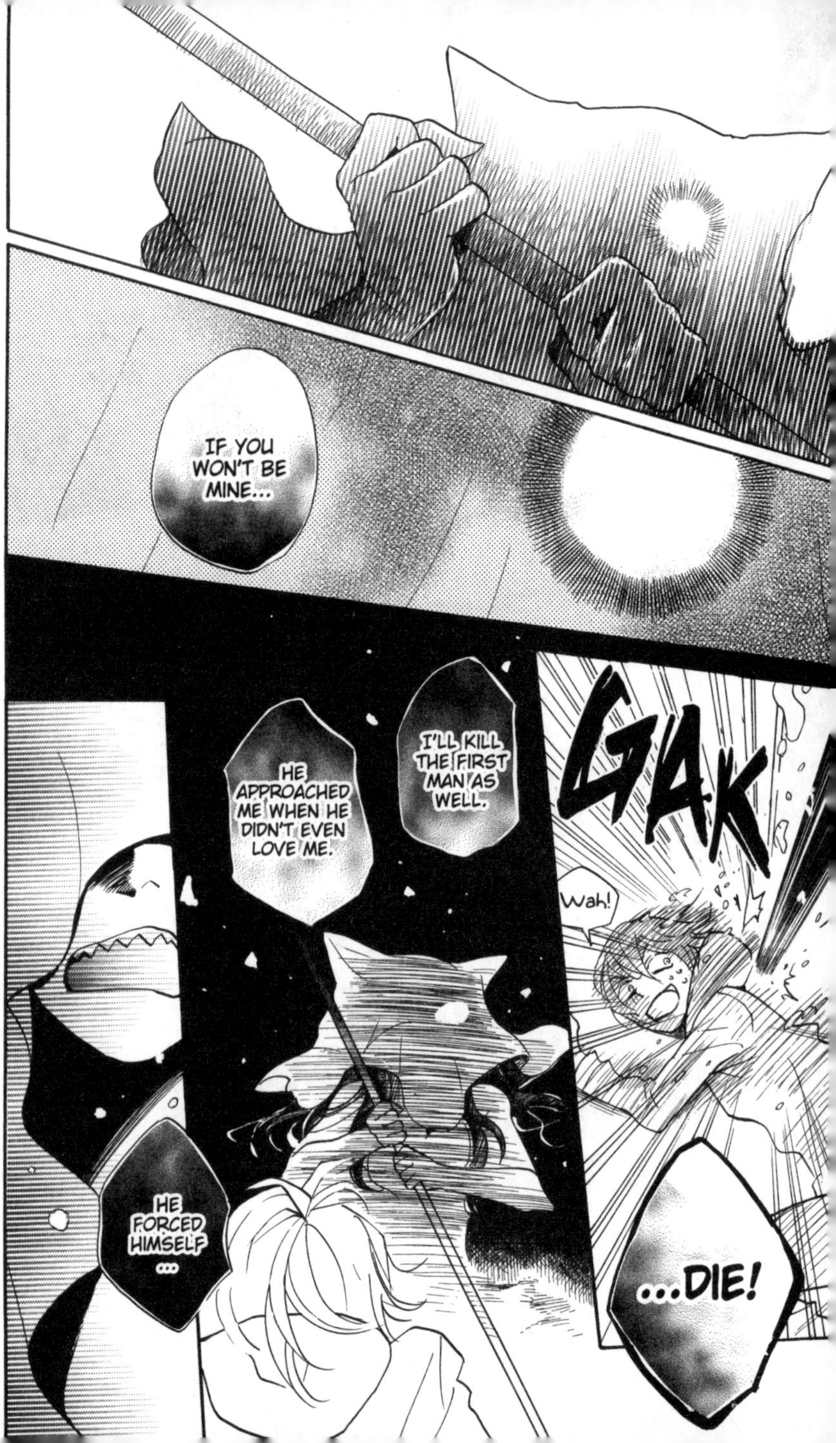
IF YOU WON'T BE MINE...
GAK
Wah!
...DIE!
I'LL KILL THE FIRST MAN AS WELL.
HE APPROACHED ME WHEN HE DIDN'T EVEN LOVE ME.
HE FORCED HIMSELF...

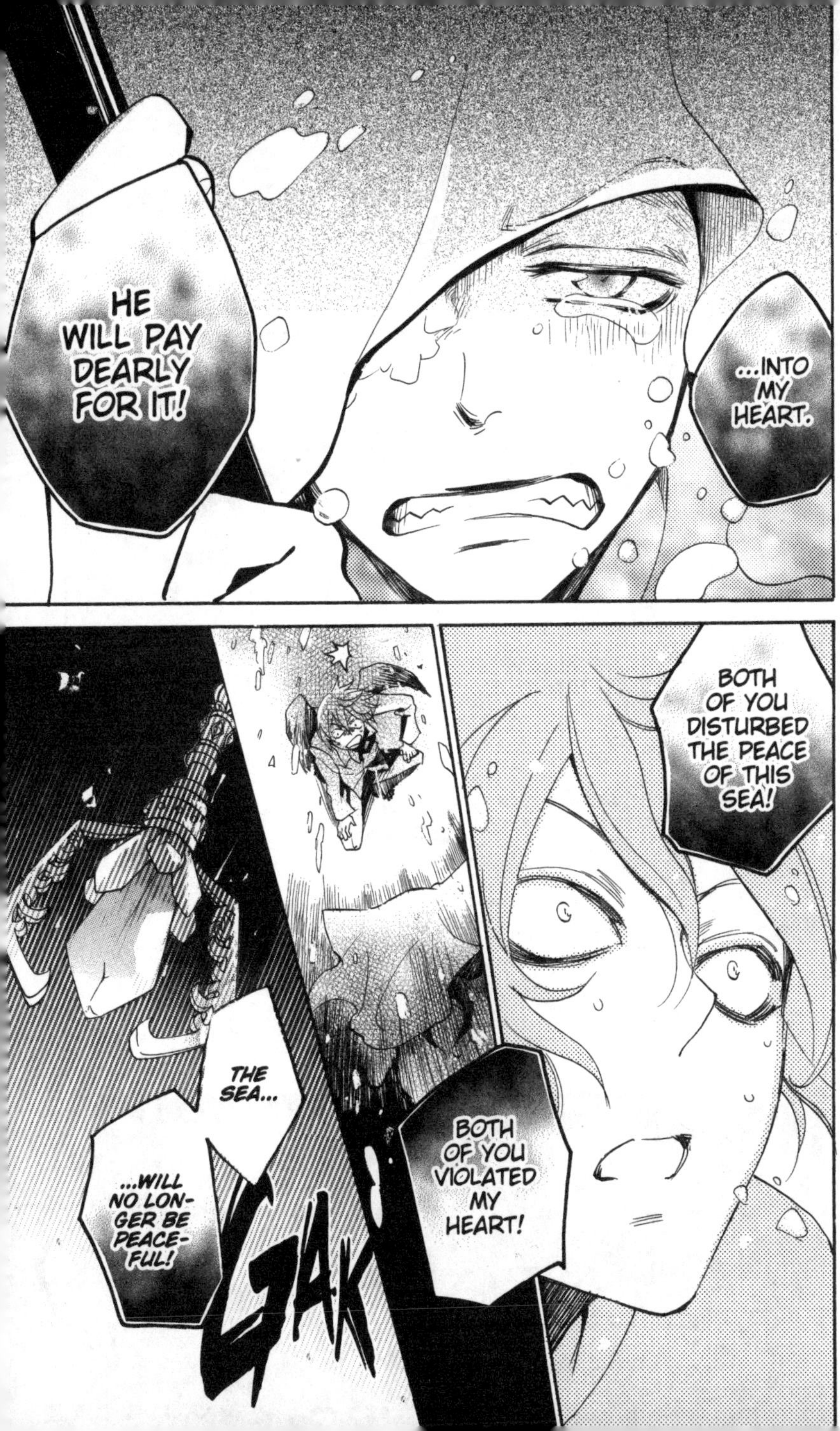
...INTO MY HEART.
HE WILL PAY DEARLY FOR IT!
BOTH OF YOU DISTURBED THE PEACE OF THIS SEA!
BOTH OF YOU VIOLATED MY HEART!
THE SEA...
...WILL NO LONGER BE PEACEFUL!
GAK

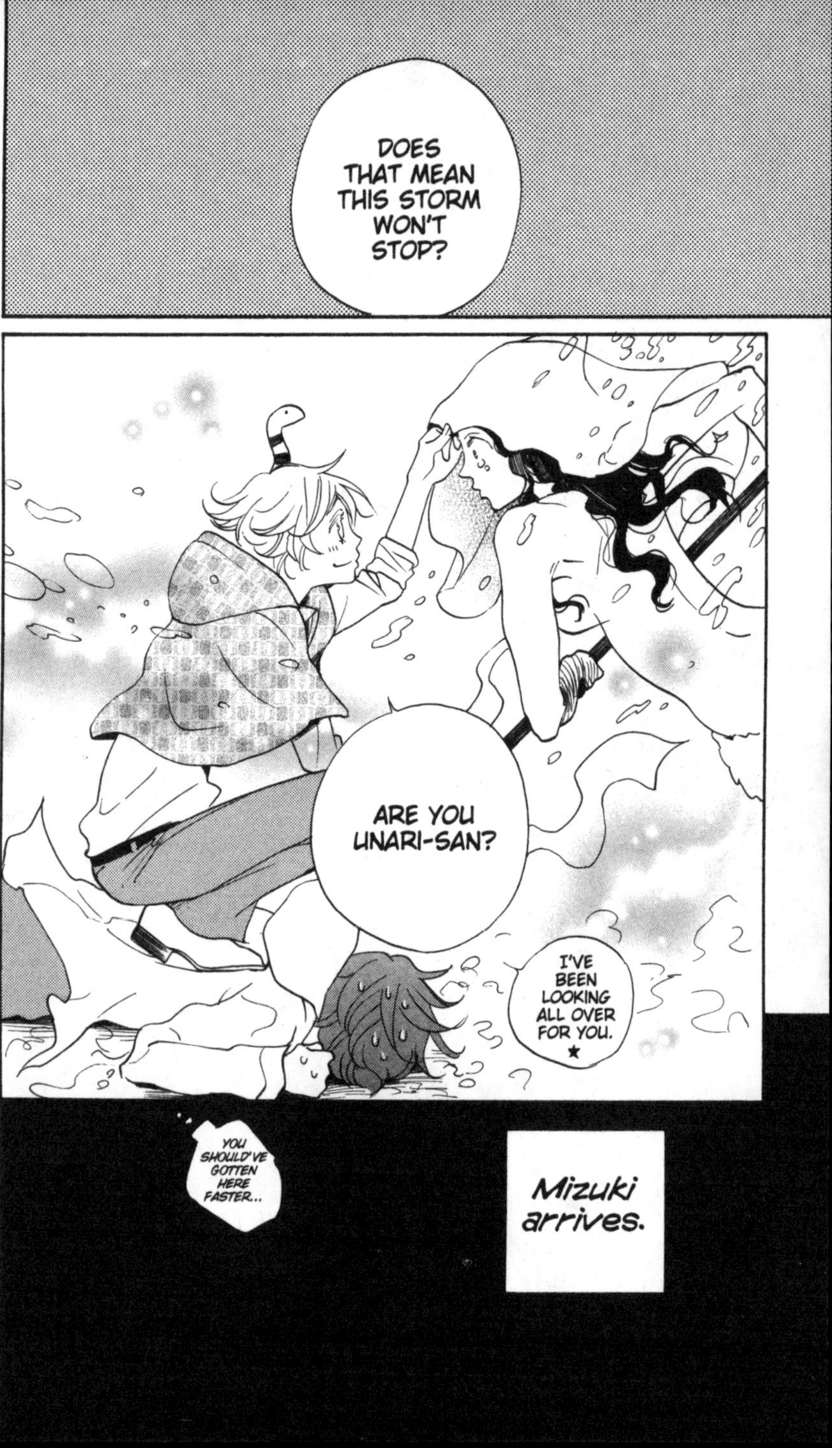
DOES THAT MEAN THIS STORM WON'T STOP?
ARE YOU UNARI-SAN?
I'VE BEEN LOOKING ALL OVER FOR YOU. ★
Mizuki arrives.
YOU SHOULD'VE GOTTEN HERE FASTER...

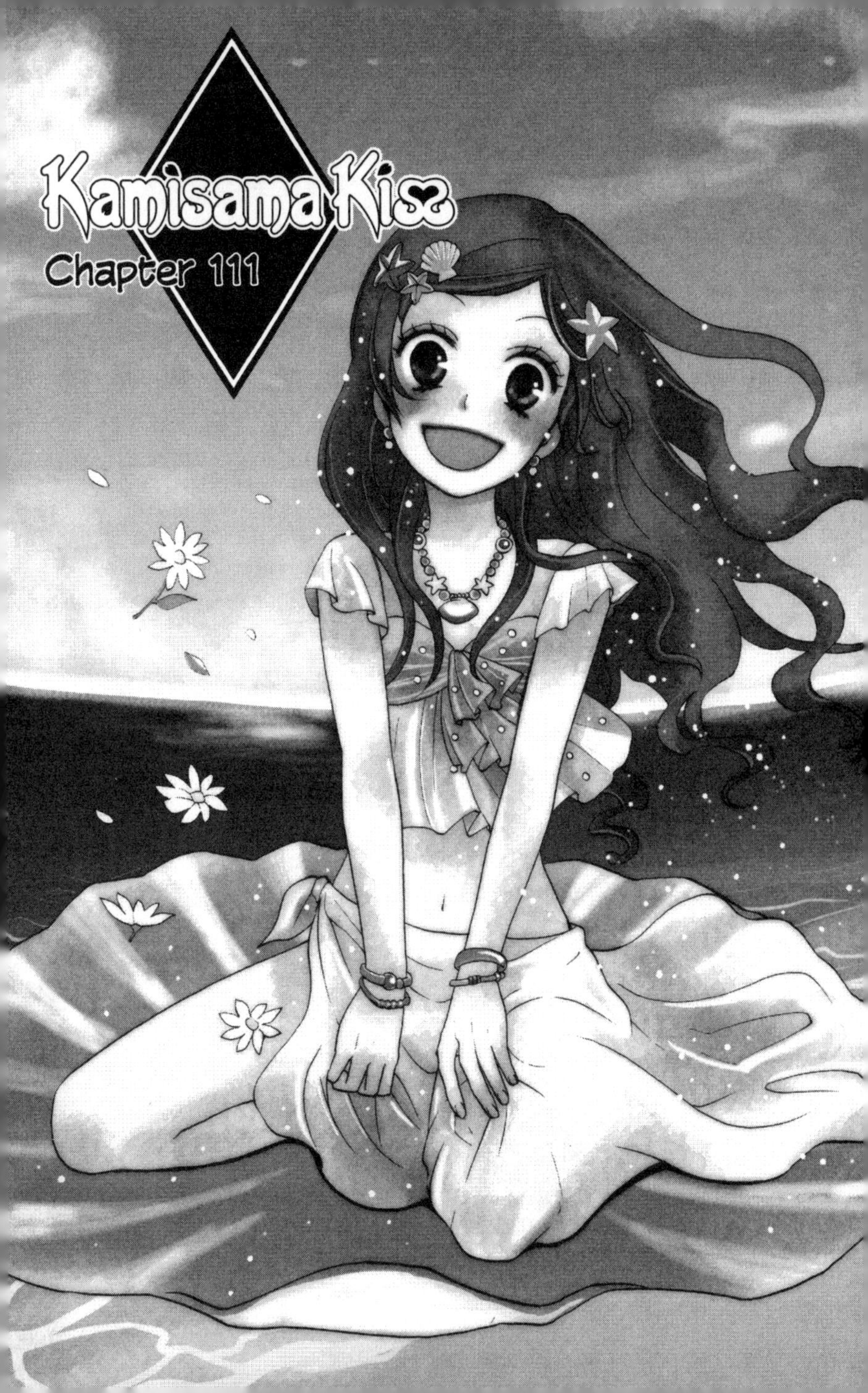
Kamisama Kiss
Chapter 111

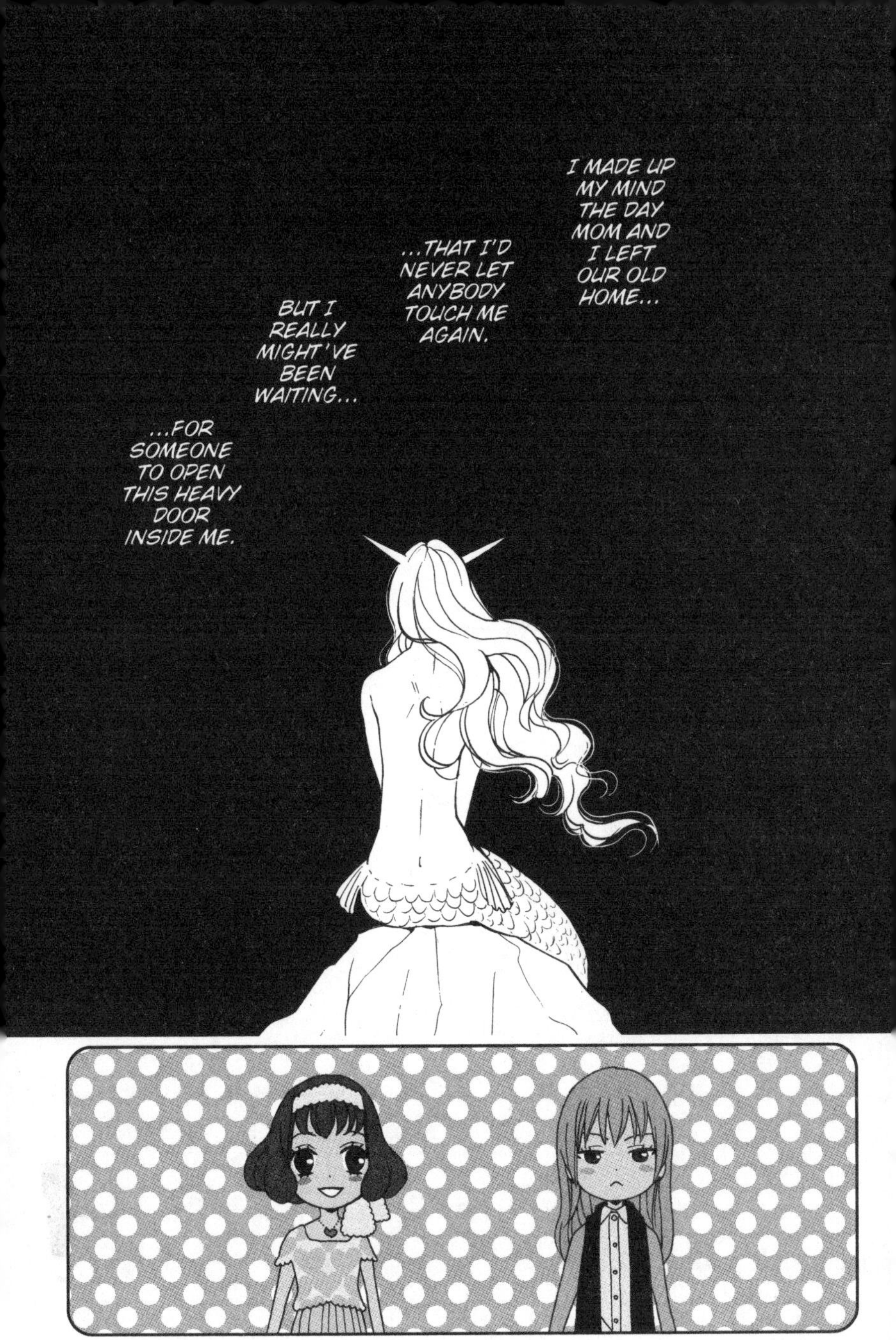
I MADE UP MY MIND THE DAY MOM AND I LEFT OUR OLD HOME...
...THAT I'D NEVER LET ANYBODY TOUCH ME AGAIN.
BUT I REALLY MIGHT'VE BEEN WAITING...
...FOR SOMEONE TO OPEN THIS HEAVY DOOR INSIDE ME.

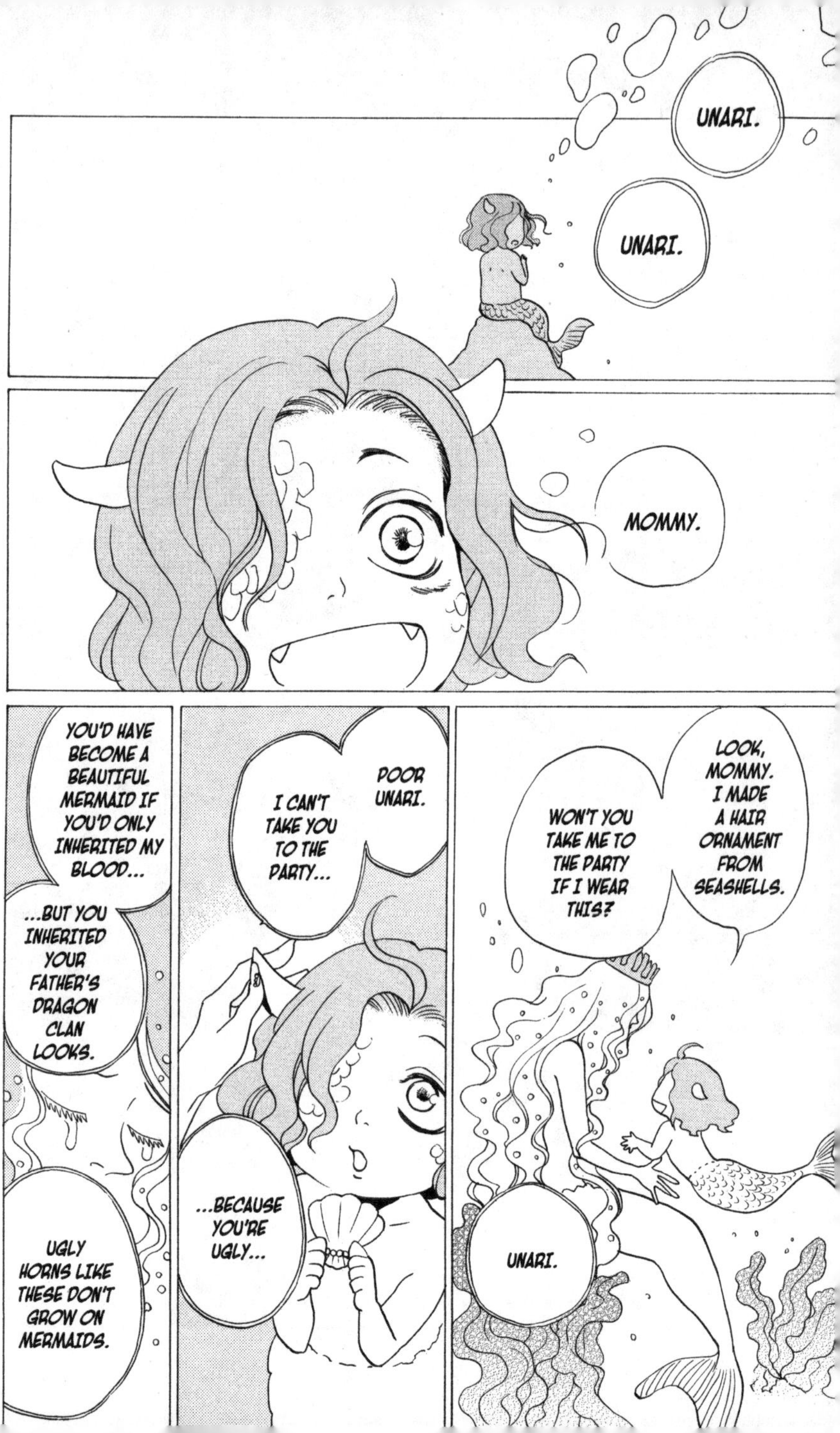
UNARI.
UNARI.
MOMMY.
LOOK, MOMMY. I MADE A HAIR ORNAMENT FROM SEASHELLS.
WON'T YOU TAKE ME TO THE PARTY IF I WEAR THIS?
UNARI.
POOR UNARI.
I CAN'T TAKE YOU TO THE PARTY...
...BECAUSE YOU'RE UGLY...
YOU'D HAVE BECOME A BEAUTIFUL MERMAID IF YOU'D ONLY INHERITED MY BLOOD...
...BUT YOU INHERITED YOUR FATHER'S DRAGON CLAN LOOKS.
UGLY HORNS LIKE THESE DON'T GROW ON MERMAIDS.

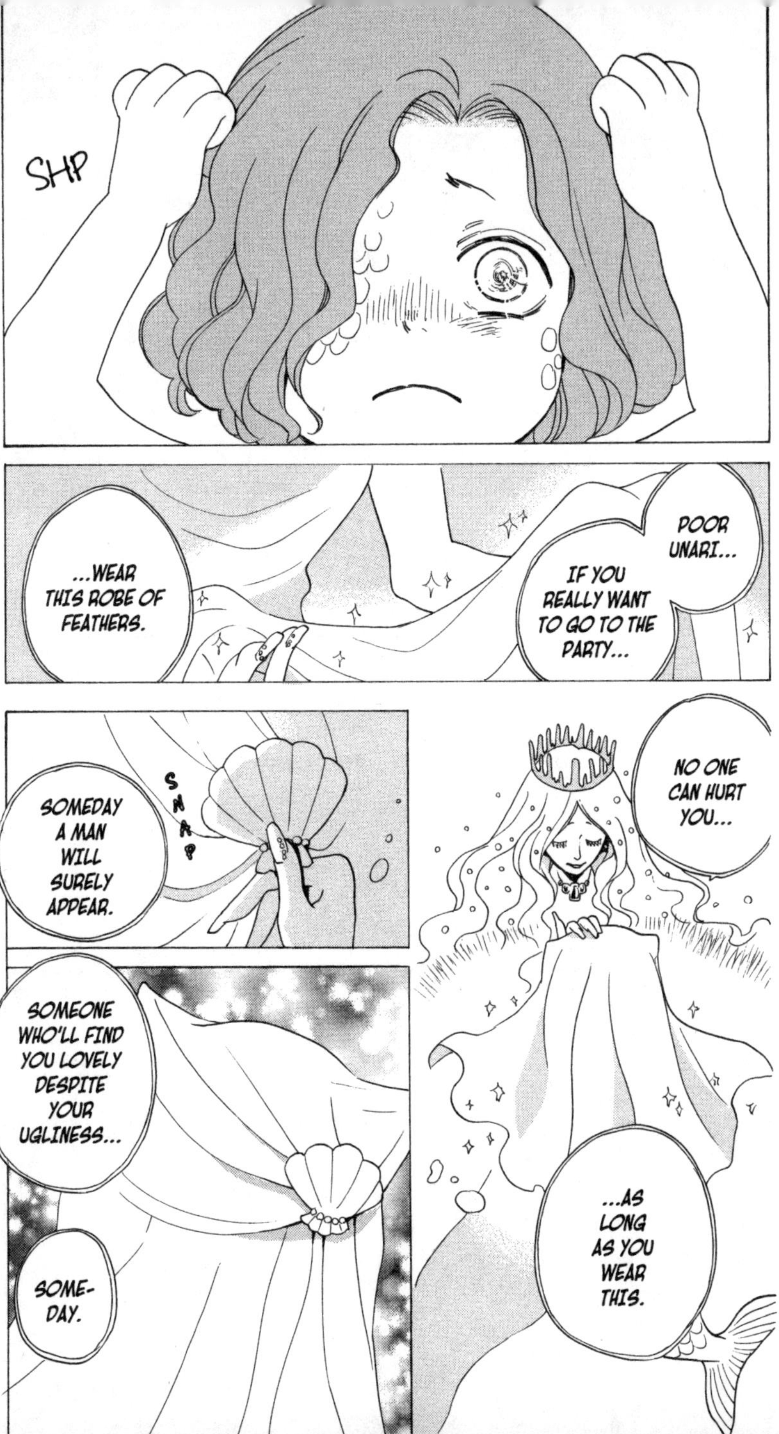
SHP
POOR UNARI...
IF YOU REALLY WANT TO GO TO THE PARTY...
...WEAR THIS ROBE OF FEATHERS.
NO ONE CAN HURT YOU...
...AS LONG AS YOU WEAR THIS.
SNAP
SOMEDAY A MAN WILL SURELY APPEAR.
SOMEONE WHO'LL FIND YOU LOVELY DESPITE YOUR UGLINESS...
SOME-DAY.

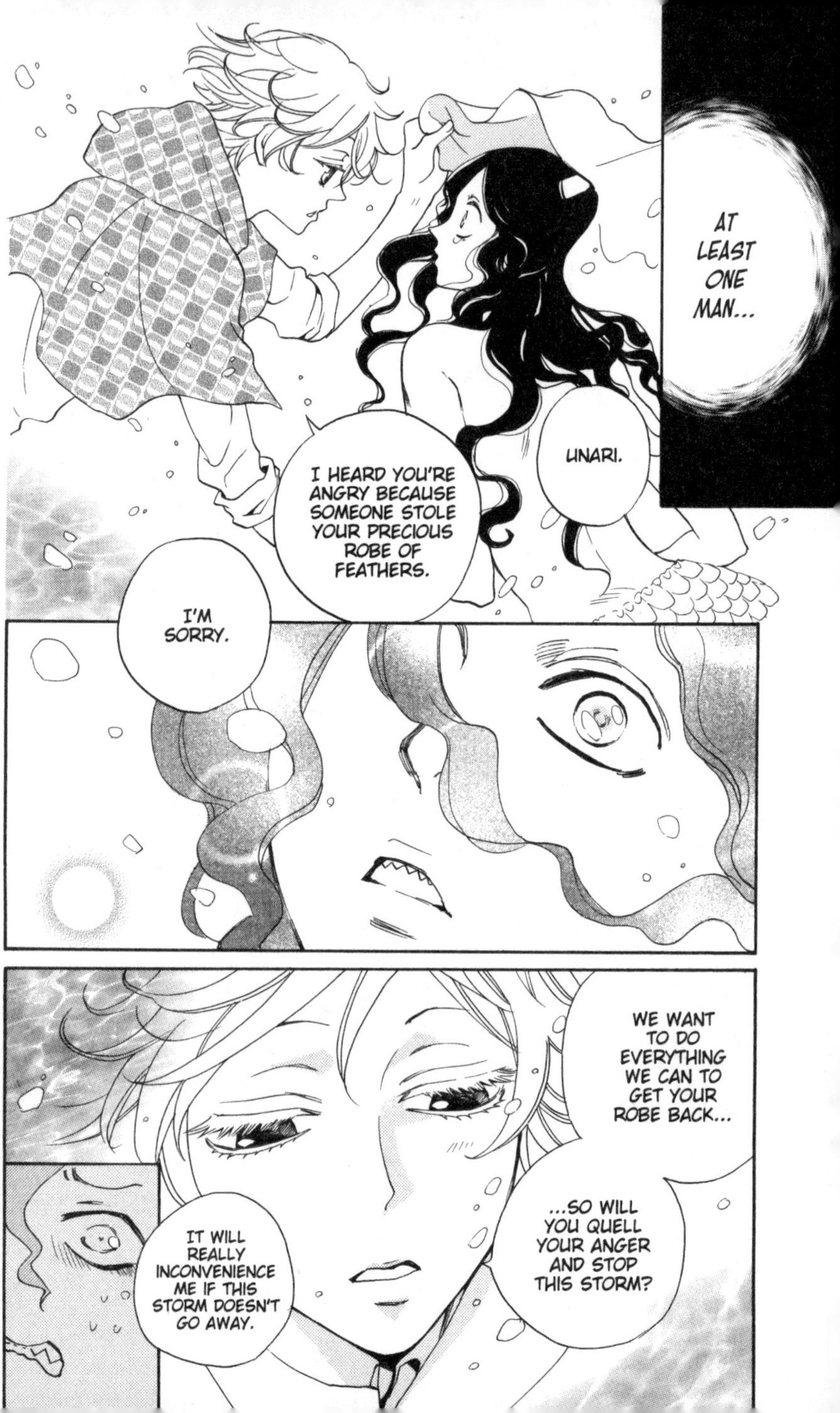
AT LEAST ONE MAN...
UNARI.
I HEARD YOU'RE ANGRY BECAUSE SOMEONE STOLE YOUR PRECIOUS ROBE OF FEATHERS.
I'M SORRY.
WE WANT TO DO EVERYTHING WE CAN TO GET YOUR ROBE BACK...
...SO WILL YOU QUELL YOUR ANGER AND STOP THIS STORM?
IT WILL REALLY INCONVENIENCE ME IF THIS STORM DOESN'T GO AWAY.

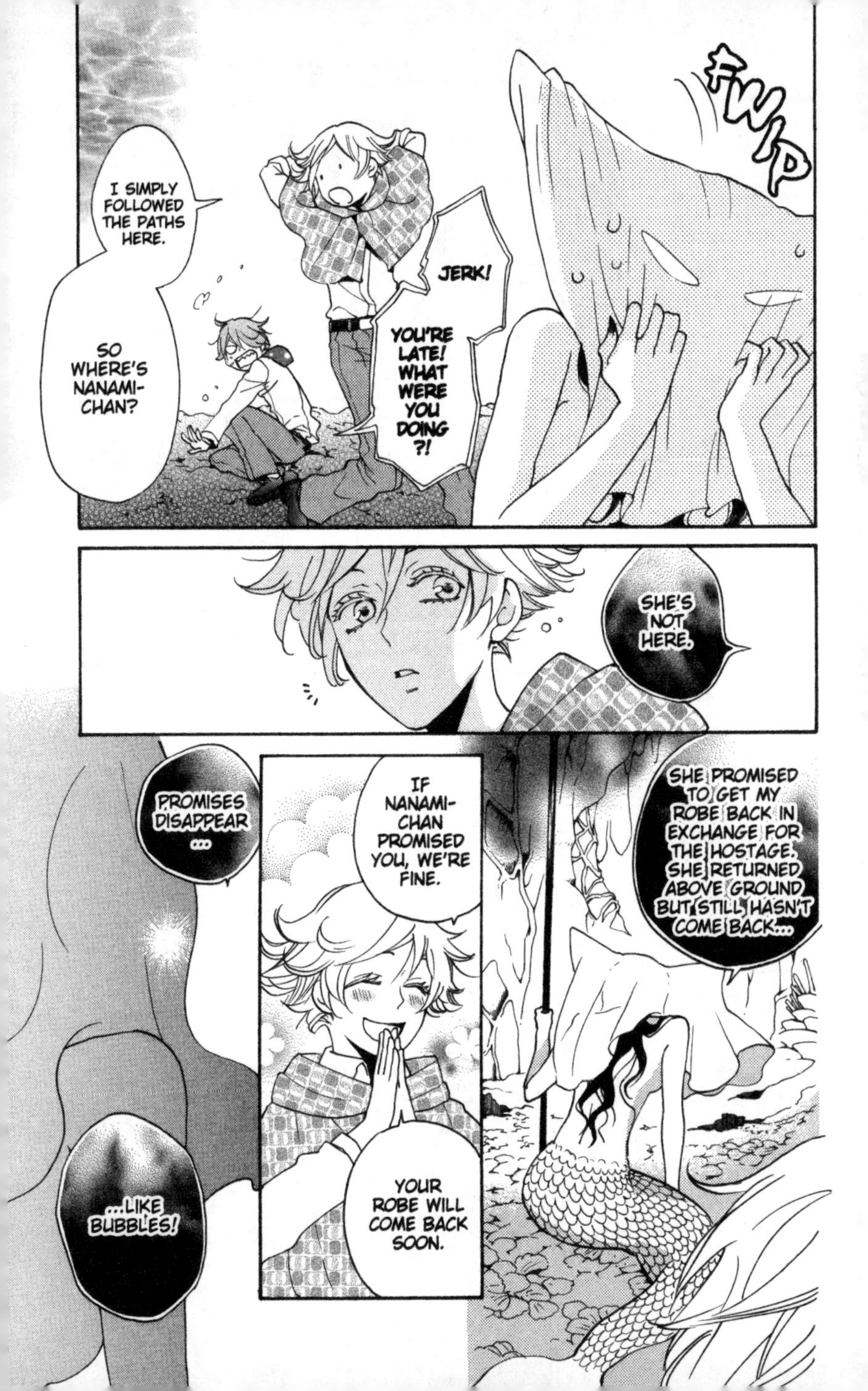
FWIP
JERK!
YOU'RE LATE! WHAT WERE YOU DOING?!
I SIMPLY FOLLOWED THE PATHS HERE.
SO WHERE'S NANAMI-CHAN?
SHE'S NOT HERE.
SHE PROMISED TO GET MY ROBE BACK IN EXCHANGE FOR THE HOSTAGE. SHE RETURNED ABOVE GROUND BUT STILL HASN'T COME BACK...
IF NANAMI-CHAN PROMISED YOU, WE'RE FINE.
YOUR ROBE WILL COME BACK SOON.
PROMISES DISAPPEAR...
...LIKE BUBBLES!

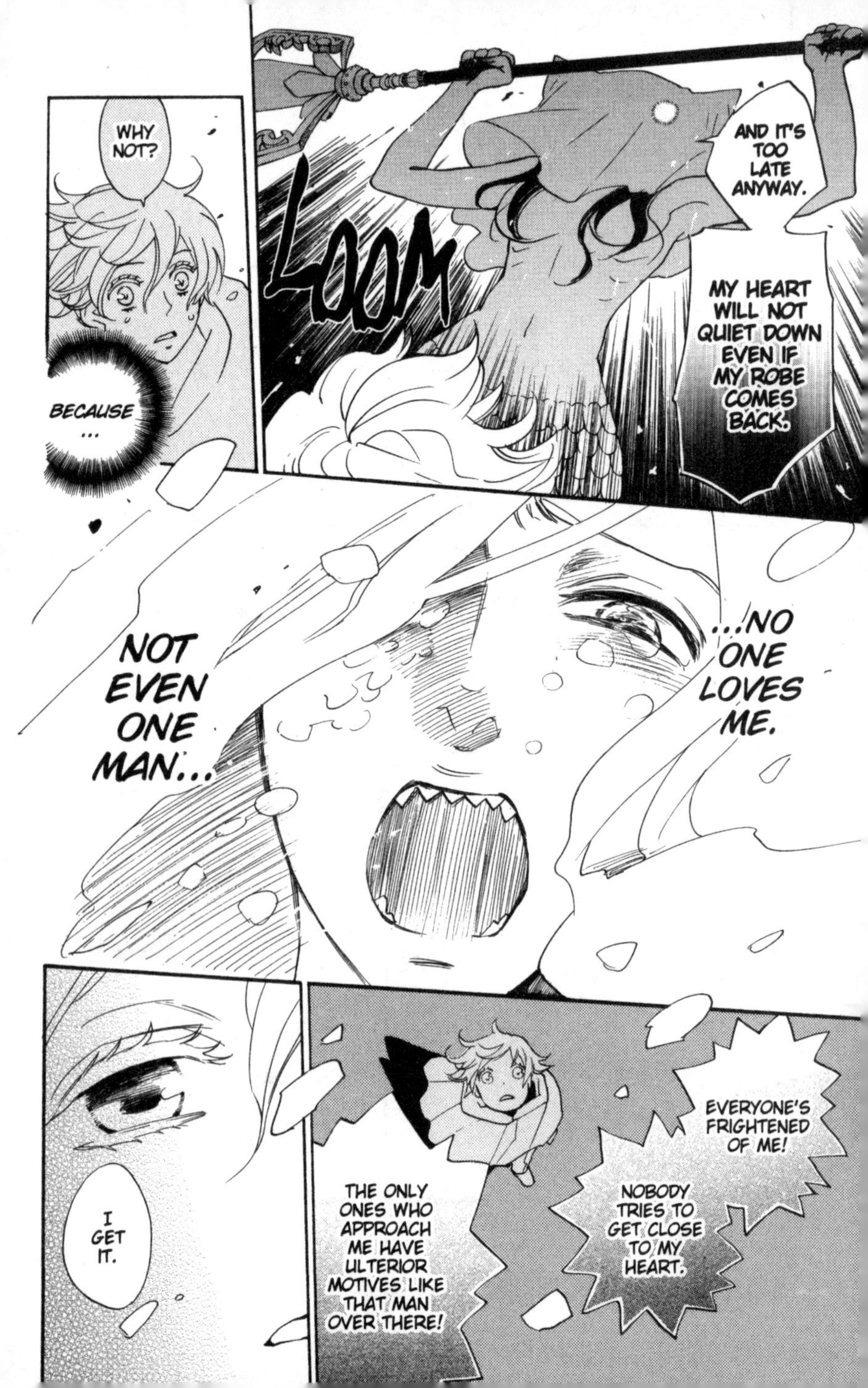
AND IT'S TOO LATE ANYWAY.
MY HEART WILL NOT QUIET DOWN EVEN IF MY ROBE COMES BACK.
LOOM
WHY NOT?
BECAUSE ...
...NO ONE LOVES ME.
NOT EVEN ONE MAN...
EVERYONE'S FRIGHTENED OF ME!
NOBODY TRIES TO GET CLOSE TO MY HEART.
THE ONLY ONES WHO APPROACH ME HAVE ULTERIOR MOTIVES LIKE THAT MAN OVER THERE!
I GET IT.

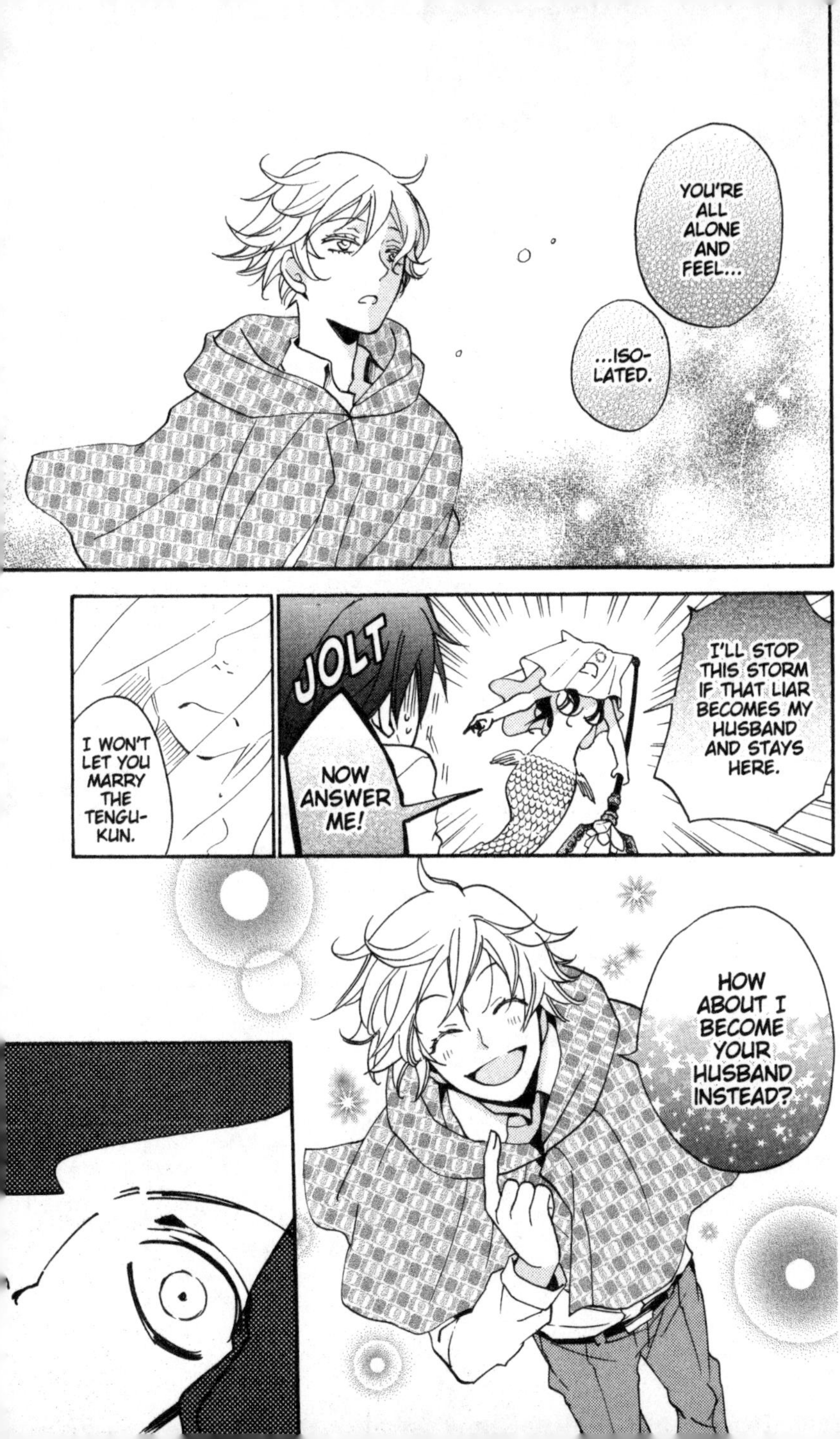
YOU'RE ALL ALONE AND FEEL...
...ISO-LATED.
I'LL STOP THIS STORM IF THAT LIAR BECOMES MY HUSBAND AND STAYS HERE.
JOLT
NOW ANSWER ME!
I WON'T LET YOU MARRY THE TENGU-KUN.
HOW ABOUT I BECOME YOUR HUSBAND INSTEAD?

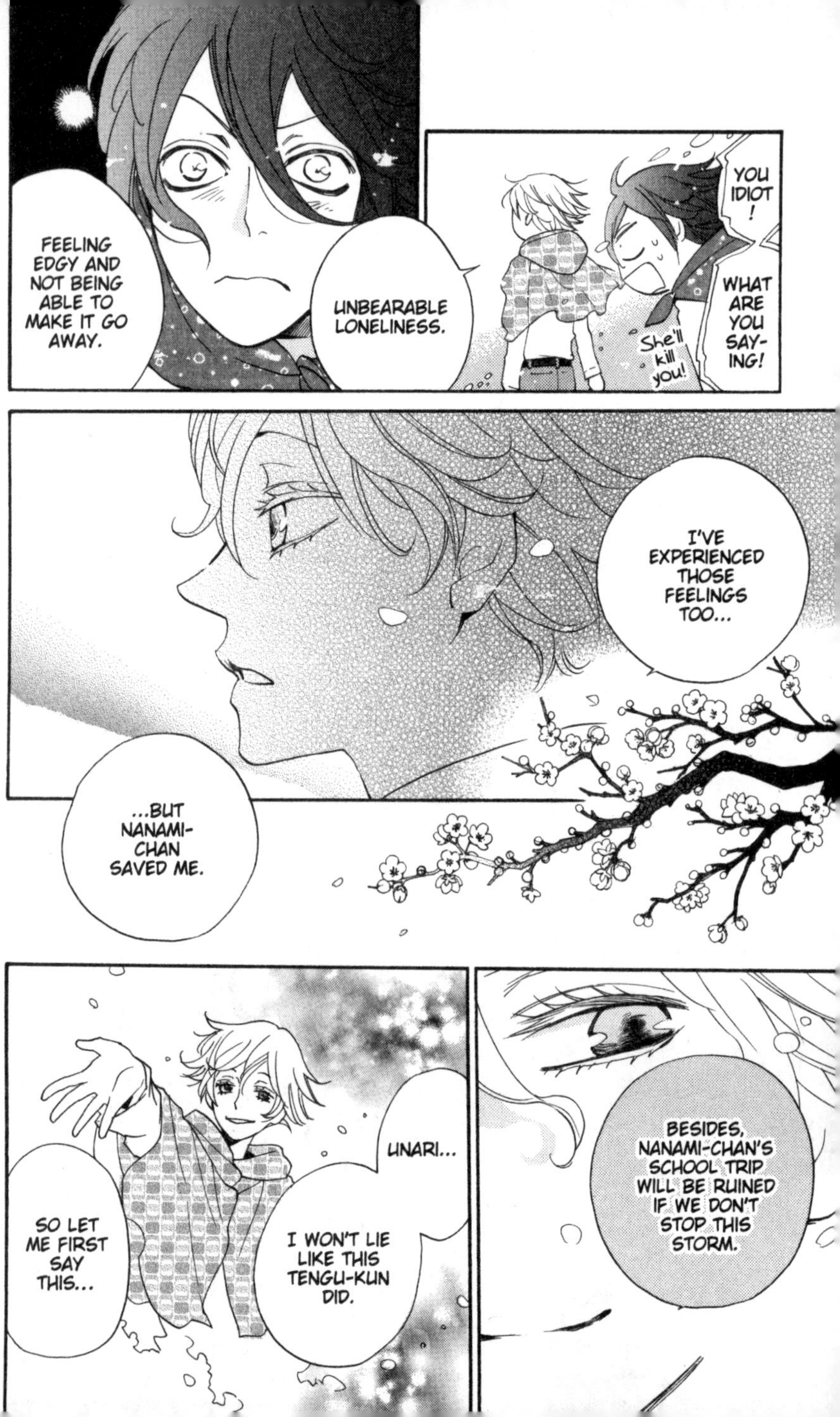
YOU IDIOT!
WHAT ARE YOU SAYING!
She'll kill you!
UNBEARABLE LONELINESS.
FEELING EDGY AND NOT BEING ABLE TO MAKE IT GO AWAY.
I'VE EXPERIENCED THOSE FEELINGS TOO...
...BUT NANAMI-CHAN SAVED ME.
BESIDES, NANAMI-CHAN'S SCHOOL TRIP WILL BE RUINED IF WE DON'T STOP THIS STORM.
UNARI...
I WON'T LIE LIKE THIS TENGU-KUN DID.
SO LET ME FIRST SAY THIS...

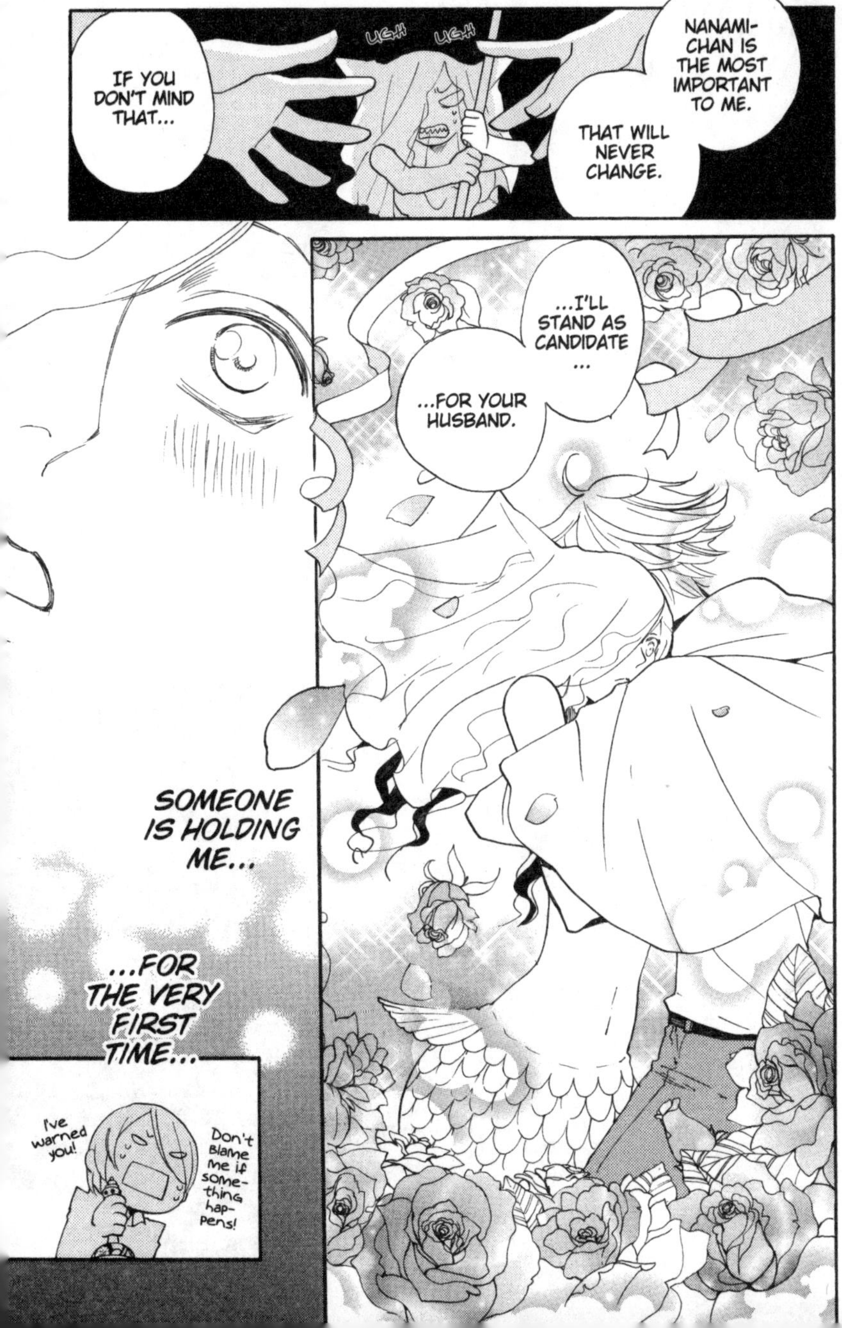
NANAMI-CHAN IS THE MOST IMPORTANT TO ME.
THAT WILL NEVER CHANGE.
UGH UGH
IF YOU DON'T MIND THAT...
...I'LL STAND AS CANDIDATE...
...FOR YOUR HUSBAND.
SOMEONE IS HOLDING ME...
...FOR THE VERY FIRST TIME...
Don't Blame me if something happens!
I've warned you!

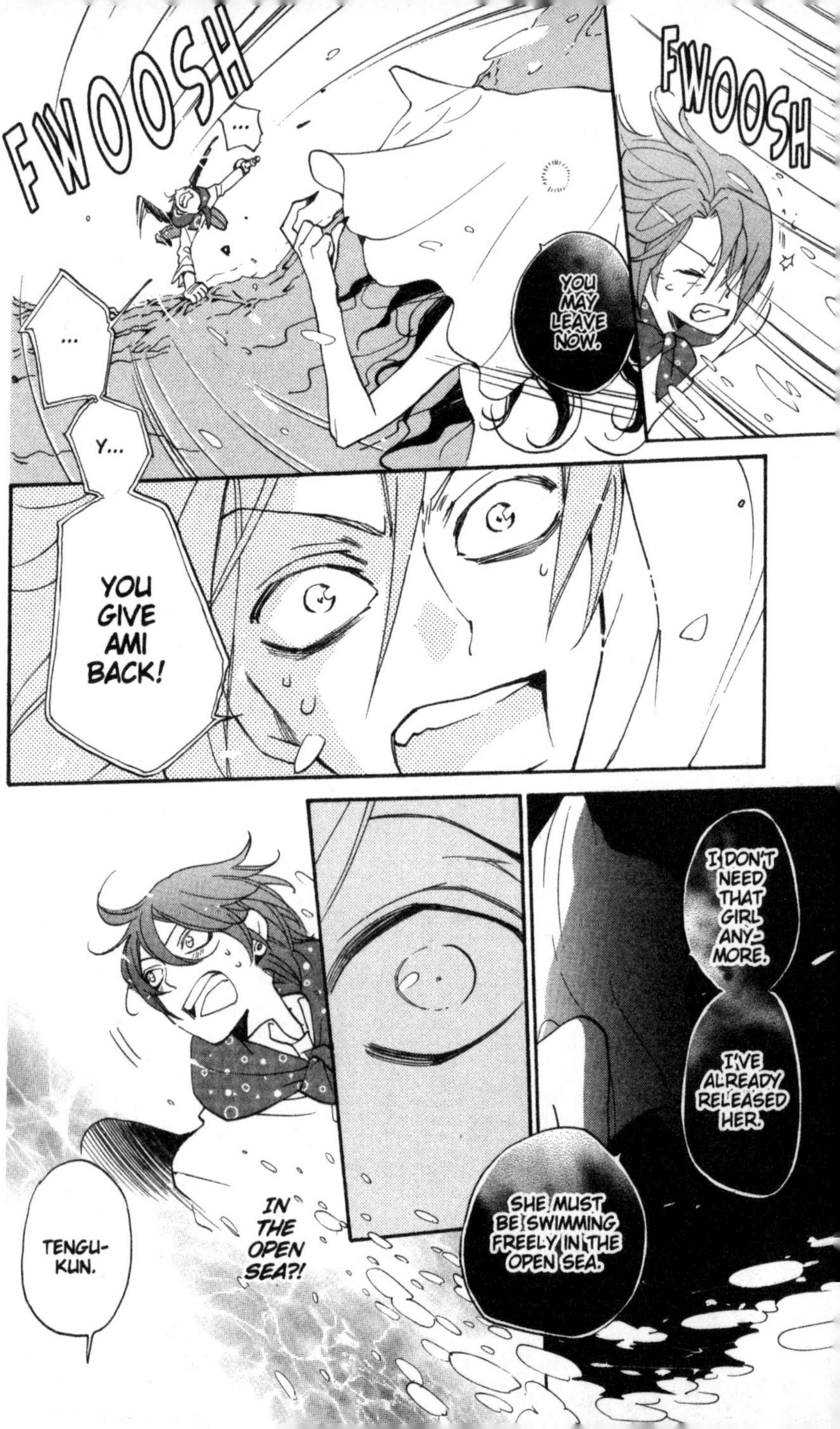
FWOOSH
YOU MAY LEAVE NOW.
FWOOSH
...
...
Y...
YOU GIVE AMI BACK!
I DON'T NEED THAT GIRL ANYMORE.
I'VE ALREADY RELEASED HER.
SHE MUST BE SWIMMING FREELY IN THE OPEN SEA.
IN THE OPEN SEA?!
TENGU-KUN.

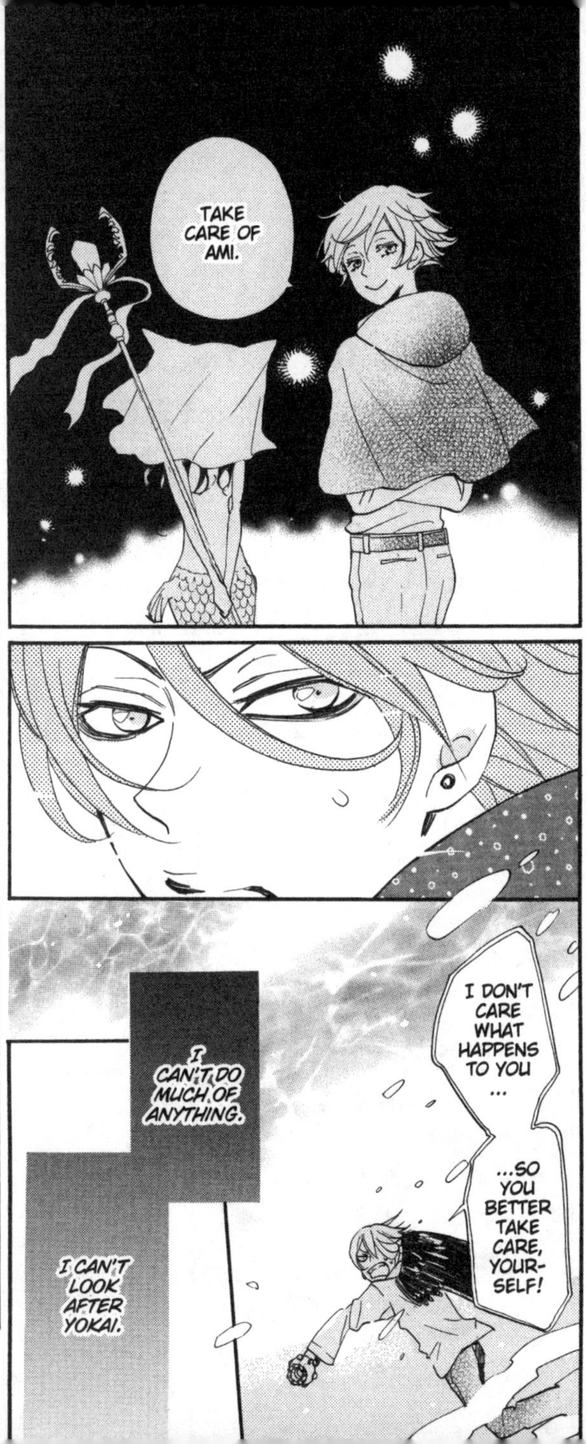
TAKE CARE OF AMI.
I DON'T CARE WHAT HAPPENS TO YOU ...
...SO YOU BETTER TAKE CARE, YOURSELF!
I CAN'T DO MUCH OF ANYTHING.
I CAN'T LOOK AFTER YOKAI.

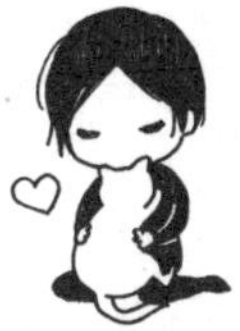

I recently felt that humans can't live unless they love something or someone.

I hope everyone's lives are filled with love.

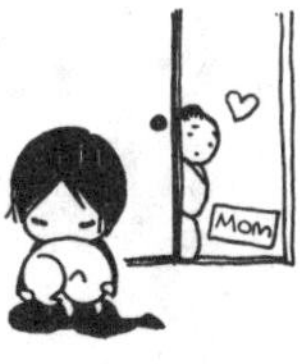
Mom

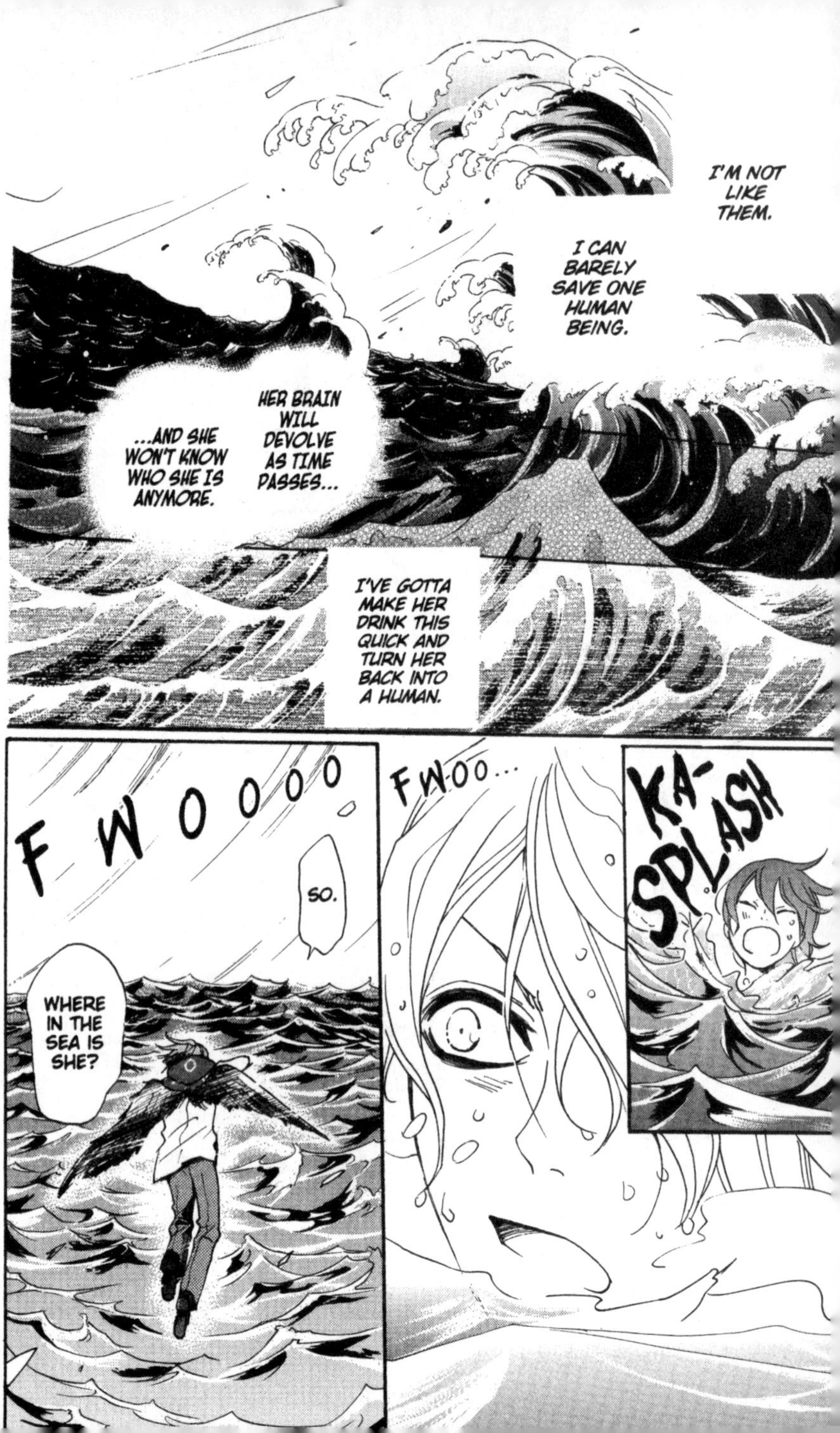

I'M NOT LIKE THEM.
I CAN BARELY SAVE ONE HUMAN BEING.
HER BRAIN WILL DEVOLVE AS TIME PASSES...
...AND SHE WON'T KNOW WHO SHE IS ANYMORE.
I'VE GOTTA MAKE HER DRINK THIS QUICK AND TURN HER BACK INTO A HUMAN.
KA-SPLASH
FWOO...
FWOOOO
SO.
WHERE IN THE SEA IS SHE?

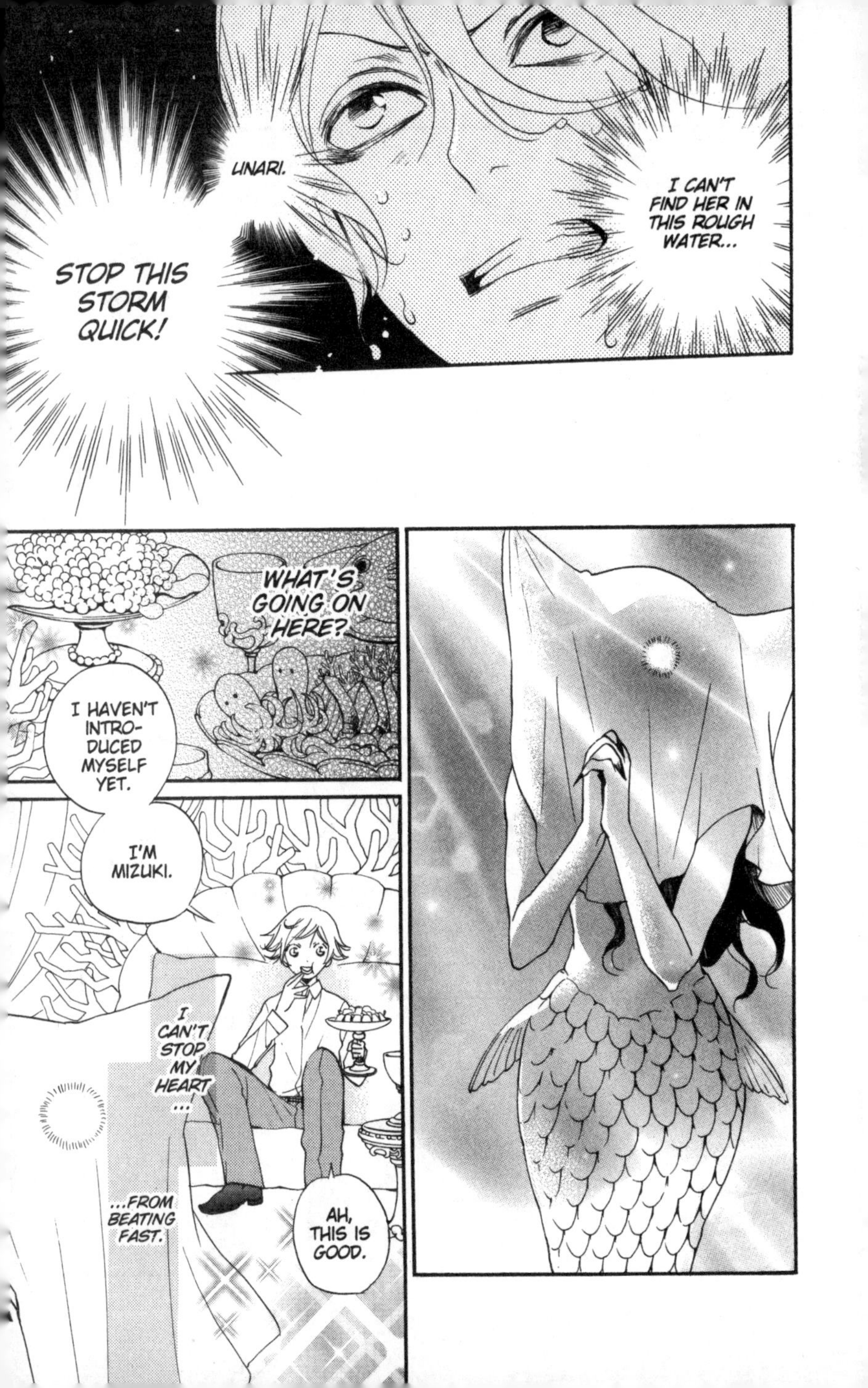
I CAN'T FIND HER IN THIS ROUGH WATER...
UNARI.
STOP THIS STORM QUICK!
WHAT'S GOING ON HERE?
I HAVEN'T INTRO-DUCED MYSELF YET.
I'M MIZUKI.
I CAN'T STOP MY HEART...
...FROM BEATING FAST.
AH, THIS IS GOOD.

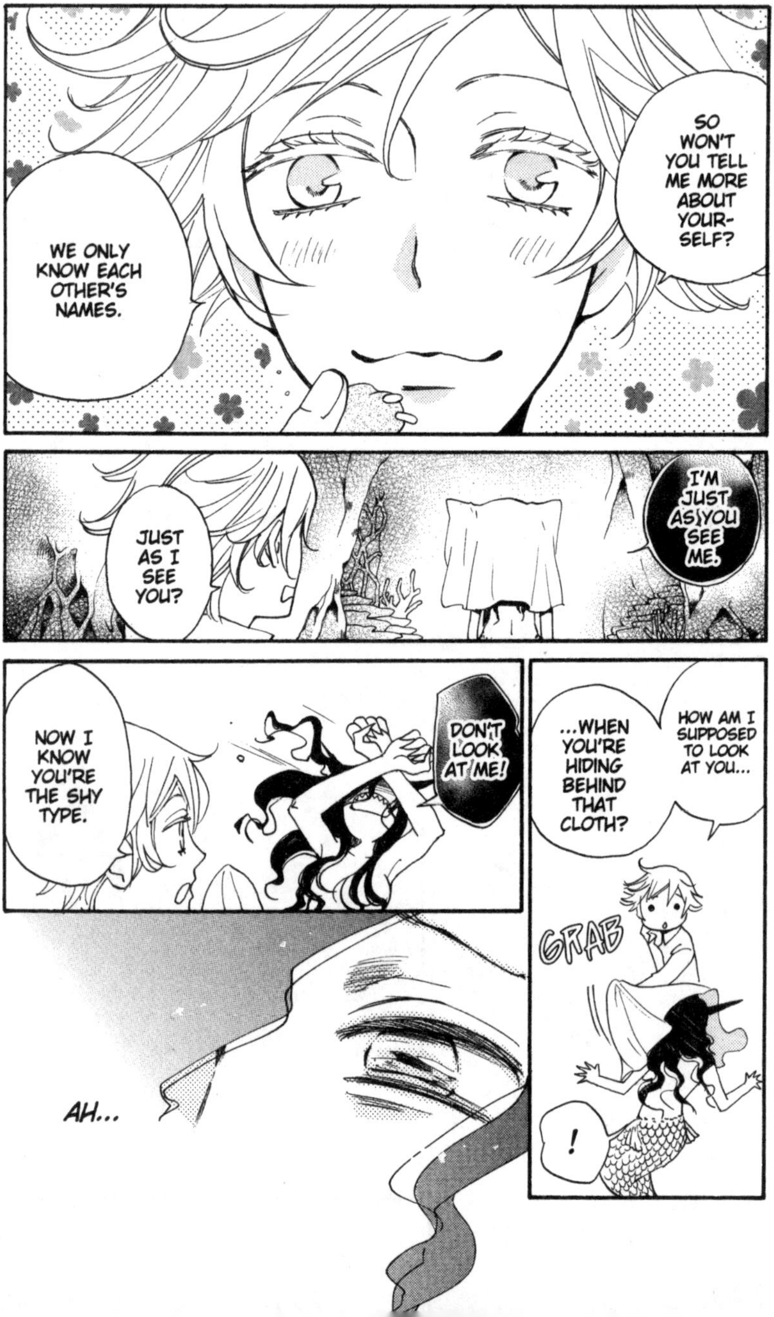
SO WON'T YOU TELL ME MORE ABOUT YOUR-SELF?
WE ONLY KNOW EACH OTHER'S NAMES.
I'M JUST AS YOU SEE ME.
JUST AS I SEE YOU?
HOW AM I SUPPOSED TO LOOK AT YOU...
...WHEN YOU'RE HIDING BEHIND THAT CLOTH?
GRAB
!
DON'T LOOK AT ME!
NOW I KNOW YOU'RE THE SHY TYPE.
AH...

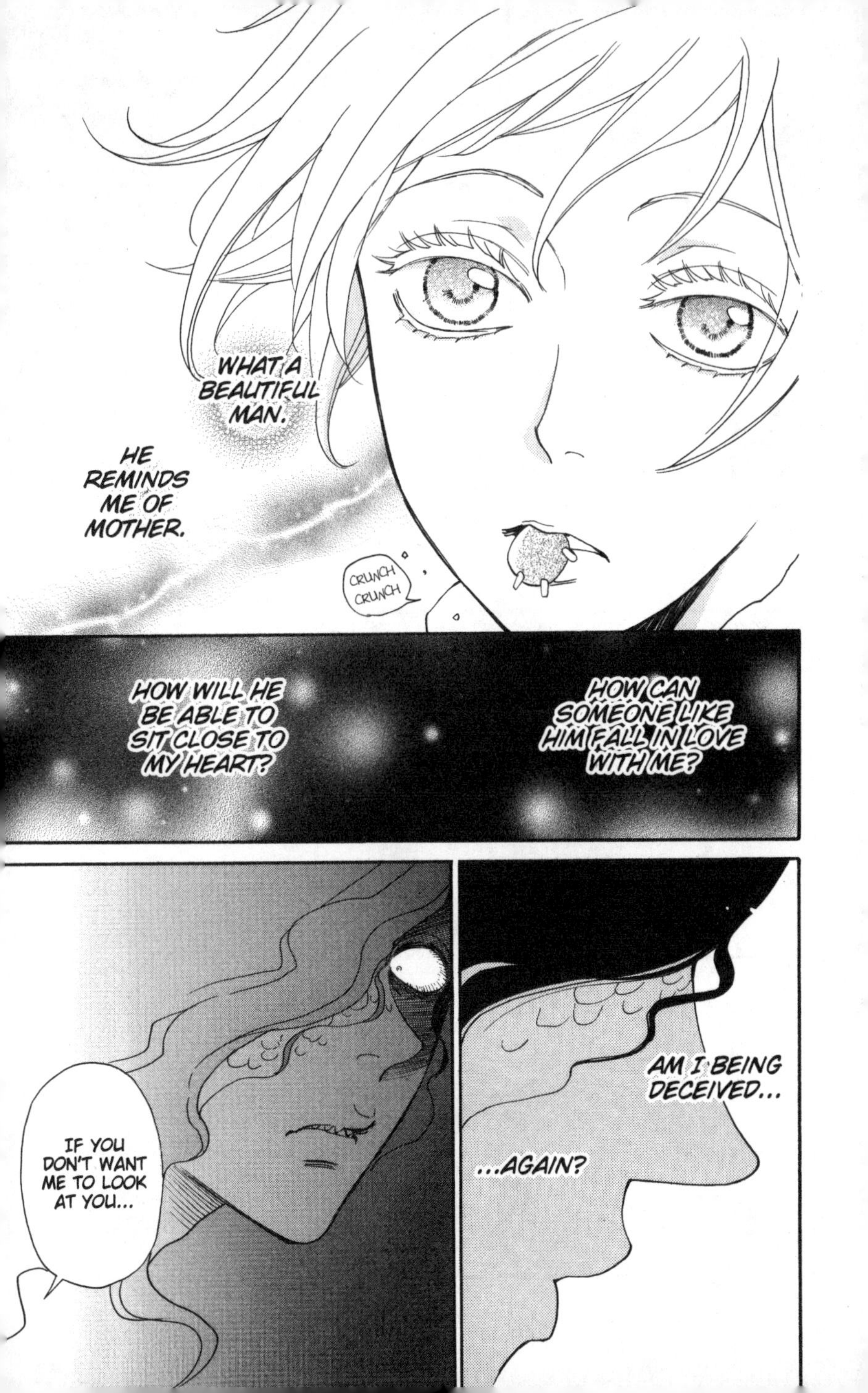
WHAT A BEAUTIFUL MAN.
HE REMINDS ME OF MOTHER.
CRUNCH CRUNCH
HOW CAN SOMEONE LIKE HIM FALL IN LOVE WITH ME?
HOW WILL HE BE ABLE TO SIT CLOSE TO MY HEART?
AM I BEING DECEIVED...
...AGAIN?
IF YOU DON'T WANT ME TO LOOK AT YOU...

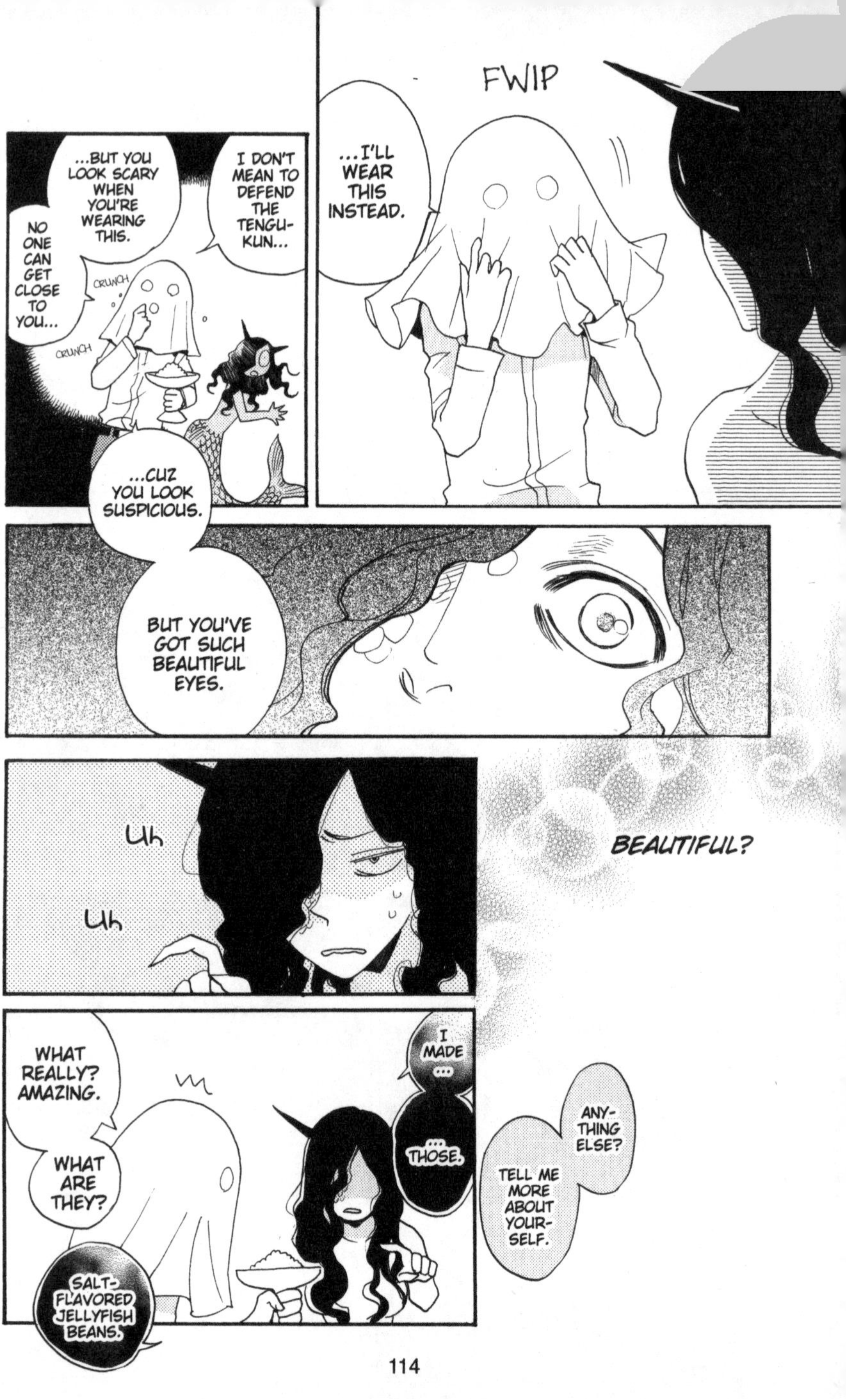
FWIP
...I'LL WEAR THIS INSTEAD.
I DON'T MEAN TO DEFEND THE TENGU-KUN...
...BUT YOU LOOK SCARY WHEN YOU'RE WEARING THIS.
NO ONE CAN GET CLOSE TO YOU...
CRUNCH
CRUNCH
...CUZ YOU LOOK SUSPICIOUS.
BUT YOU'VE GOT SUCH BEAUTIFUL EYES.
BEAUTIFUL?
Uh
Uh
ANY-THING ELSE?
TELL ME MORE ABOUT YOUR-SELF.
I MADE...
...THOSE.
WHAT REALLY? AMAZING.
WHAT ARE THEY?
SALT-FLAVORED JELLYFISH BEANS.

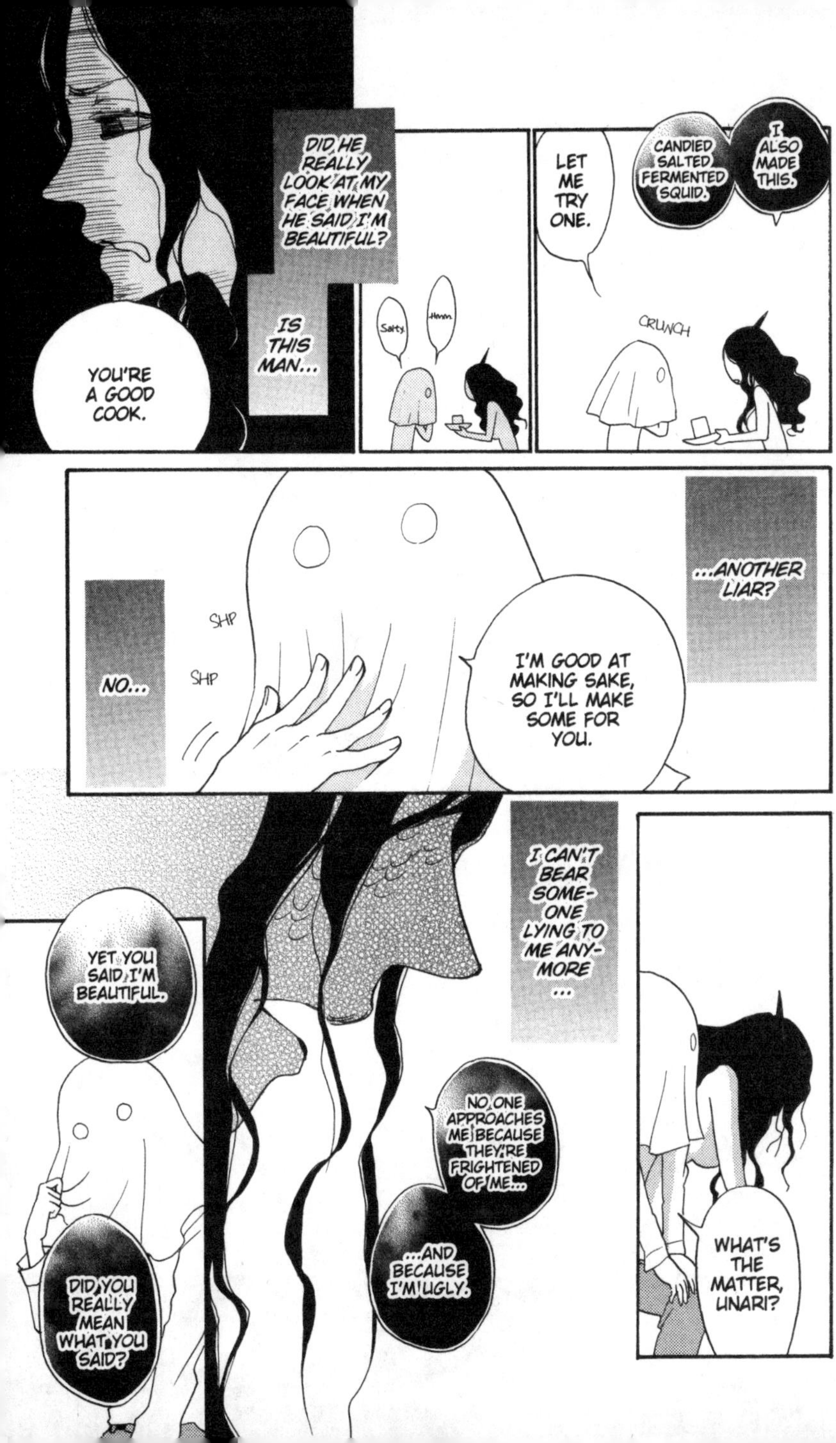
I ALSO MADE THIS.
CANDIED SALTED FERMENTED SQUID.
LET ME TRY ONE.
CRUNCH
Hmm.
Salty.
DID HE REALLY LOOK AT MY FACE WHEN HE SAID I'M BEAUTIFUL?
IS THIS MAN...
YOU'RE A GOOD COOK.
...ANOTHER LIAR?
I'M GOOD AT MAKING SAKE, SO I'LL MAKE SOME FOR YOU.
SHP
SHP
NO...
I CAN'T BEAR SOME-ONE LYING TO ME ANY-MORE...
WHAT'S THE MATTER, UNARI?
NO ONE APPROACHES ME BECAUSE THEY'RE FRIGHTENED OF ME...
...AND BECAUSE I'M UGLY.
YET YOU SAID I'M BEAUTIFUL.
DID YOU REALLY MEAN WHAT YOU SAID?

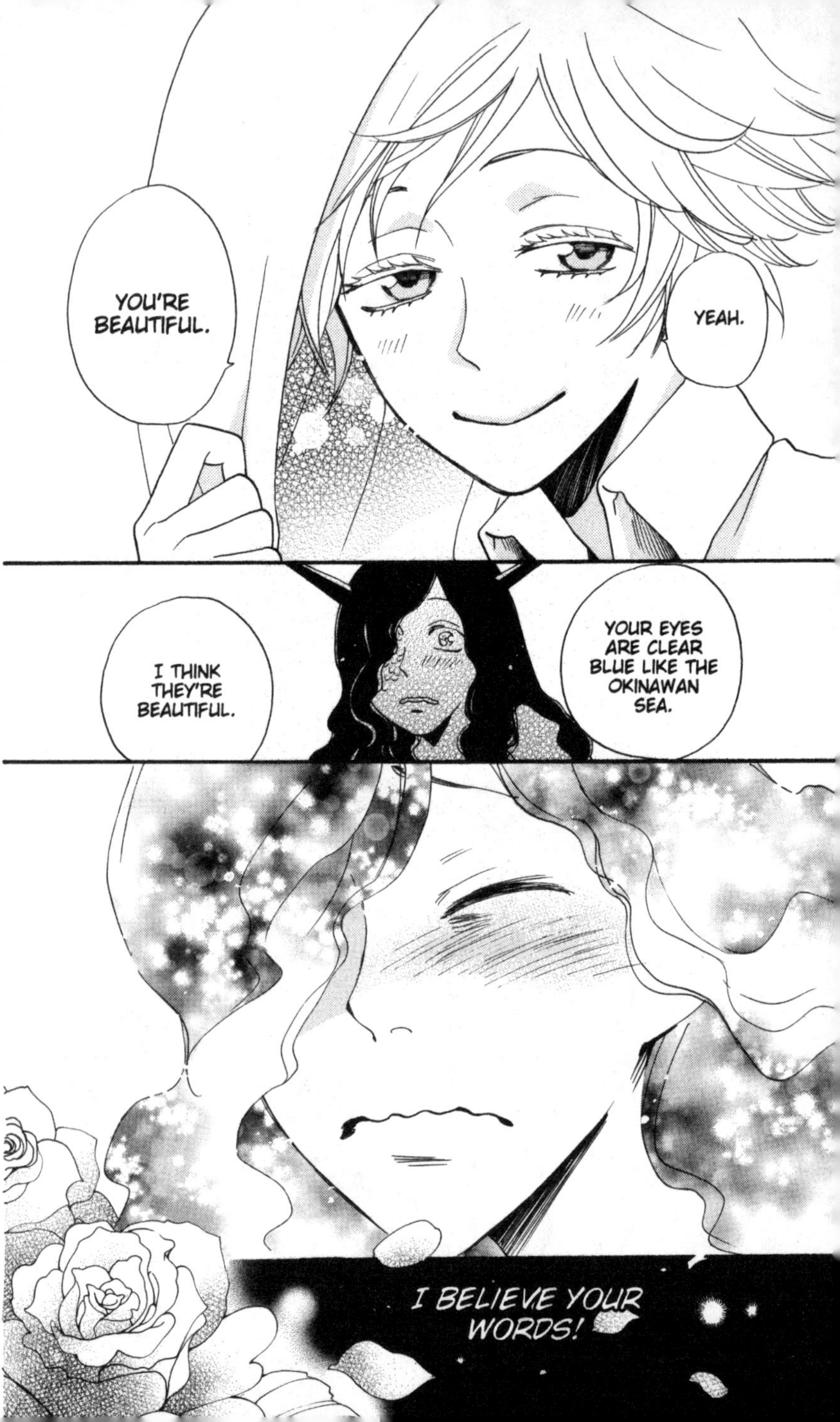
YEAH.
YOU'RE BEAUTIFUL.
YOUR EYES ARE CLEAR BLUE LIKE THE OKINAWAN SEA.
I THINK THEY'RE BEAUTIFUL.
I BELIEVE YOUR WORDS!

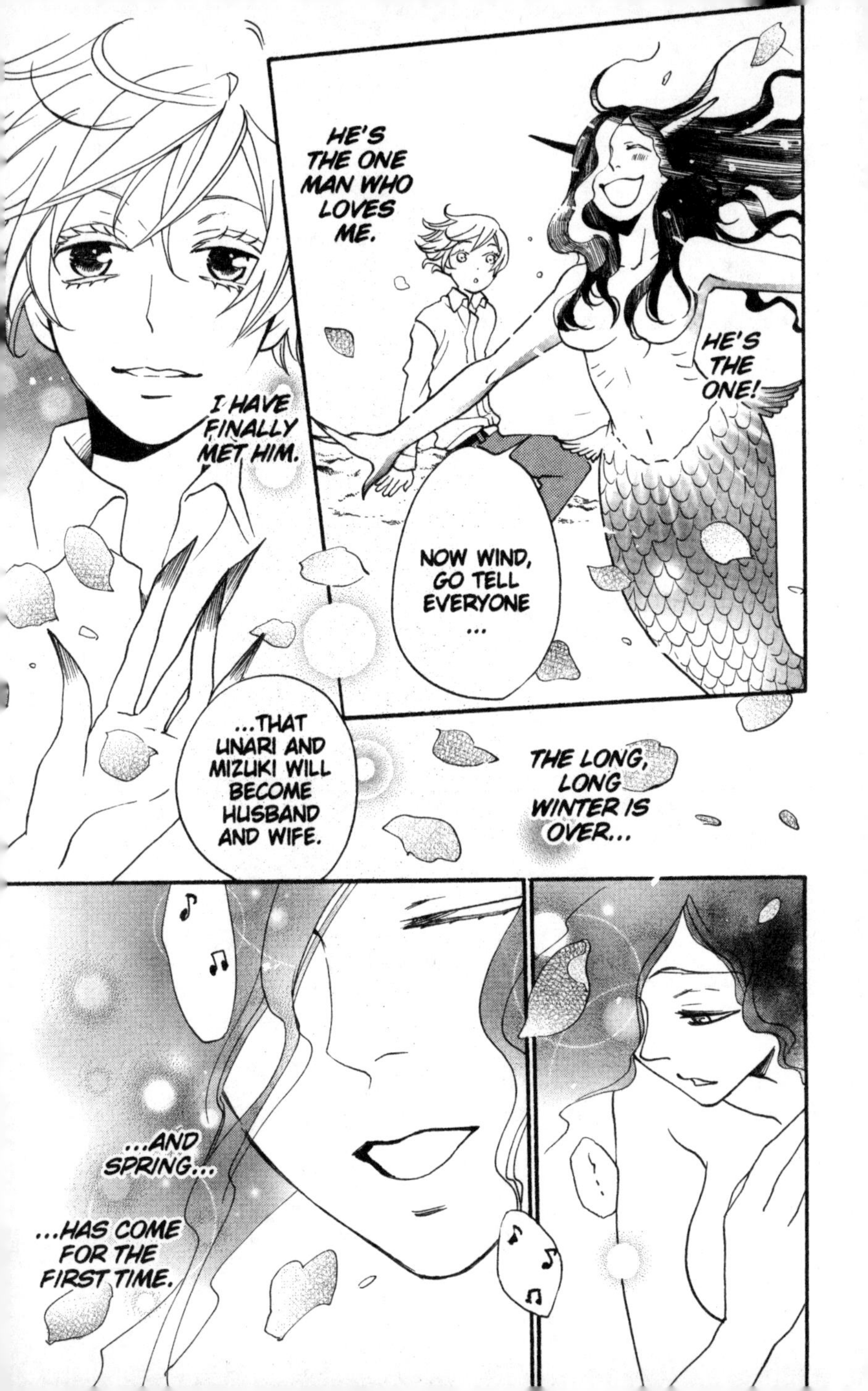
HE'S THE ONE MAN WHO LOVES ME.
HE'S THE ONE!
NOW WIND, GO TELL EVERYONE ...
...THAT UNARI AND MIZUKI WILL BECOME HUSBAND AND WIFE.
THE LONG, LONG WINTER IS OVER...
I HAVE FINALLY MET HIM.
...
...AND SPRING...
...HAS COME FOR THE FIRST TIME.

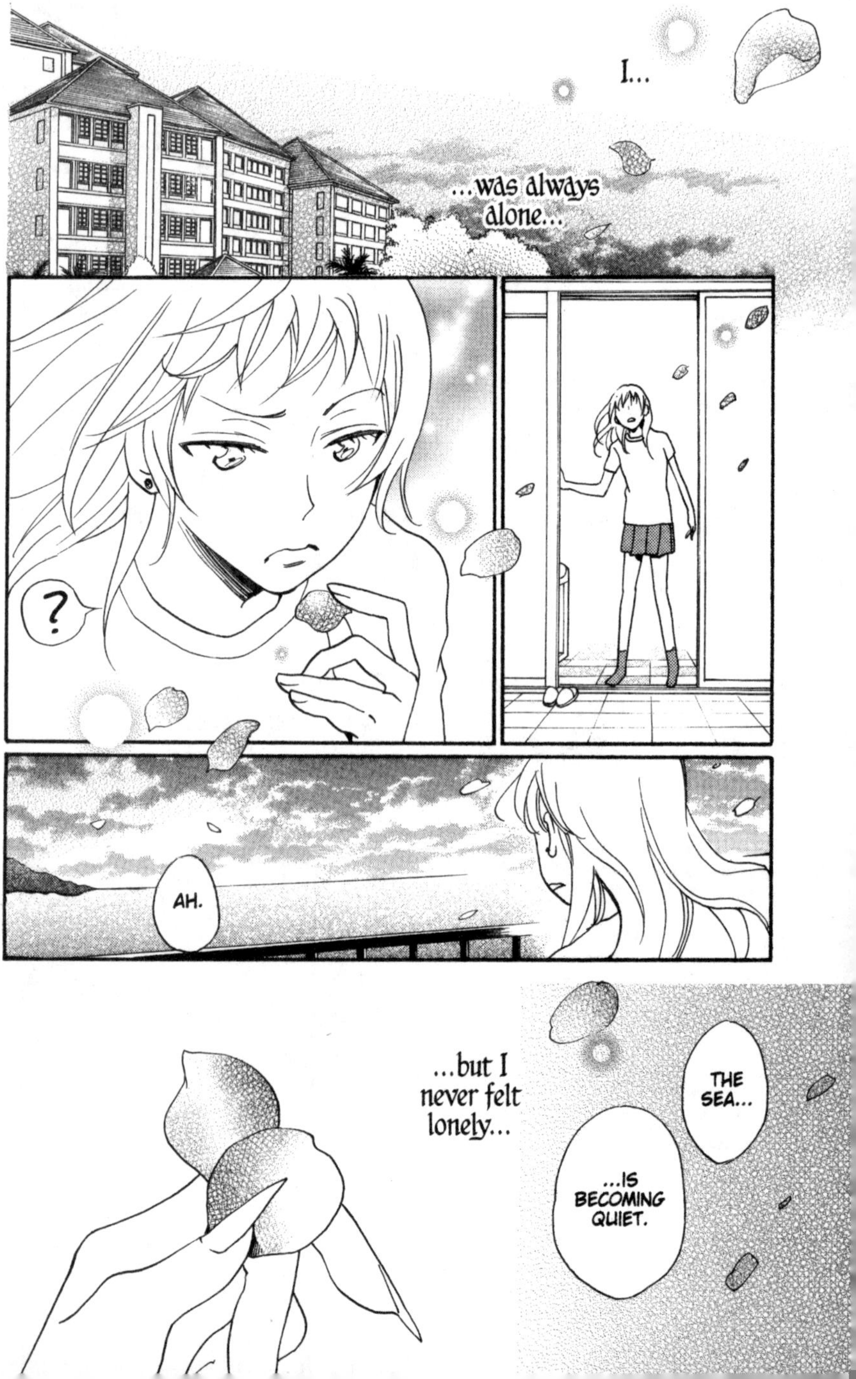
I...
...was always alone...
?
AH.
THE SEA...
...IS BECOMING QUIET.
...but I never felt lonely...

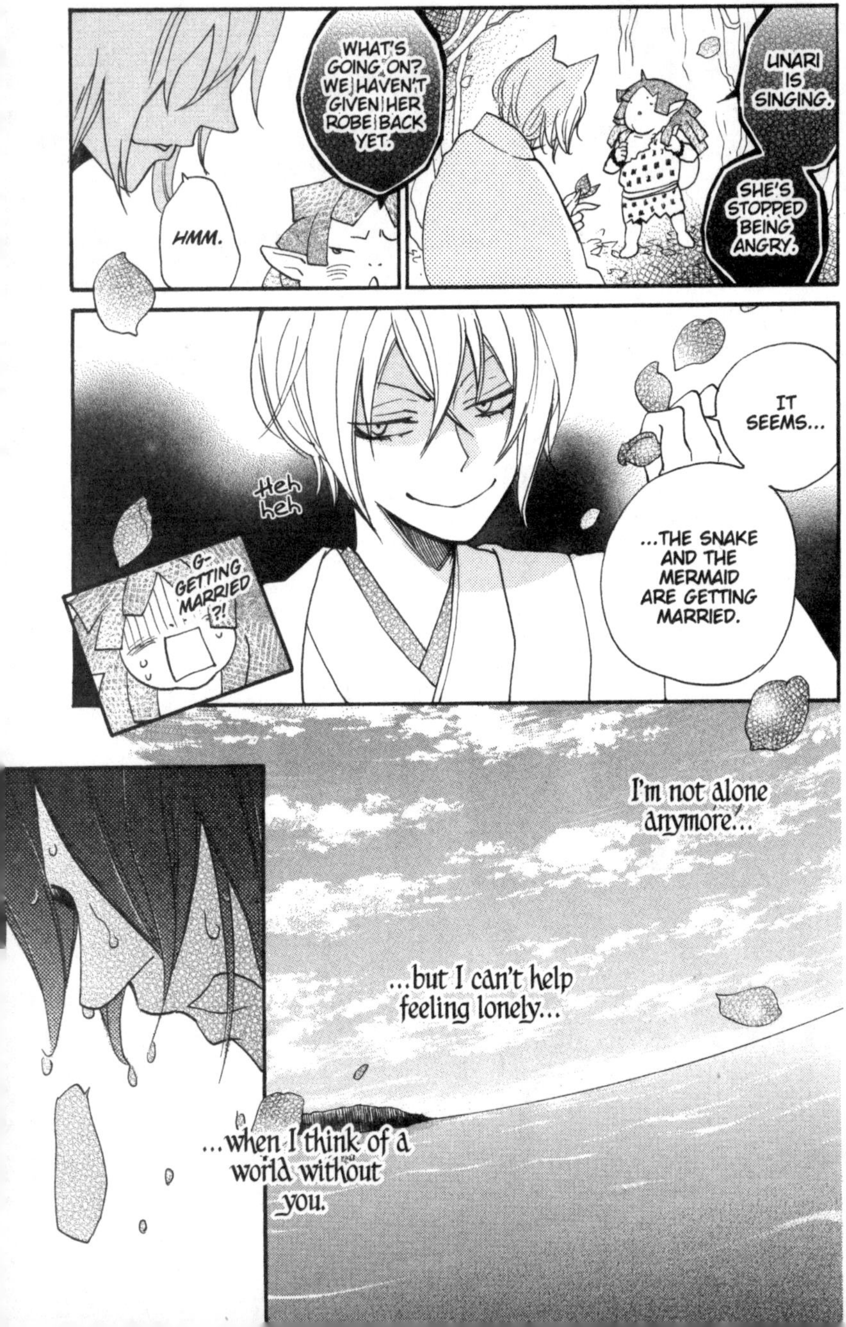
UNARI IS SINGING.
SHE'S STOPPED BEING ANGRY.
WHAT'S GOING ON? WE HAVEN'T GIVEN HER ROBE BACK YET.
HMM.
IT SEEMS...
...THE SNAKE AND THE MERMAID ARE GETTING MARRIED.
Heh heh
G-GETTING MARRIED?!
I'm not alone anymore...
...but I can't help feeling lonely...
...when I think of a world without you.

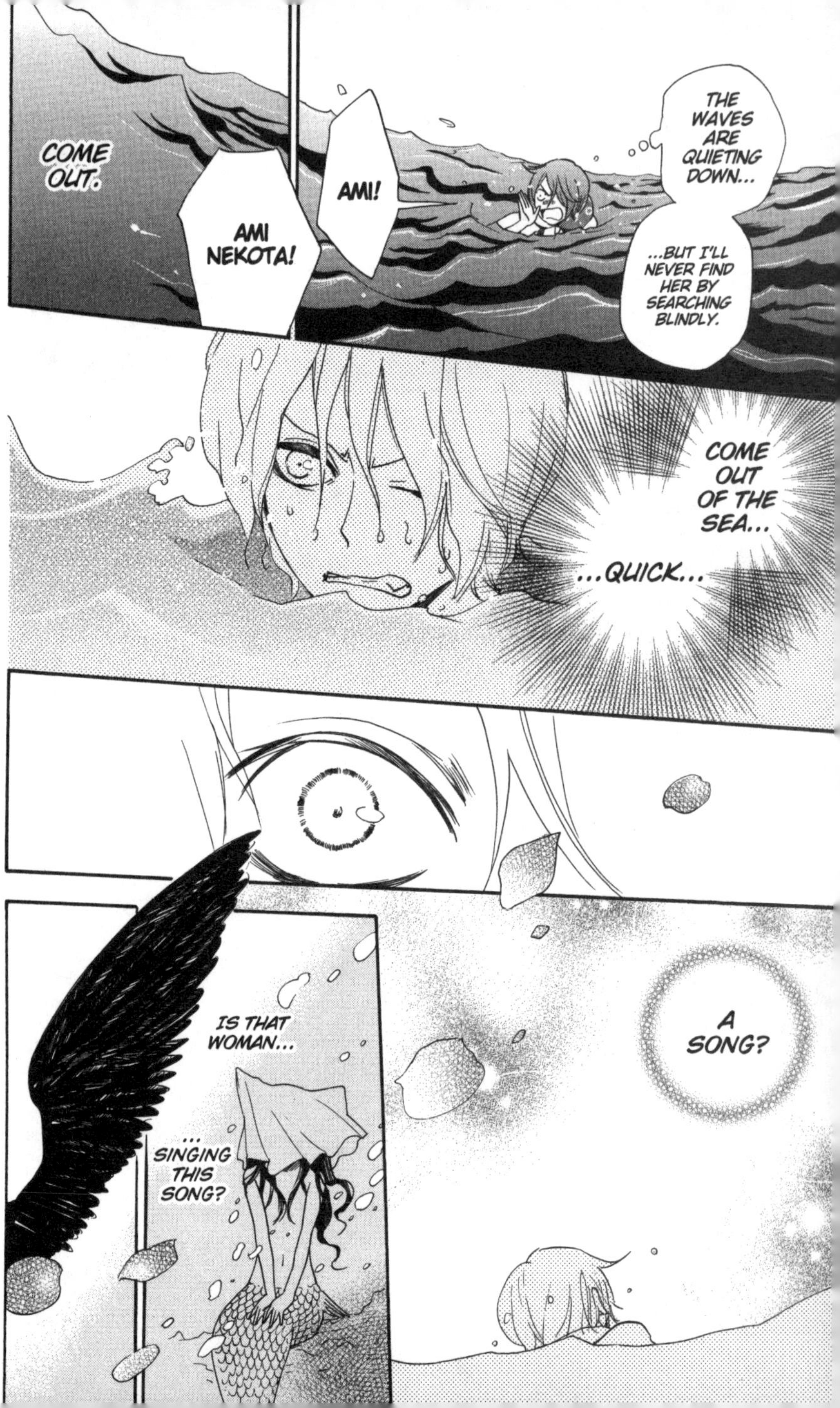
THE WAVES ARE QUIETING DOWN...
...BUT I'LL NEVER FIND HER BY SEARCHING BLINDLY.
AMI!
AMI NEKOTA!
COME OUT.
COME OUT OF THE SEA...
...QUICK...
A SONG?
IS THAT WOMAN...
...SINGING THIS SONG?

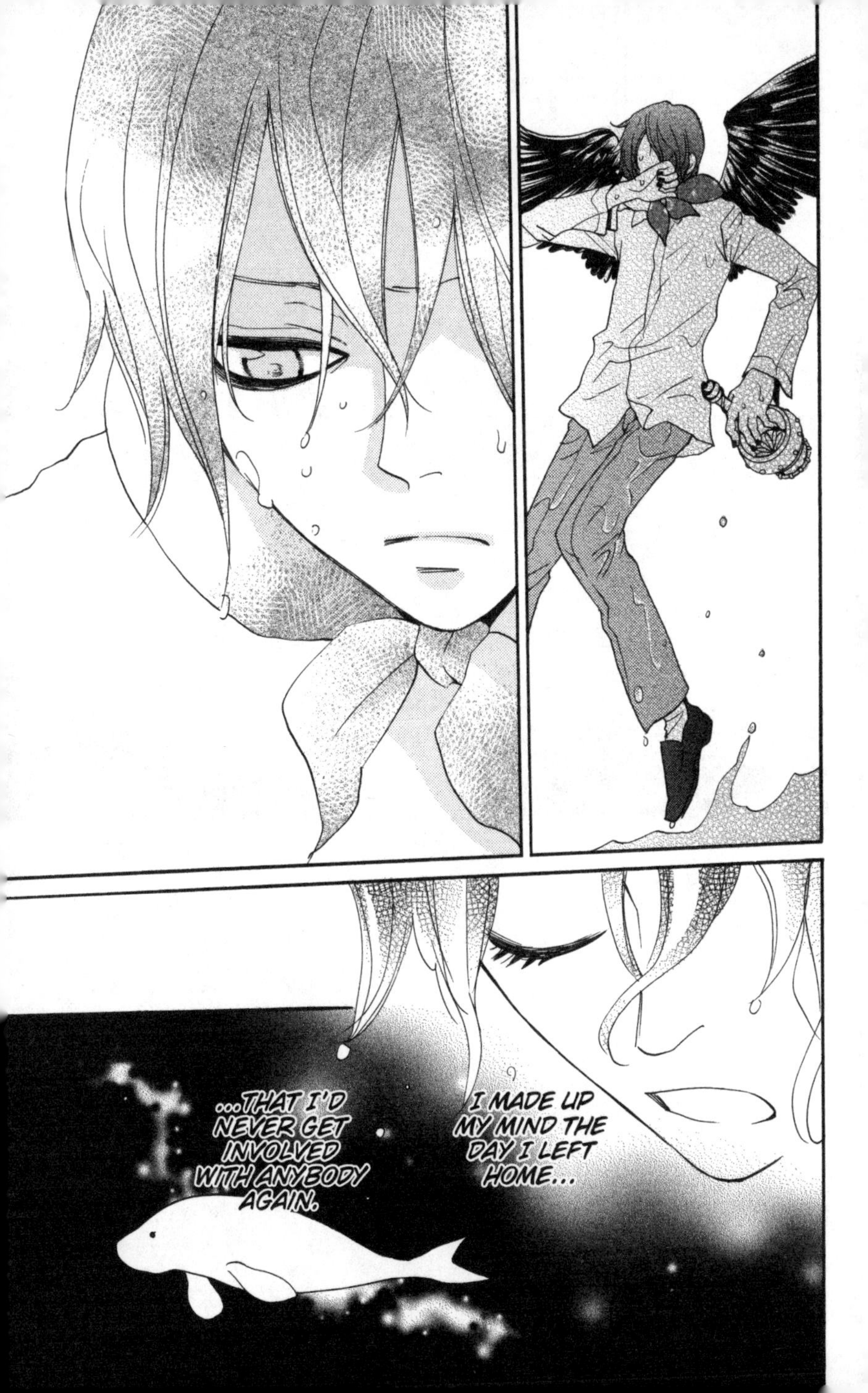
I MADE UP MY MIND THE DAY I LEFT HOME...
...THAT I'D NEVER GET INVOLVED WITH ANYBODY AGAIN.

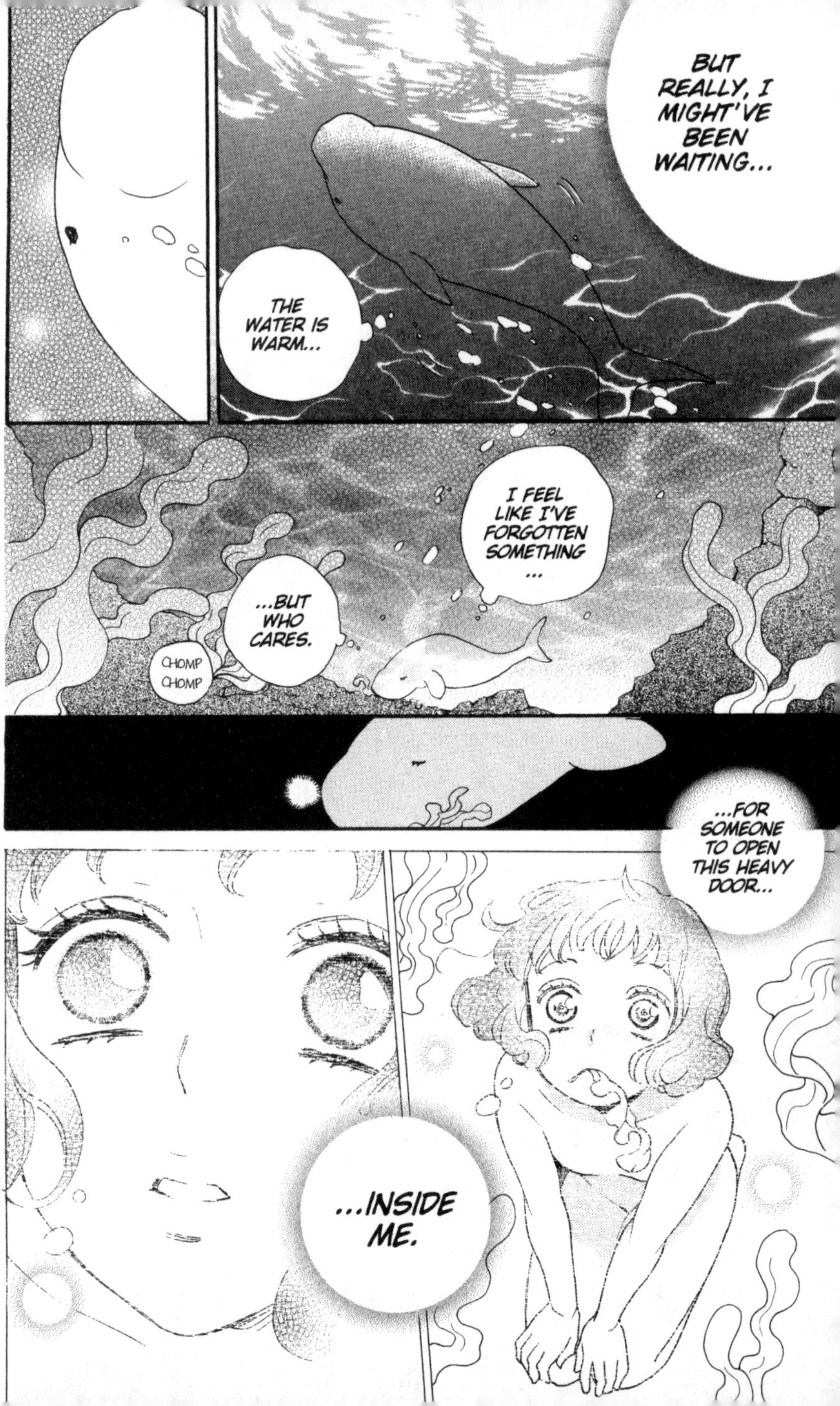
BUT REALLY, I MIGHT'VE BEEN WAITING...
THE WATER IS WARM...
I FEEL LIKE I'VE FORGOTTEN SOMETHING...
...BUT WHO CARES.
CHOMP CHOMP
...FOR SOMEONE TO OPEN THIS HEAVY DOOR...
...INSIDE ME.

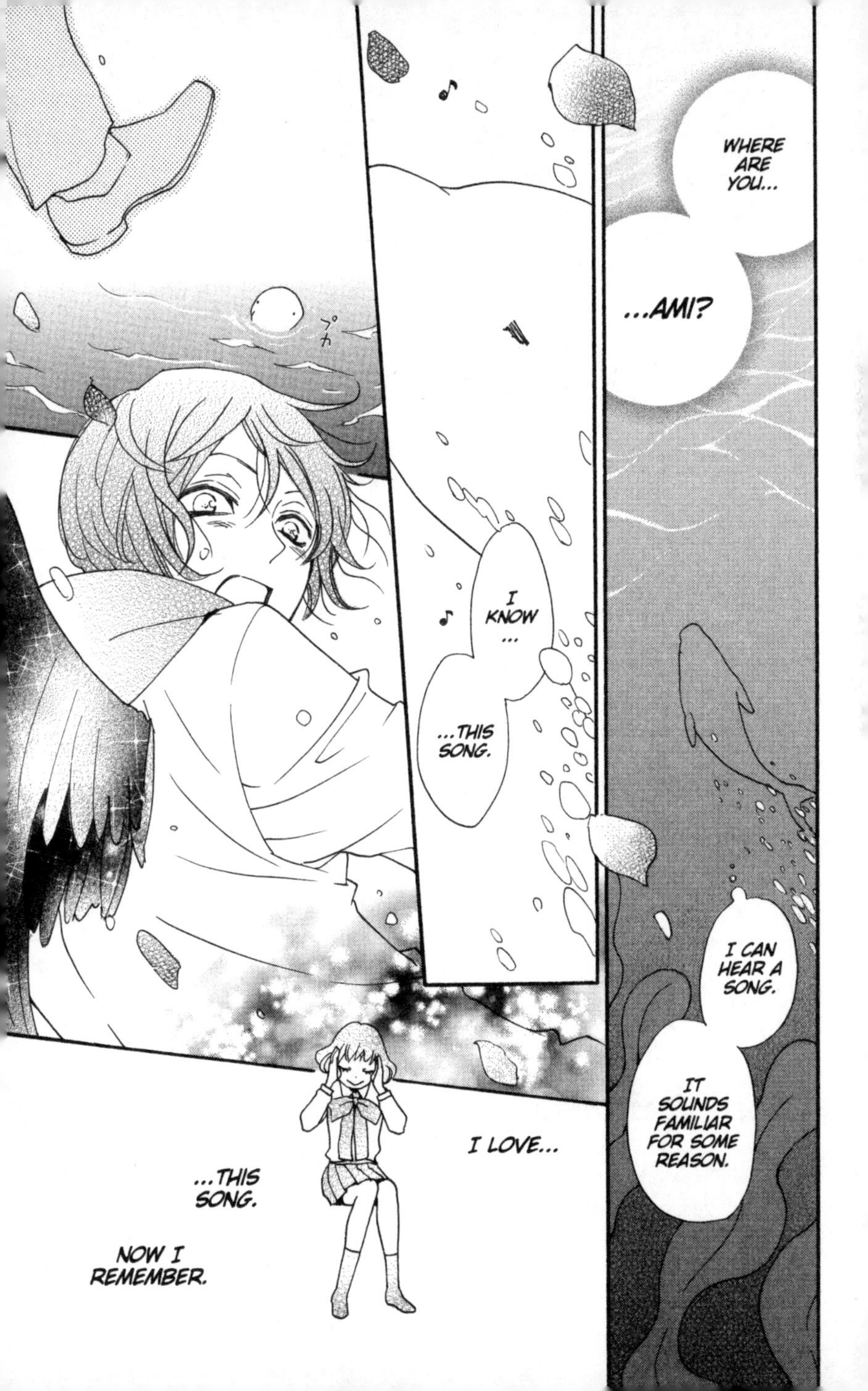
WHERE ARE YOU...
...AMI?
I CAN HEAR A SONG.
IT SOUNDS FAMILIAR FOR SOME REASON.
I KNOW...
...THIS SONG.
プカ
I LOVE...
...THIS SONG.
NOW I REMEMBER.

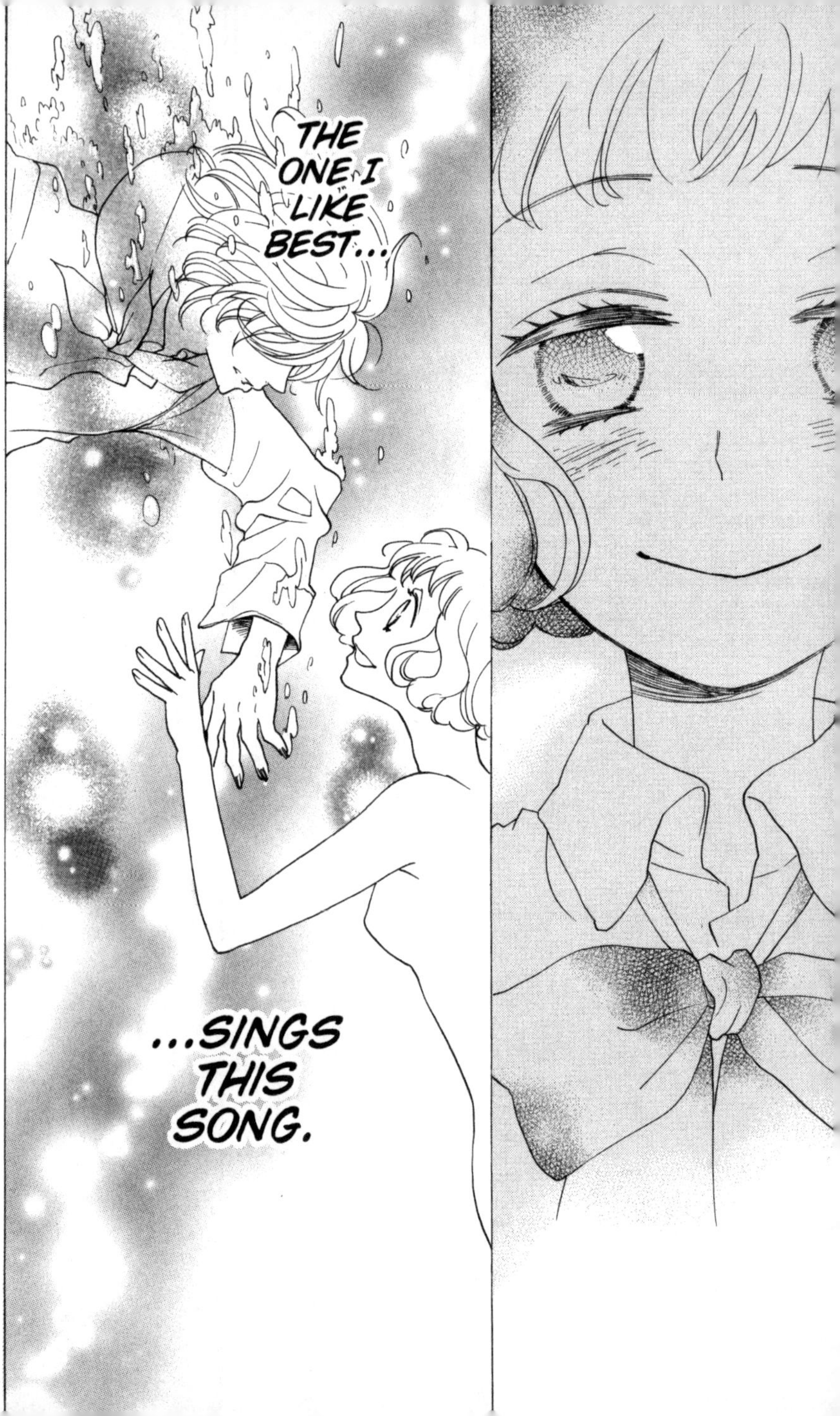
THE ONE I LIKE BEST...
...SINGS THIS SONG.

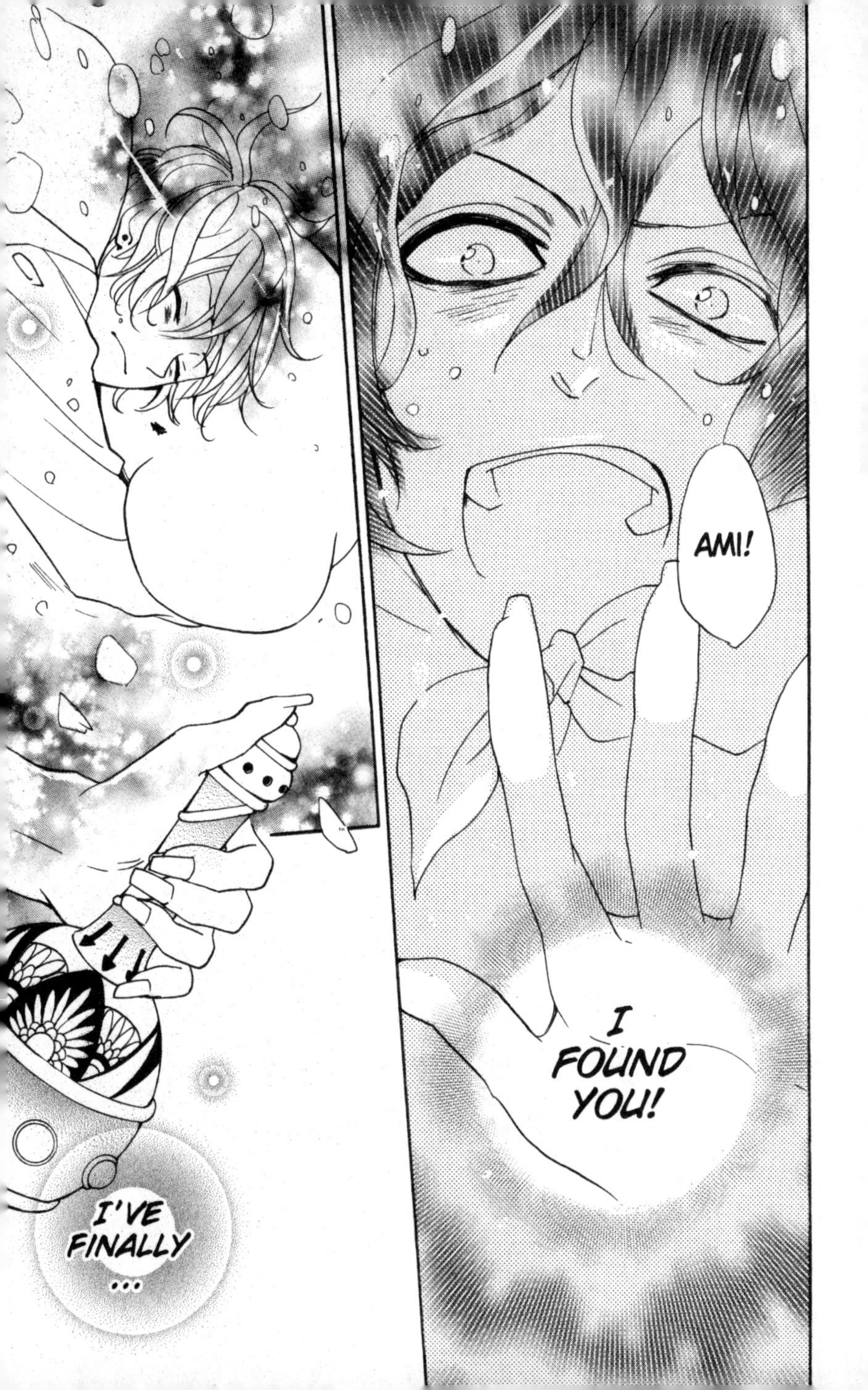
AMI!
I FOUND YOU!
I'VE FINALLY ...

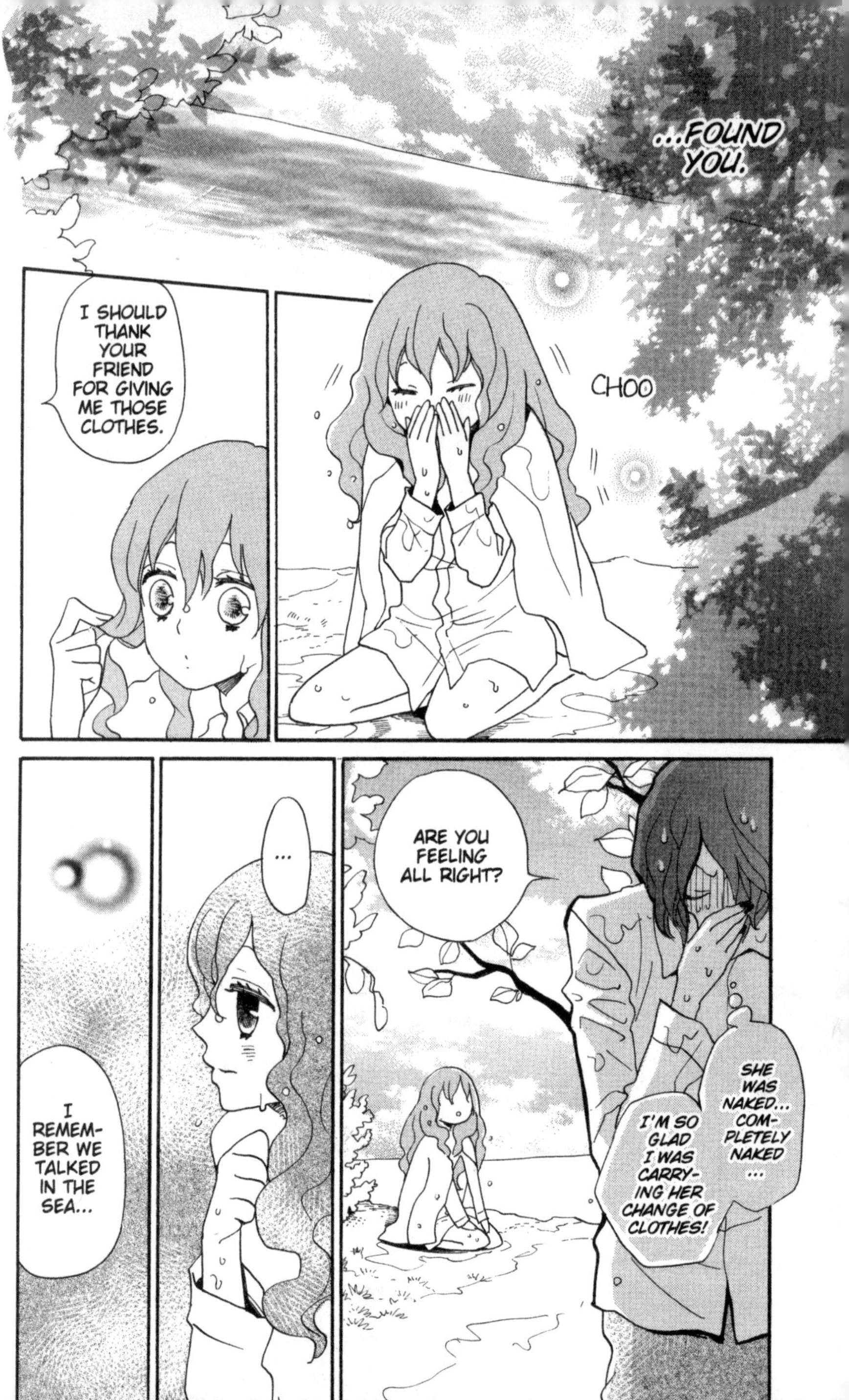
...FOUND YOU.
CHOO
I SHOULD THANK YOUR FRIEND FOR GIVING ME THOSE CLOTHES.
ARE YOU FEELING ALL RIGHT?
SHE WAS NAKED... COMPLETELY NAKED...
I'M SO GLAD I WAS CARRYING HER CHANGE OF CLOTHES!
...
I REMEMBER WE TALKED IN THE SEA...

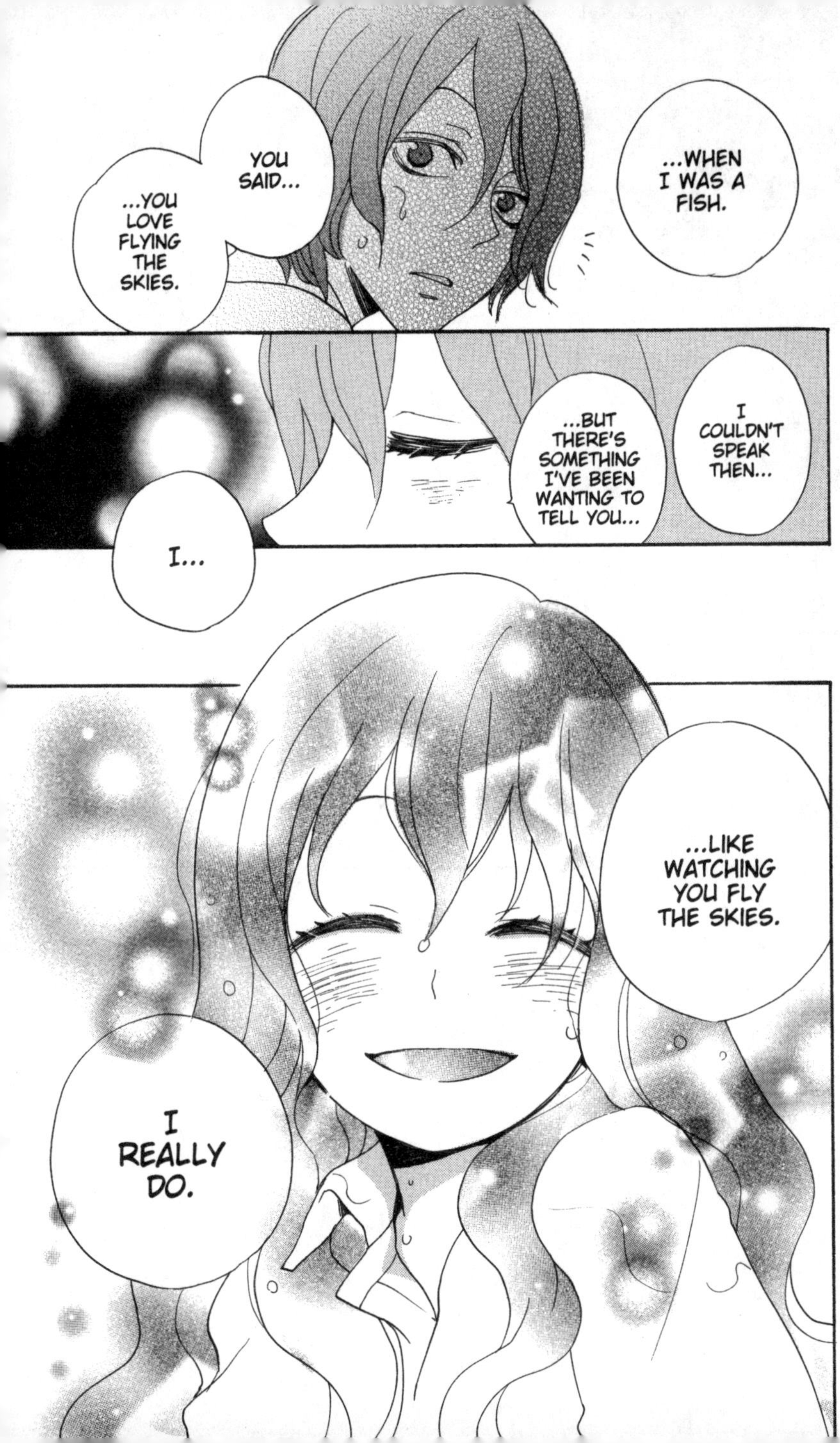
...WHEN I WAS A FISH.
YOU SAID...
...YOU LOVE FLYING THE SKIES.
I COULDN'T SPEAK THEN...
...BUT THERE'S SOMETHING I'VE BEEN WANTING TO TELL YOU...
I...
...LIKE WATCHING YOU FLY THE SKIES.
I REALLY DO.

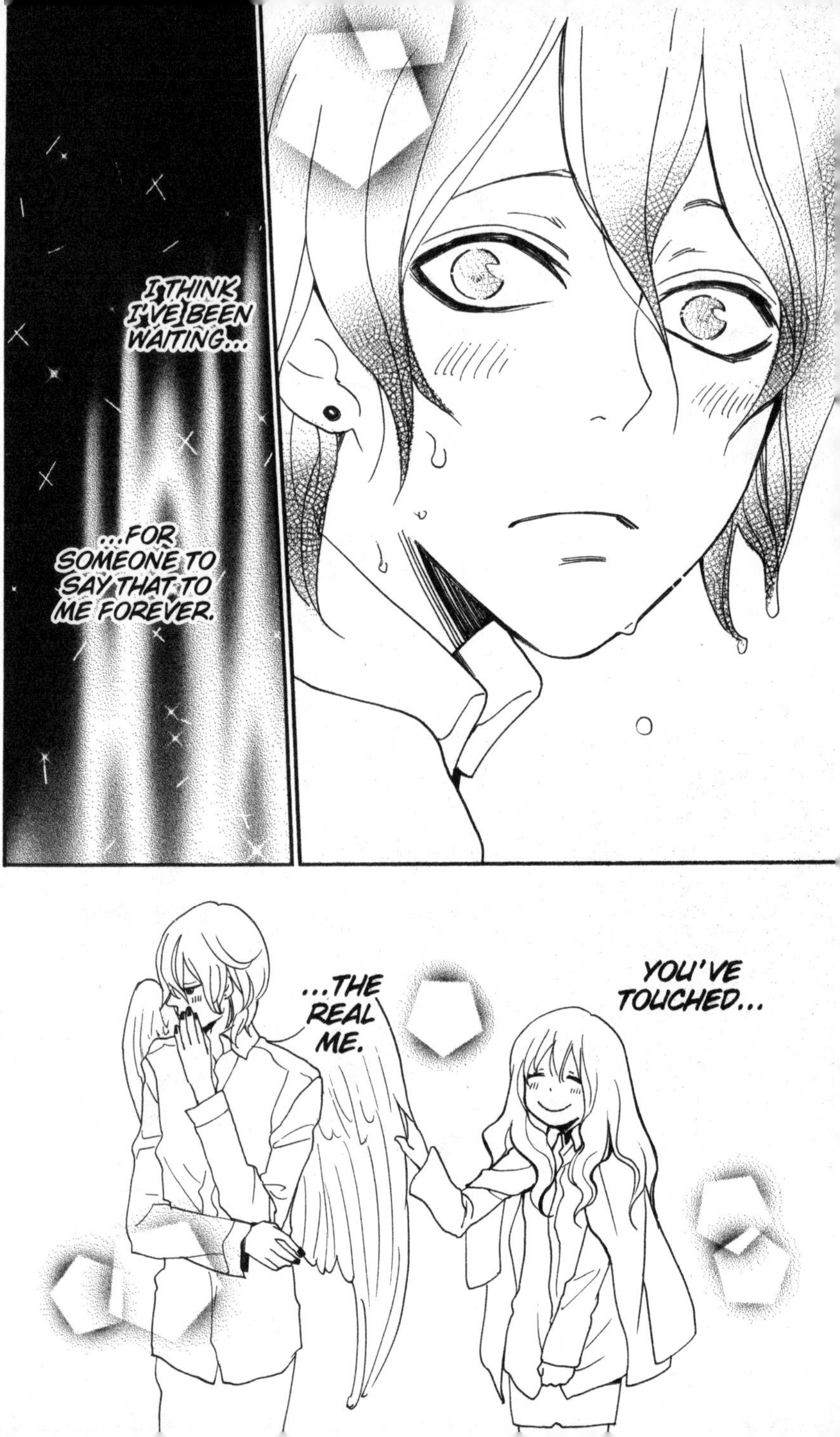
I THINK I'VE BEEN WAITING...
...FOR SOMEONE TO SAY THAT TO ME FOREVER.
YOU'VE TOUCHED...
...THE REAL ME.

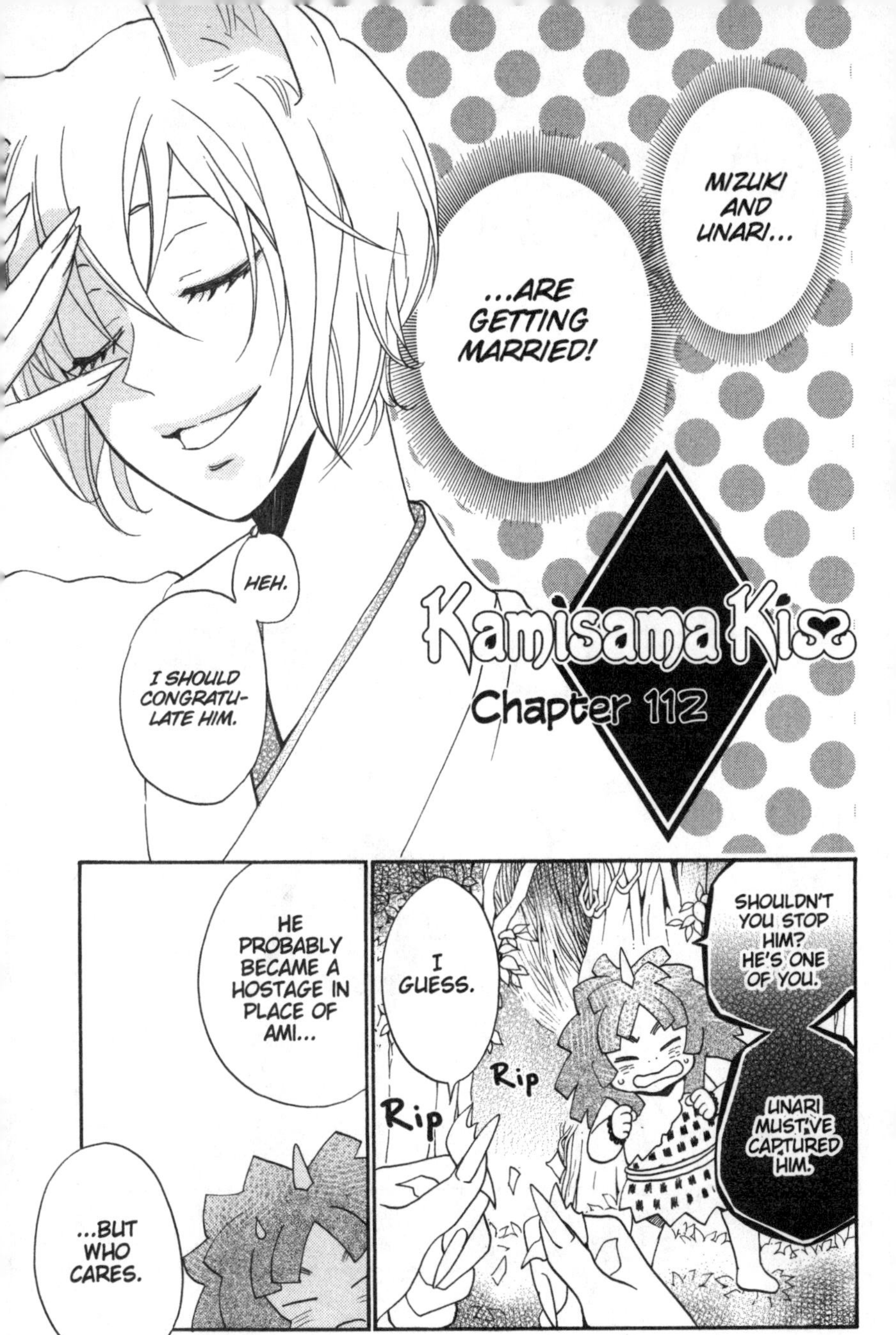
MIZUKI AND UNARI...
...ARE GETTING MARRIED!
Kamisama Kiss
Chapter 112
HEH.
I SHOULD CONGRATULATE HIM.
SHOULDN'T YOU STOP HIM? HE'S ONE OF YOU.
UNARI MUST'VE CAPTURED HIM.
I GUESS.
Rip
Rip
HE PROBABLY BECAME A HOSTAGE IN PLACE OF AMI...
...BUT WHO CARES.

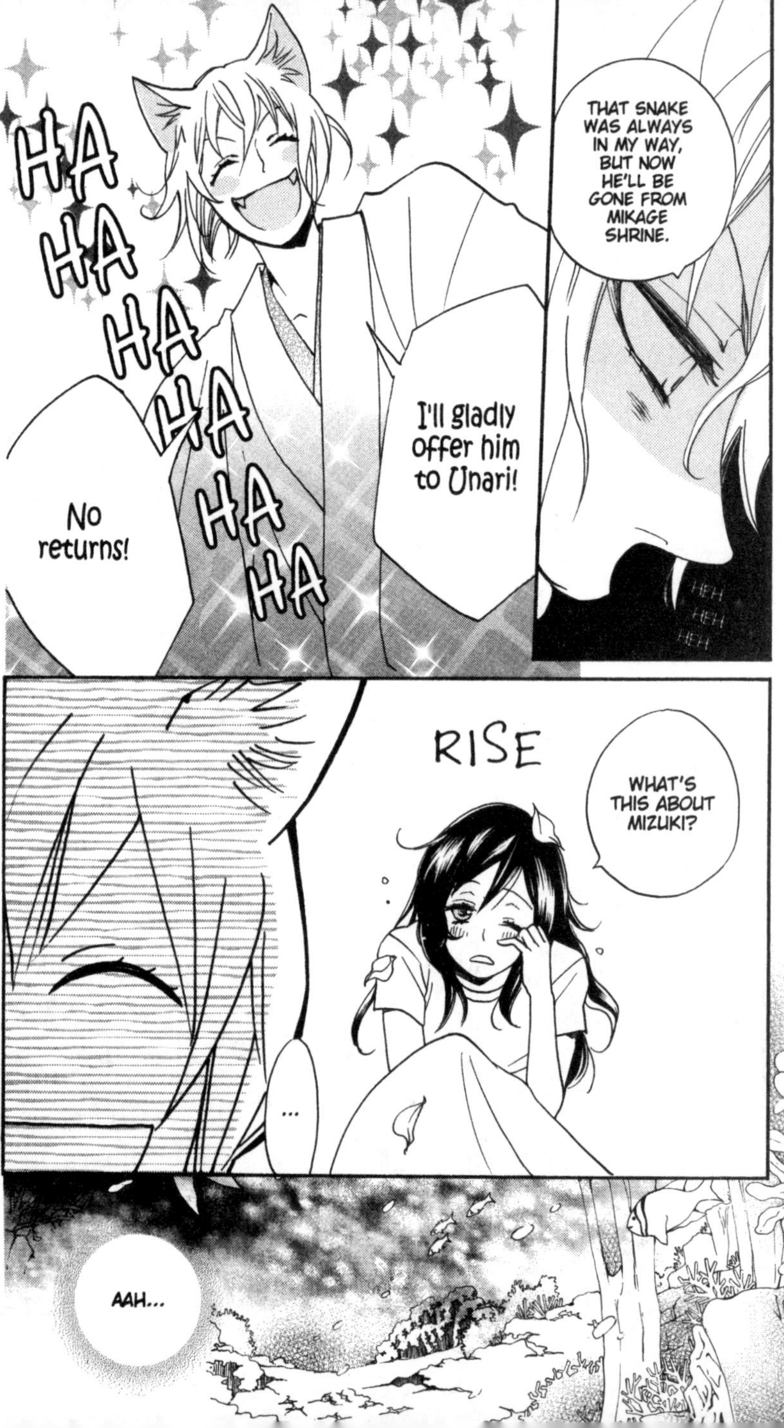
THAT SNAKE WAS ALWAYS IN MY WAY, BUT NOW HE'LL BE GONE FROM MIKAGE SHRINE.
HEH HEH HEH
I'll gladly offer him to Unari!
HA HA HA HA HA HA HA
No returns!
RISE
WHAT'S THIS ABOUT MIZUKI?
...
AAH...

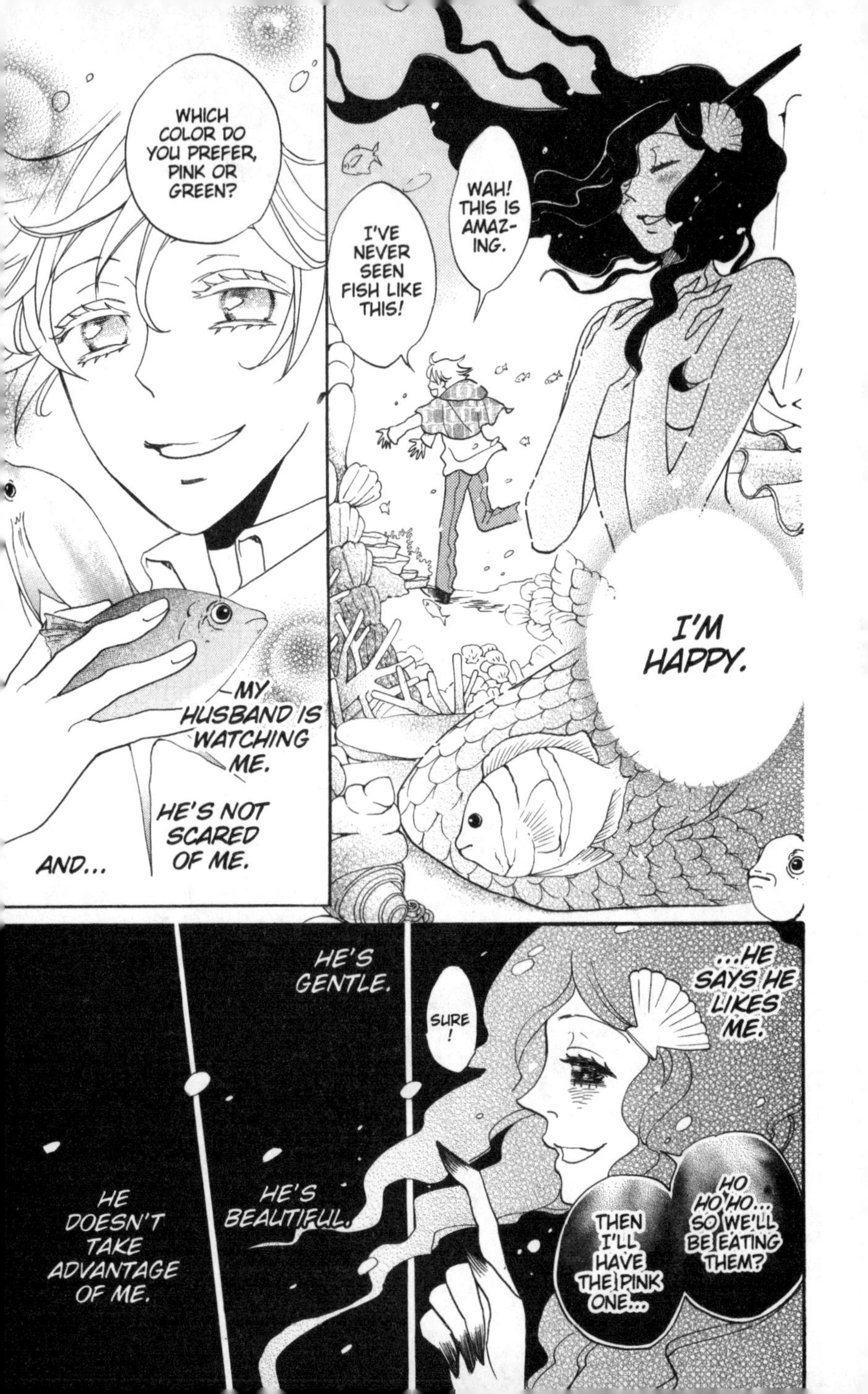

WAH! THIS IS AMAZ-ING.
I'VE NEVER SEEN FISH LIKE THIS!
I'M HAPPY.
WHICH COLOR DO YOU PREFER, PINK OR GREEN?
MY HUSBAND IS WATCHING ME.
HE'S NOT SCARED OF ME.
AND...
...HE SAYS HE LIKES ME.
HO HO HO... SO WE'LL BE EATING THEM?
THEN I'LL HAVE THE PINK ONE...
SURE!
HE'S GENTLE.
HE'S BEAUTIFUL.
HE DOESN'T TAKE ADVANTAGE OF ME.

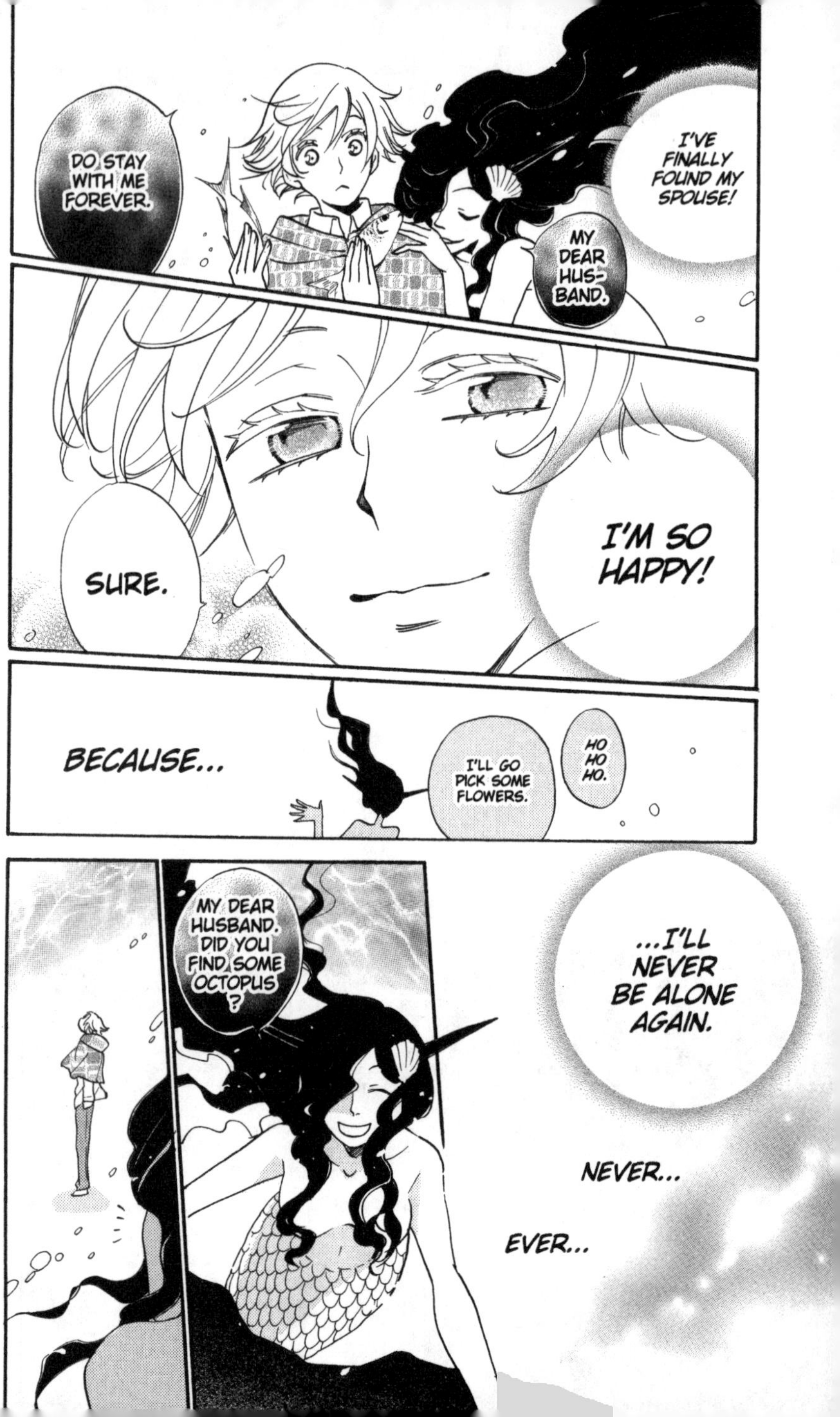
I'VE FINALLY FOUND MY SPOUSE!
MY DEAR HUS-BAND.
DO STAY WITH ME FOREVER.
I'M SO HAPPY!
SURE.
HO HO HO.
I'LL GO PICK SOME FLOWERS.
BECAUSE...
...I'LL NEVER BE ALONE AGAIN.
NEVER...
EVER...
MY DEAR HUSBAND. DID YOU FIND SOME OCTOPUS?

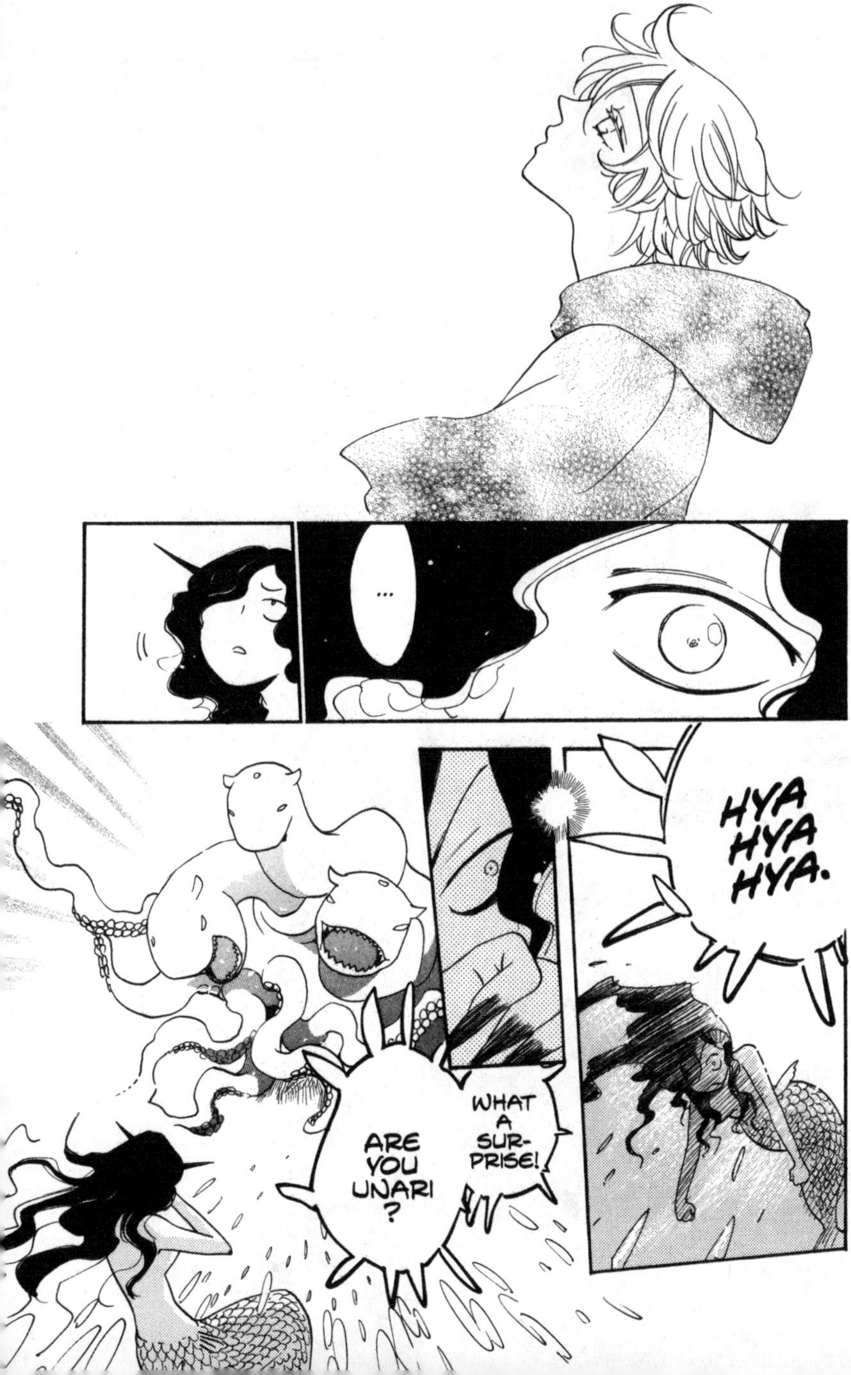
...
HYA HYA HYA.
WHAT A SUR-PRISE!
ARE YOU UNARI?

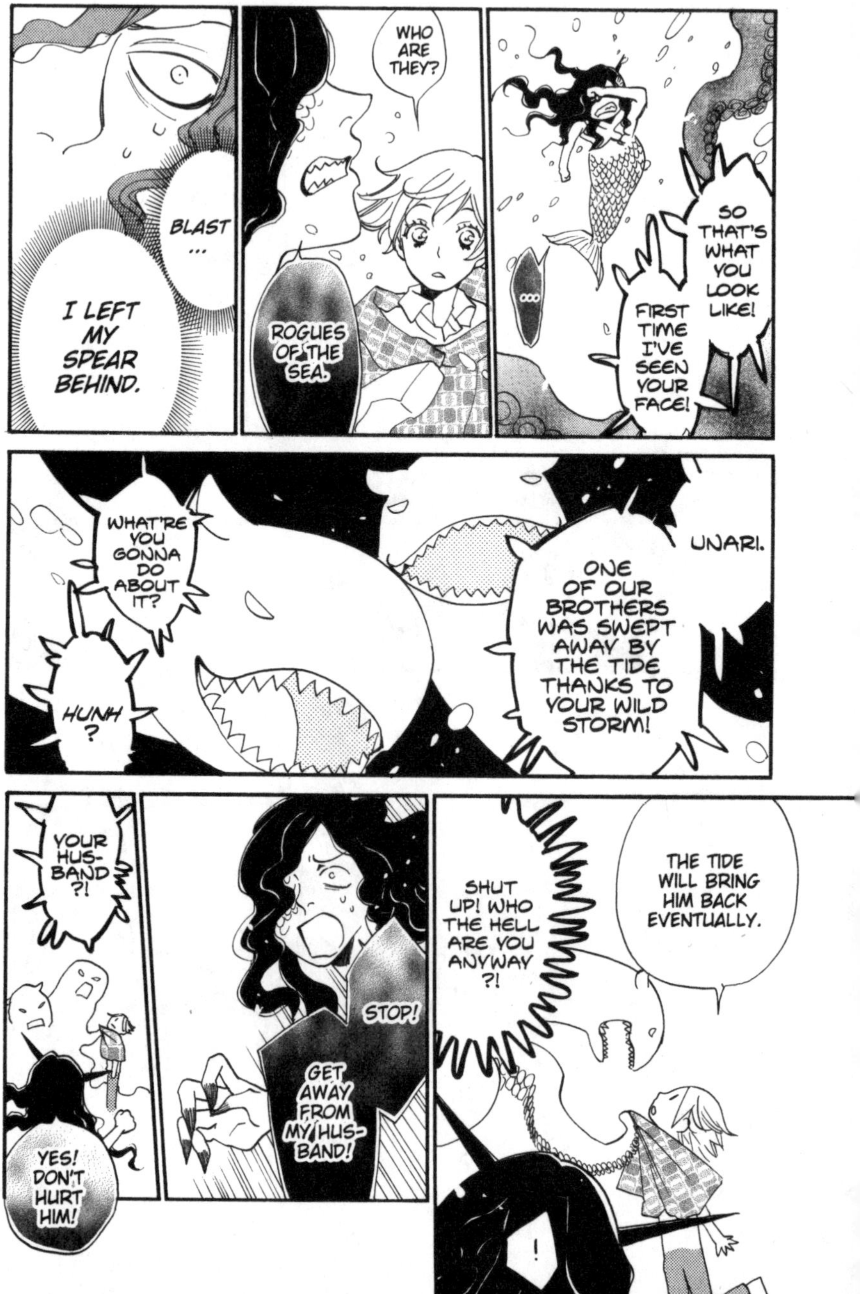
SO THAT'S WHAT YOU LOOK LIKE!
FIRST TIME I'VE SEEN YOUR FACE!
...
WHO ARE THEY?
ROGUES OF THE SEA.
BLAST...
I LEFT MY SPEAR BEHIND.
UNARI.
ONE OF OUR BROTHERS WAS SWEPT AWAY BY THE TIDE THANKS TO YOUR WILD STORM!
WHAT'RE YOU GONNA DO ABOUT IT?
HUNH?
THE TIDE WILL BRING HIM BACK EVENTUALLY.
SHUT UP! WHO THE HELL ARE YOU ANYWAY?!
!
STOP!
GET AWAY FROM MY HUS-BAND!
YOUR HUS-BAND?!
YES! DON'T HURT HIM!

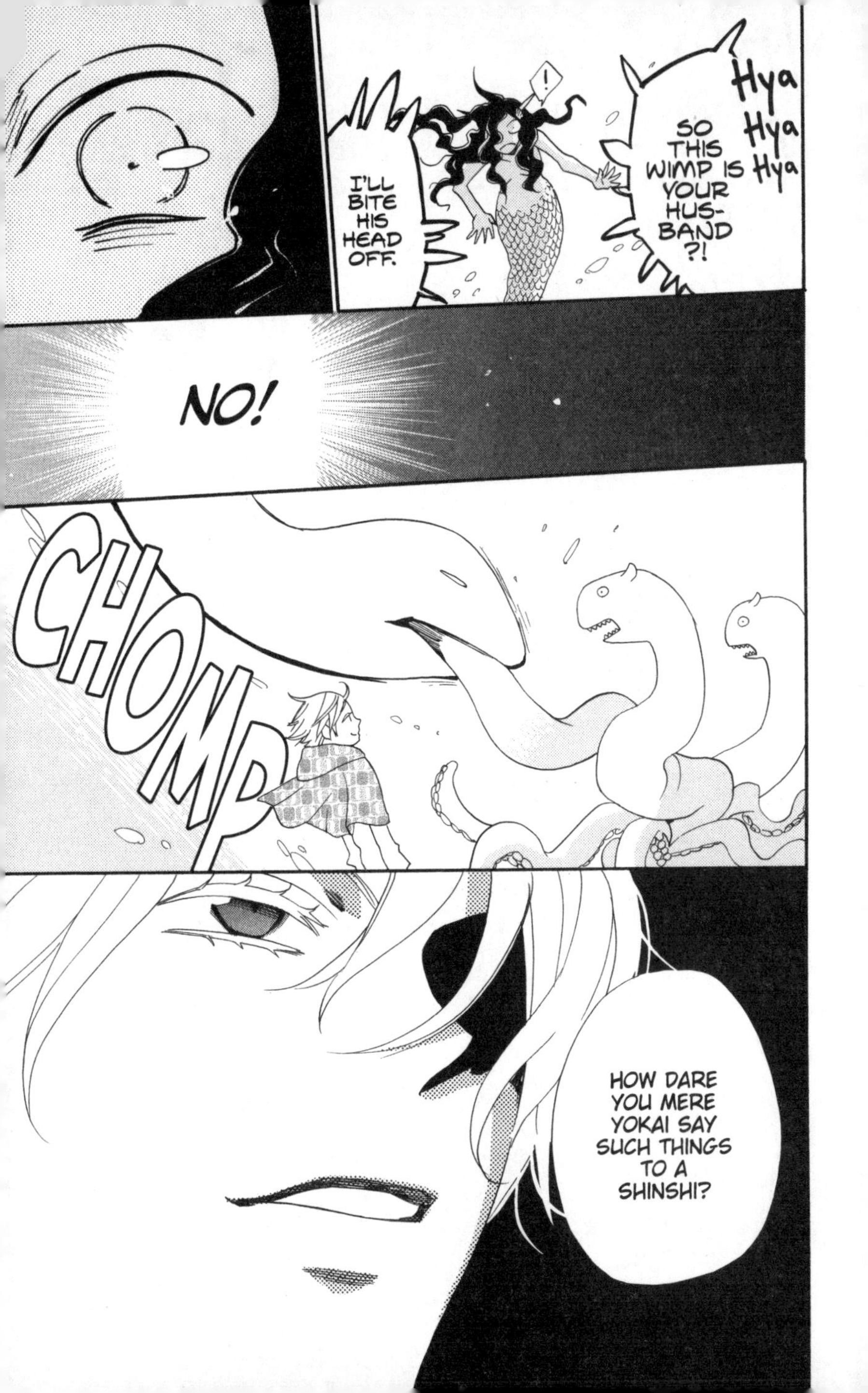
Hya Hya Hya
SO THIS WIMP IS YOUR HUS-BAND ?!
!
I'LL BITE HIS HEAD OFF.
NO!
CHOMP
HOW DARE YOU MERE YOKAI SAY SUCH THINGS TO A SHINSHI?

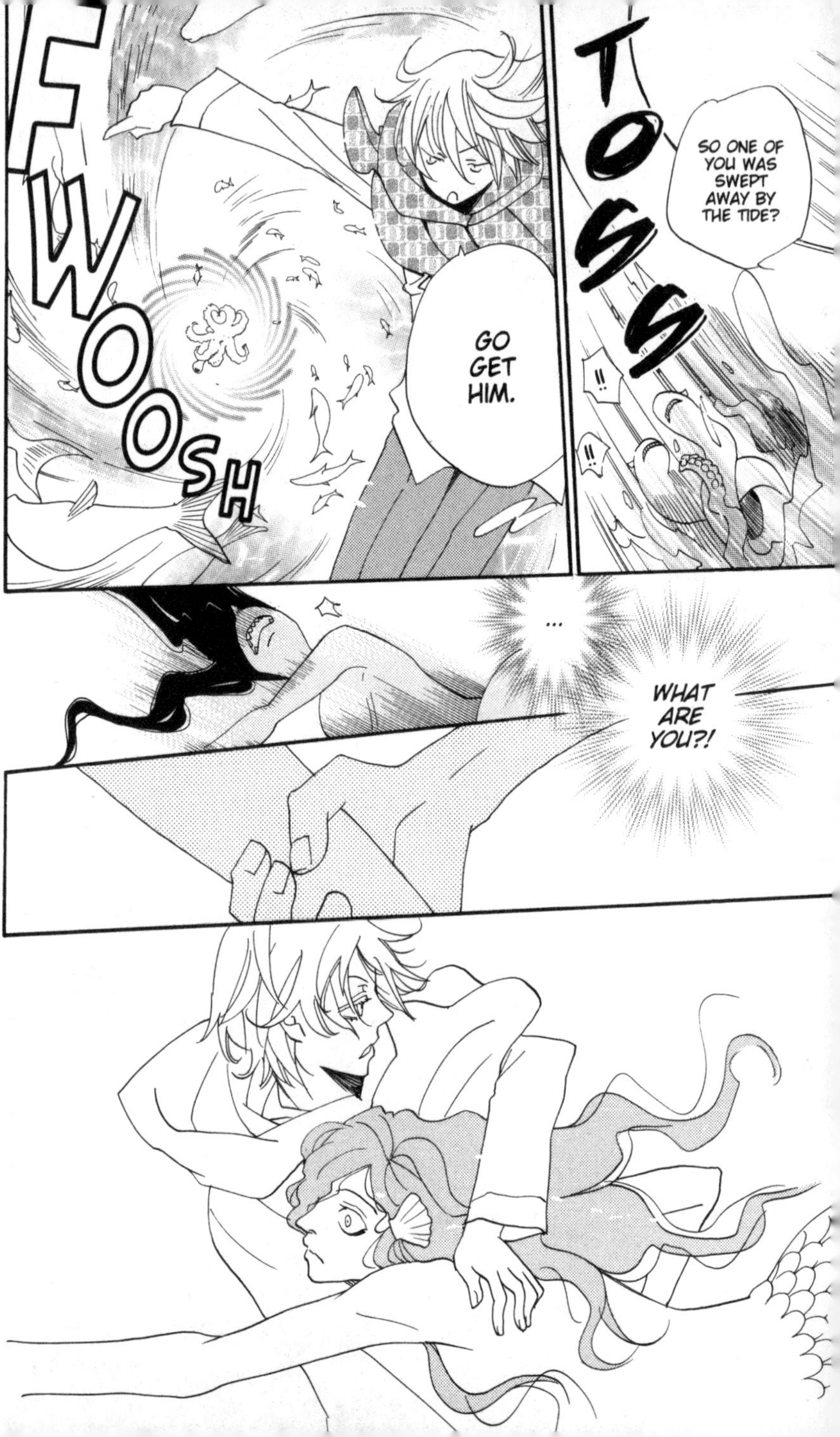
TOSS
SO ONE OF YOU WAS SWEPT AWAY BY THE TIDE?
!!
!!
FWOOSH
GO GET HIM.
...
WHAT ARE YOU?!

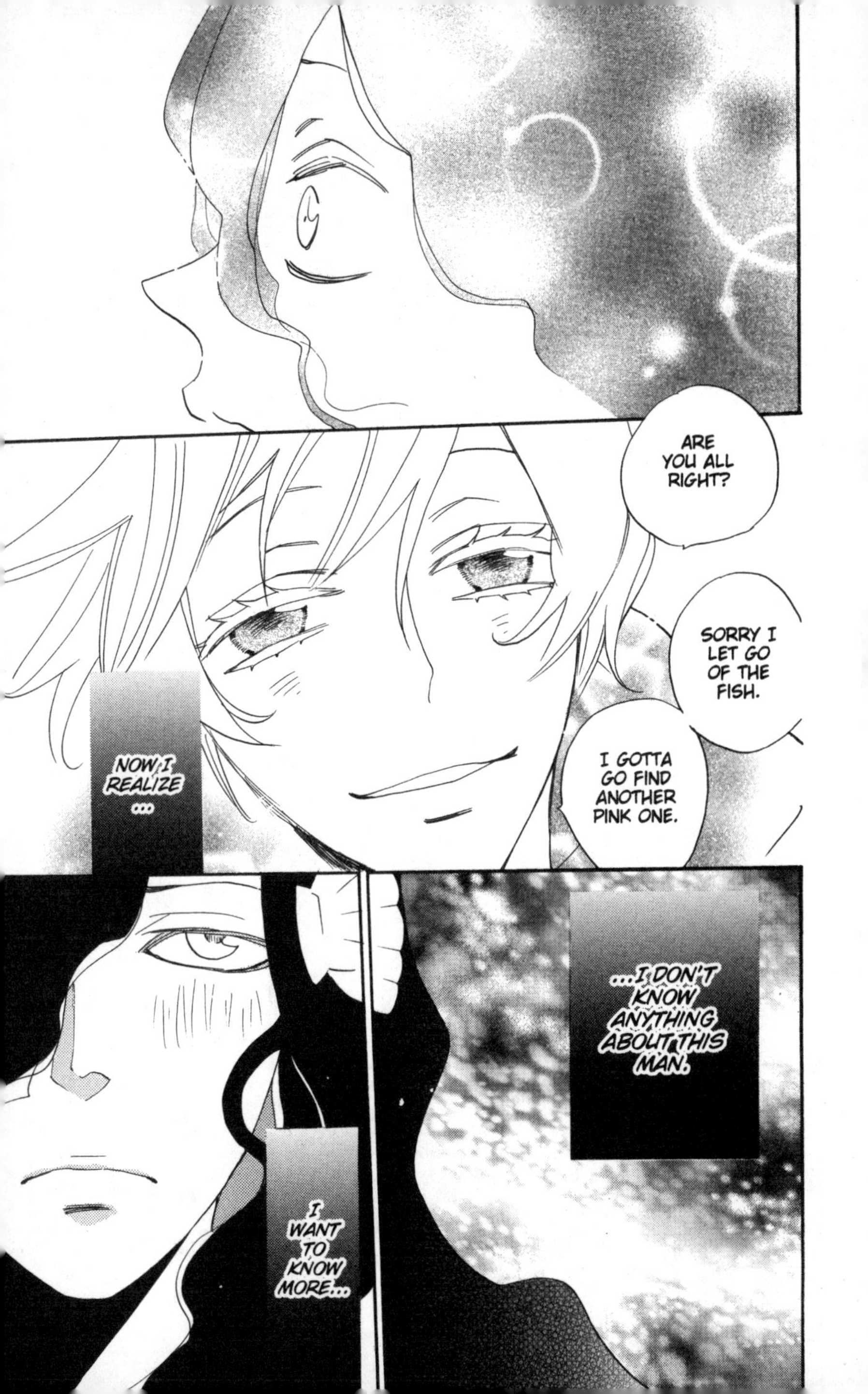
ARE YOU ALL RIGHT?
SORRY I LET GO OF THE FISH.
I GOTTA GO FIND ANOTHER PINK ONE.
NOW I REALIZE ...
...I DON'T KNOW ANYTHING ABOUT THIS MAN.
I WANT TO KNOW MORE...

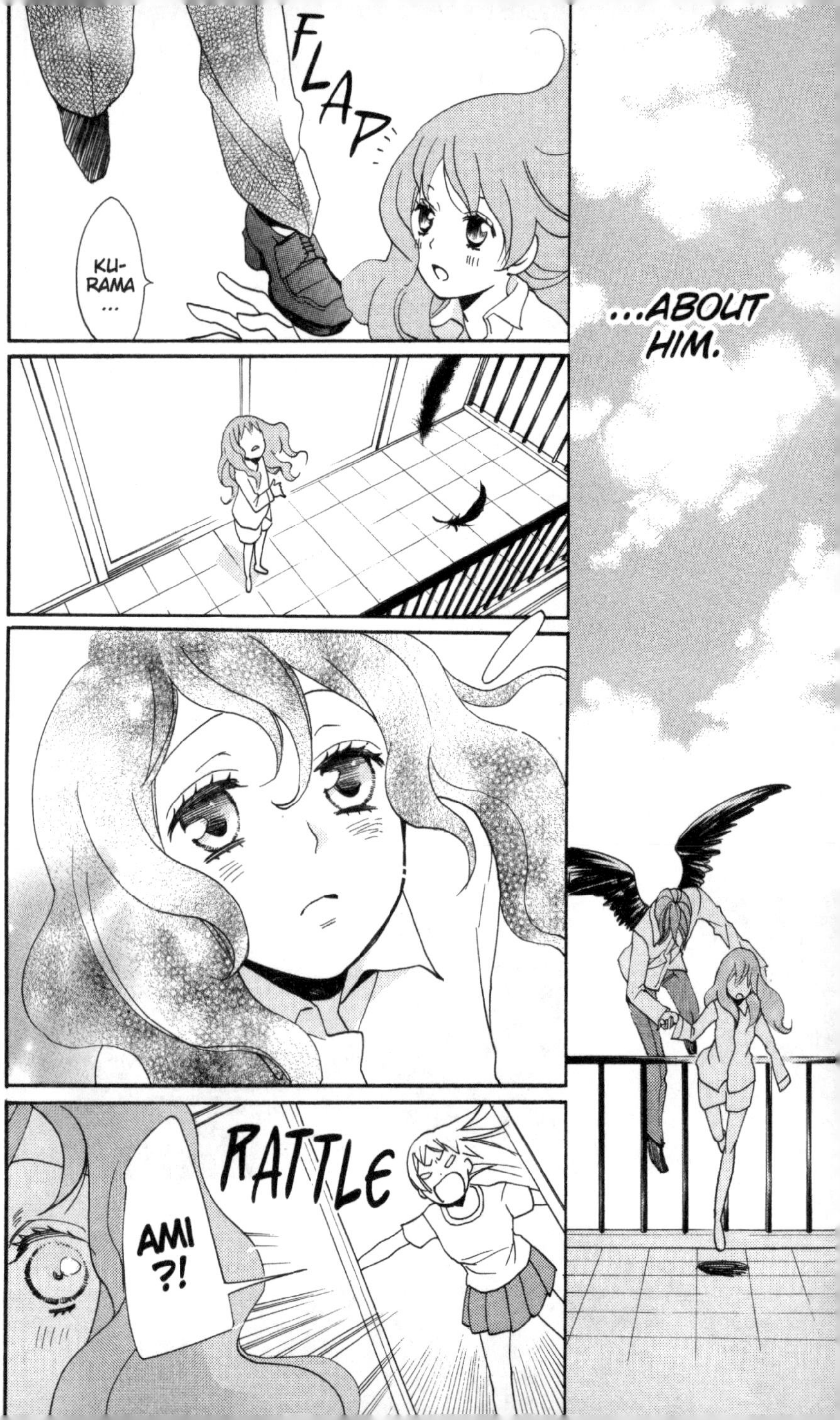
...ABOUT HIM.
FLAP
KU-RAMA ...
RATTLE
AMI ?!

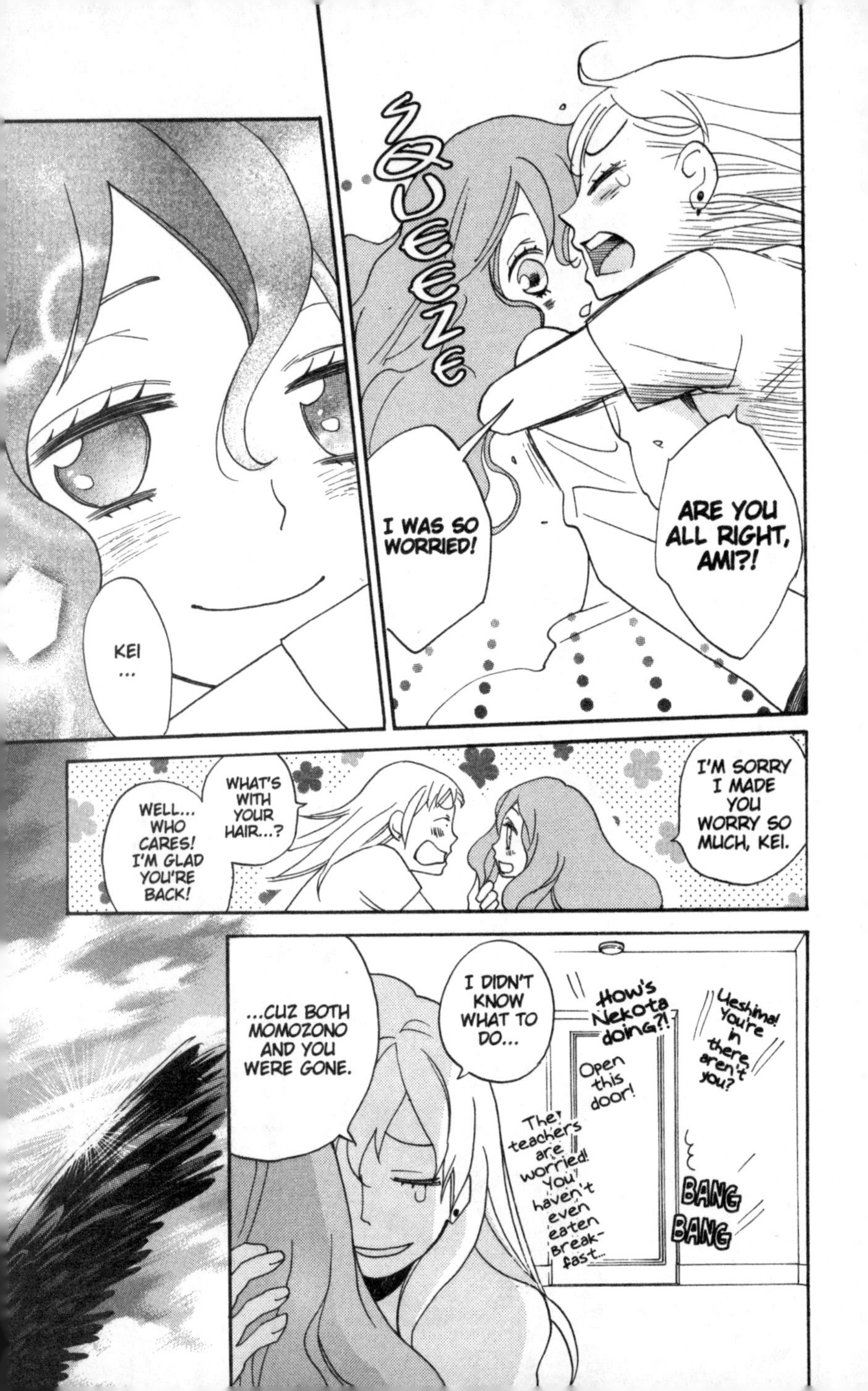
SQUEEZE
ARE YOU ALL RIGHT, AMI?!
I WAS SO WORRIED!
KEI...
I'M SORRY I MADE YOU WORRY SO MUCH, KEI.
WHAT'S WITH YOUR HAIR...?
WELL... WHO CARES! I'M GLAD YOU'RE BACK!
Ueshima! You're in there, aren't you?
How's Nekota doing?!
Open this door!
The teachers are worried! You haven't even eaten breakfast...
BANG BANG
I DIDN'T KNOW WHAT TO DO...
...CUZ BOTH MOMOZONO AND YOU WERE GONE.

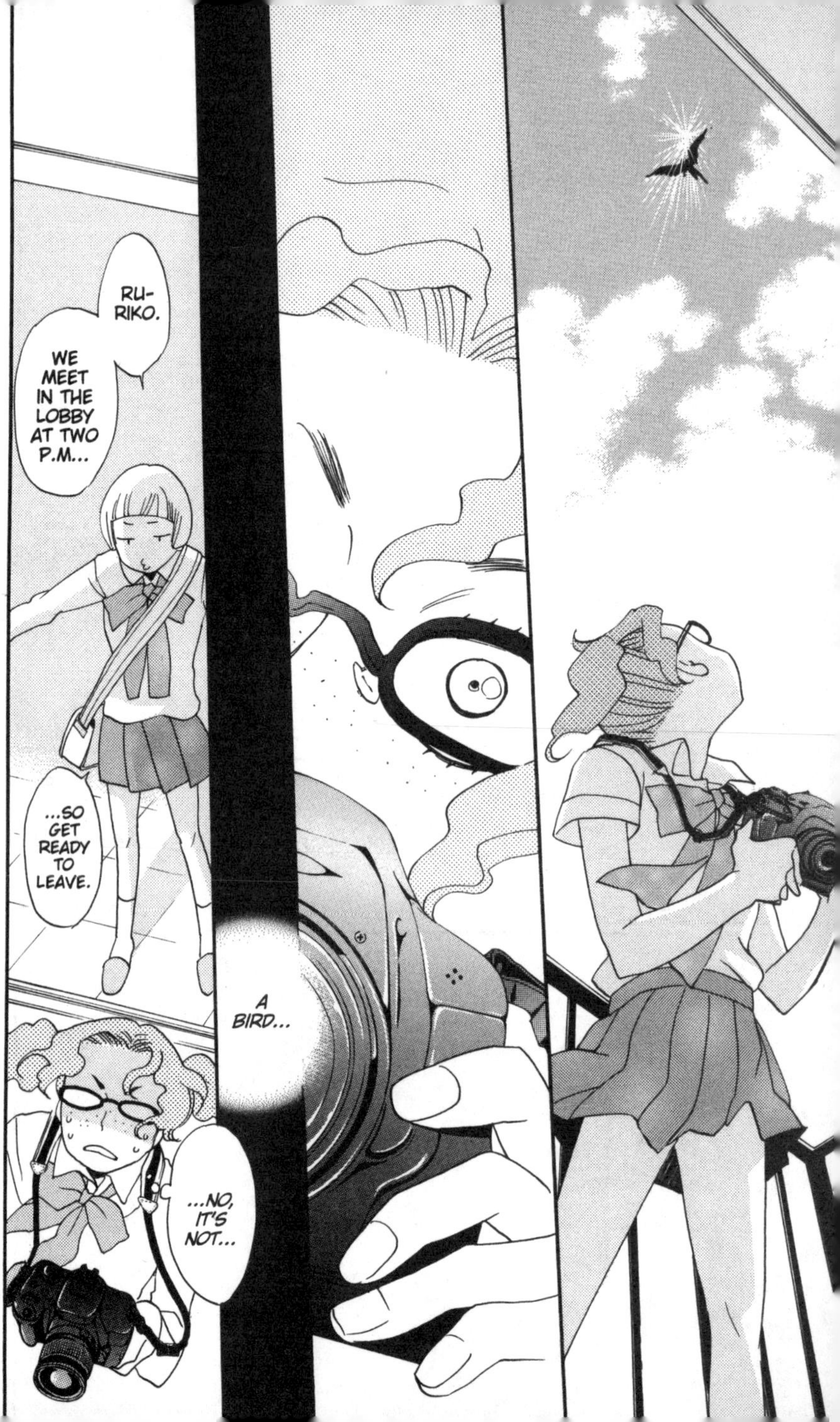
A BIRD...
RU-RIKO.
WE MEET IN THE LOBBY AT TWO P.M...
...SO GET READY TO LEAVE.
...NO, IT'S NOT...

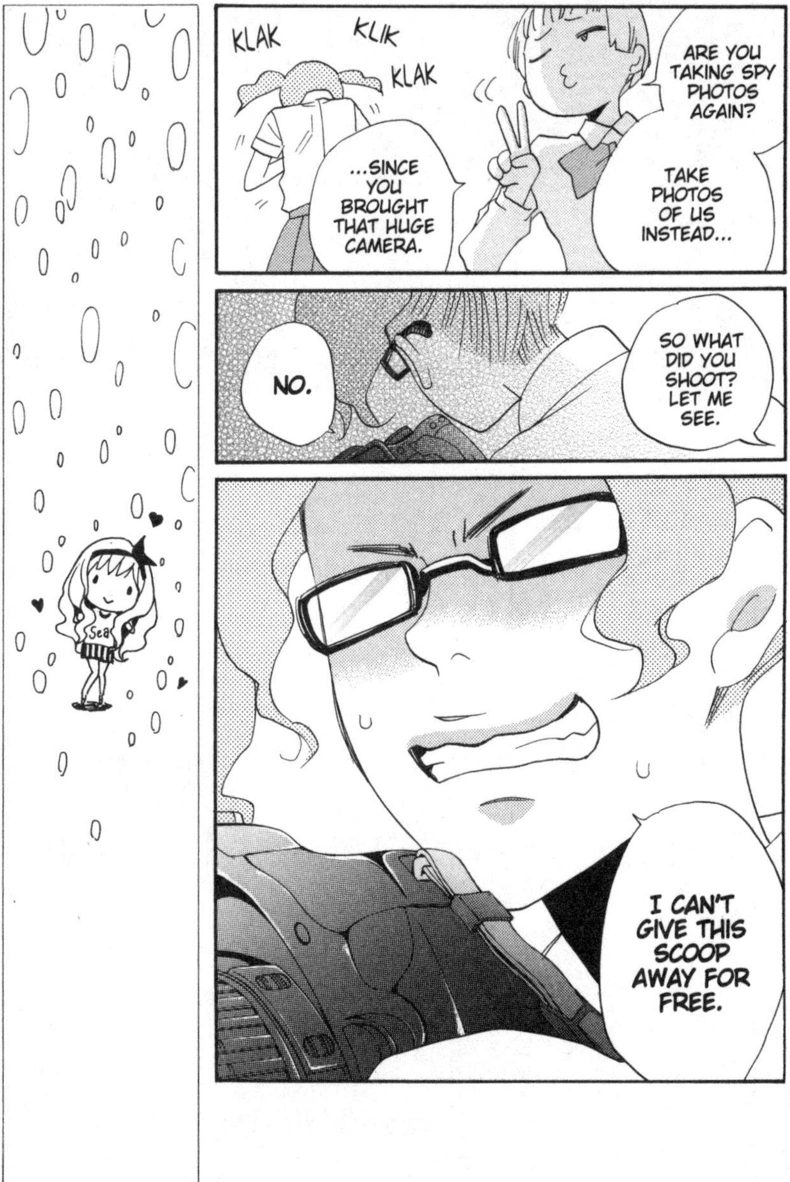
ARE YOU TAKING SPY PHOTOS AGAIN?
TAKE PHOTOS OF US INSTEAD...
KLIK
KLAK
KLAK
...SINCE YOU BROUGHT THAT HUGE CAMERA.
SO WHAT DID YOU SHOOT? LET ME SEE.
NO.
I CAN'T GIVE THIS SCOOP AWAY FOR FREE.
Sea

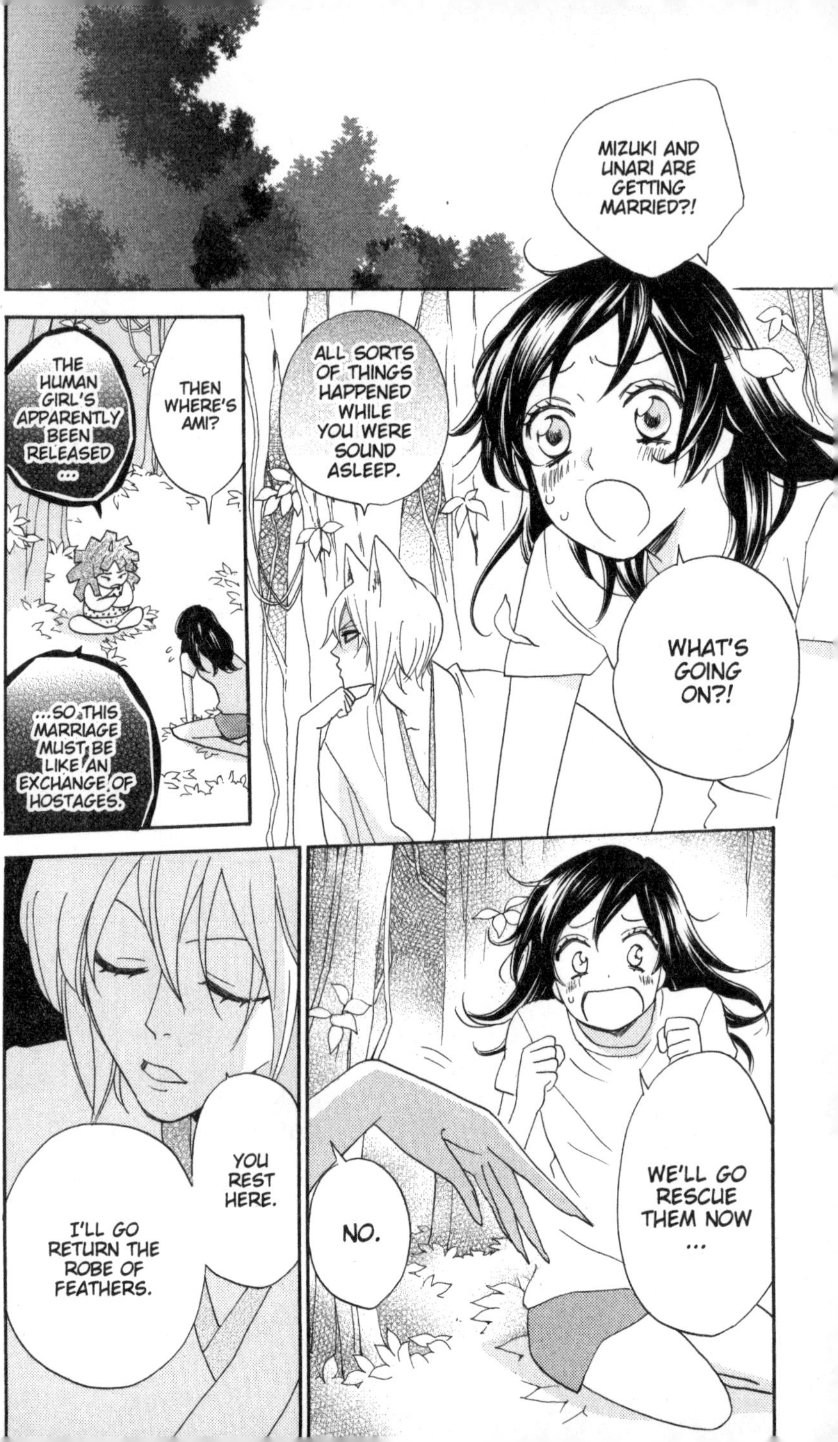
MIZUKI AND UNARI ARE GETTING MARRIED?!
WHAT'S GOING ON?!
ALL SORTS OF THINGS HAPPENED WHILE YOU WERE SOUND ASLEEP.
THEN WHERE'S AMI?
THE HUMAN GIRL'S APPARENTLY BEEN RELEASED ...
...SO THIS MARRIAGE MUST BE LIKE AN EXCHANGE OF HOSTAGES.
WE'LL GO RESCUE THEM NOW ...
NO.
YOU REST HERE.
I'LL GO RETURN THE ROBE OF FEATHERS.

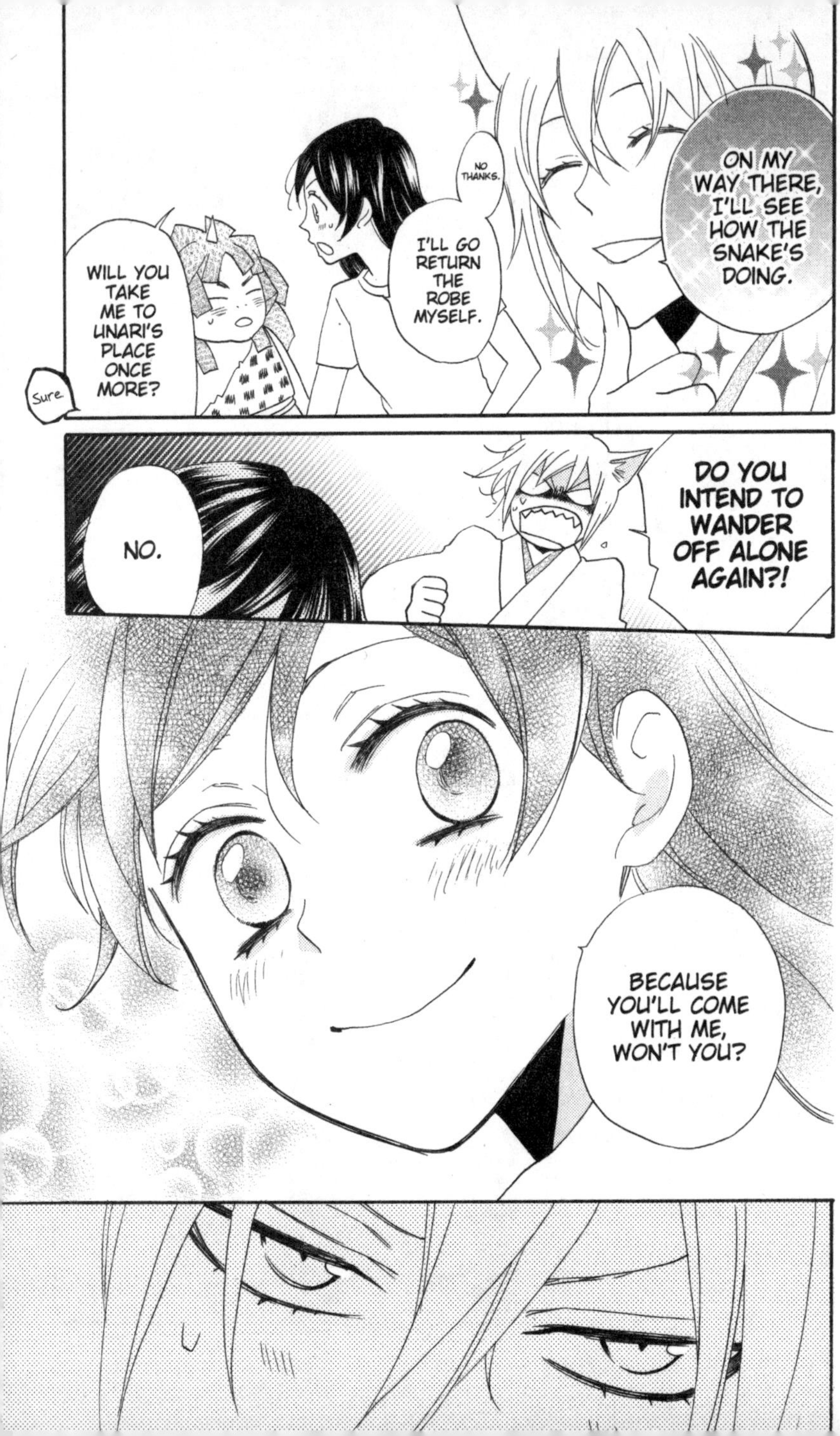
ON MY WAY THERE, I'LL SEE HOW THE SNAKE'S DOING.
NO THANKS.
I'LL GO RETURN THE ROBE MYSELF.
WILL YOU TAKE ME TO UNARI'S PLACE ONCE MORE?
Sure.
DO YOU INTEND TO WANDER OFF ALONE AGAIN?!
NO.
BECAUSE YOU'LL COME WITH ME, WON'T YOU?

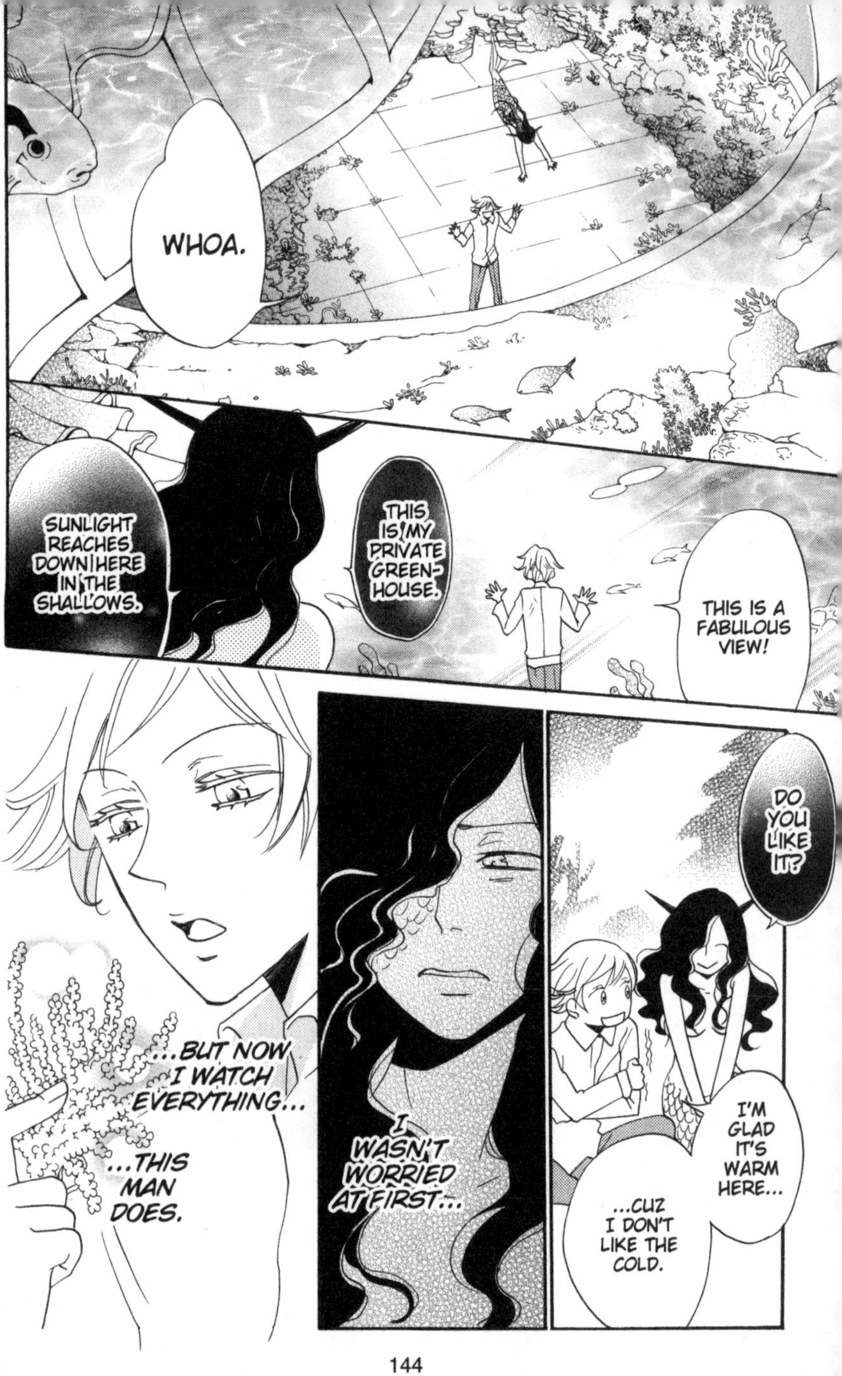
WHOA.
THIS IS A FABULOUS VIEW!
THIS IS MY PRIVATE GREENHOUSE.
SUNLIGHT REACHES DOWN HERE IN THE SHALLOWS.
DO YOU LIKE IT?
I'M GLAD IT'S WARM HERE...
...CUZ I DON'T LIKE THE COLD.
I WASN'T WORRIED AT FIRST...
...BUT NOW I WATCH EVERYTHING...
...THIS MAN DOES.

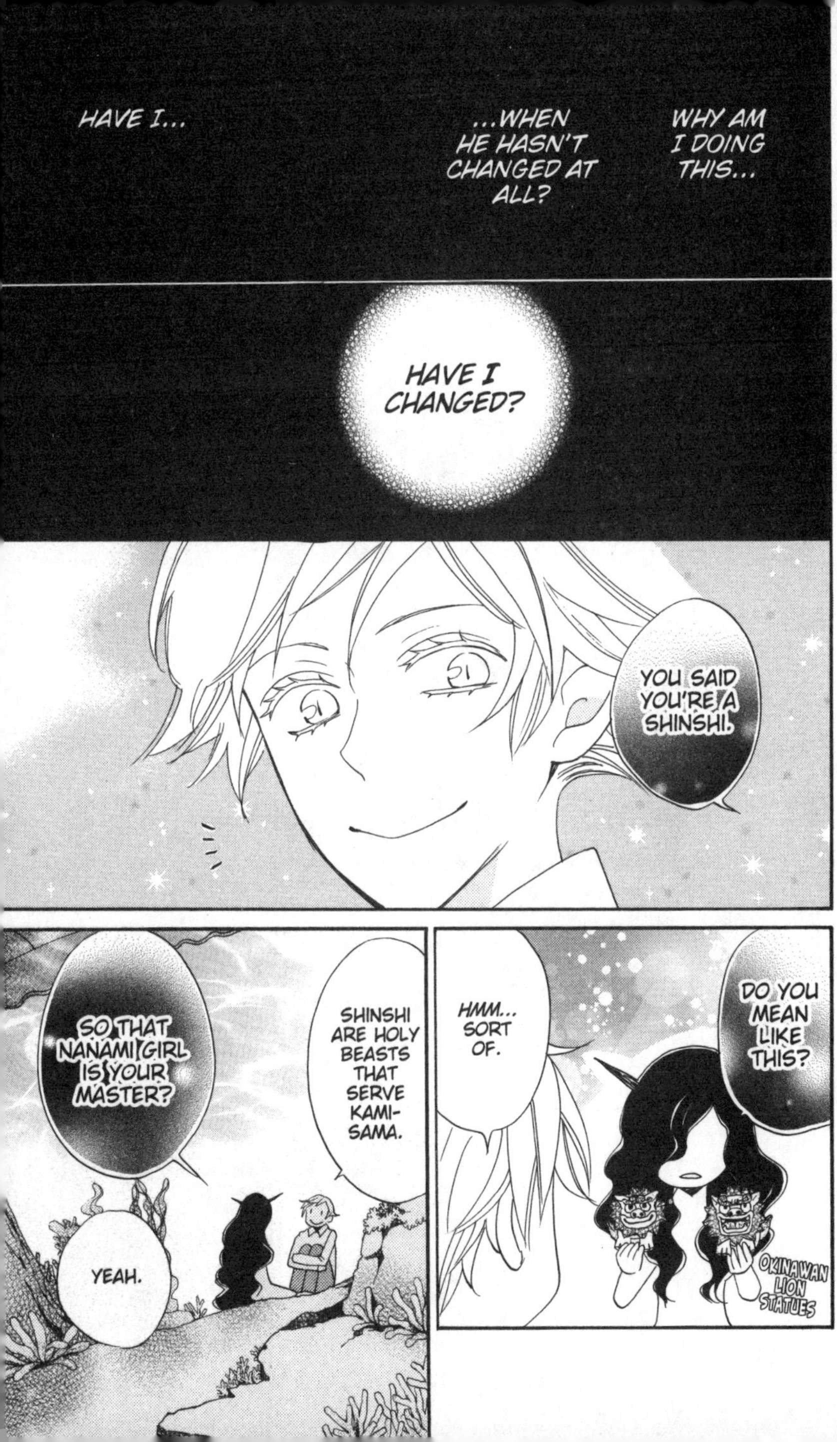
WHY AM I DOING THIS...
...WHEN HE HASN'T CHANGED AT ALL?
HAVE I...
HAVE I CHANGED?
YOU SAID YOU'RE A SHINSHI.
DO YOU MEAN LIKE THIS?
HMM... SORT OF.
OKINAWAN LION STATUES
SHINSHI ARE HOLY BEASTS THAT SERVE KAMI-SAMA.
SO THAT NANAMI GIRL IS YOUR MASTER?
YEAH.

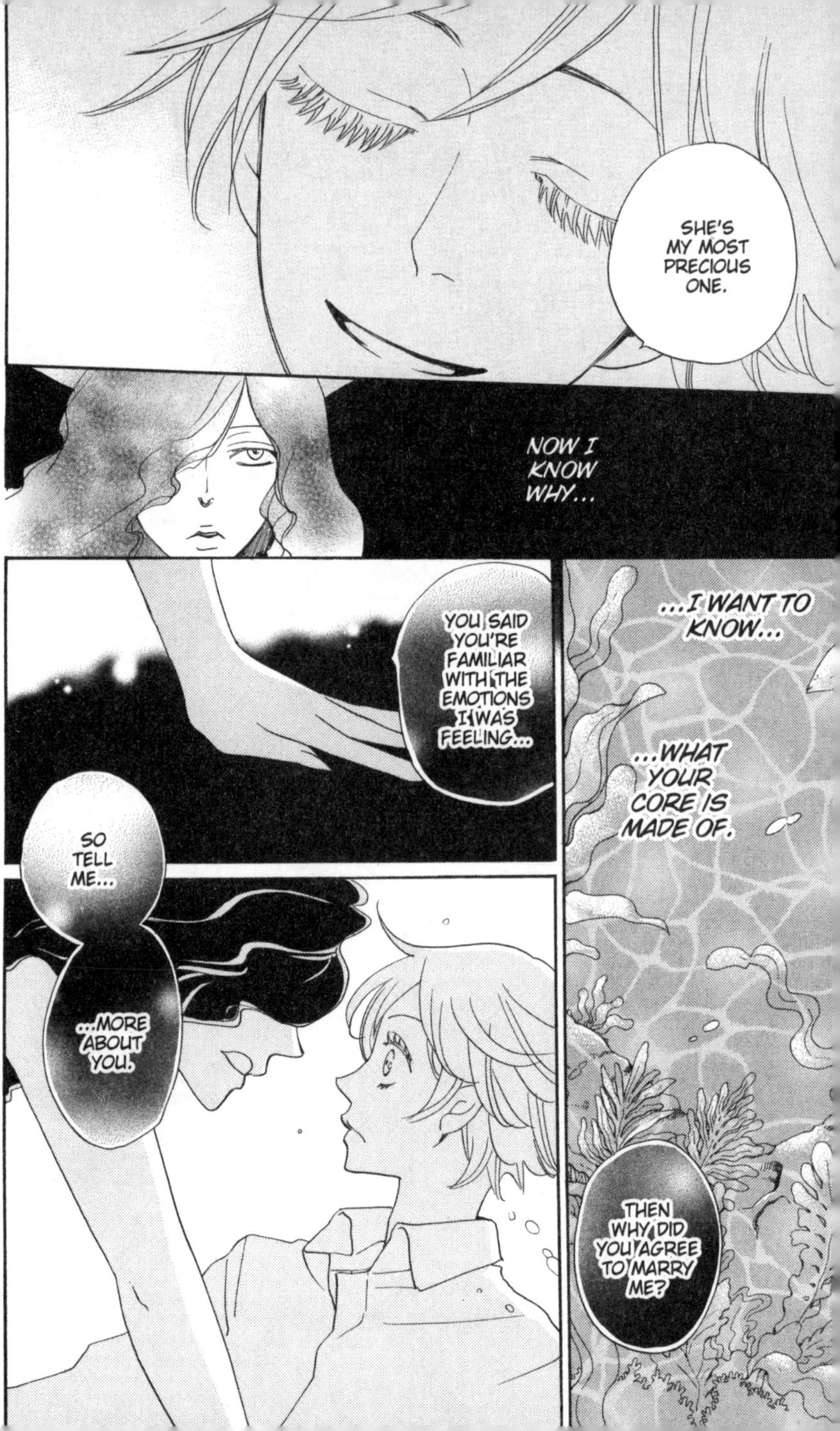
SHE'S MY MOST PRECIOUS ONE.
NOW I KNOW WHY...
YOU SAID YOU'RE FAMILIAR WITH THE EMOTIONS I WAS FEELING...
SO TELL ME...
...MORE ABOUT YOU.
...I WANT TO KNOW...
...WHAT YOUR CORE IS MADE OF.
THEN WHY DID YOU AGREE TO MARRY ME?

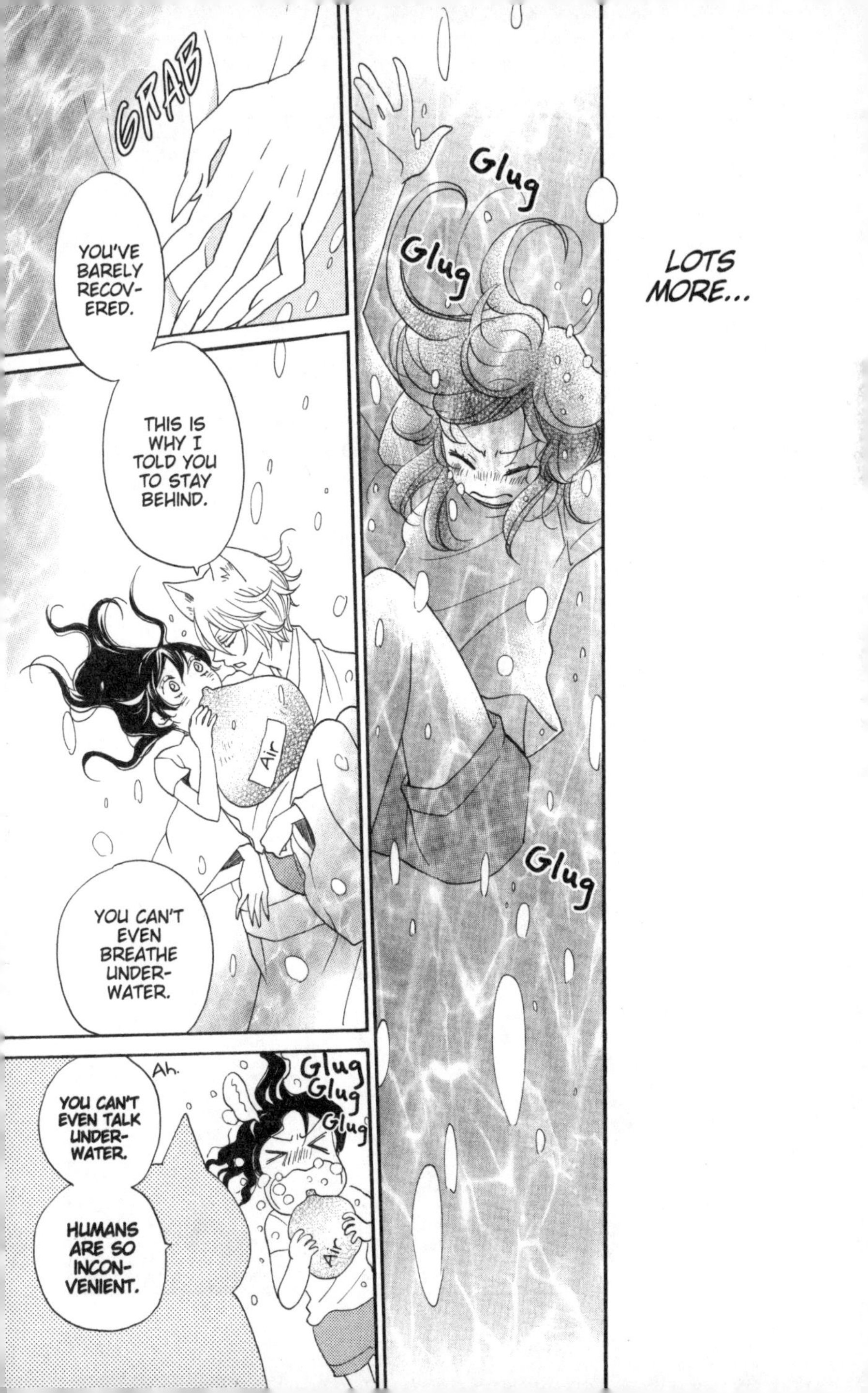
LOTS MORE...
Glug
Glug
Glug
GRAB
YOU'VE BARELY RECOV-ERED.
THIS IS WHY I TOLD YOU TO STAY BEHIND.
Air
YOU CAN'T EVEN BREATHE UNDER-WATER.
Glug Glug Glug
Ah.
YOU CAN'T EVEN TALK UNDER-WATER.
HUMANS ARE SO INCON-VENIENT.
Air

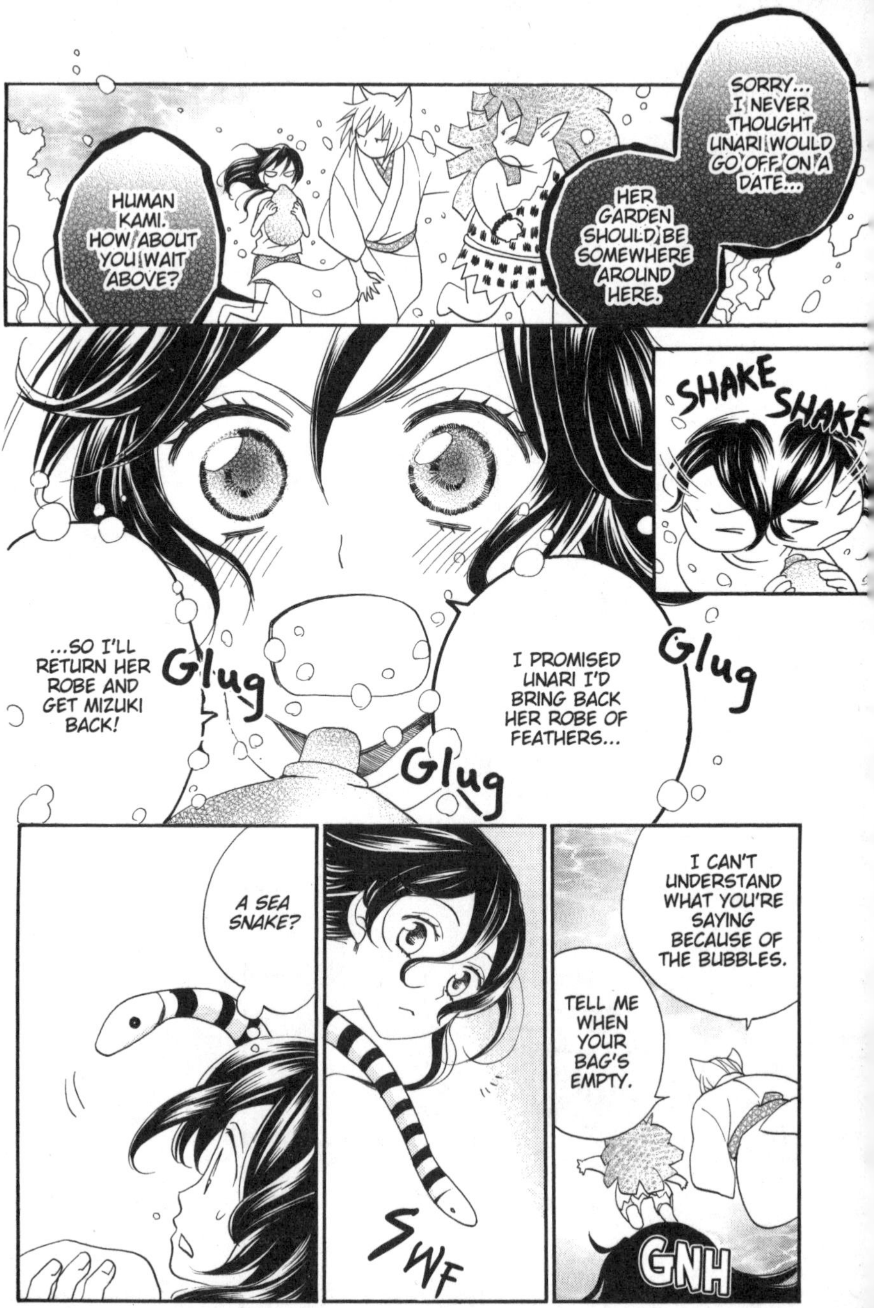
SORRY... I NEVER THOUGHT UNARI WOULD GO OFF ON A DATE...
HER GARDEN SHOULD BE SOMEWHERE AROUND HERE.
HUMAN KAMI. HOW ABOUT YOU WAIT ABOVE?
SHAKE SHAKE
Glug
I PROMISED UNARI I'D BRING BACK HER ROBE OF FEATHERS...
Glug
Glug
...SO I'LL RETURN HER ROBE AND GET MIZUKI BACK!
I CAN'T UNDERSTAND WHAT YOU'RE SAYING BECAUSE OF THE BUBBLES.
TELL ME WHEN YOUR BAG'S EMPTY.
GNH
SWF
A SEA SNAKE?

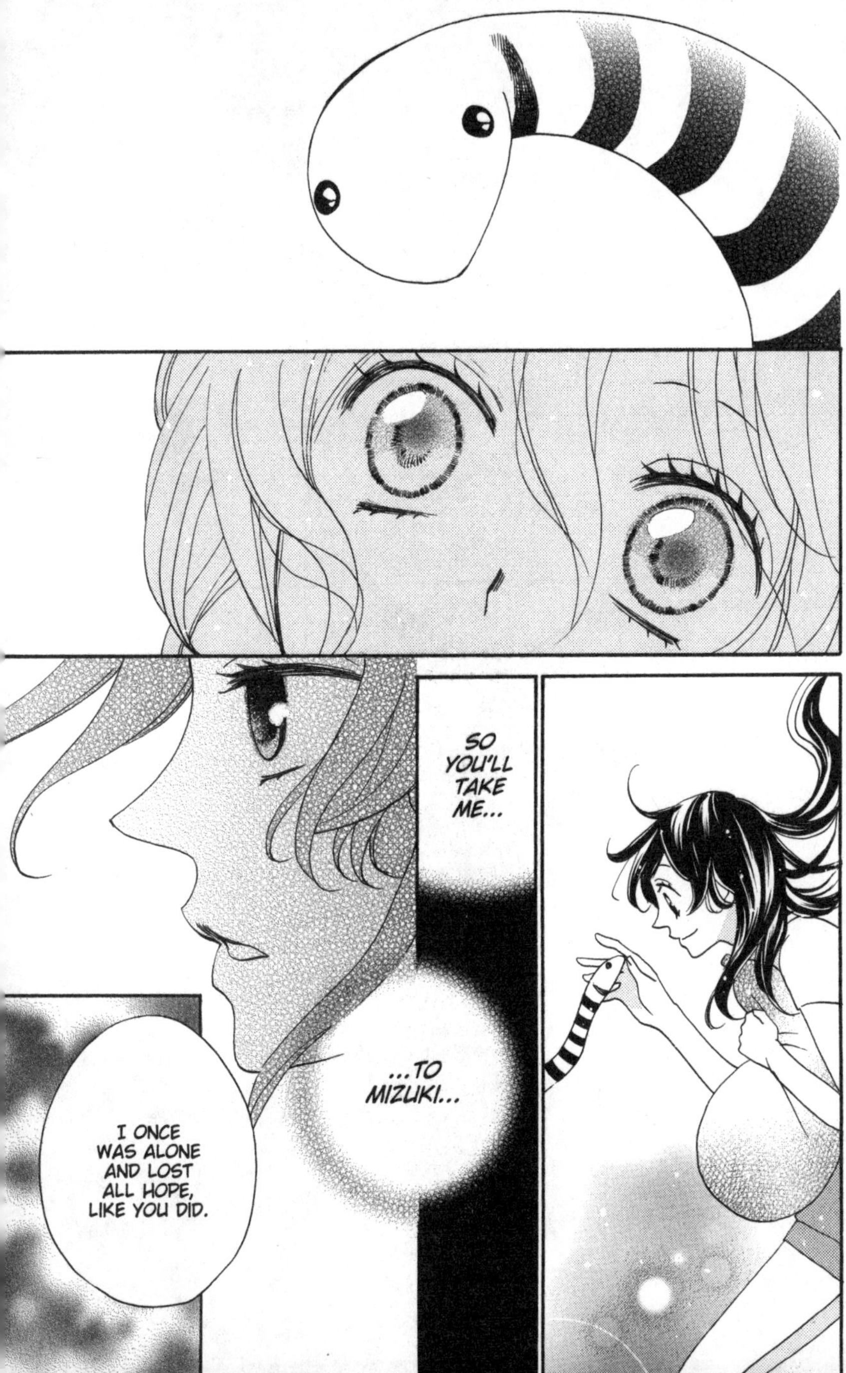
SO YOU'LL TAKE ME...
...TO MIZUKI...
I ONCE WAS ALONE AND LOST ALL HOPE, LIKE YOU DID.

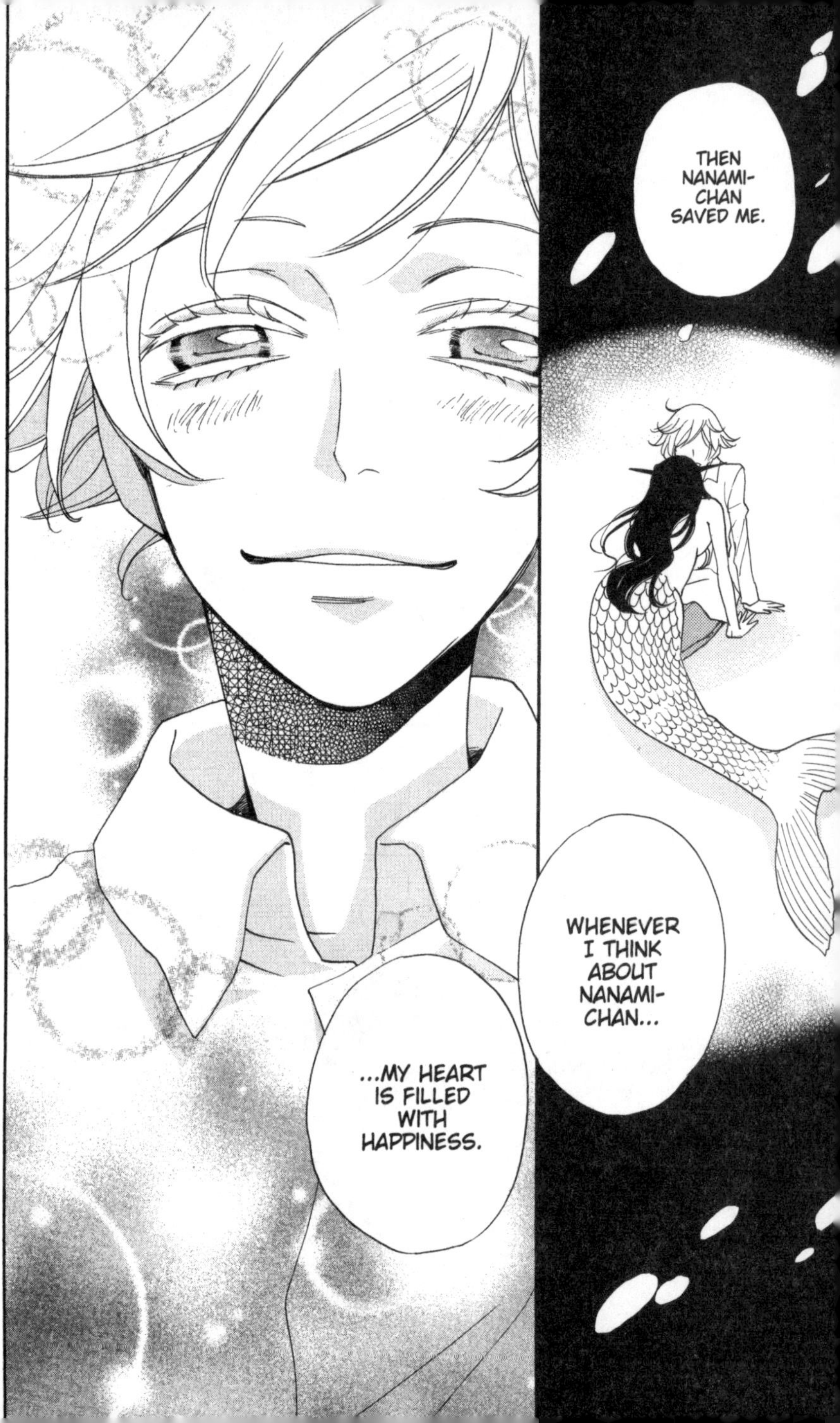
THEN NANAMI-CHAN SAVED ME.
WHENEVER I THINK ABOUT NANAMI-CHAN...
...MY HEART IS FILLED WITH HAPPINESS.

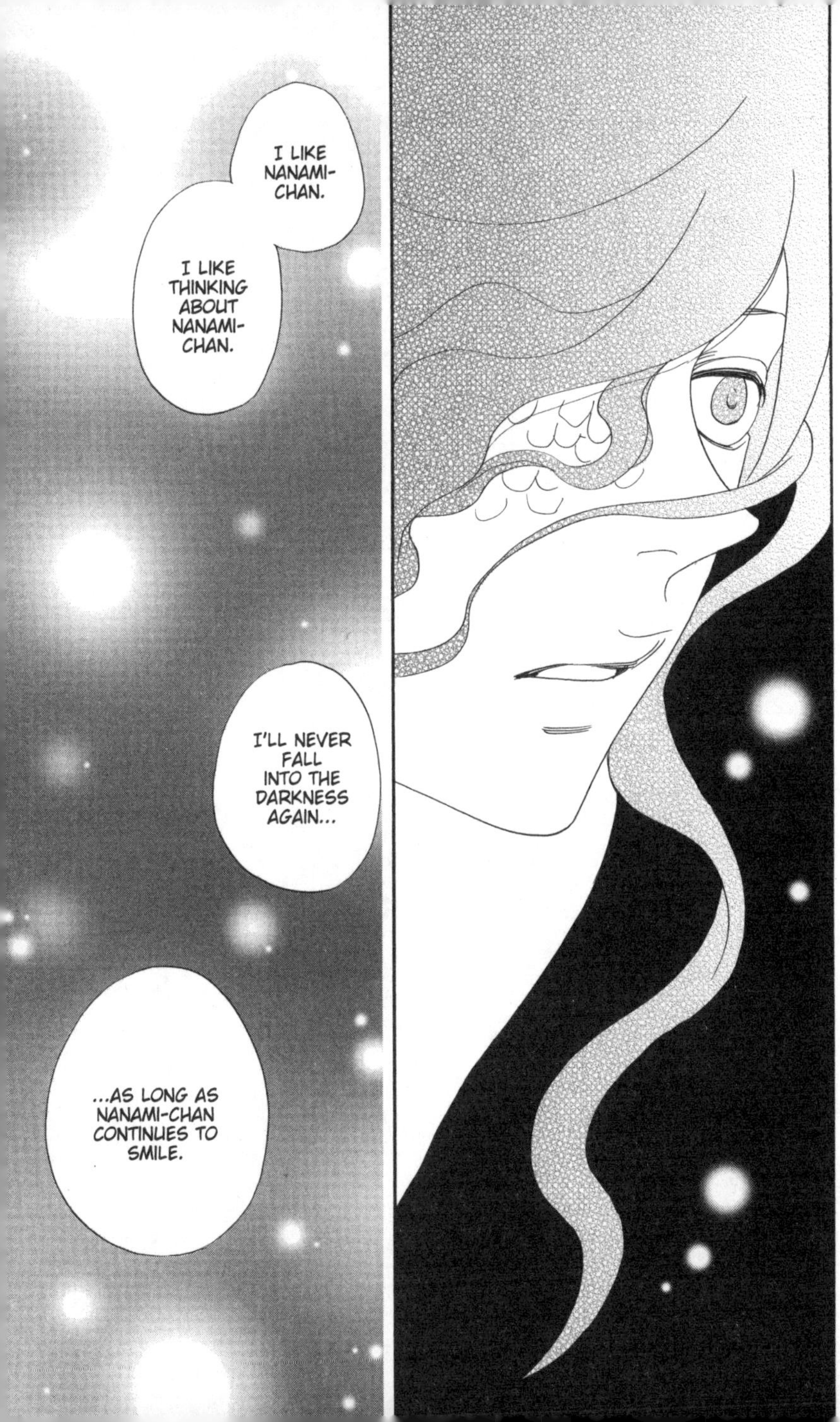
I LIKE NANAMI-CHAN.
I LIKE THINKING ABOUT NANAMI-CHAN.
I'LL NEVER FALL INTO THE DARKNESS AGAIN...
...AS LONG AS NANAMI-CHAN CONTINUES TO SMILE.

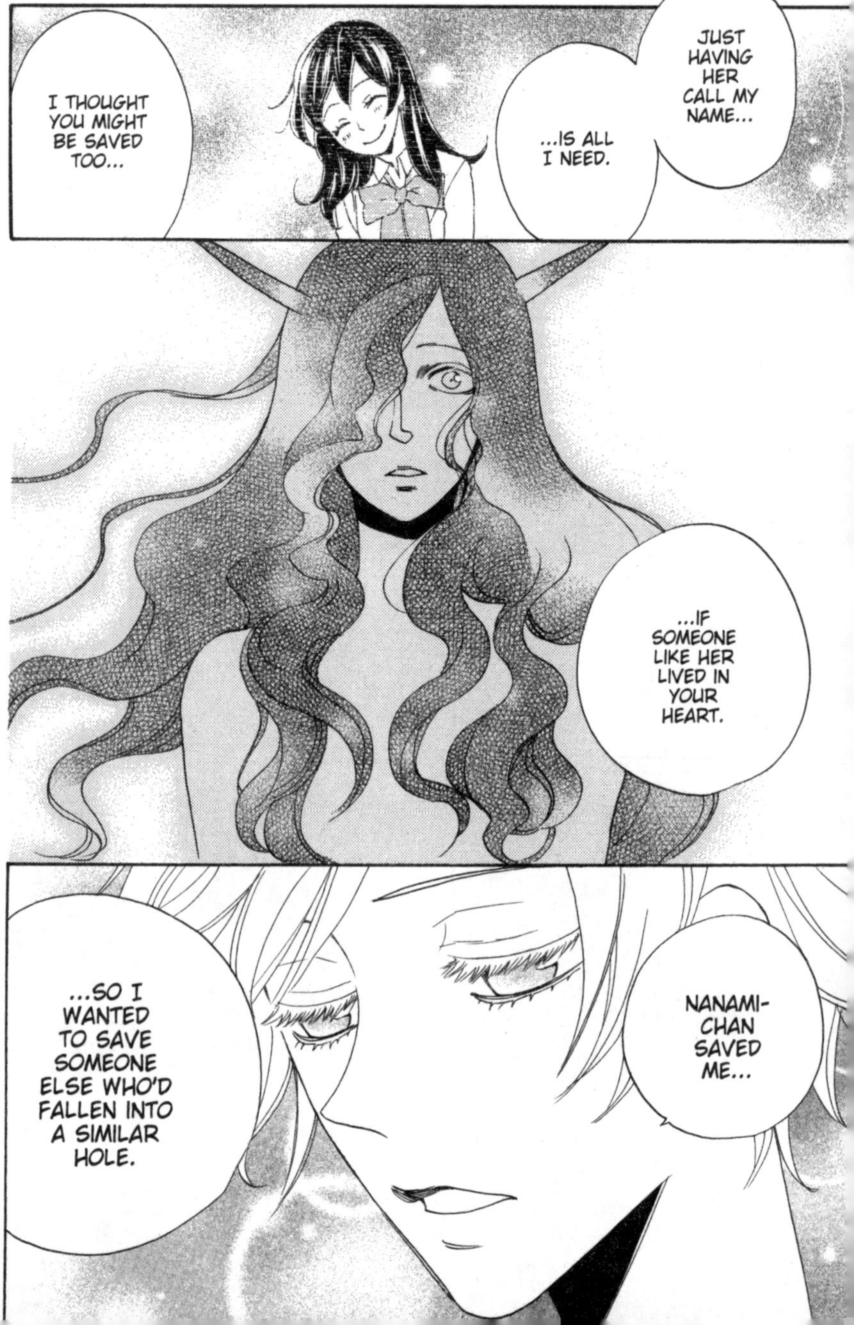
JUST HAVING HER CALL MY NAME...
...IS ALL I NEED.
I THOUGHT YOU MIGHT BE SAVED TOO...
...IF SOMEONE LIKE HER LIVED IN YOUR HEART.
NANAMI-CHAN SAVED ME...
...SO I WANTED TO SAVE SOMEONE ELSE WHO'D FALLEN INTO A SIMILAR HOLE.

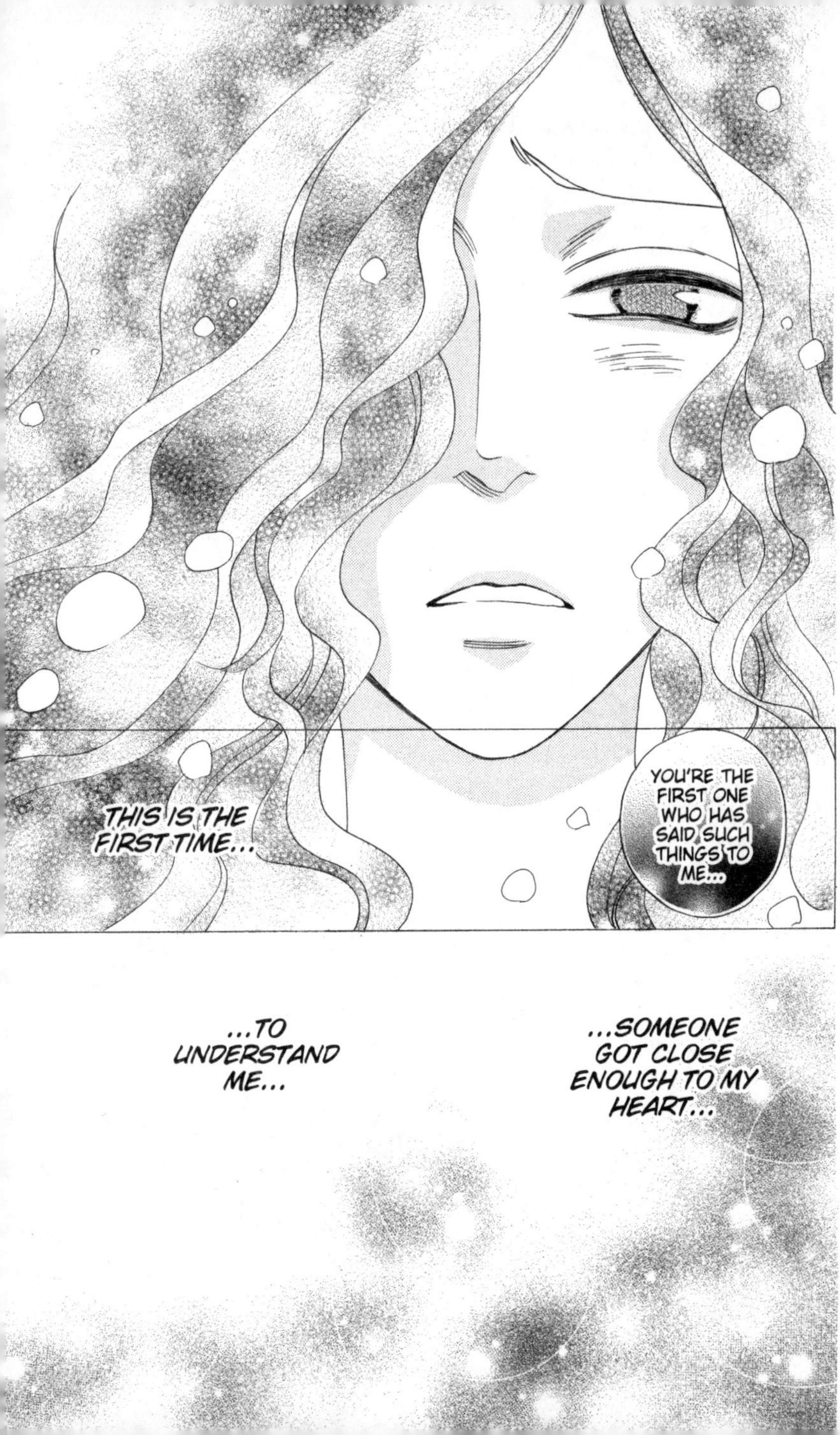
YOU'RE THE FIRST ONE WHO HAS SAID SUCH THINGS TO ME...
THIS IS THE FIRST TIME...
...SOMEONE GOT CLOSE ENOUGH TO MY HEART...
...TO UNDERSTAND ME...

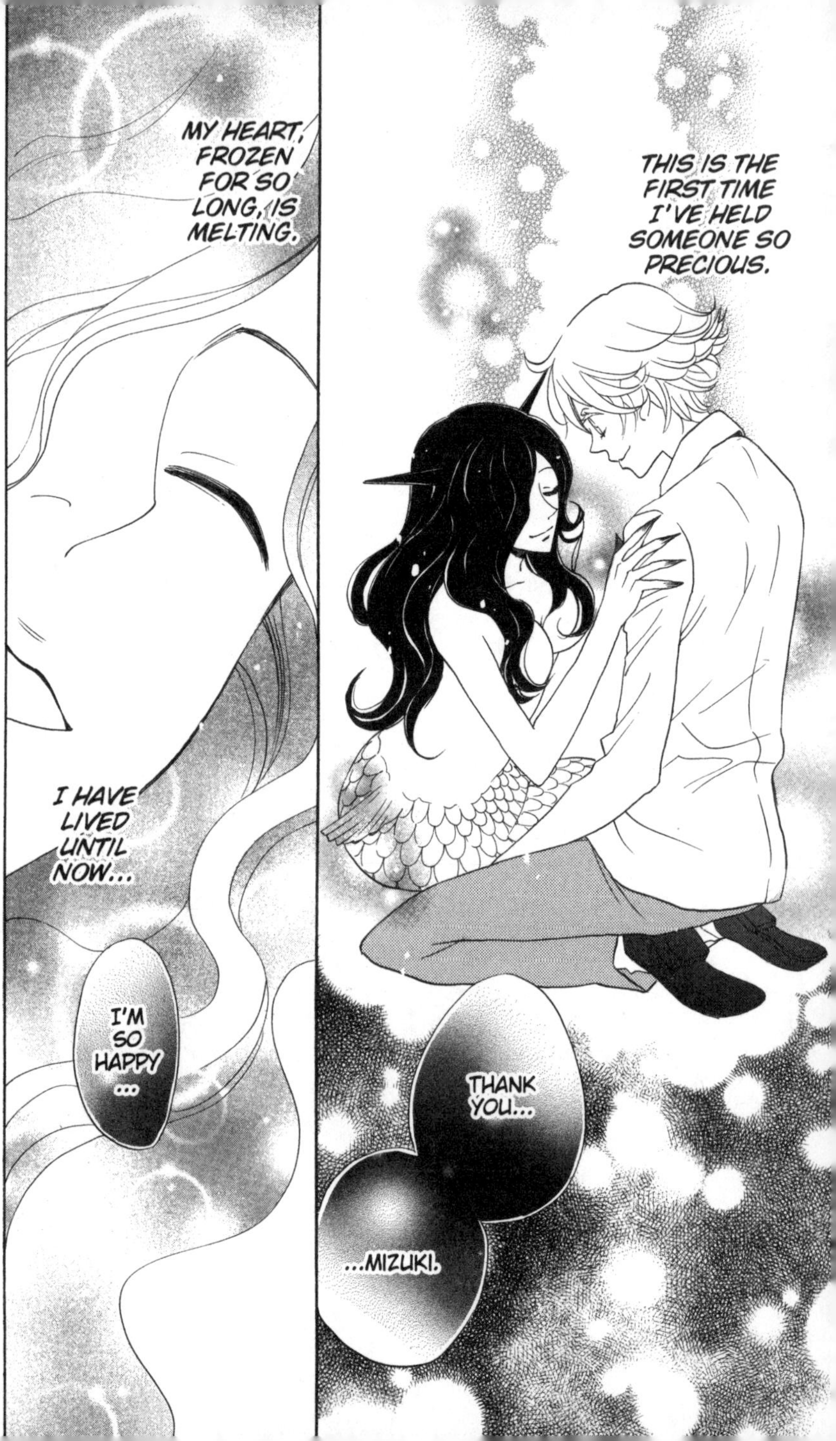
THIS IS THE FIRST TIME I'VE HELD SOMEONE SO PRECIOUS.
THANK YOU...
...MIZUKI.
MY HEART, FROZEN FOR SO LONG, IS MELTING.
I HAVE LIVED UNTIL NOW...
I'M SO HAPPY...

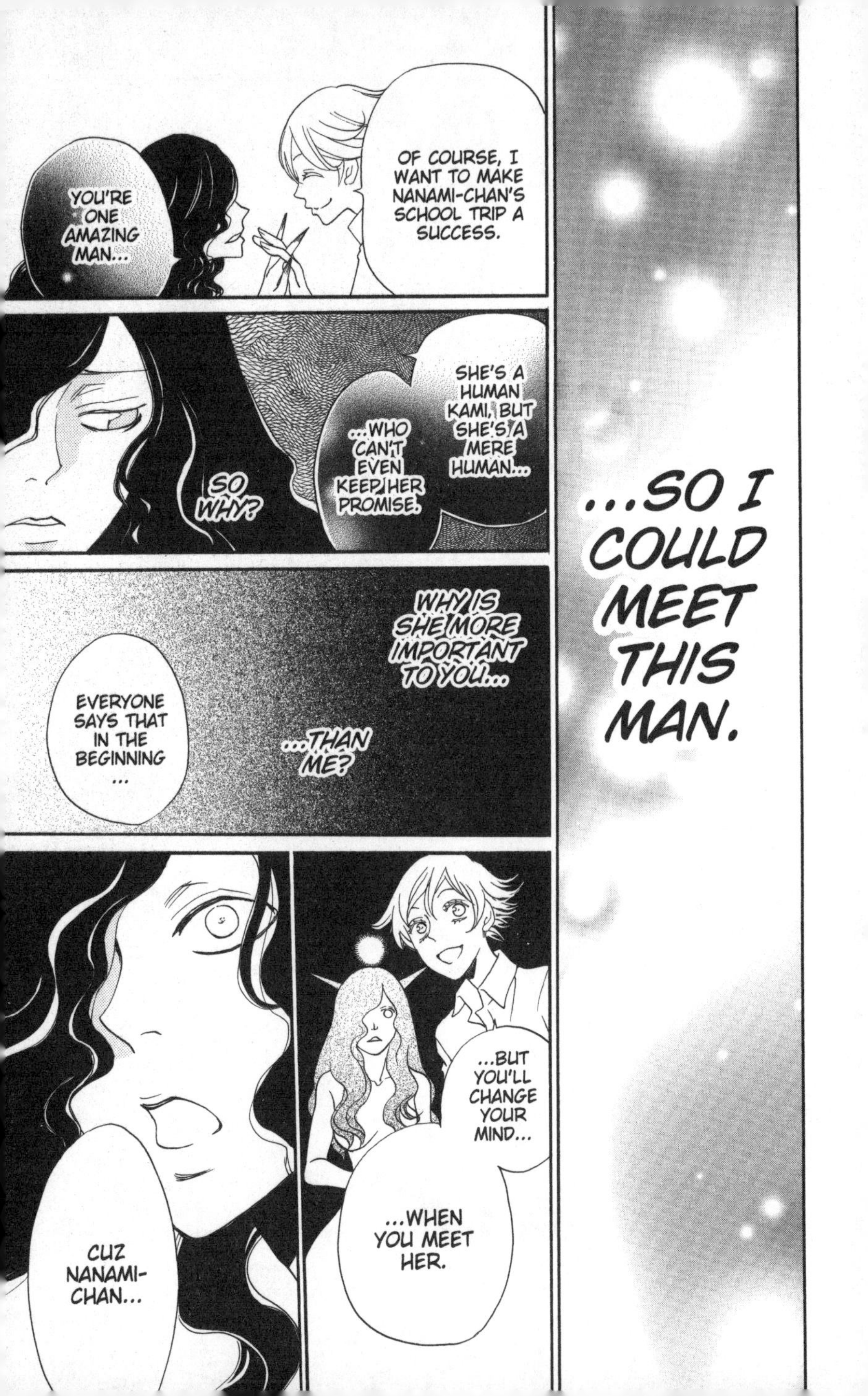
...SO I COULD MEET THIS MAN.
OF COURSE, I WANT TO MAKE NANAMI-CHAN'S SCHOOL TRIP A SUCCESS.
YOU'RE ONE AMAZING MAN...
SHE'S A HUMAN KAMI, BUT SHE'S A MERE HUMAN...
...WHO CAN'T EVEN KEEP HER PROMISE.
SO WHY?
WHY IS SHE MORE IMPORTANT TO YOU...
...THAN ME?
EVERYONE SAYS THAT IN THE BEGINNING...
...BUT YOU'LL CHANGE YOUR MIND...
...WHEN YOU MEET HER.
CUZ NANAMI-CHAN...

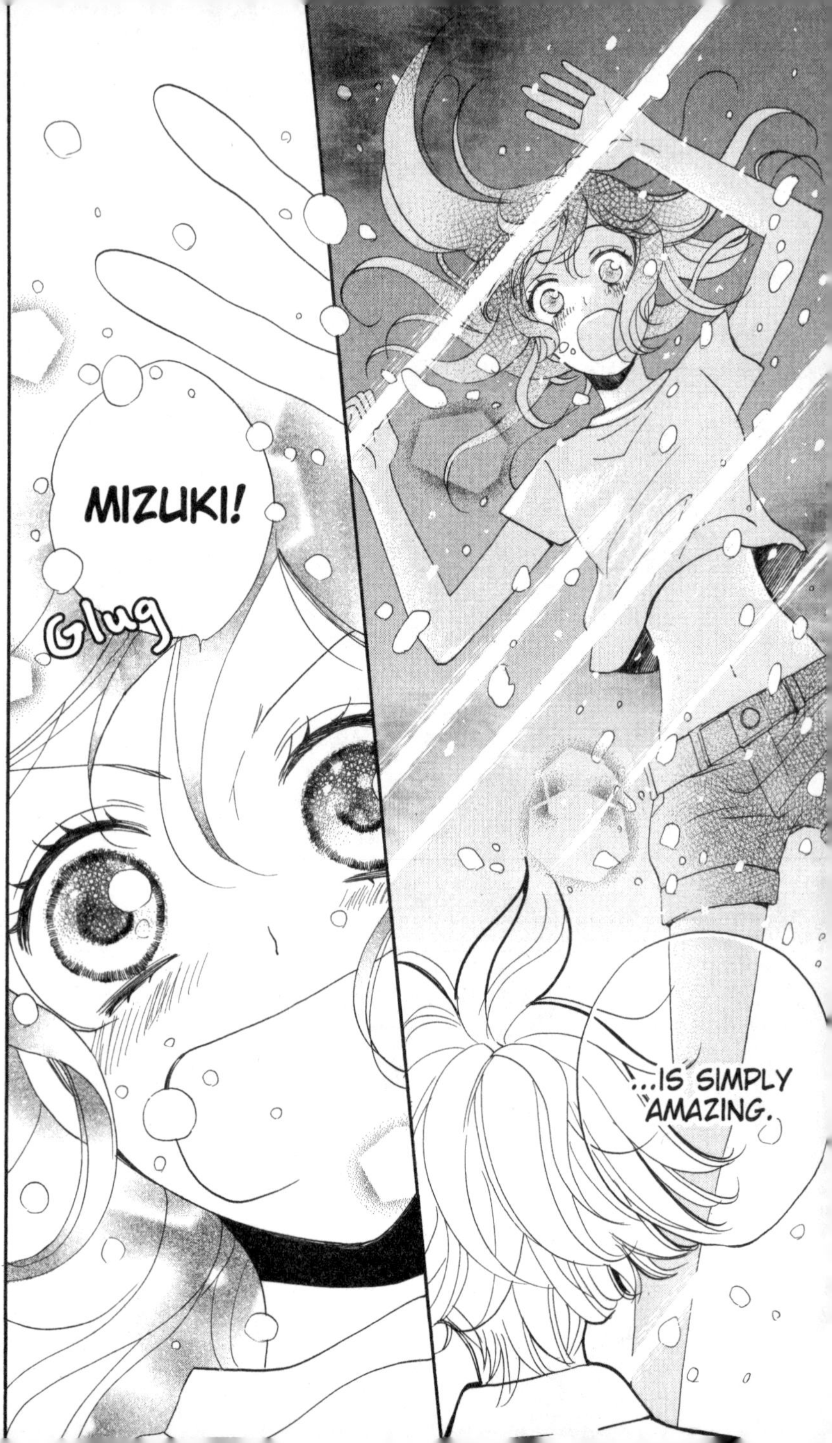
...IS SIMPLY AMAZING.
MIZUKI!
Glug

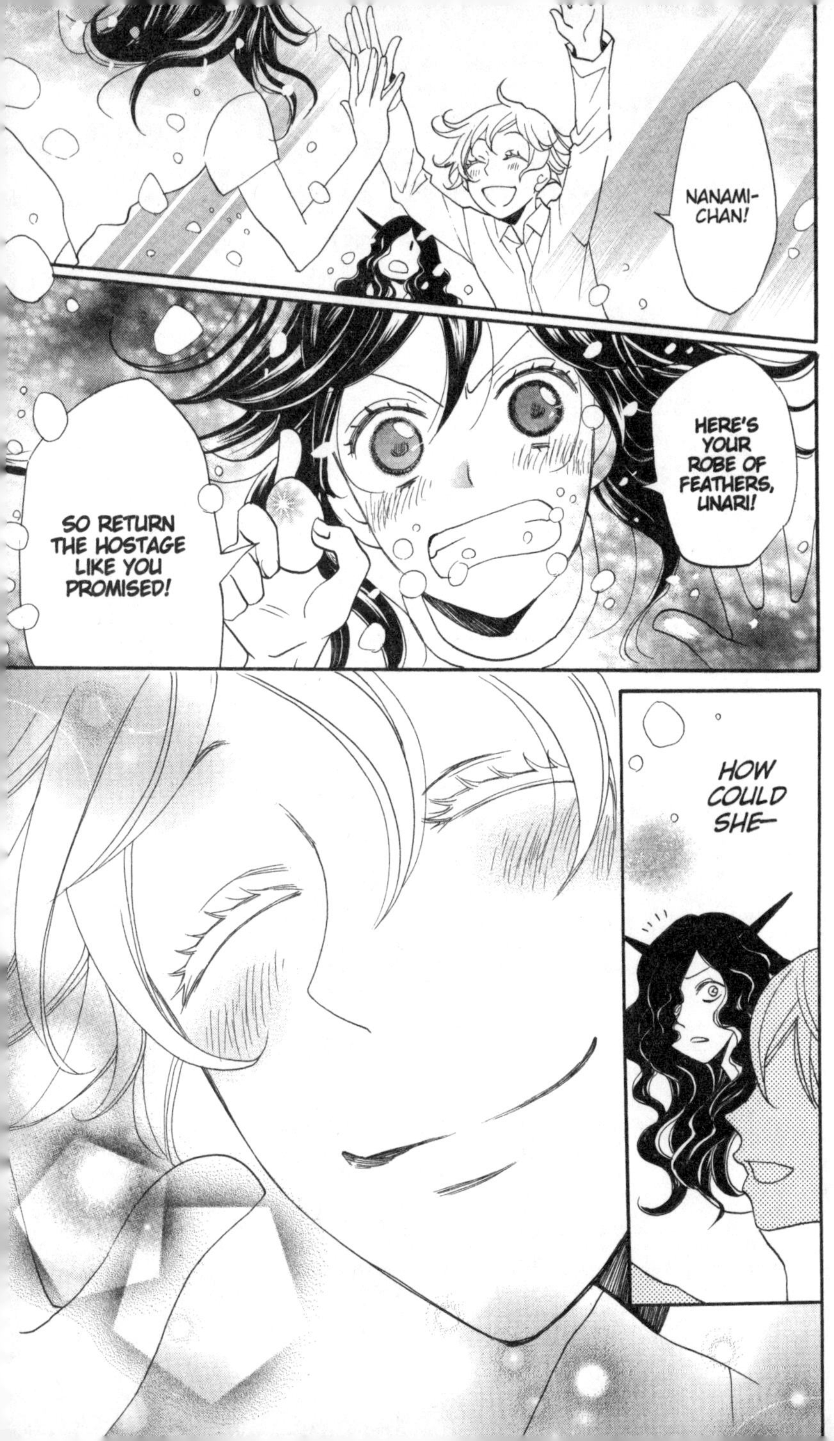
NANAMI-CHAN!
HERE'S YOUR ROBE OF FEATHERS, UNARI!
SO RETURN THE HOSTAGE LIKE YOU PROMISED!
HOW COULD SHE—

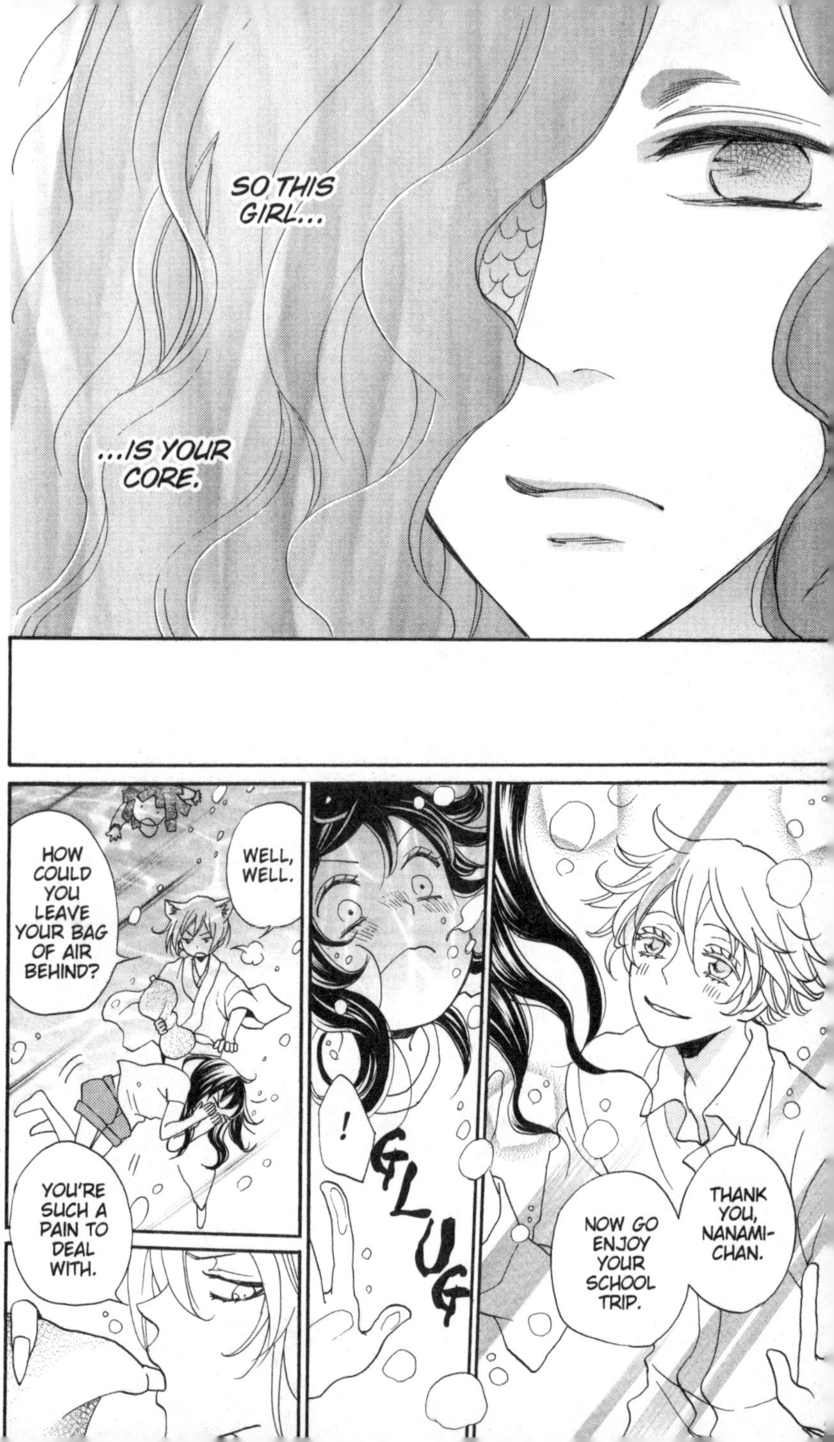
SO THIS GIRL...
...IS YOUR CORE.
THANK YOU, NANAMI-CHAN.
NOW GO ENJOY YOUR SCHOOL TRIP.
!
GLUG
WELL, WELL.
HOW COULD YOU LEAVE YOUR BAG OF AIR BEHIND?
YOU'RE SUCH A PAIN TO DEAL WITH.

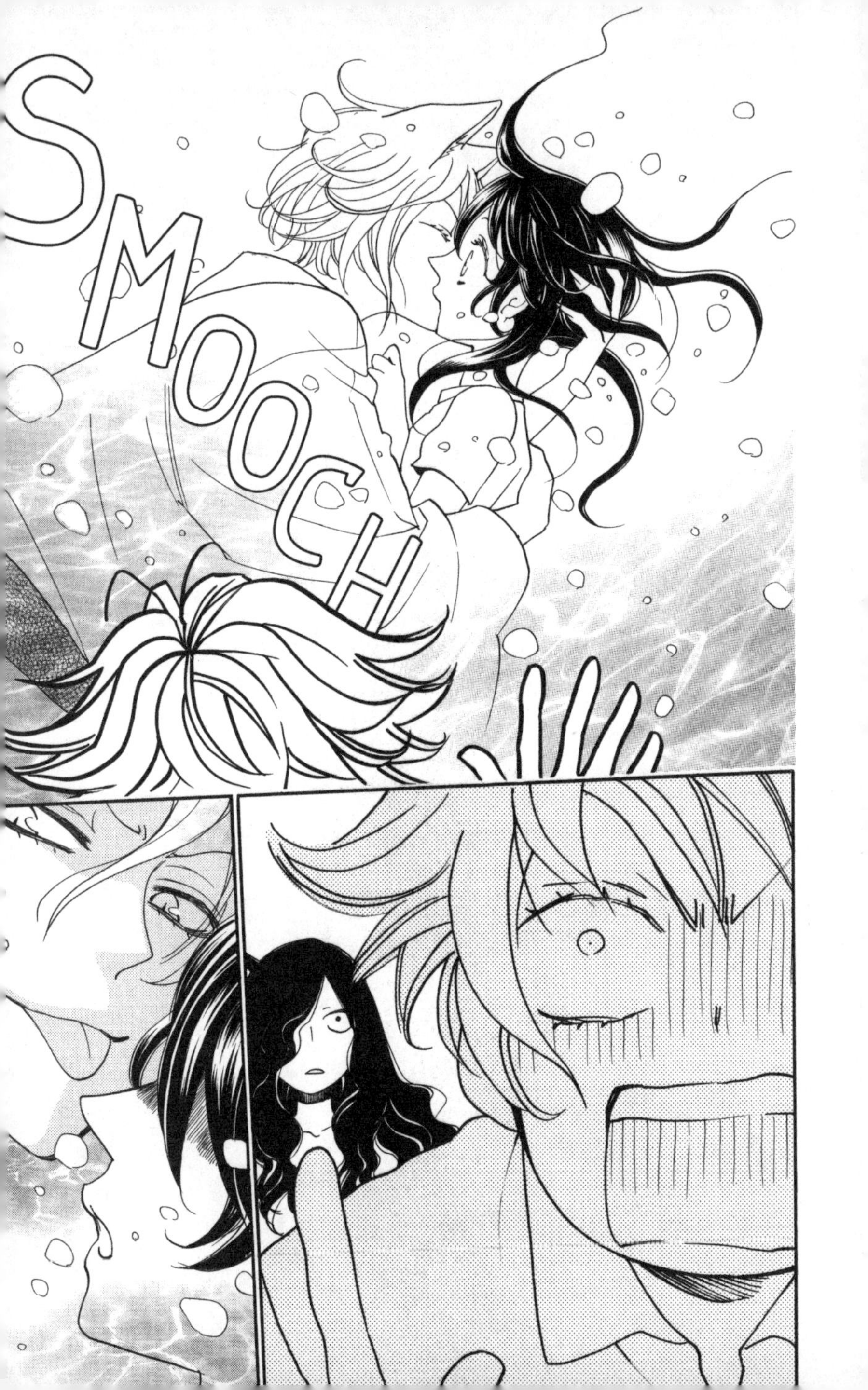
SMOOCH

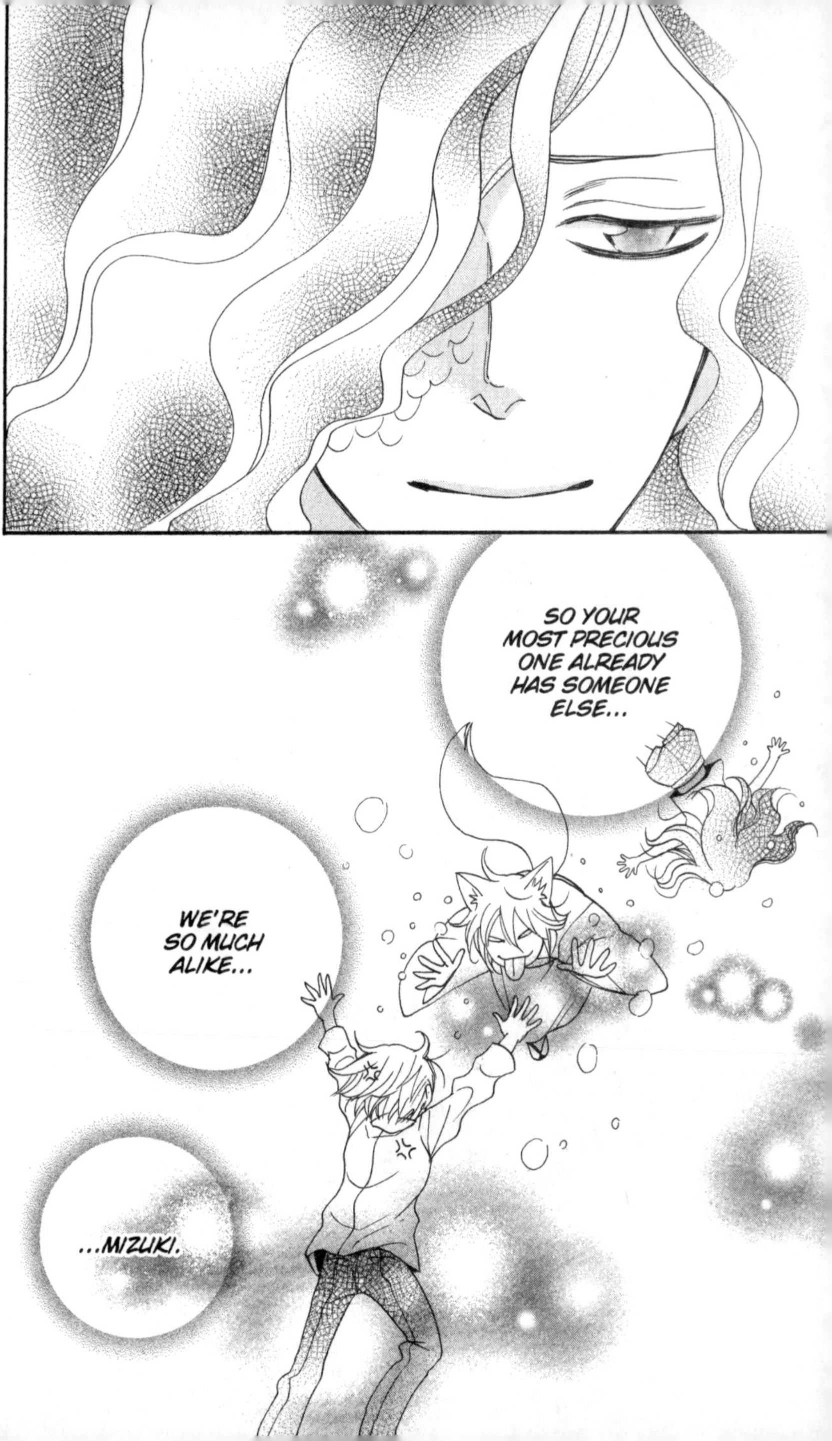
SO YOUR MOST PRECIOUS ONE ALREADY HAS SOMEONE ELSE...
WE'RE SO MUCH ALIKE...
...MIZUKI.

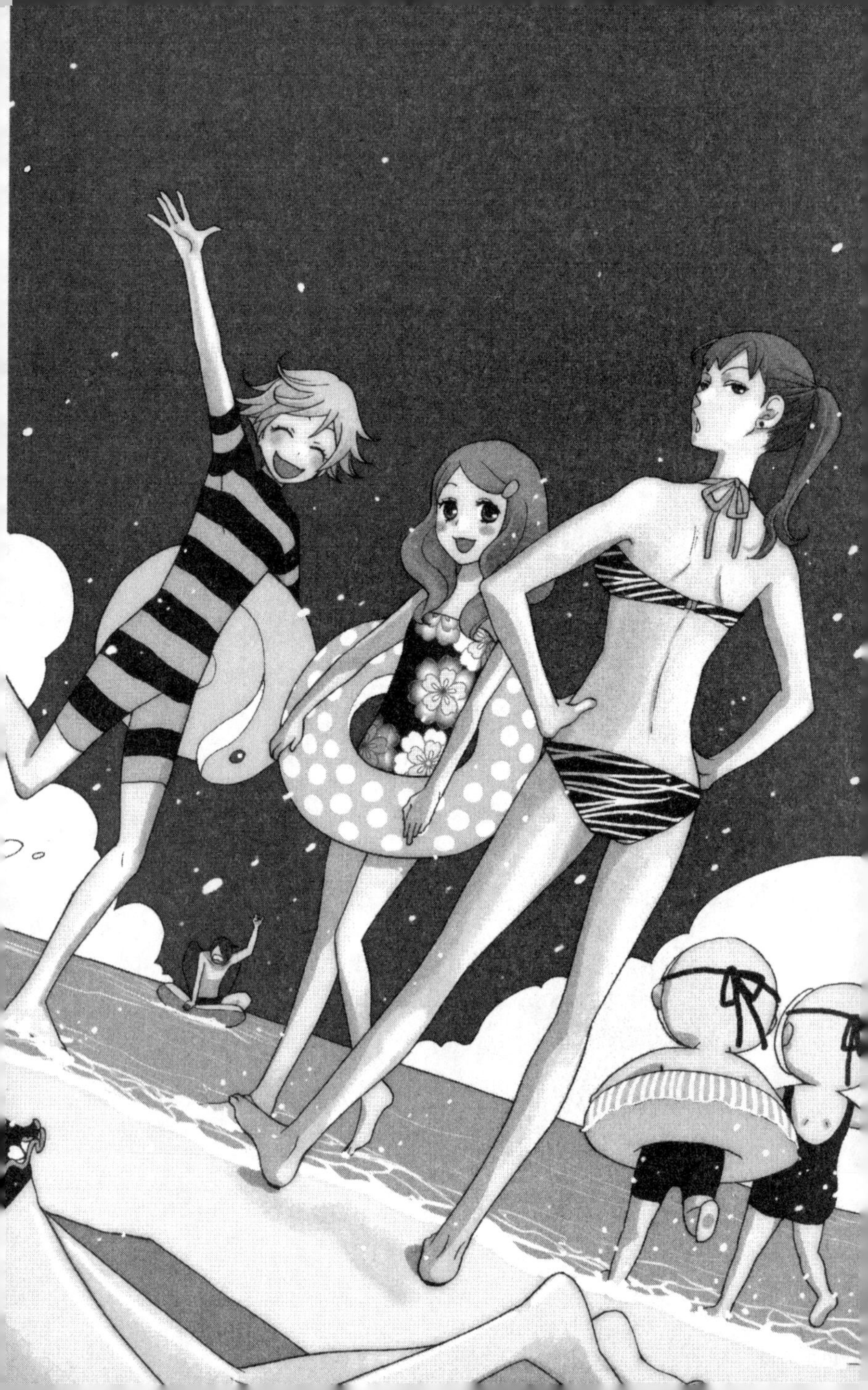

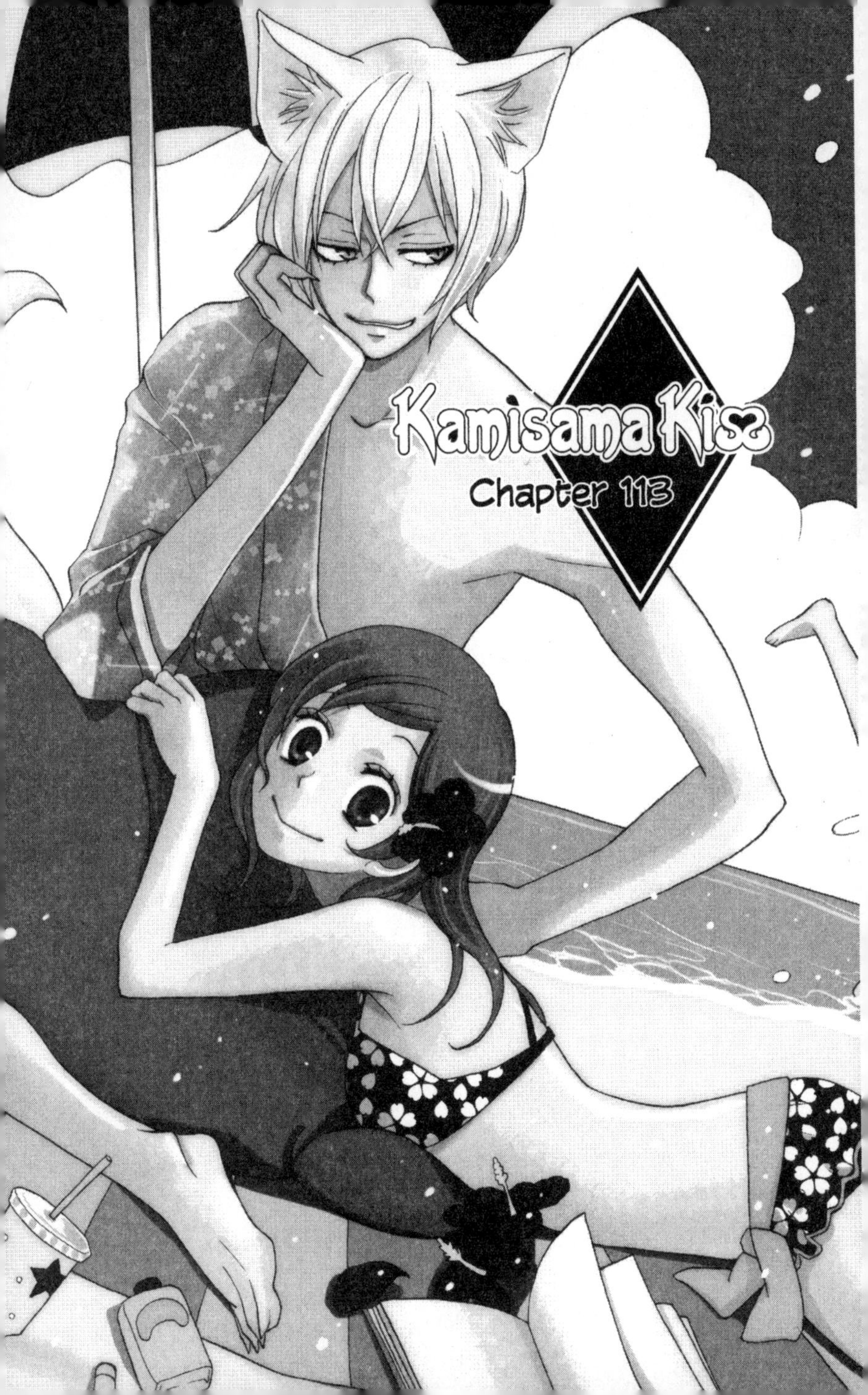
Kamisama Kiss
Chapter 113

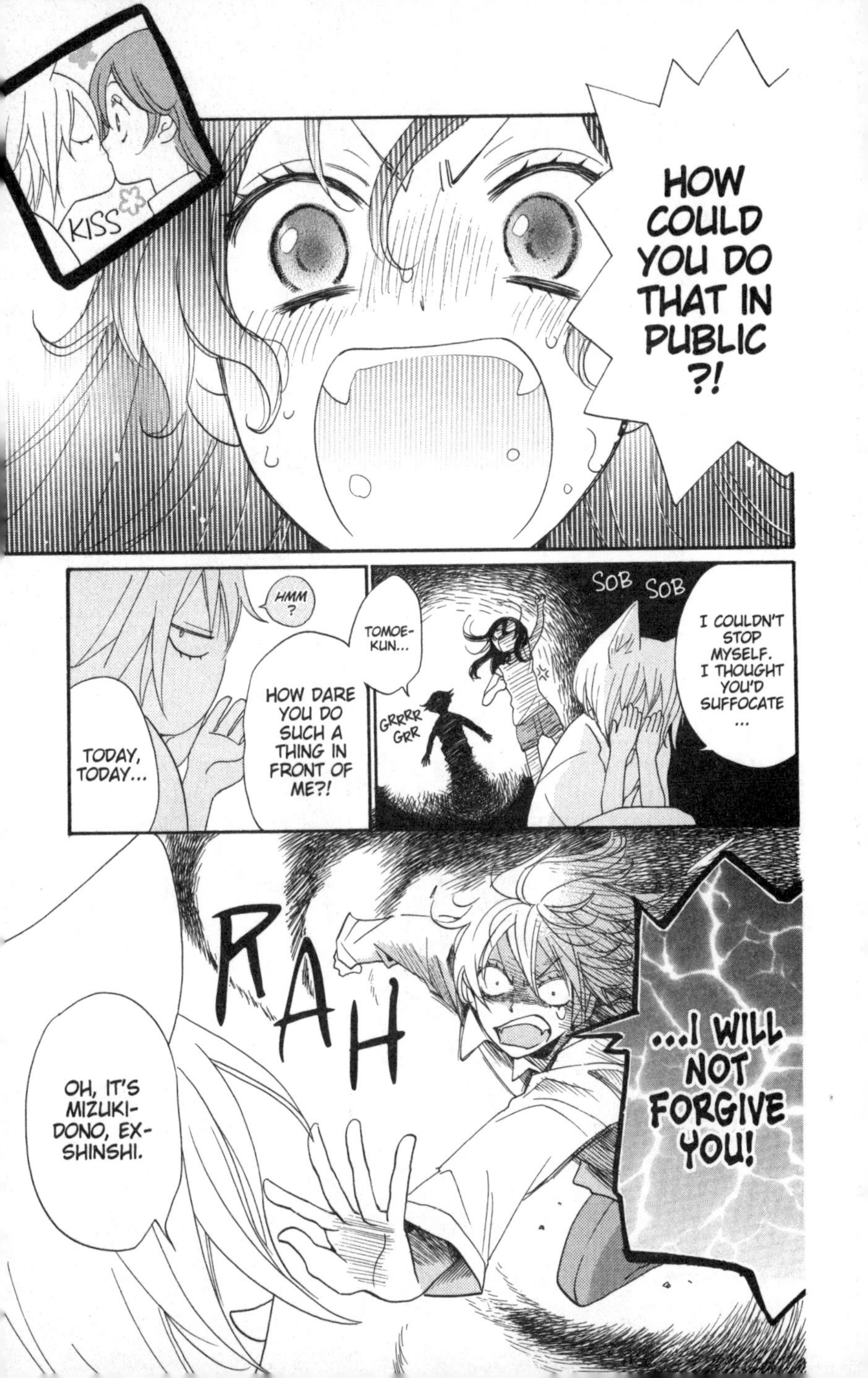
HOW COULD YOU DO THAT IN PUBLIC?!
KISS
SOB SOB
I COULDN'T STOP MYSELF. I THOUGHT YOU'D SUFFOCATE...
TOMOE-KUN...
GRRRR GRR
HOW DARE YOU DO SUCH A THING IN FRONT OF ME?!
HMM?
TODAY, TODAY...
...I WILL NOT FORGIVE YOU!
RAH
OH, IT'S MIZUKI-DONO, EX-SHINSHI.

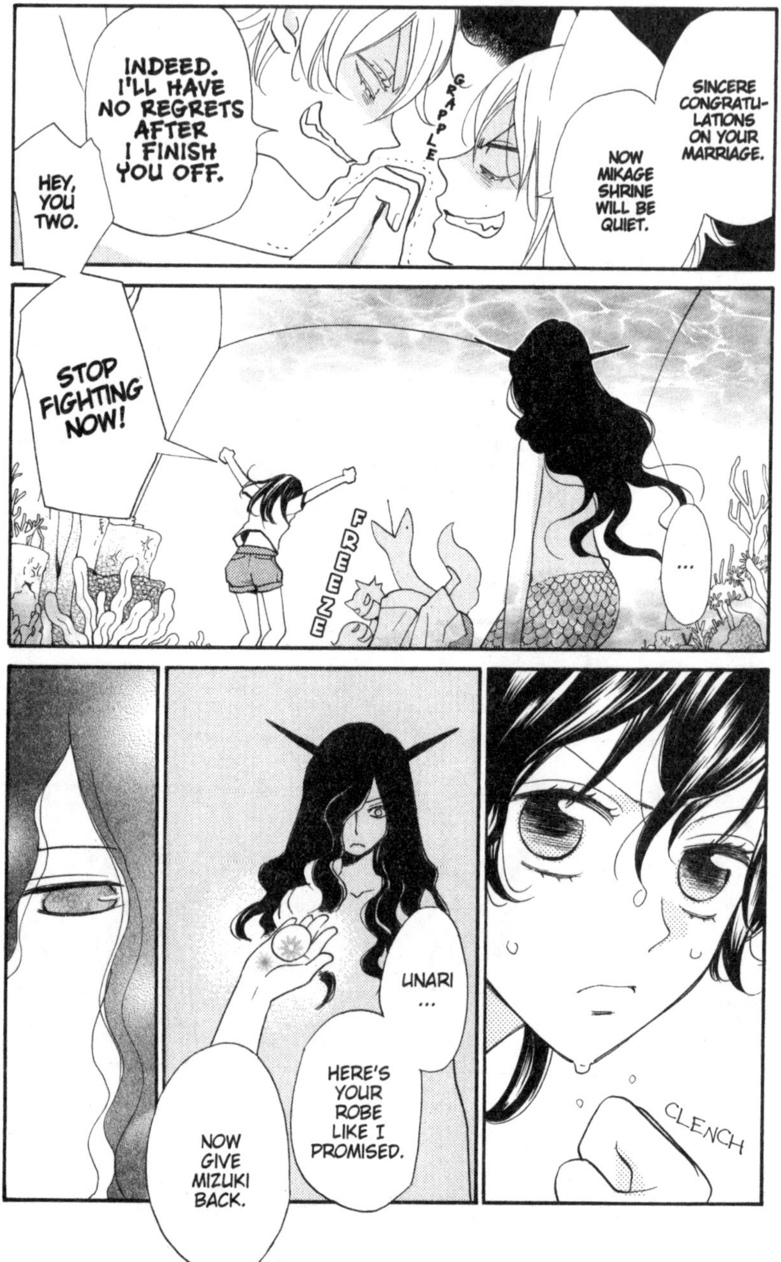
SINCERE CONGRATULATIONS ON YOUR MARRIAGE.
NOW MIKAGE SHRINE WILL BE QUIET.
GRAPPLE
INDEED. I'LL HAVE NO REGRETS AFTER I FINISH YOU OFF.
HEY, YOU TWO.
...
FREEZE
STOP FIGHTING NOW!
CLENCH
UNARI ...
HERE'S YOUR ROBE LIKE I PROMISED.
NOW GIVE MIZUKI BACK.

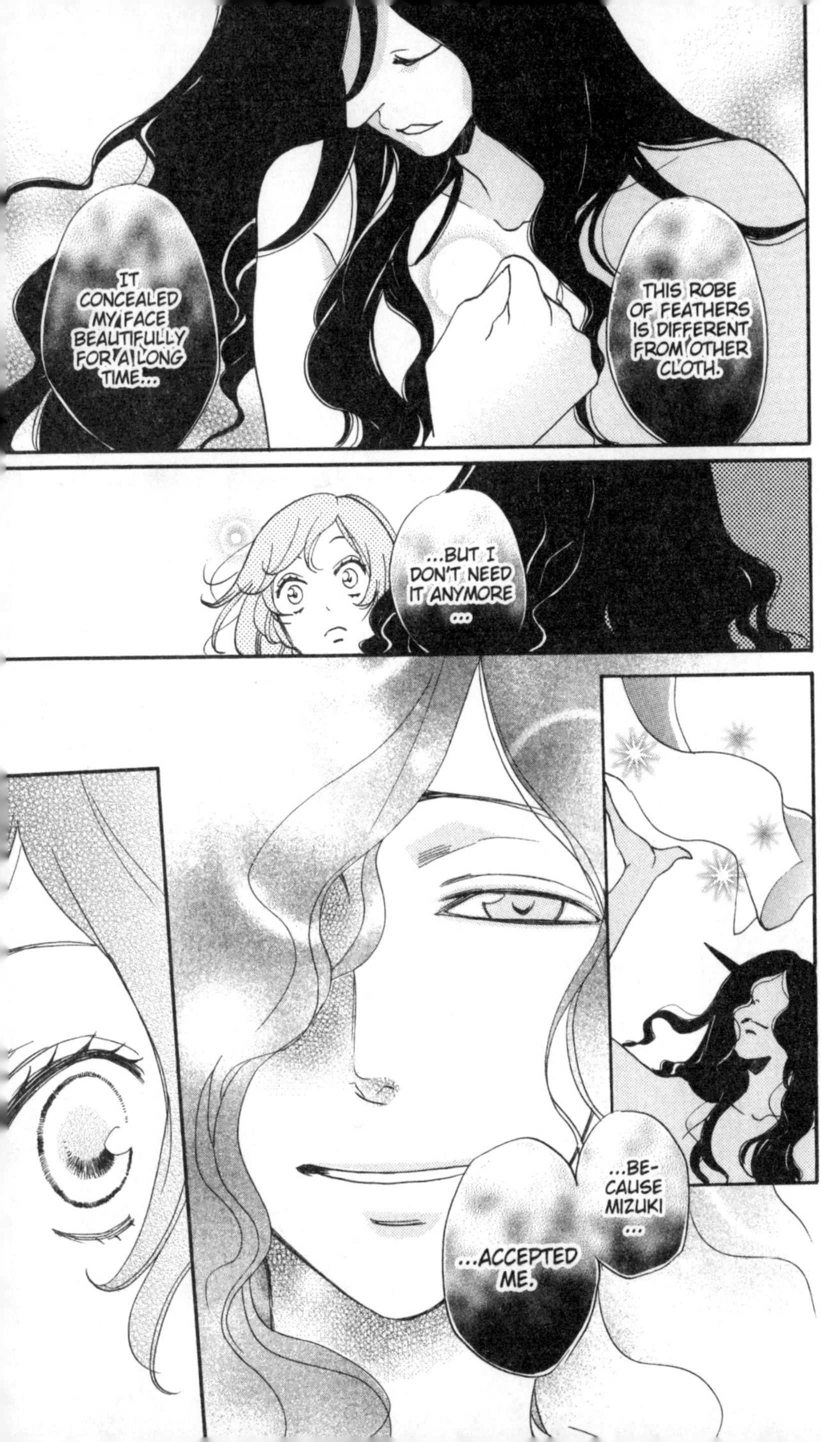
THIS ROBE OF FEATHERS IS DIFFERENT FROM OTHER CLOTH.
IT CONCEALED MY FACE BEAUTIFULLY FOR A LONG TIME...
...BUT I DON'T NEED IT ANYMORE ...
...BE-CAUSE MIZUKI ...
...ACCEPTED ME.

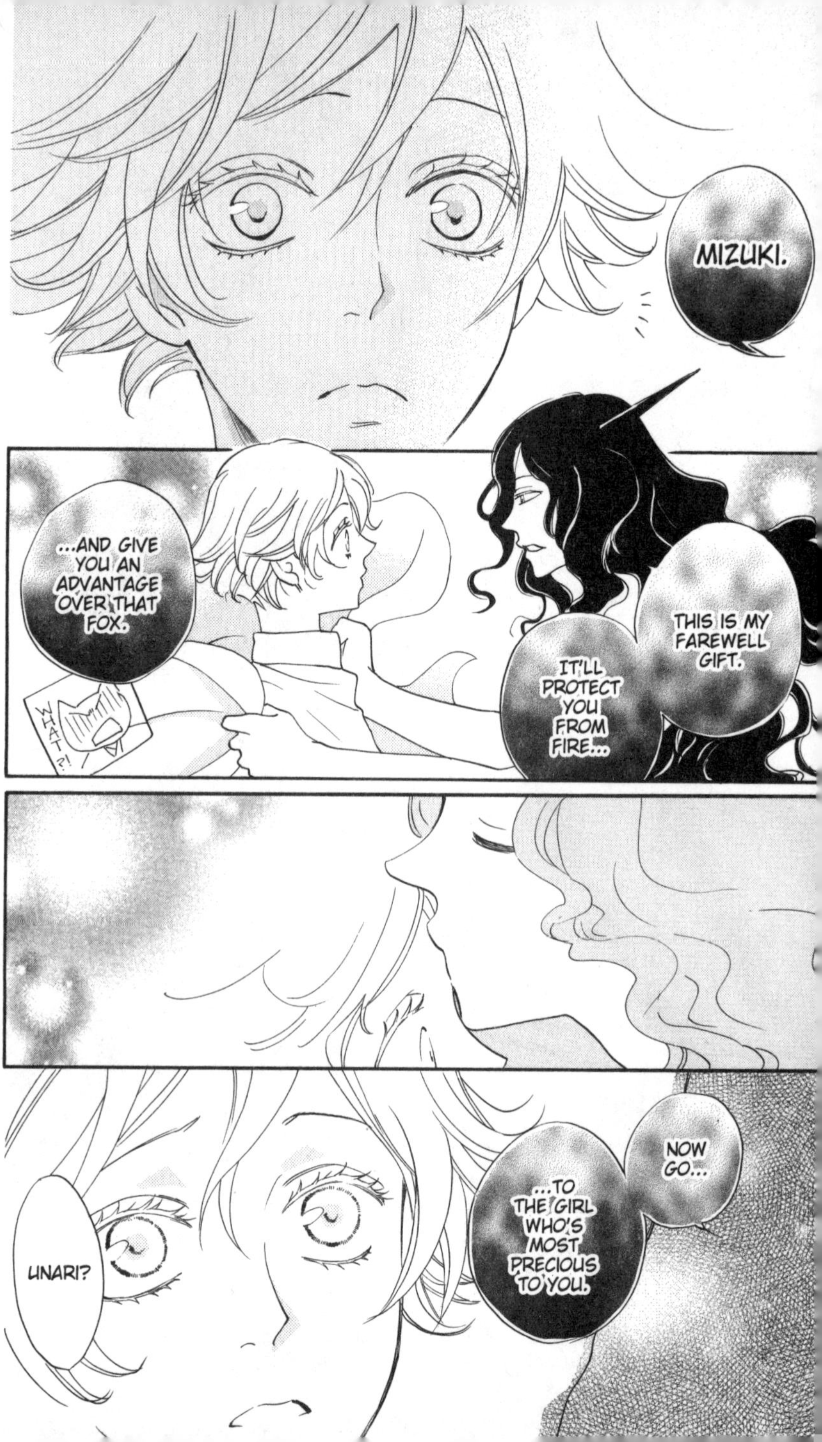
MIZUKI.
THIS IS MY FAREWELL GIFT.
IT'LL PROTECT YOU FROM FIRE...
...AND GIVE YOU AN ADVANTAGE OVER THAT FOX.
WHAT?!
NOW GO...
...TO THE GIRL WHO'S MOST PRECIOUS TO YOU.
UNARI?

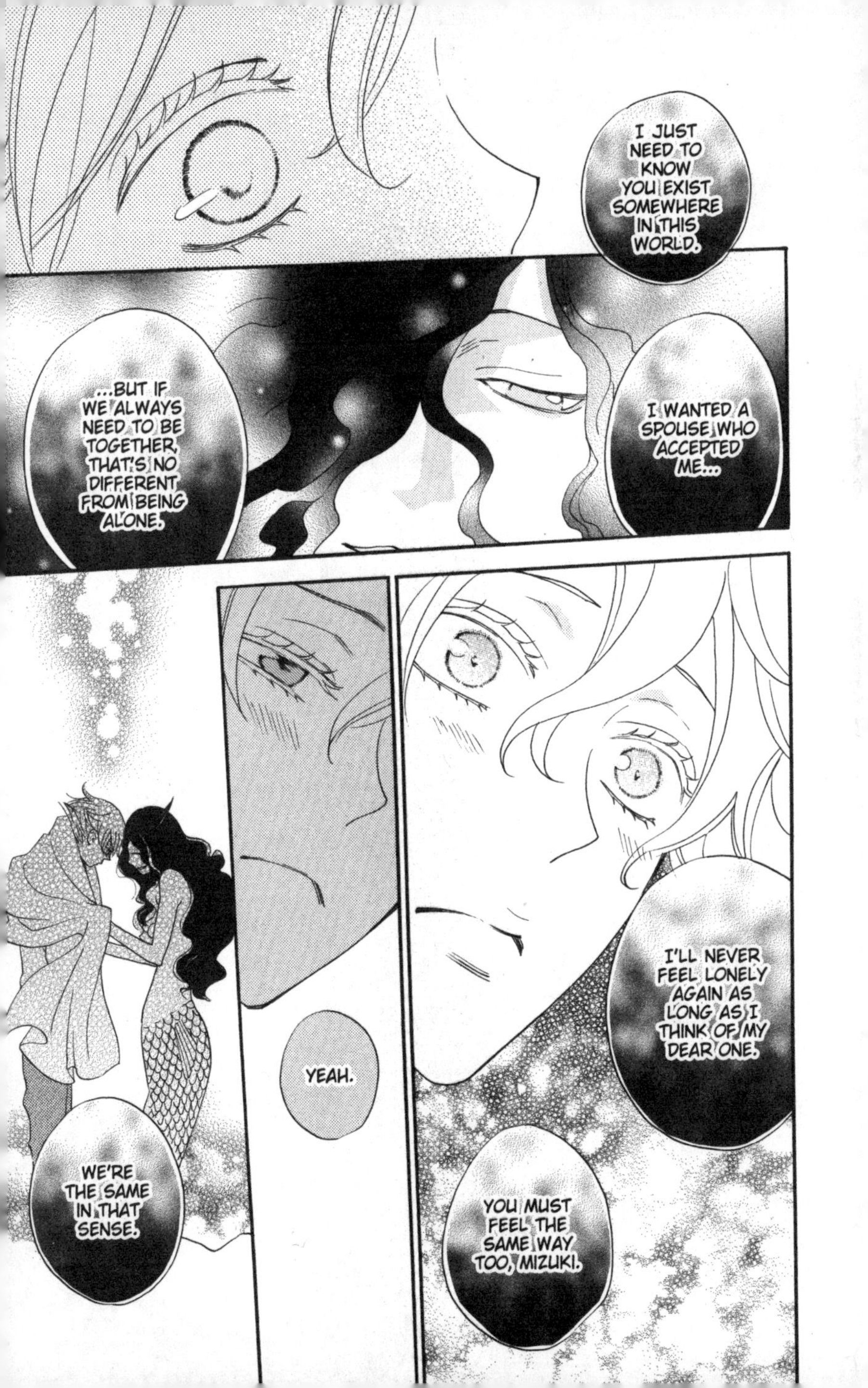
I JUST NEED TO KNOW YOU EXIST SOMEWHERE IN THIS WORLD.
I WANTED A SPOUSE WHO ACCEPTED ME...
...BUT IF WE ALWAYS NEED TO BE TOGETHER, THAT'S NO DIFFERENT FROM BEING ALONE.
I'LL NEVER FEEL LONELY AGAIN AS LONG AS I THINK OF MY DEAR ONE.
YOU MUST FEEL THE SAME WAY TOO, MIZUKI.
YEAH.
WE'RE THE SAME IN THAT SENSE.

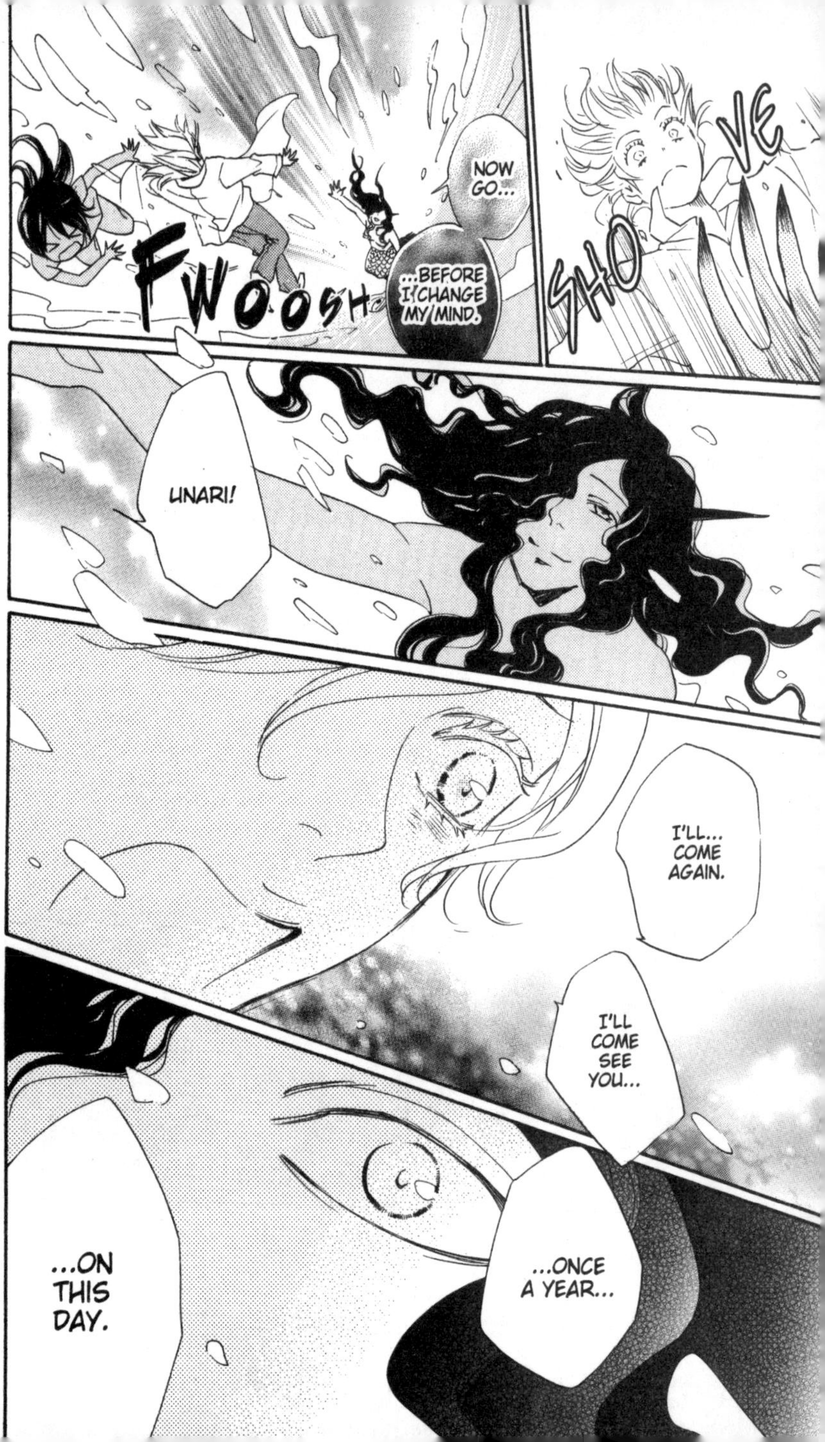
SHOVE
NOW GO...
...BEFORE I CHANGE MY MIND.
FWOOSH
UNARI!
I'LL... COME AGAIN.
I'LL COME SEE YOU...
...ONCE A YEAR...
...ON THIS DAY.

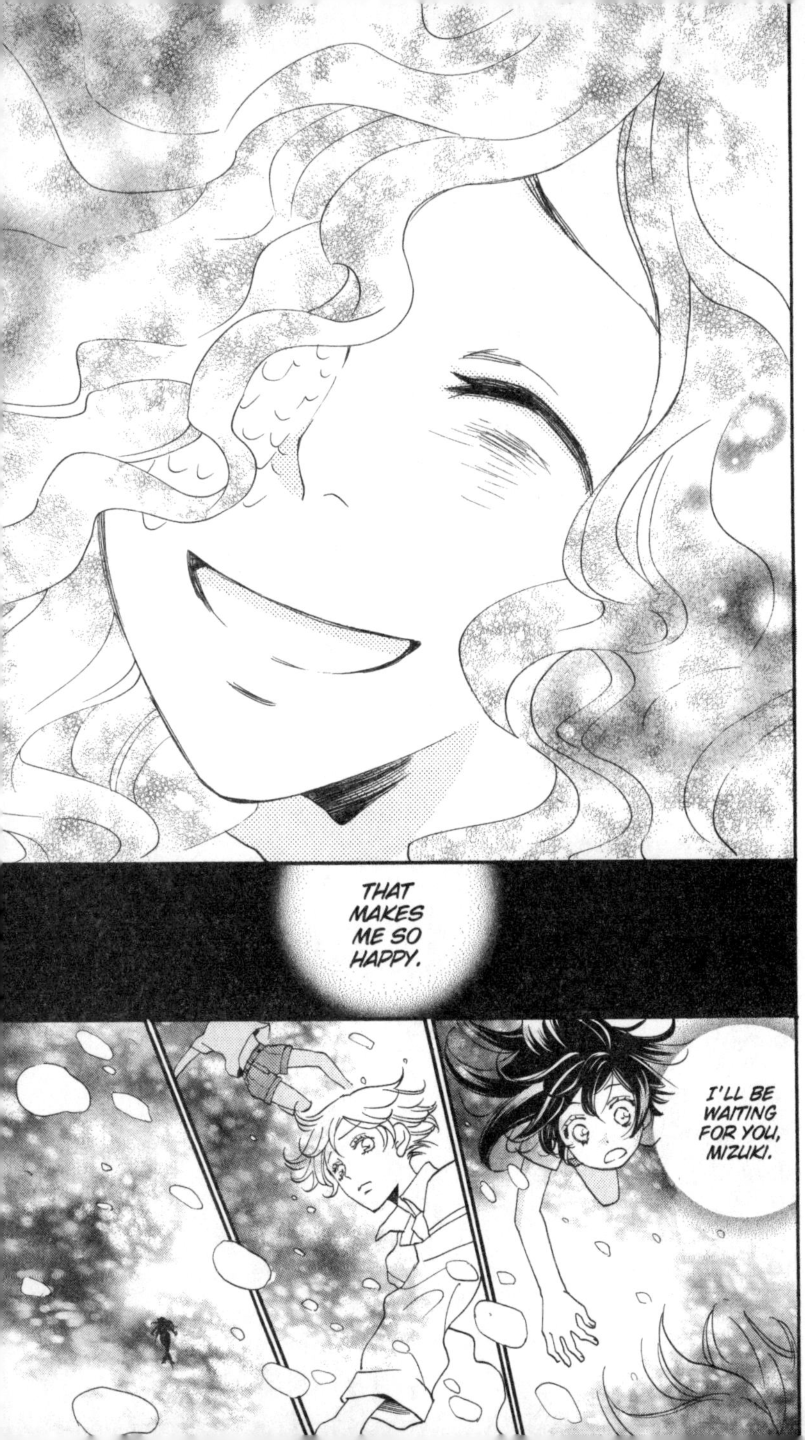
THAT MAKES ME SO HAPPY.
I'LL BE WAITING FOR YOU, MIZUKI.

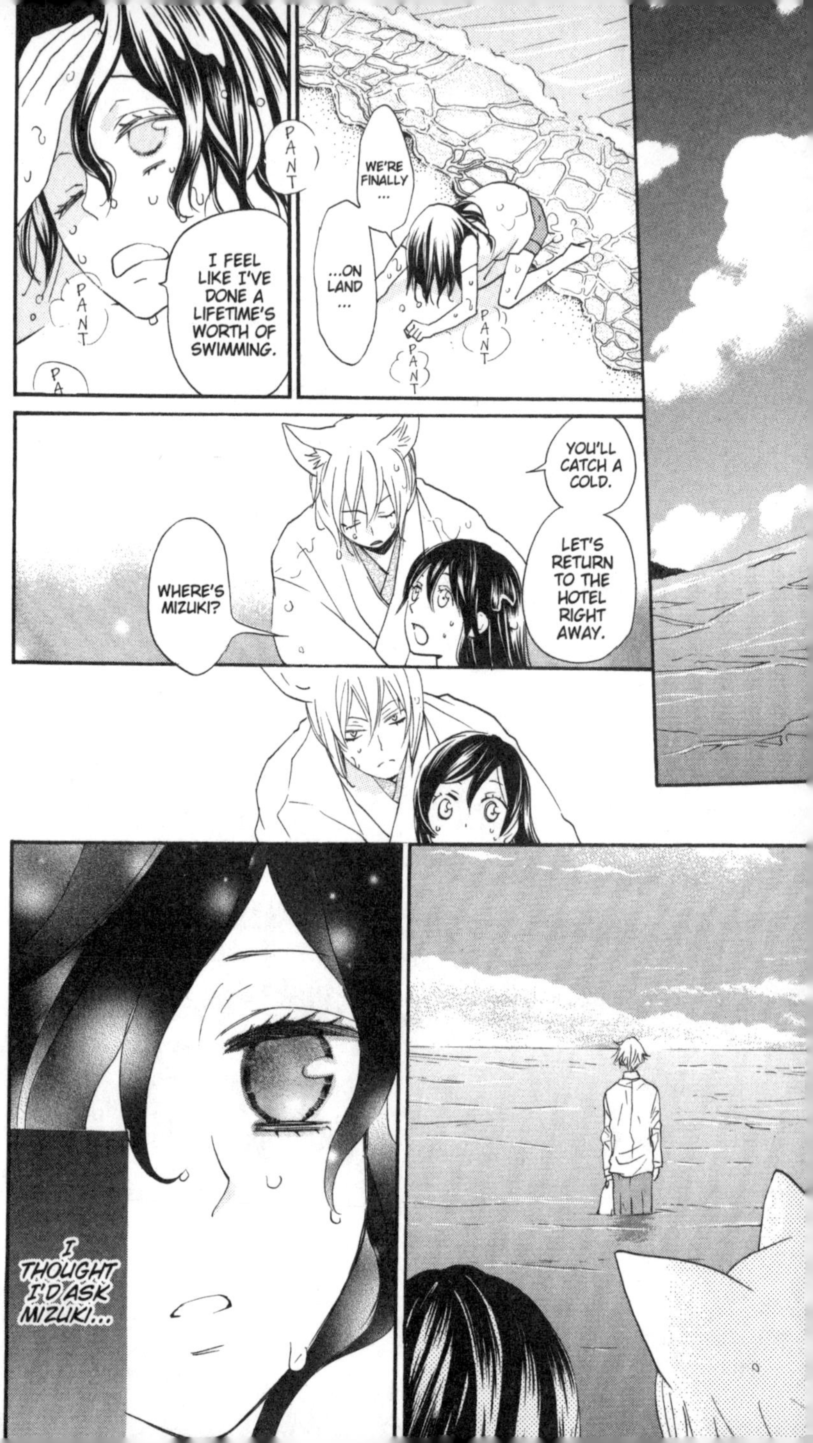

WE'RE FINALLY...
...ON LAND...
PANT
PANT
PANT
I FEEL LIKE I'VE DONE A LIFETIME'S WORTH OF SWIMMING.
PANT
YOU'LL CATCH A COLD.
LET'S RETURN TO THE HOTEL RIGHT AWAY.
WHERE'S MIZUKI?
I THOUGHT I'D ASK MIZUKI...

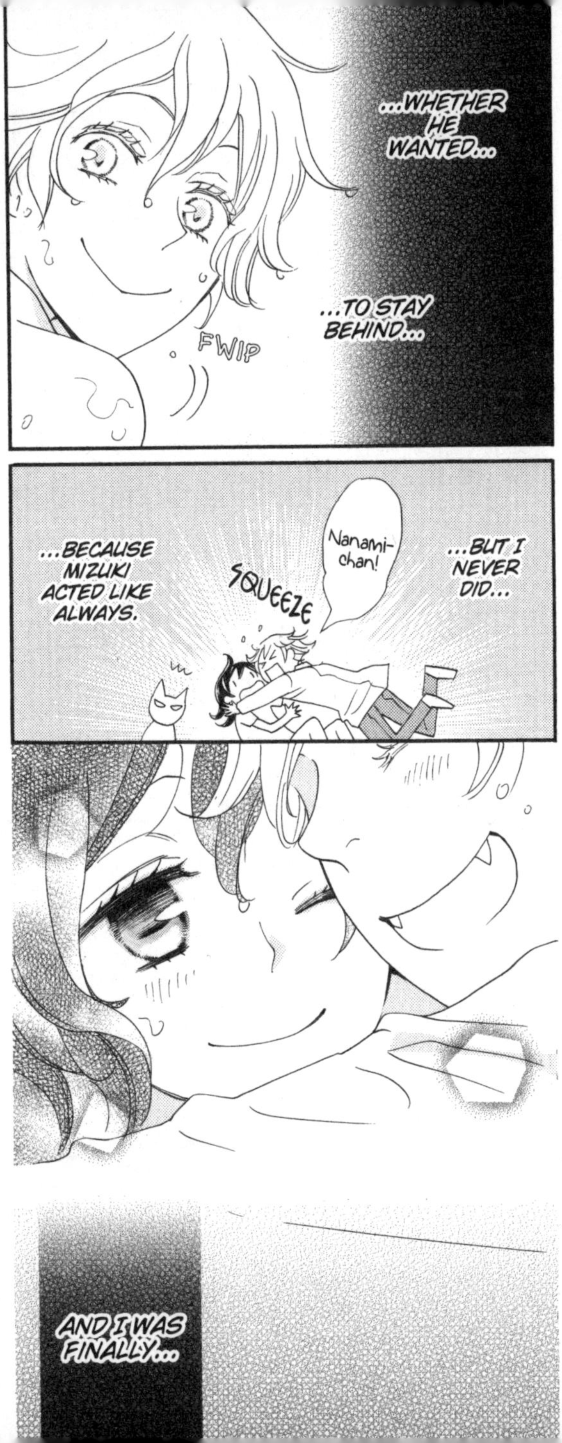
...WHETHER HE WANTED...
...TO STAY BEHIND...
FWIP
...BUT I NEVER DID...
Nanami-chan!
SQUEEZE
...BECAUSE MIZUKI ACTED LIKE ALWAYS.
AND I WAS FINALLY...

Thank you for reading this far!

If you have any comments and thoughts about volume 19, do let me hear from you!

The address is...

Julietta Suzuki
c/o Shojo Beat
VIZ Media, LLC
P.O. Box 77010
San Francisco
CA 94107

I'll be waiting. ☺

I hope we'll be able to meet again in the next volume...

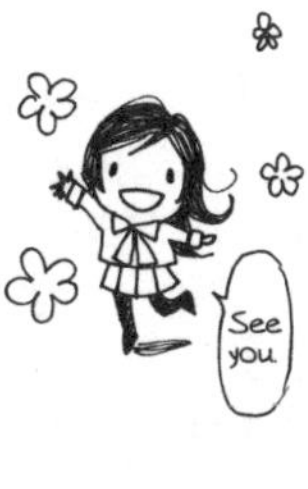
See you

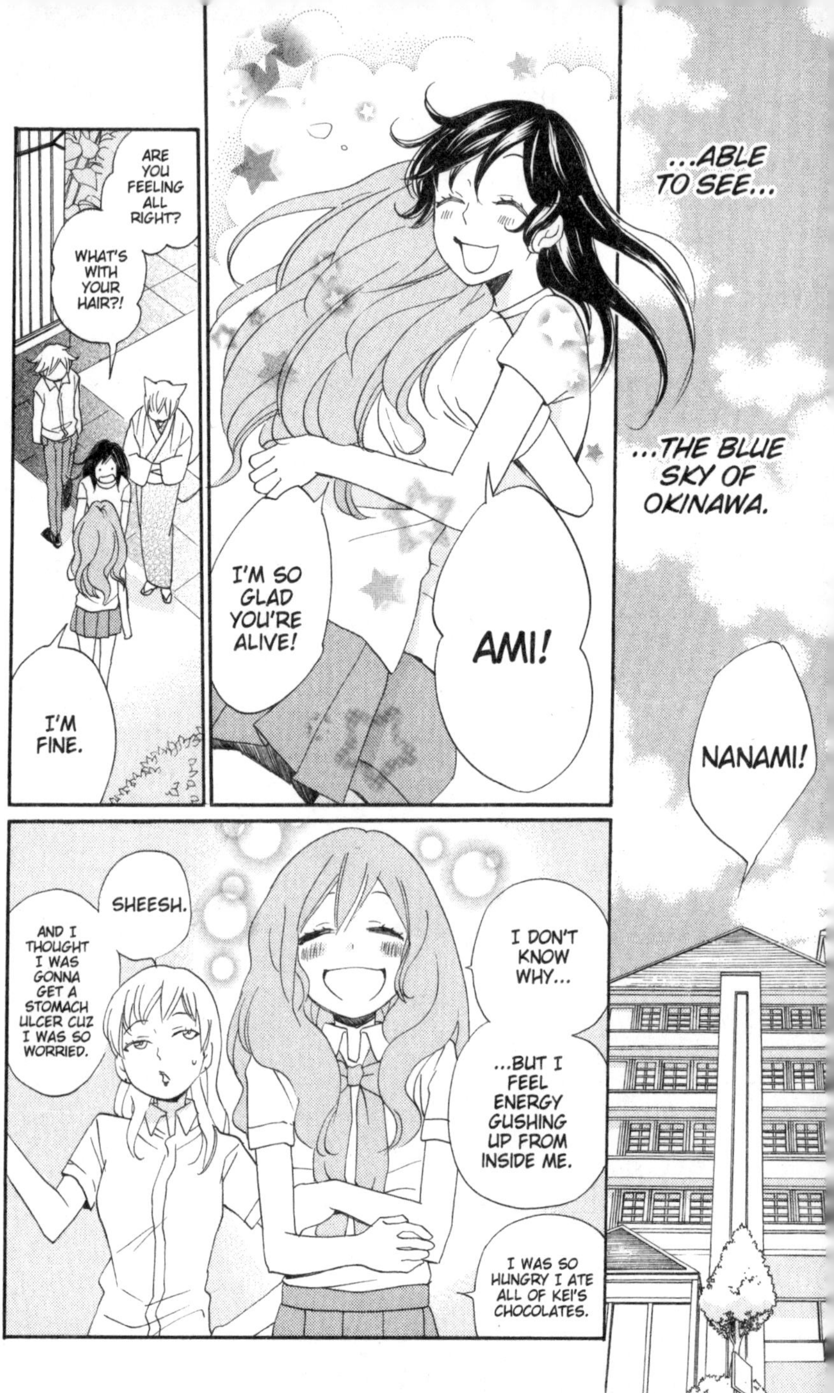
...ABLE TO SEE...
...THE BLUE SKY OF OKINAWA.
NANAMI!
AMI!
I'M SO GLAD YOU'RE ALIVE!
ARE YOU FEELING ALL RIGHT?
WHAT'S WITH YOUR HAIR?!
I'M FINE.
I DON'T KNOW WHY...
...BUT I FEEL ENERGY GUSHING UP FROM INSIDE ME.
I WAS SO HUNGRY I ATE ALL OF KEI'S CHOCOLATES.
SHEESH.
AND I THOUGHT I WAS GONNA GET A STOMACH ULCER CUZ I WAS SO WORRIED.

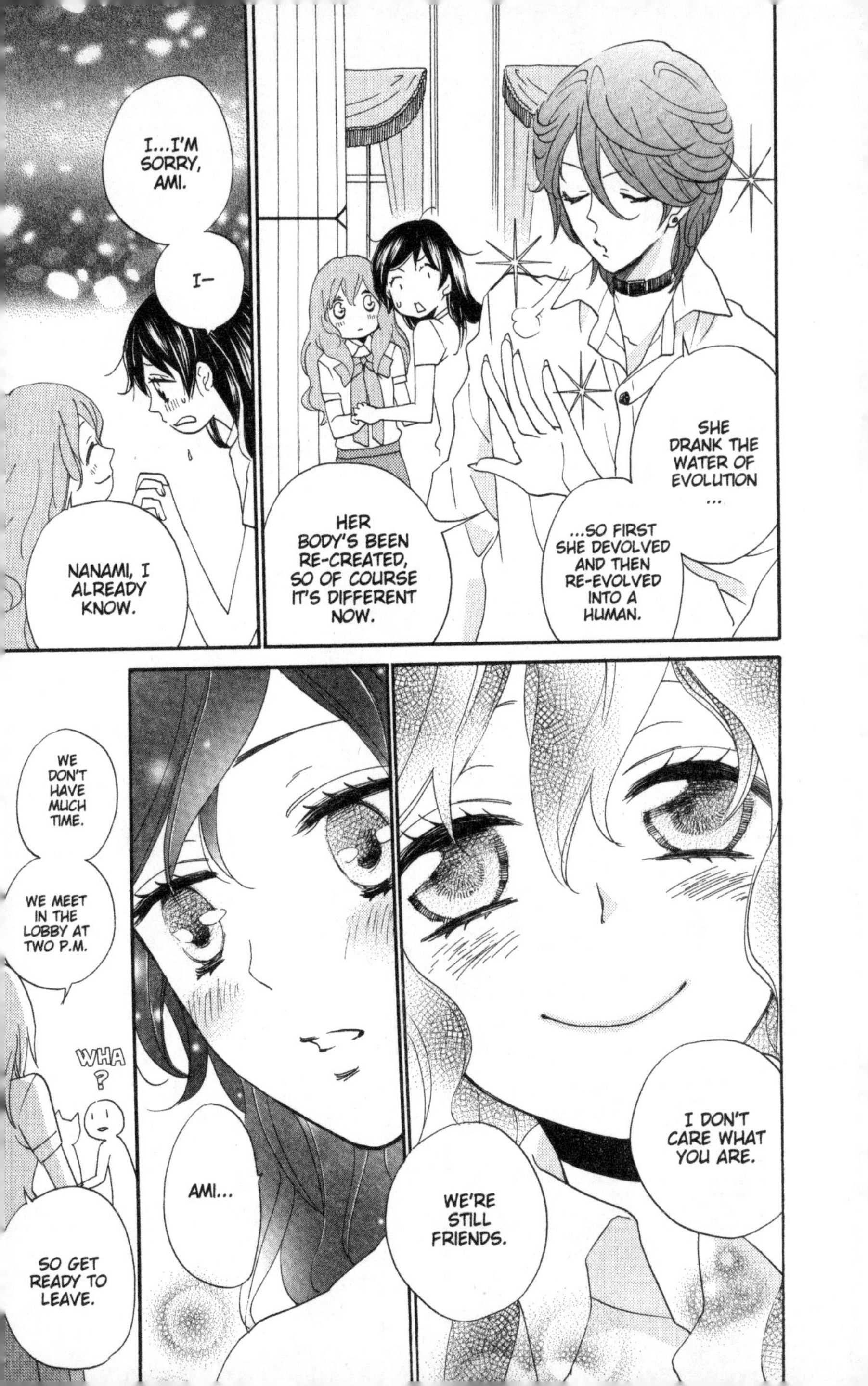
SHE DRANK THE WATER OF EVOLUTION...
...SO FIRST SHE DEVOLVED AND THEN RE-EVOLVED INTO A HUMAN.
HER BODY'S BEEN RE-CREATED, SO OF COURSE IT'S DIFFERENT NOW.
I...I'M SORRY, AMI.
I—
NANAMI, I ALREADY KNOW.
I DON'T CARE WHAT YOU ARE.
WE'RE STILL FRIENDS.
AMI...
WE DON'T HAVE MUCH TIME.
WE MEET IN THE LOBBY AT TWO P.M.
WHA?
SO GET READY TO LEAVE.

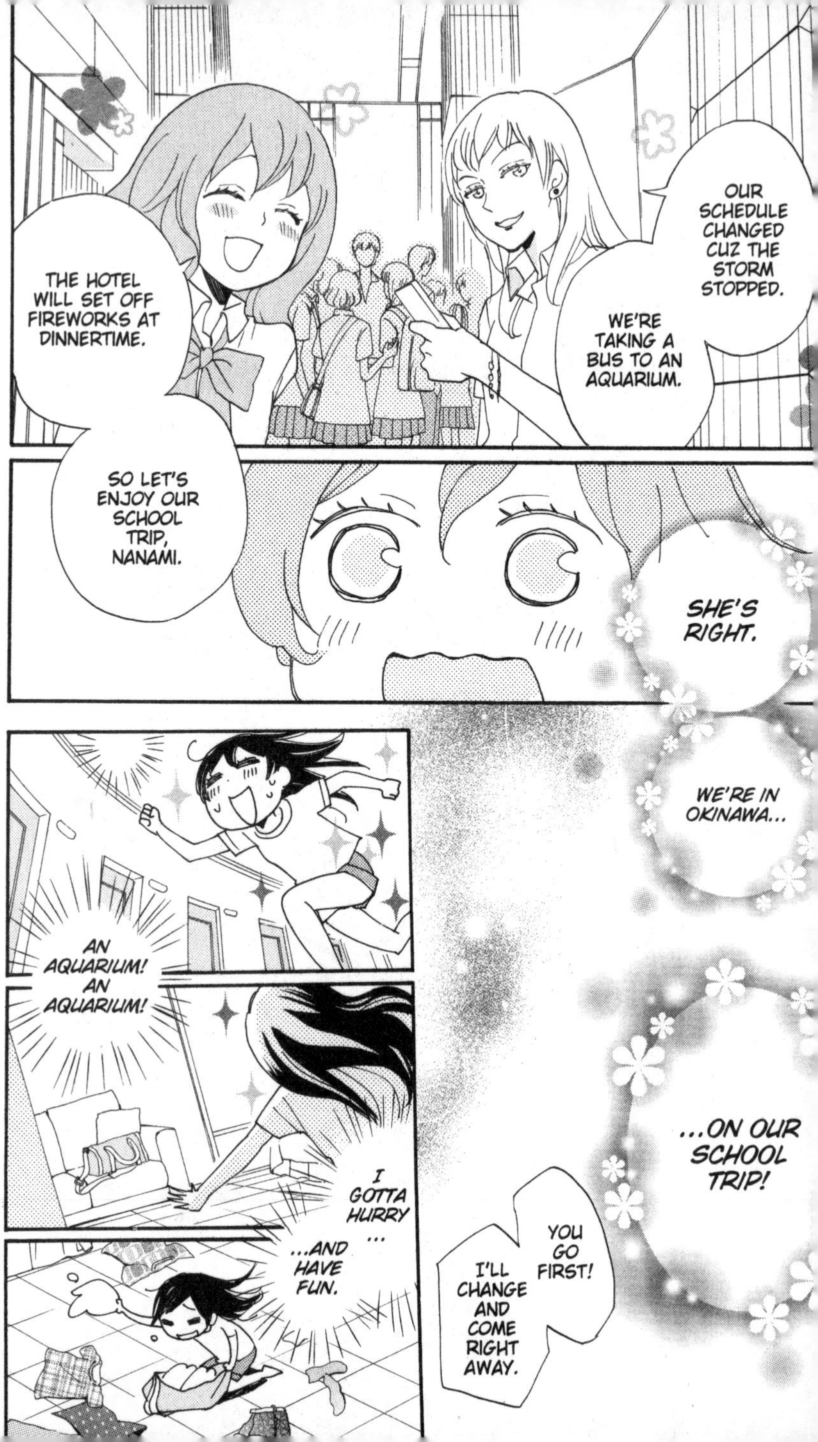
OUR SCHEDULE CHANGED CUZ THE STORM STOPPED.
WE'RE TAKING A BUS TO AN AQUARIUM.
THE HOTEL WILL SET OFF FIREWORKS AT DINNERTIME.
SO LET'S ENJOY OUR SCHOOL TRIP, NANAMI.
SHE'S RIGHT.
WE'RE IN OKINAWA...
...ON OUR SCHOOL TRIP!
AN AQUARIUM! AN AQUARIUM!
I GOTTA HURRY...
...AND HAVE FUN.
YOU GO FIRST!
I'LL CHANGE AND COME RIGHT AWAY.

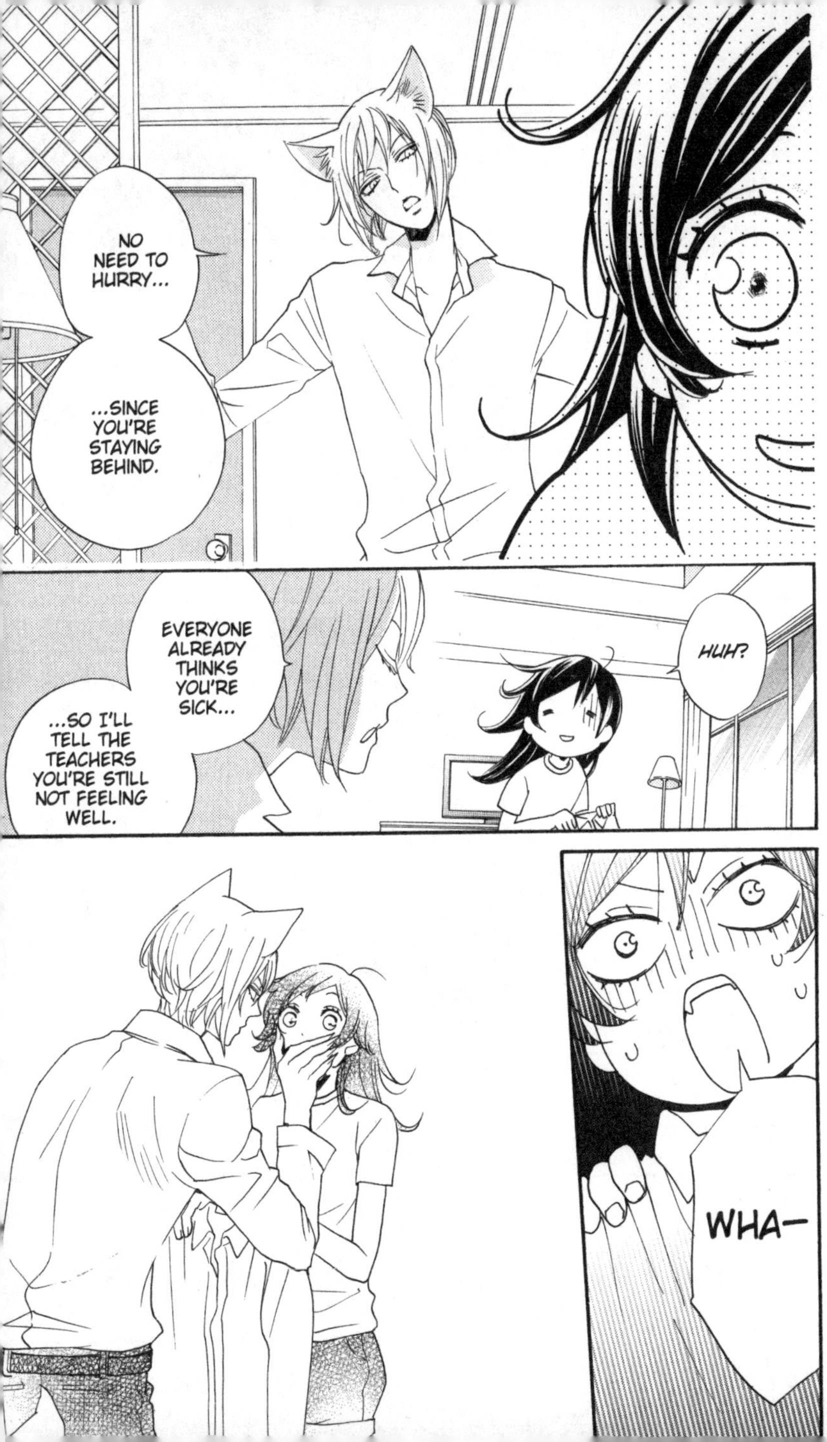
NO NEED TO HURRY...
...SINCE YOU'RE STAYING BEHIND.
HUH?
EVERYONE ALREADY THINKS YOU'RE SICK...
...SO I'LL TELL THE TEACHERS YOU'RE STILL NOT FEELING WELL.
WHA-

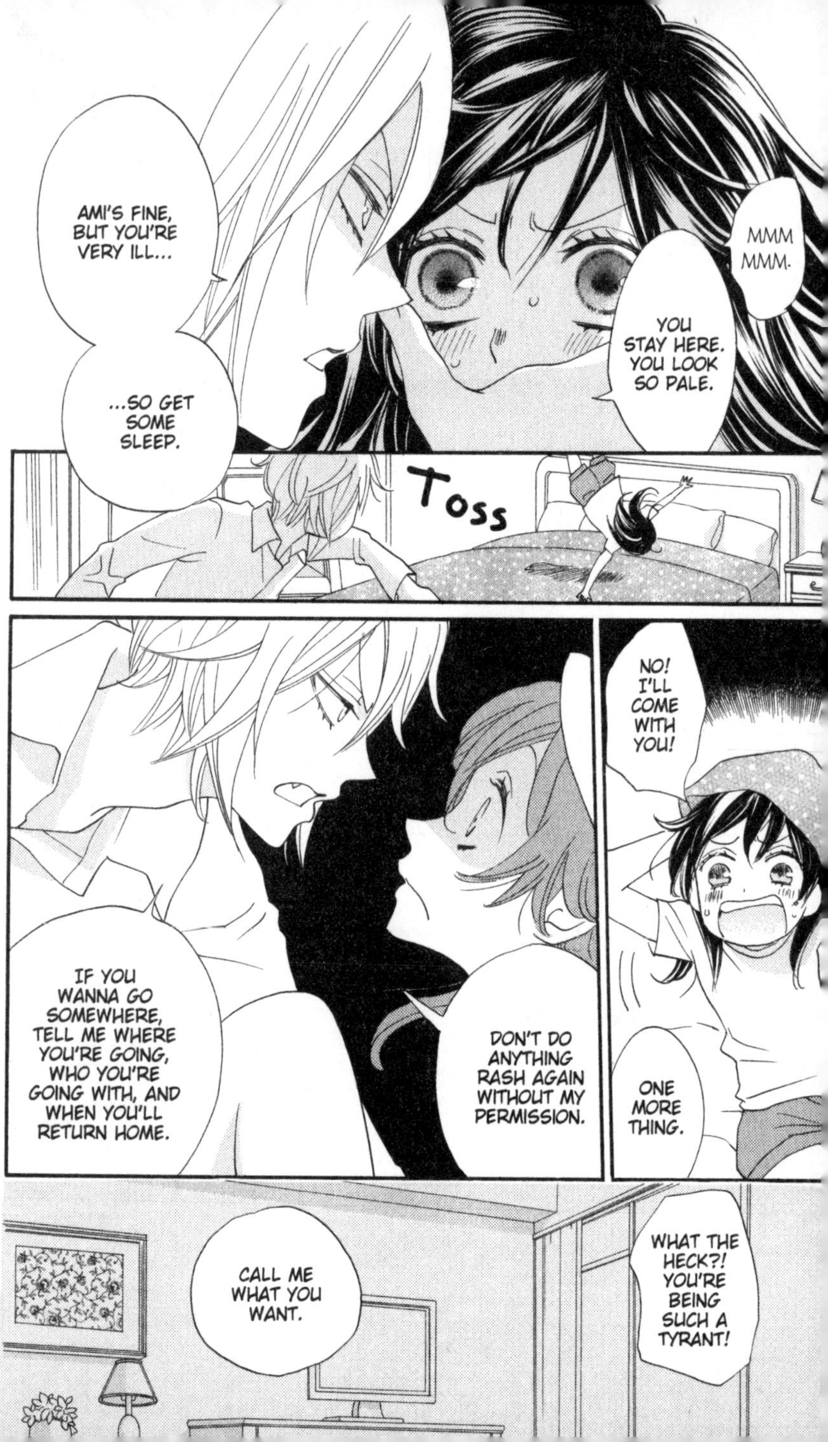
MMM MMM.
YOU STAY HERE. YOU LOOK SO PALE.
AMI'S FINE, BUT YOU'RE VERY ILL...
...SO GET SOME SLEEP.
TOSS
NO! I'LL COME WITH YOU!
ONE MORE THING.
DON'T DO ANYTHING RASH AGAIN WITHOUT MY PERMISSION.
IF YOU WANNA GO SOMEWHERE, TELL ME WHERE YOU'RE GOING, WHO YOU'RE GOING WITH, AND WHEN YOU'LL RETURN HOME.
WHAT THE HECK?! YOU'RE BEING SUCH A TYRANT!
CALL ME WHAT YOU WANT.

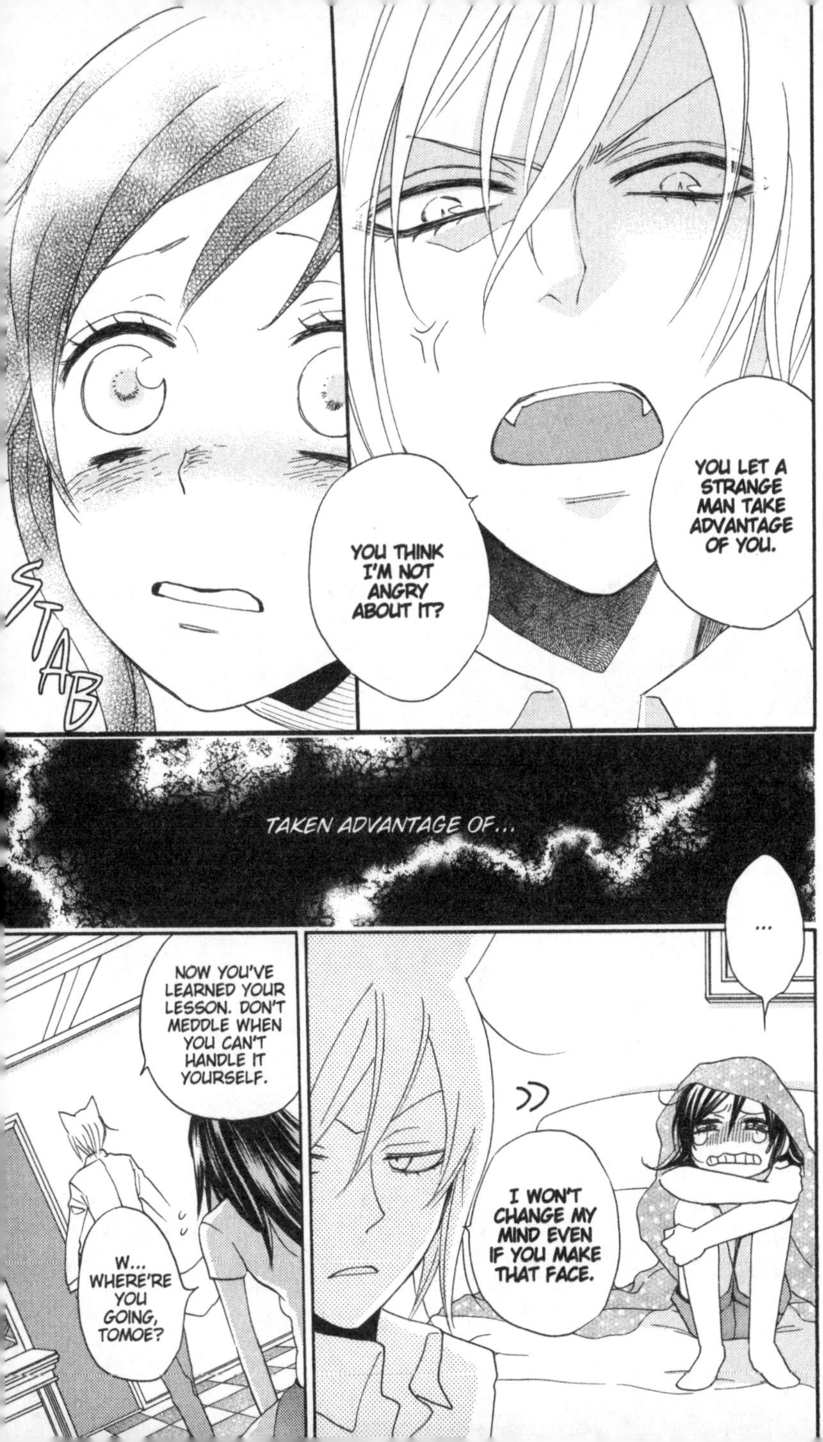
YOU LET A STRANGE MAN TAKE ADVANTAGE OF YOU.
YOU THINK I'M NOT ANGRY ABOUT IT?
STAB
TAKEN ADVANTAGE OF...
...
I WON'T CHANGE MY MIND EVEN IF YOU MAKE THAT FACE.
NOW YOU'VE LEARNED YOUR LESSON. DON'T MEDDLE WHEN YOU CAN'T HANDLE IT YOURSELF.
W... WHERE'RE YOU GOING, TOMOE?

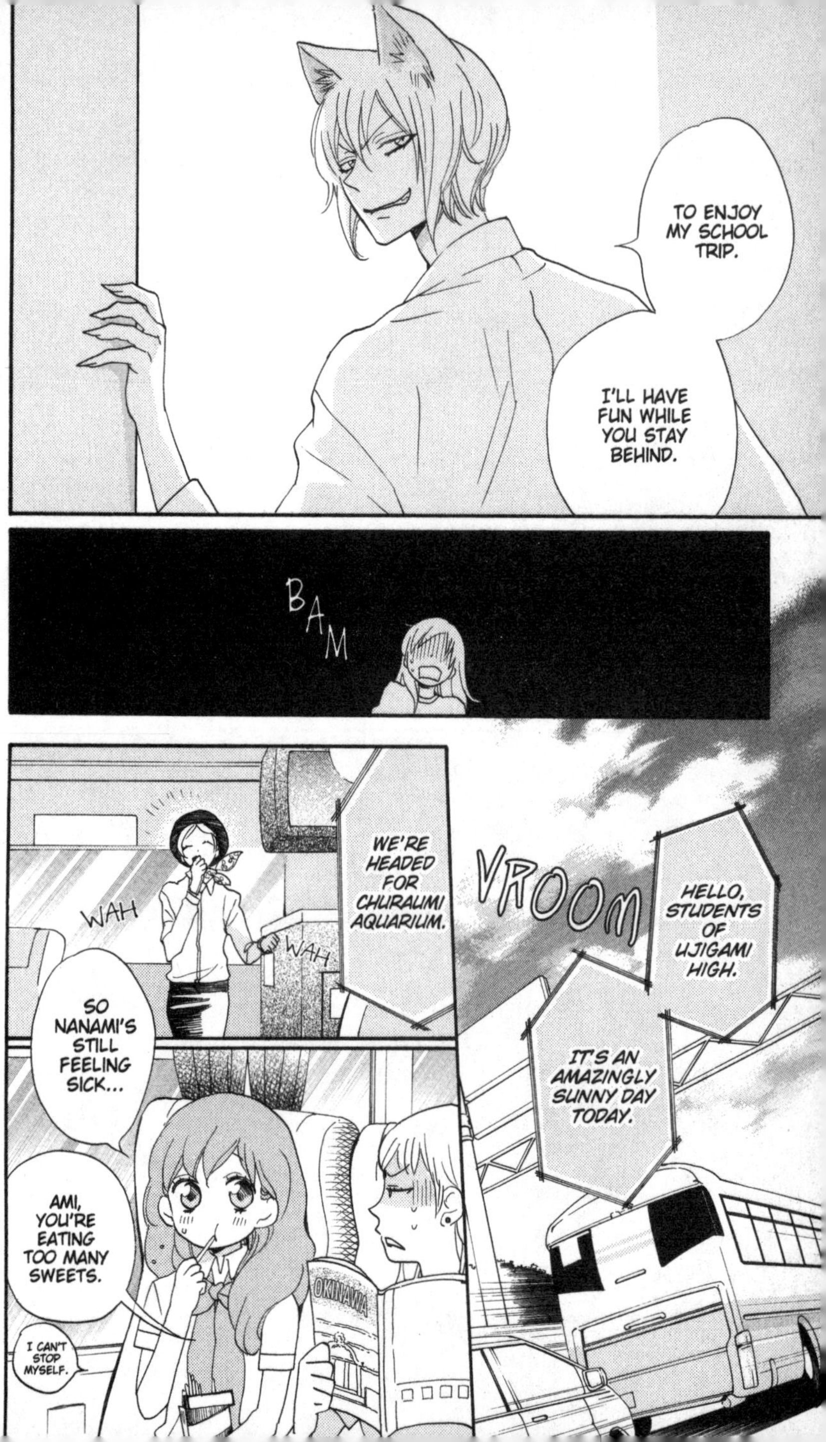
TO ENJOY MY SCHOOL TRIP.
I'LL HAVE FUN WHILE YOU STAY BEHIND.
BAM
VROOM
HELLO, STUDENTS OF UJIGAMI HIGH.
IT'S AN AMAZINGLY SUNNY DAY TODAY.
WE'RE HEADED FOR CHURAUMI AQUARIUM.
WAH
WAH
SO NANAMI'S STILL FEELING SICK...
AMI, YOU'RE EATING TOO MANY SWEETS.
I CAN'T STOP MYSELF.
OKINAWA

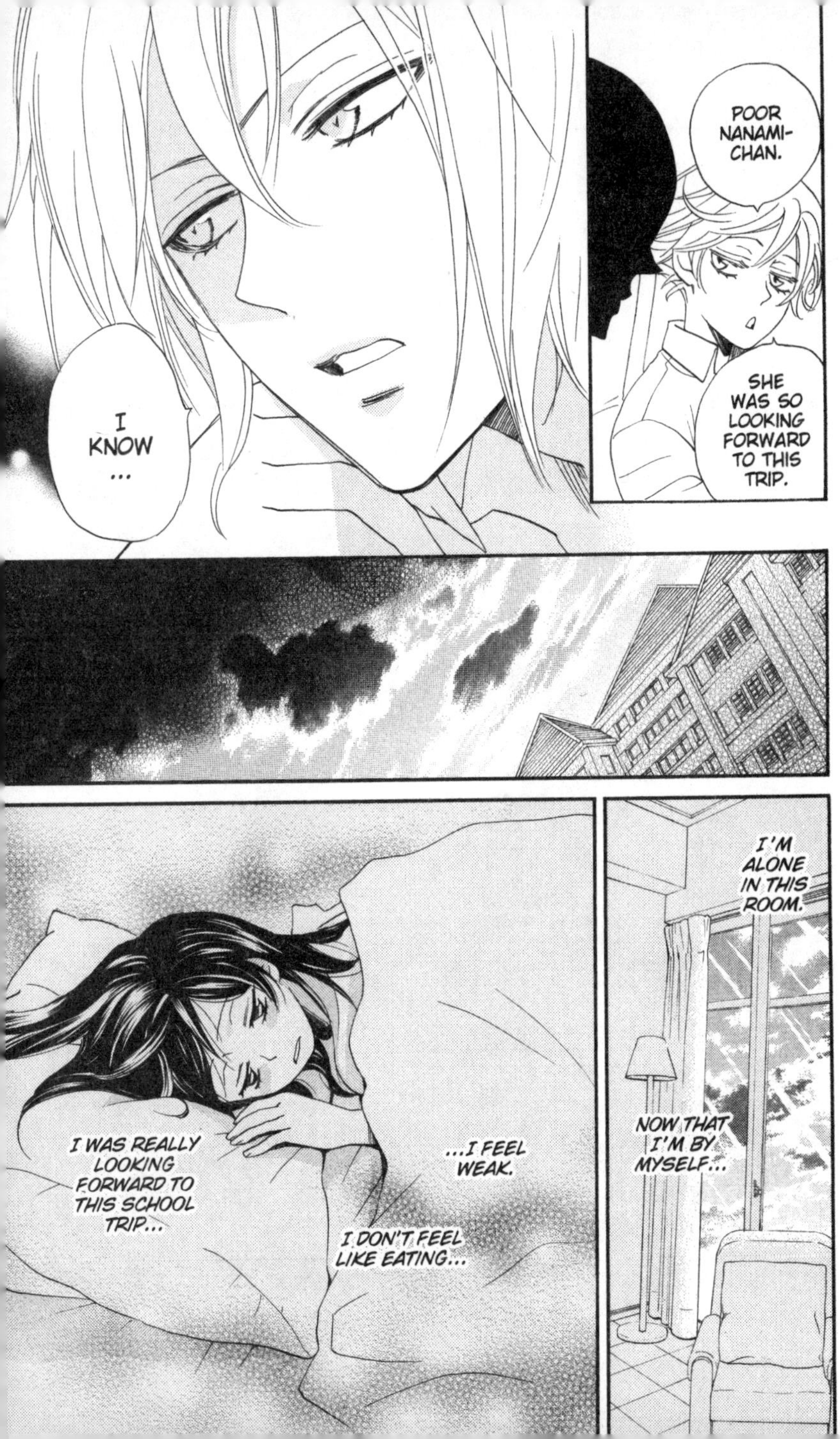
POOR NANAMI-CHAN.
SHE WAS SO LOOKING FORWARD TO THIS TRIP.
I KNOW ...
I'M ALONE IN THIS ROOM.
NOW THAT I'M BY MYSELF...
...I FEEL WEAK.
I WAS REALLY LOOKING FORWARD TO THIS SCHOOL TRIP...
I DON'T FEEL LIKE EATING...

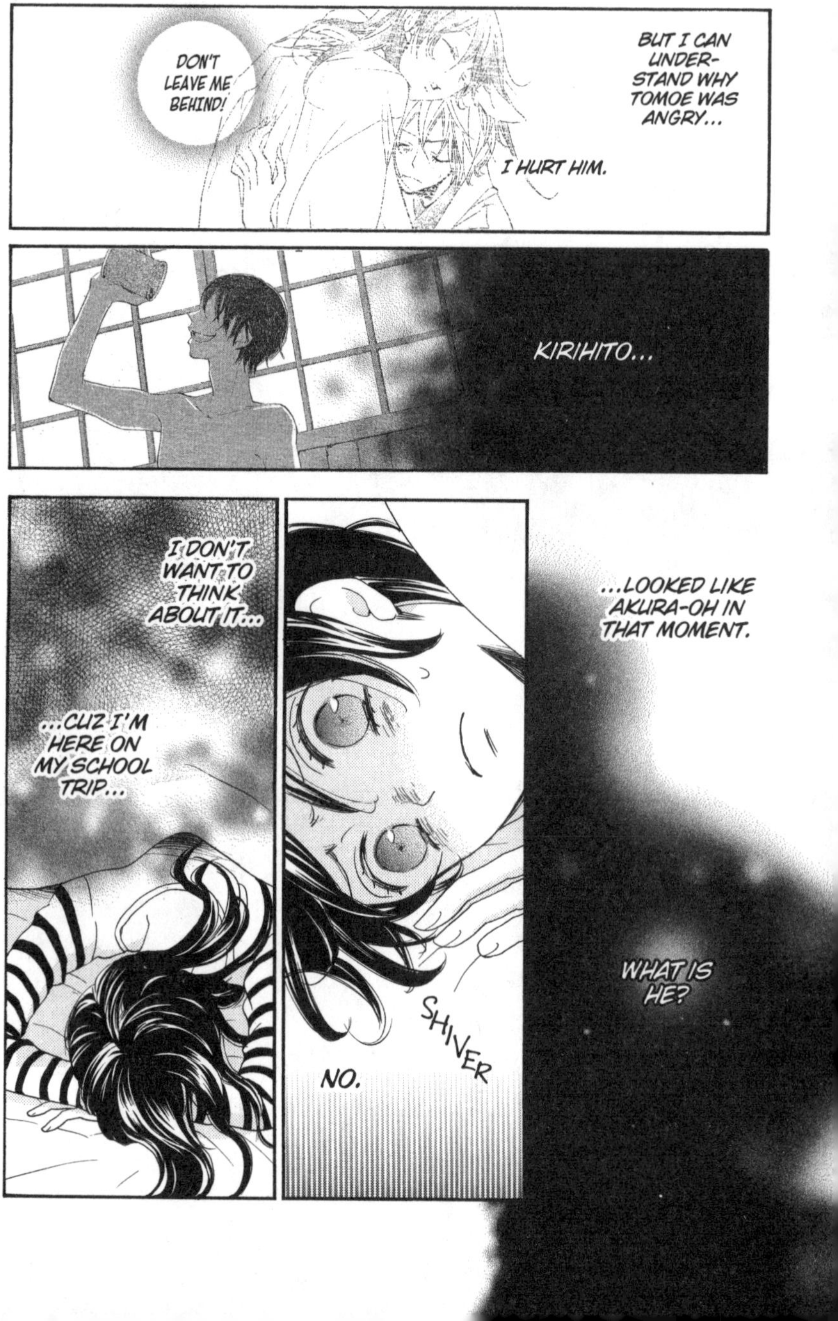
BUT I CAN UNDER-STAND WHY TOMOE WAS ANGRY...
I HURT HIM.
DON'T LEAVE ME BEHIND!
KIRIHITO...
...LOOKED LIKE AKURA-OH IN THAT MOMENT.
WHAT IS HE?
SHIVER
NO.
I DON'T WANT TO THINK ABOUT IT...
...CUZ I'M HERE ON MY SCHOOL TRIP...

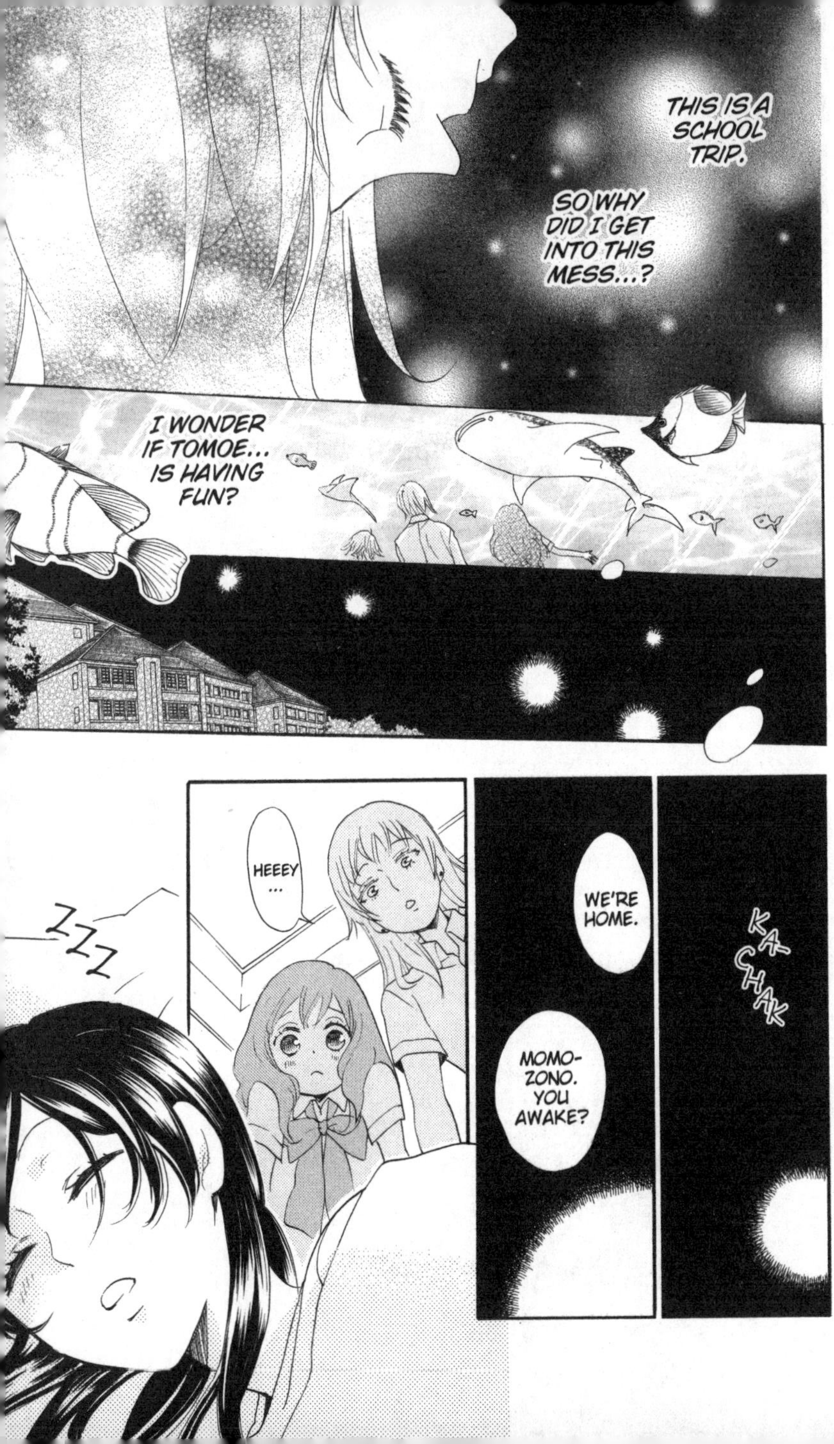
THIS IS A SCHOOL TRIP.
SO WHY DID I GET INTO THIS MESS...?
I WONDER IF TOMOE... IS HAVING FUN?
KA-CHAK
WE'RE HOME.
MOMO-ZONO. YOU AWAKE?
HEEEY...
ZZZ

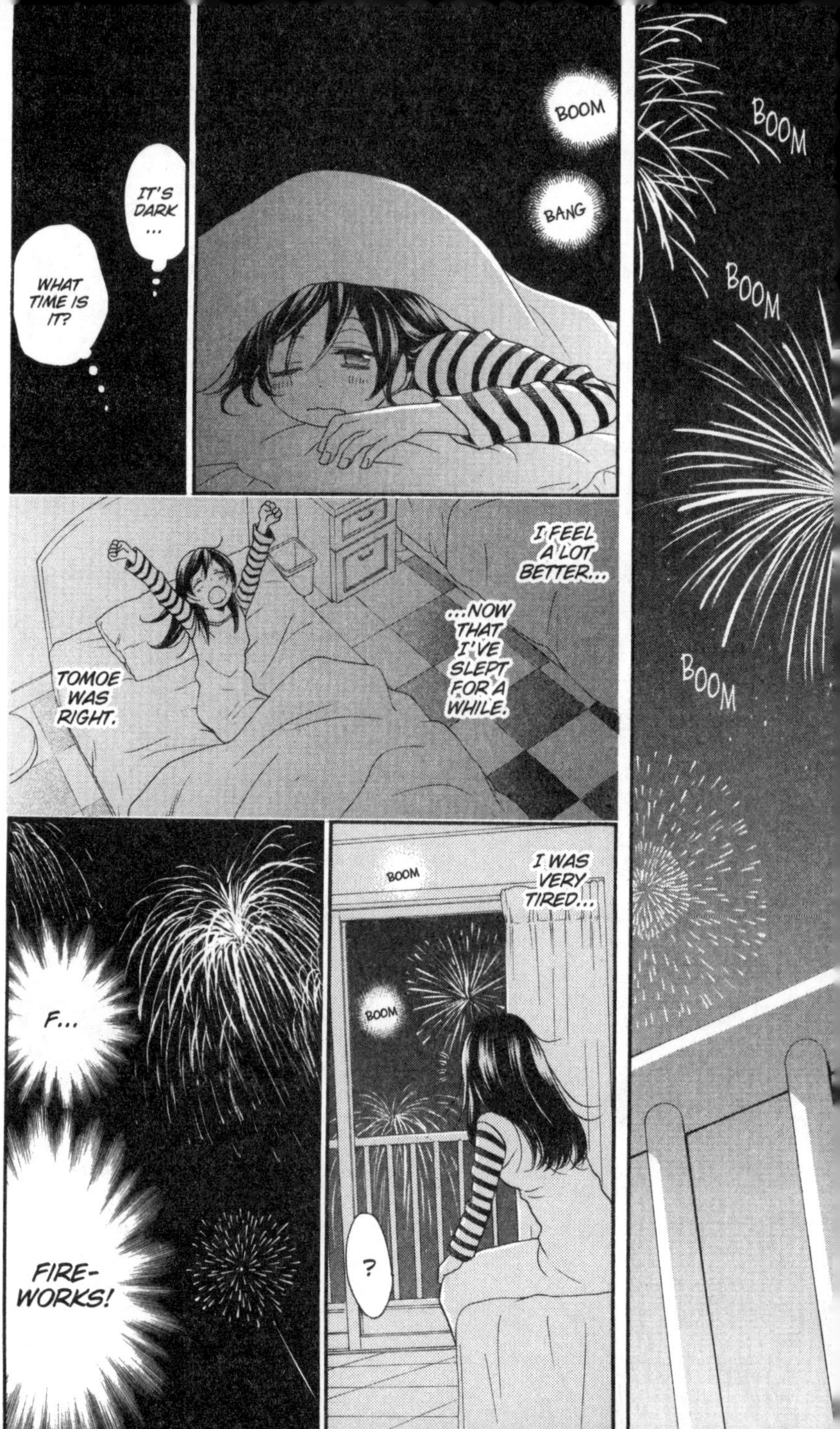
BOOM
BOOM
BOOM
BOOM
BANG
IT'S DARK...
WHAT TIME IS IT?
I FEEL A LOT BETTER...
...NOW THAT I'VE SLEPT FOR A WHILE.
TOMOE WAS RIGHT.
I WAS VERY TIRED...
BOOM
BOOM
?
F...
FIRE-WORKS!

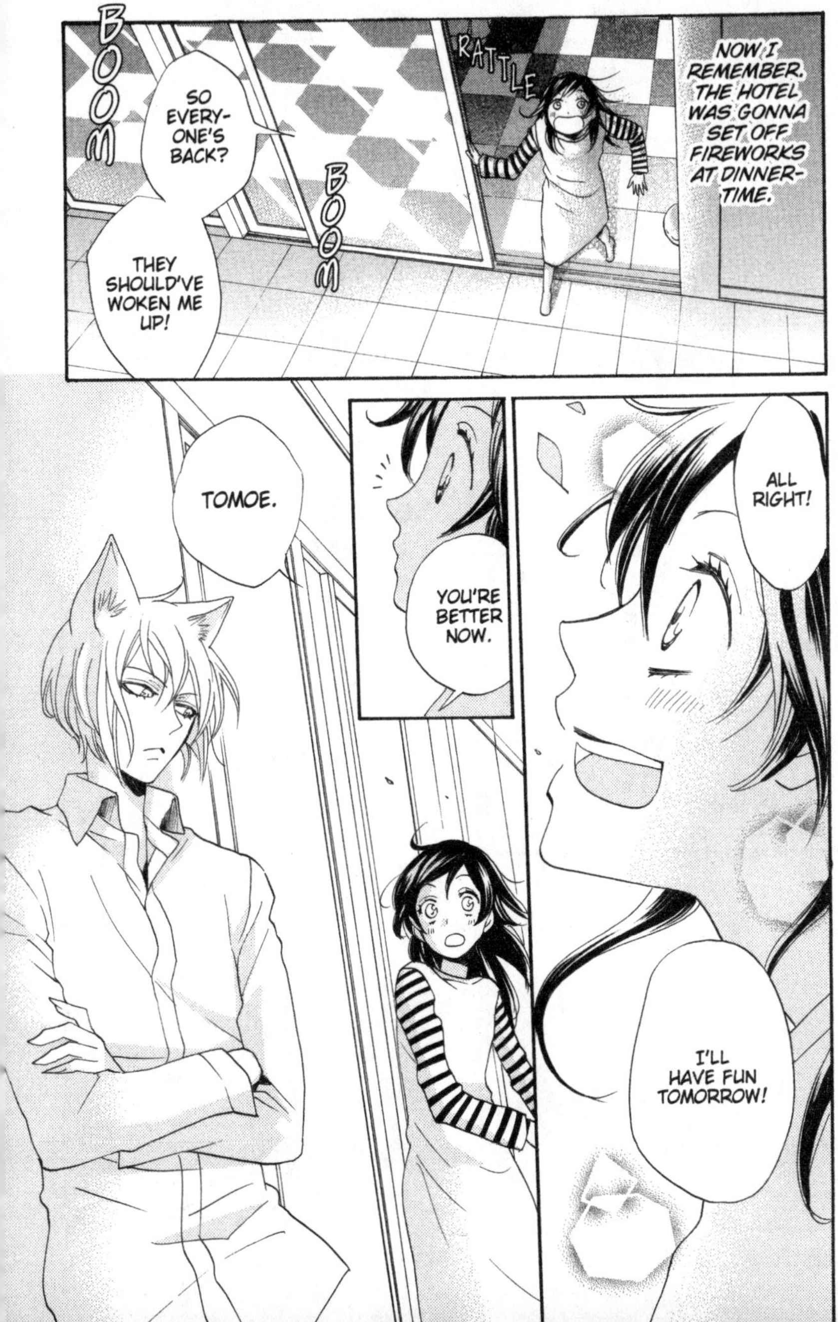
NOW I REMEMBER. THE HOTEL WAS GONNA SET OFF FIREWORKS AT DINNER-TIME.
RATTLE
BOOM
SO EVERY-ONE'S BACK?
THEY SHOULD'VE WOKEN ME UP!
BOOM
ALL RIGHT!
I'LL HAVE FUN TOMORROW!
YOU'RE BETTER NOW.
TOMOE.

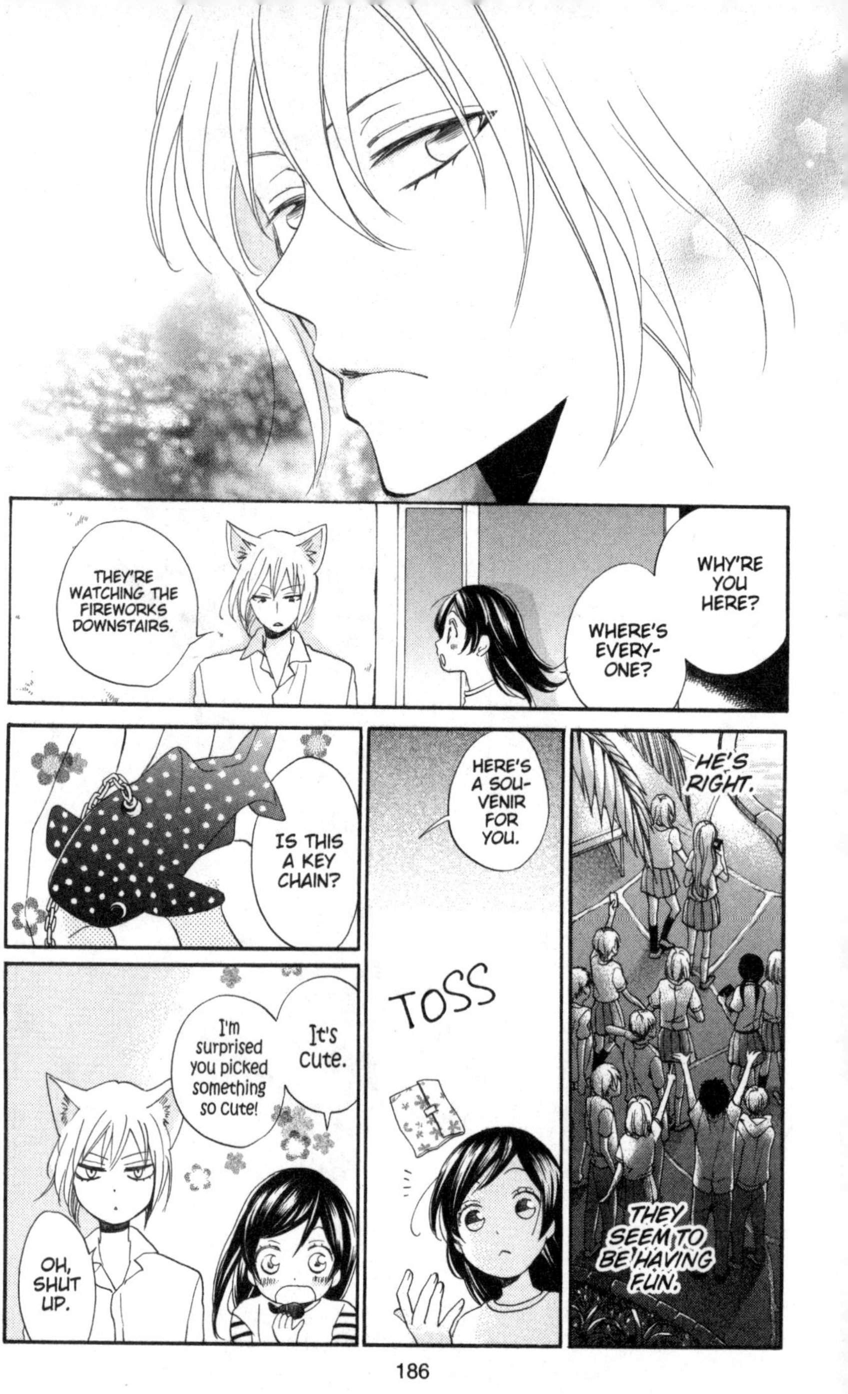
WHY'RE YOU HERE?
WHERE'S EVERY-ONE?
THEY'RE WATCHING THE FIREWORKS DOWNSTAIRS.
HE'S RIGHT.
THEY SEEM TO BE HAVING FUN.
HERE'S A SOU-VENIR FOR YOU.
TOSS
IS THIS A KEY CHAIN?
It's cute.
I'm surprised you picked something so cute!
OH, SHUT UP.

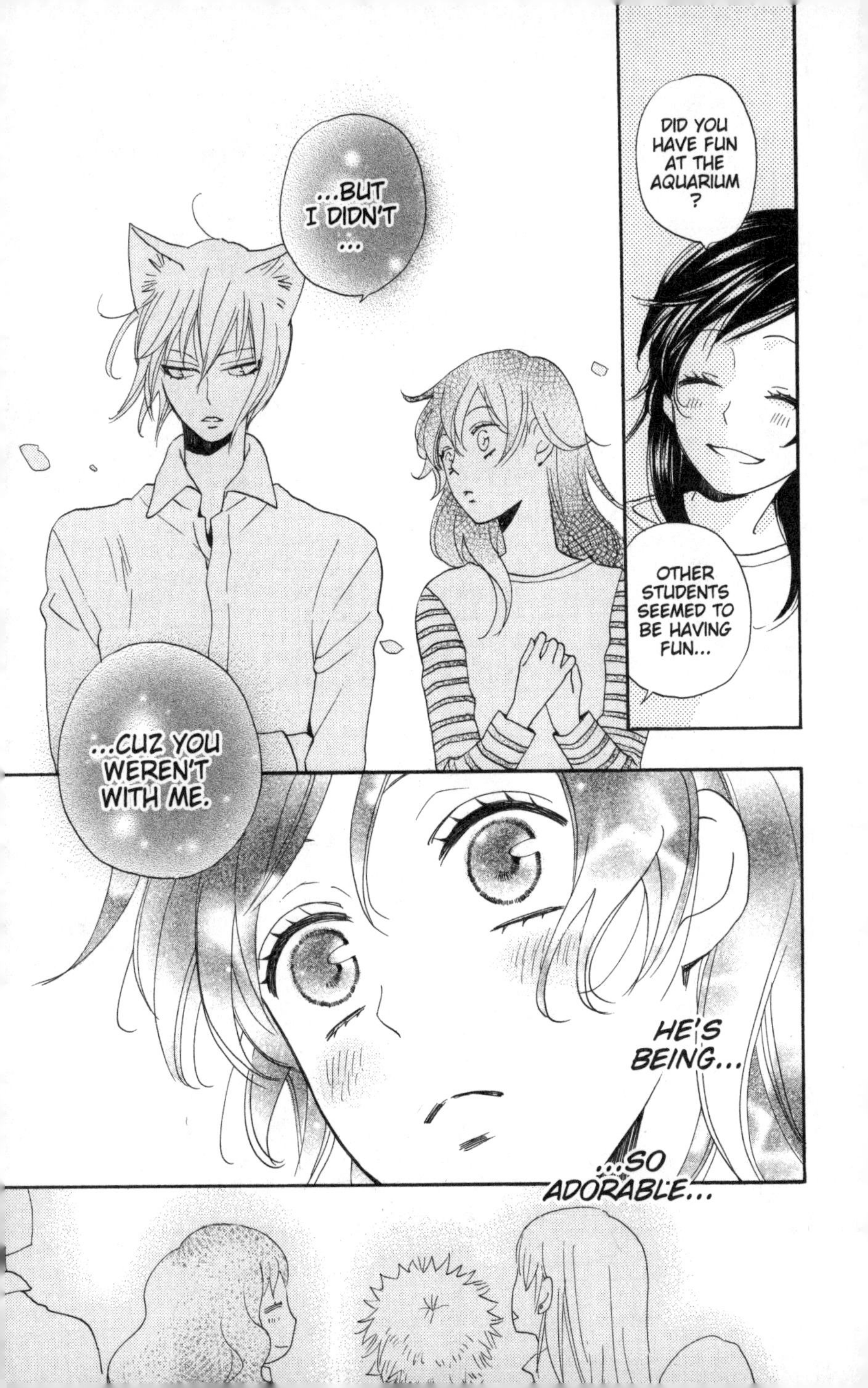
DID YOU HAVE FUN AT THE AQUARIUM?
OTHER STUDENTS SEEMED TO BE HAVING FUN...
...BUT I DIDN'T...
...CUZ YOU WEREN'T WITH ME.
HE'S BEING...
...SO ADORABLE...

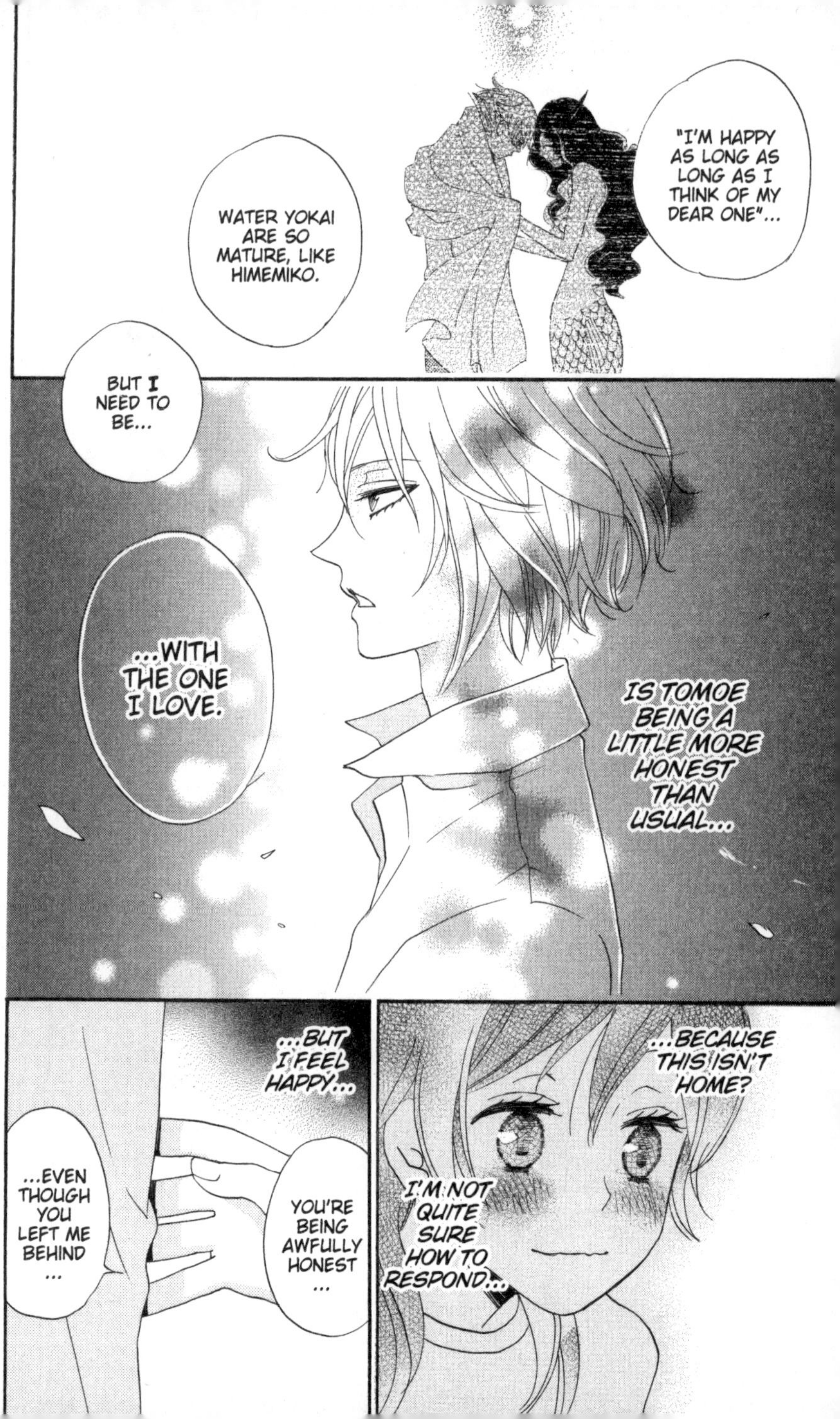
"I'M HAPPY AS LONG AS LONG AS I THINK OF MY DEAR ONE"...
WATER YOKAI ARE SO MATURE, LIKE HIMEMIKO.
BUT I NEED TO BE...
...WITH THE ONE I LOVE.
IS TOMOE BEING A LITTLE MORE HONEST THAN USUAL...
...BECAUSE THIS ISN'T HOME?
I'M NOT QUITE SURE HOW TO RESPOND...
...BUT I FEEL HAPPY...
YOU'RE BEING AWFULLY HONEST...
...EVEN THOUGH YOU LEFT ME BEHIND...

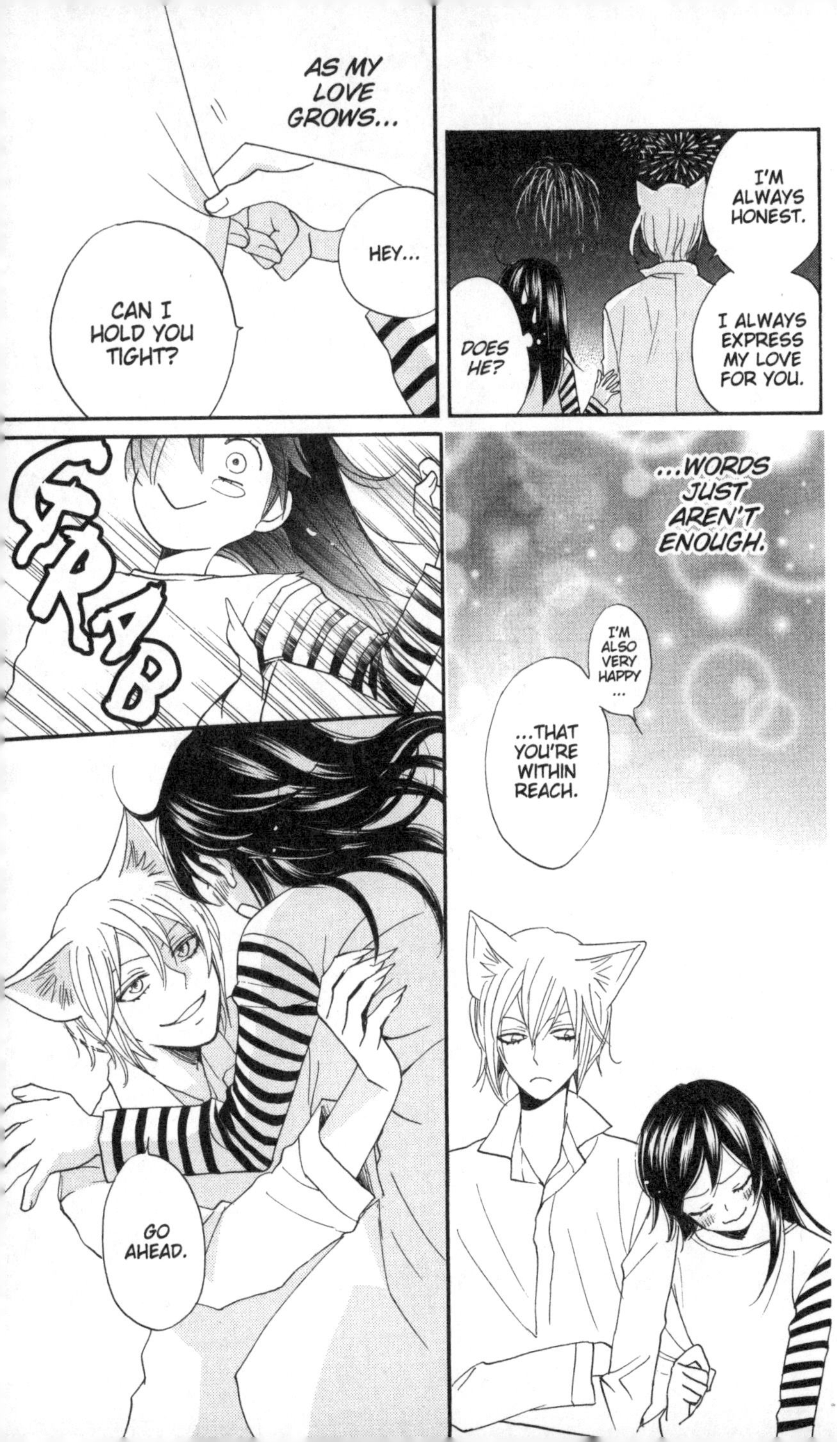
I'M ALWAYS HONEST.
I ALWAYS EXPRESS MY LOVE FOR YOU.
DOES HE?
AS MY LOVE GROWS...
HEY...
CAN I HOLD YOU TIGHT?
...WORDS JUST AREN'T ENOUGH.
I'M ALSO VERY HAPPY...
...THAT YOU'RE WITHIN REACH.
GRAB
GO AHEAD.

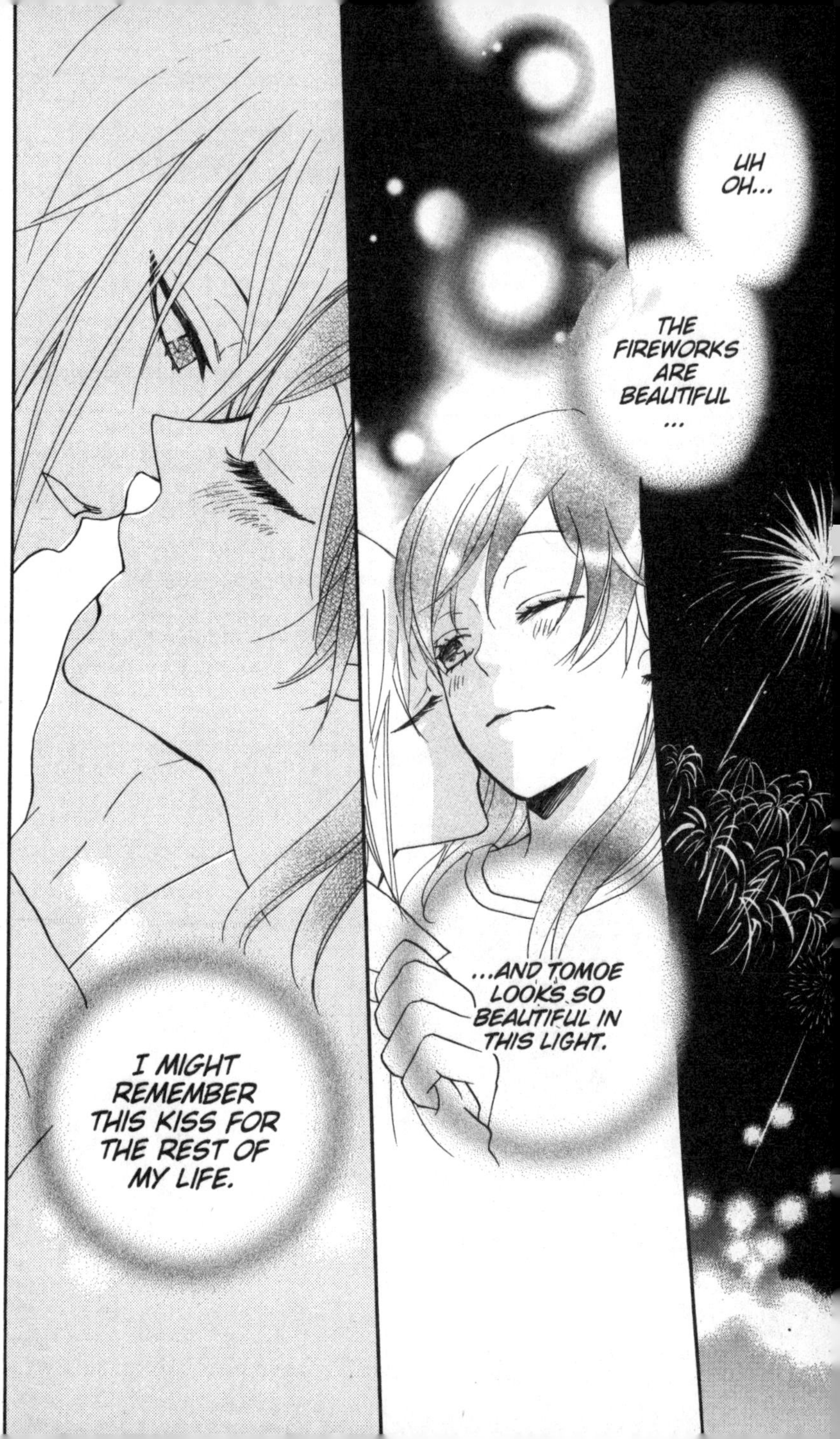
UH OH...
THE FIREWORKS ARE BEAUTIFUL ...
...AND TOMOE LOOKS SO BEAUTIFUL IN THIS LIGHT.
I MIGHT REMEMBER THIS KISS FOR THE REST OF MY LIFE.

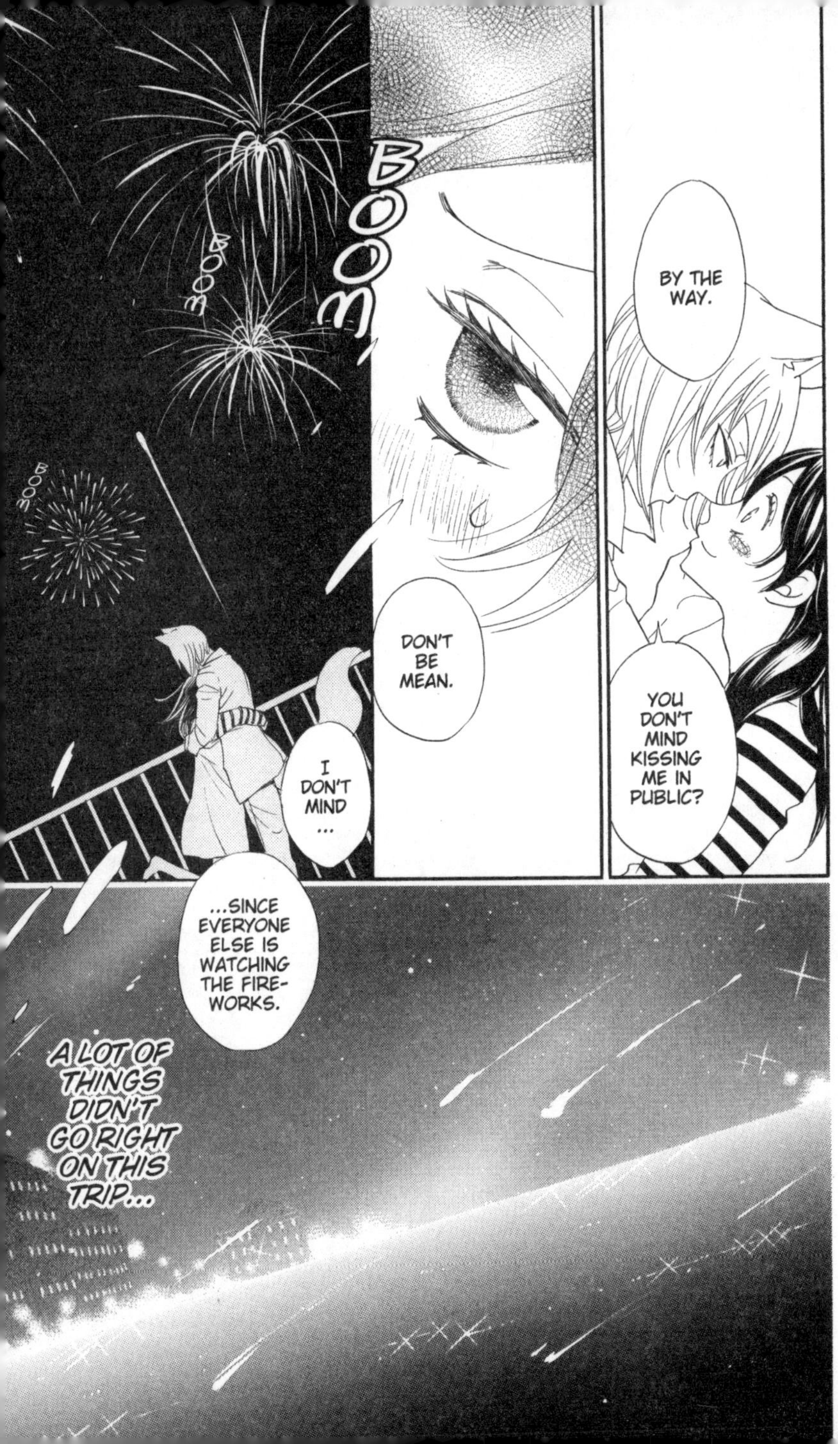
BY THE WAY.
YOU DON'T MIND KISSING ME IN PUBLIC?
DON'T BE MEAN.
BOOM
BOOM
BOOM
I DON'T MIND...
...SINCE EVERYONE ELSE IS WATCHING THE FIRE-WORKS.
A LOT OF THINGS DIDN'T GO RIGHT ON THIS TRIP...

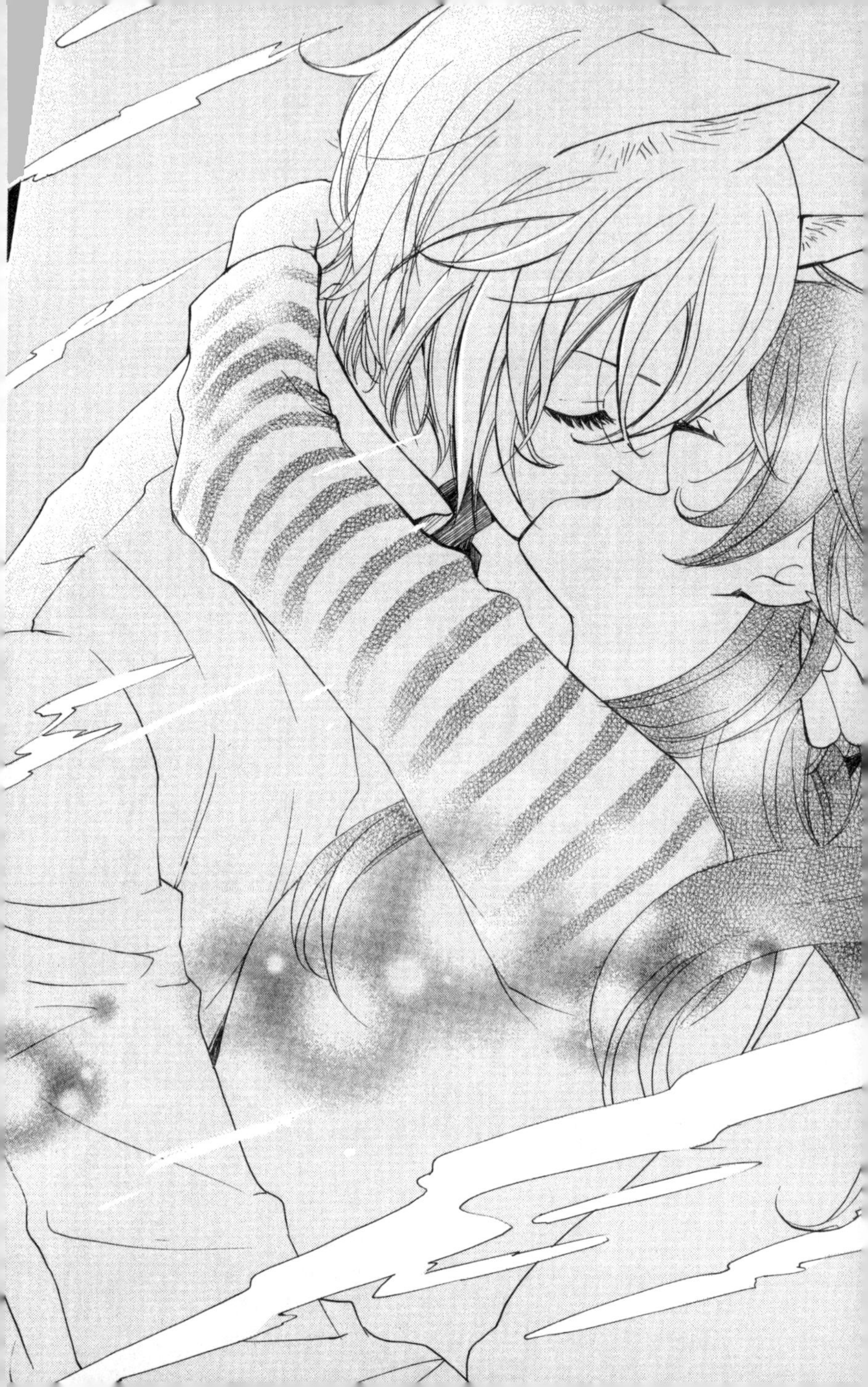

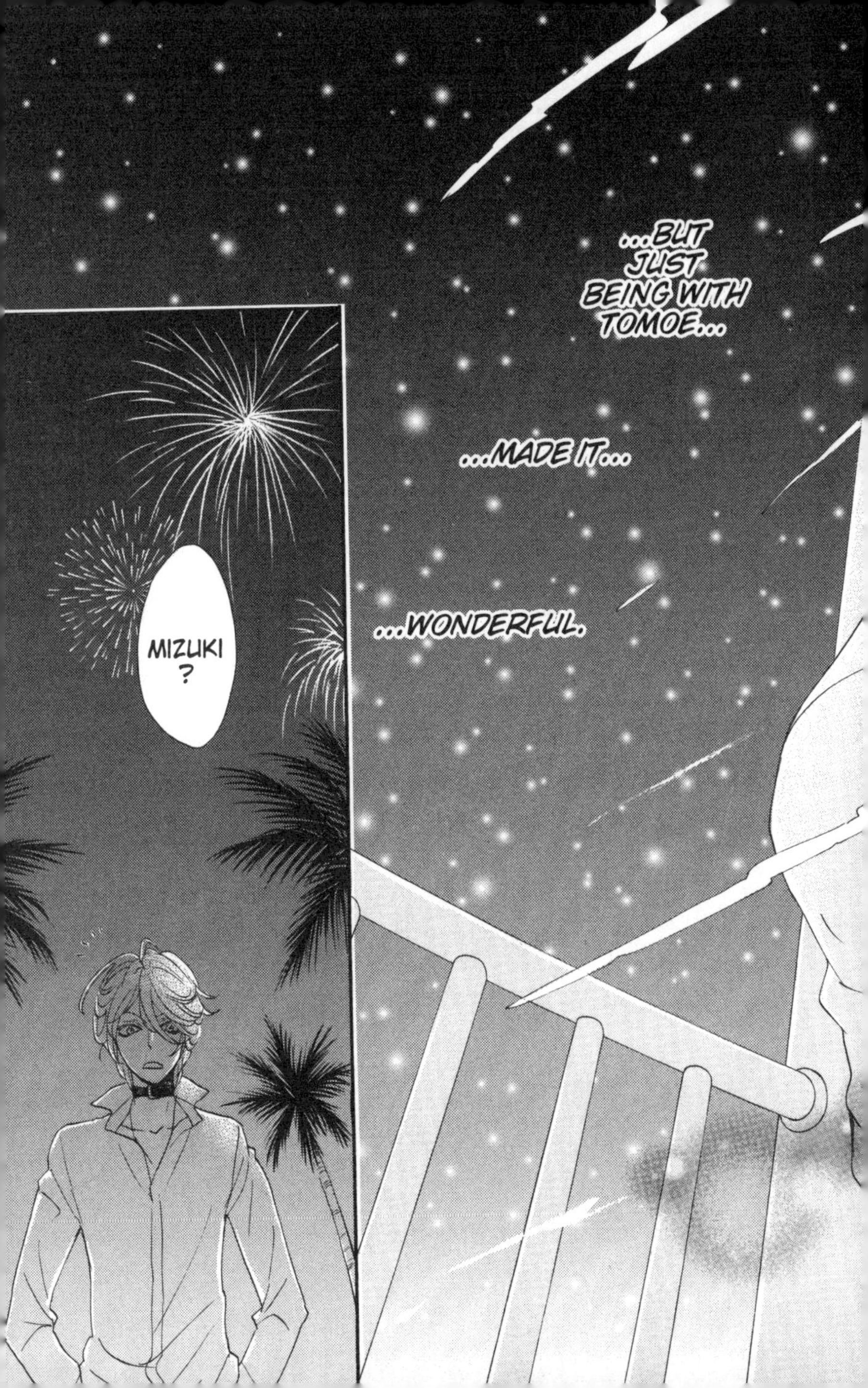
...BUT JUST BEING WITH TOMOE...
...MADE IT...
...WONDERFUL.
MIZUKI ?

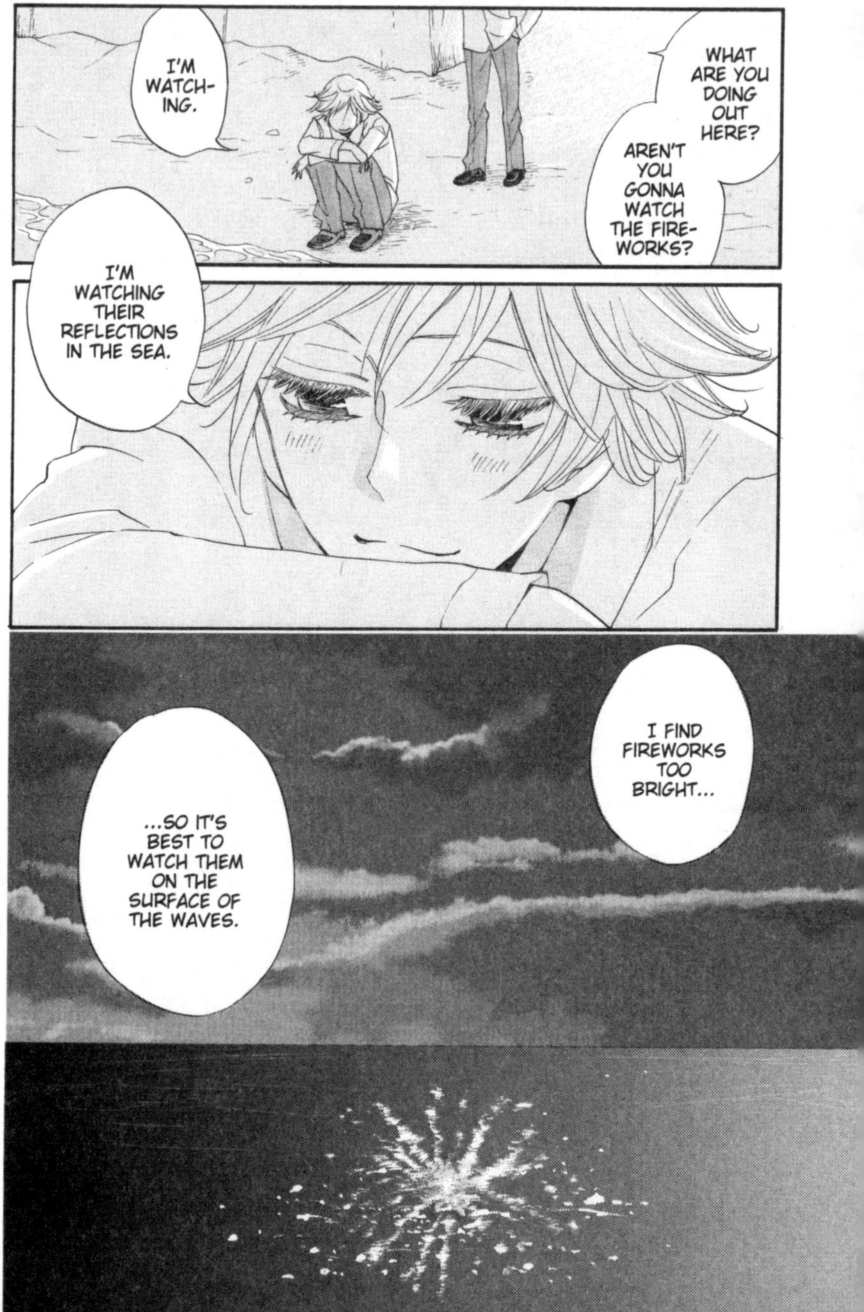
WHAT ARE YOU DOING OUT HERE?
AREN'T YOU GONNA WATCH THE FIRE-WORKS?
I'M WATCH-ING.
I'M WATCHING THEIR REFLECTIONS IN THE SEA.
I FIND FIREWORKS TOO BRIGHT...
...SO IT'S BEST TO WATCH THEM ON THE SURFACE OF THE WAVES.

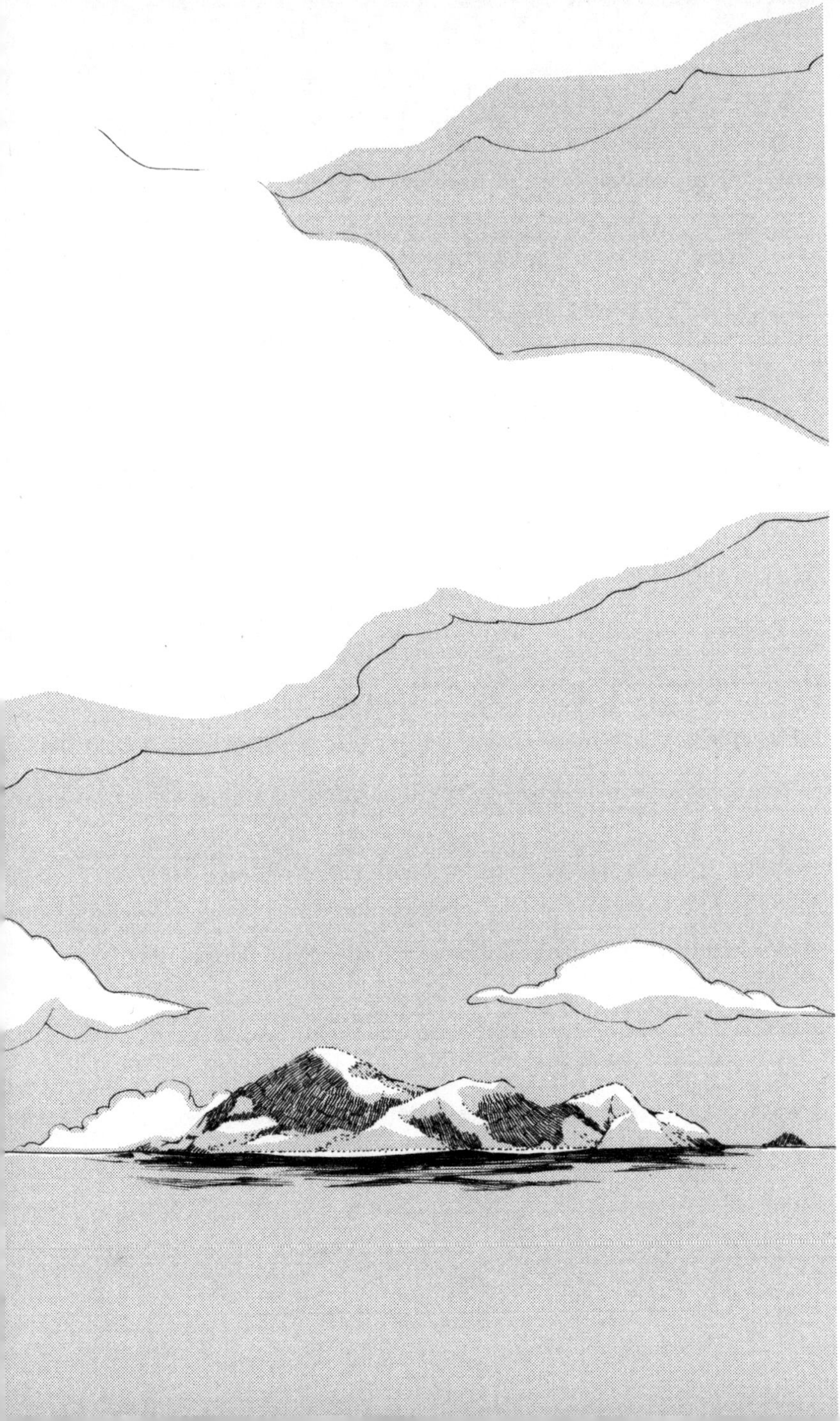

The Otherworld

Ayakashi is an archaic term for yokai.

Kami are Shinto deities or spirits. The word can be used for a range of creatures, from nature spirits to strong and dangerous gods.

Komainu are a pair of guardian statues placed at the gate of a shrine, usually carved of stone. Depending on the shrine, they can be lions, foxes or cows.

Onibi-warashi are like will-o'-the-wisps.

Shinshi are birds, beasts, insects or fish that have a special relationship with a kami.

Tengu are a type of yokai. They are sometimes associated with excess pride.

Tochigami (or *jinushigami*) are deities of a specific area of land.

Yokai are demons, monsters or goblins.

Honorifics

-chan is a diminutive most often used with babies, children or teenage girls.

-dono roughly means "my lord," although not in the aristocratic sense.

-kun is used by persons of superior rank to their juniors. It can sometimes have a familiar connotation.

-san is a standard honorific similar to Mr., Mrs., Miss or Ms.

-sama is used with people of much higher rank.

Julietta Suzuki's debut manga *Hoshi ni Naru Hi* (The Day One Becomes a Star) appeared in the 2004 *Hana to Yume Plus*. Her other books include *Akuma to Dolce* (The Devil and Sweets) and *Karakuri Odette*. Born in December in Fukuoka Prefecture, she enjoys having movies play in the background while she works on her manga.

KAMISAMA KISS
VOL. 19
Shojo Beat Edition

STORY AND ART BY
Julietta Suzuki

English Translation & Adaptation/Tomo Kimura
Touch-up Art & Lettering/Joanna Estep
Design/Yukiko Whitley
Editor/Pancha Diaz

KAMISAMA HAJIMEMASHITA by Julietta Suzuki
© Julietta Suzuki 2014
All rights reserved.
First published in Japan in 2014 by HAKUSENSHA, Inc., Tokyo.
English language translation rights arranged with
HAKUSENSHA, Inc., Tokyo.

The stories, characters and incidents mentioned
in this publication are entirely fictional.

Printed in Italy

Published by VIZ Media, LLC
P.O. Box 77010
San Francisco, CA 94107

10 9 8 7 6
First printing, October 2015
Sixth printing, March 2024

viz.com   shojobeat.com

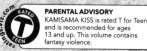

This is the last page.

In keeping with the original Japanese comic format, this book reads from right to left—so action, sound effects, and word balloons are completely reversed. This preserves the orientation of the original artwork—plus, it's fun! Check out the diagram shown here to get the hang of things, and then turn to the other side of the book to get started!